Knowledge Discovery for Counterterrorism and Law Enforcement

Chapman & Hall/CRC
Data Mining and Knowledge Discovery Series

SERIES EDITOR

Vipin Kumar

University of Minnesota
Department of Computer Science and Engineering
Minneapolis, Minnesota, U.S.A

AIMS AND SCOPE

This series aims to capture new developments and applications in data mining and knowledge discovery, while summarizing the computational tools and techniques useful in data analysis. This series encourages the integration of mathematical, statistical, and computational methods and techniques through the publication of a broad range of textbooks, reference works, and handbooks. The inclusion of concrete examples and applications is highly encouraged. The scope of the series includes, but is not limited to, titles in the areas of data mining and knowledge discovery methods and applications, modeling, algorithms, theory and foundations, data and knowledge visualization, data mining systems and tools, and privacy and security issues.

PUBLISHED TITLES

UNDERSTANDING COMPLEX DATASETS: Data Mining with Matrix
Decompositions
David Skillicorn

COMPUTATIONAL METHODS OF FEATURE SELECTION
Huan Liu and Hiroshi Motoda

CONSTRAINED CLUSTERING: Advances in Algorithms, Theory,
and Applications
Sugato Basu, Ian Davidson, and Kiri L. Wagstaff

KNOWLEDGE DISCOVERY FOR COUNTERTERRORISM AND
LAW ENFORCEMENT
David Skillicorn

Chapman & Hall/CRC
Data Mining and Knowledge Discovery Series

Knowledge Discovery for Counterterrorism and Law Enforcement

David Skillicorn

CRC Press
Taylor & Francis Group
Boca Raton London New York

CRC Press is an imprint of the
Taylor & Francis Group, an **informa** business
A CHAPMAN & HALL BOOK

CRC Press
Taylor & Francis Group
6000 Broken Sound Parkway NW, Suite 300
Boca Raton, FL 33487-2742

First issued in paperback 2019

© 2009 by Taylor & Francis Group, LLC
CRC Press is an imprint of Taylor & Francis Group, an Informa business

No claim to original U.S. Government works

ISBN-13: 978-1-4200-7399-7 (hbk)
ISBN-13: 978-0-367-38644-3 (pbk)

Visit the Taylor & Francis Web site at
http://www.taylorandfrancis.com

and the CRC Press Web site at
http://www.crcpress.com

Dedicated to the memory of those innocent people
who lost their lives in the first Bali bombing,
October 12th 2002.

Contents

10 The Bottom Line   301

Bibliography   317

Index   327

Preface

Humans are exceedingly good at taking large amounts of data and 'making sense' of it, that is working out the significant content within it and its implications. For example, our eyes receive a vast stream of input in the form of photons and our visual system and brain extract from it the presence and properties of objects in the outside world. Our abilities to make sense out of such large amounts of data are not simply something passive either. We can prime our senses to attend to and interpret particular kinds of stimuli. For example, if we are thinking of buying a particular kind of car, we notice them everywhere we go.

Knowledge discovery mimics these natural human abilities using computer algorithms. Given large amounts of data, we want to 'make sense' of them algorithmically, that is to extract the significant content in the same way that we do as humans. Data represented by text is an interesting example. Humans are, of course, good at understanding the content of a text, provided it forms some sort of coherent narrative. However, they are much less effective at understanding the mental state of the author of the text, or whether two texts have been written by the same author. Algorithms, as we shall see, are quite good at these latter problems, but not so good at understanding the 'meaning' of a text.

Knowledge discovery, therefore, opens up new possibilities for extracting knowledge from data, both larger data than humans can handle well, and data in forms that do not match human strengths. Algorithmic knowledge discovery is most effective when it works symbiotically with human abilities, supplementing them in the cases where humans perform poorly, and relying on them in the cases where humans perform well. The area of algorithmic knowledge discovery, sometimes called knowledge discovery in data (KDD) or data mining, is a rapidly growing area that overlaps with statistics, computer science, and psychology.

The subject of this book is knowledge discovery in situations where some groups of people are motivated to manipulate either the data that is collected or the analysis process to hide themselves or their actions, or to subvert the outcome of the knowledge discovery in other ways. For example, criminals will attempt, when they can, to prevent discovery of their actions by simple things, such as wearing ski masks to prevent their faces being captured by closed-circuit TV, or by complex things, such as altering an accounting system to hide their financial manipulations. Terrorists will attempt to conceal themselves, their target, and the actions they take from intelligence analysts as they prepare for an attack.

All knowledge-discovery systems have vulnerabilities that can potentially be exploited. Even our brains have such vulnerabilities. For example, optical illusions show how it is possible for us to see things that are not there; and a card with two spots on it can be used to show the existence of our blind spots, where we don't see things that are there. Many parts of our world are explicitly designed to exploit the way our data-analysis brain works: an LCD TV screen displays a large number of colored dots and, from this digital display, we miraculously 'see' objects. Moreover, unless we stop and think about it, these objects appear to be three-dimensional. The builders of the Parthenon in Athens exploited the way we 'see' to make the columns seem taller than they actually are.

All knowledge-discovery systems are susceptible to manipulation. In this adversarial knowledge-discovery setting, designers and users of algorithmic knowledge-discovery systems must be aware of the existence of potential opponents, and include this awareness in the way that the systems work. It turns out that the possibility of manipulation completely changes the way that knowledge discovery must be done – mainstream knowledge-discovery algorithms are individually quite fragile and open to subversion. However, progress can be made on two fronts: 'hardening' algorithms so that they are harder to subvert; and arranging them into larger systems to create a defence in depth. How this can be done is the focus of this book.

The primary audience for this book is professionals in intelligence, counterterrorism, law enforcement, fraud detection, and justice who think about these issues, and work with tools that, in one way or another, extract knowledge from data. Increasingly organizations are having to protect themselves from malfeasance as well, so professionals in counter-industrial espionage, accounting and auditing may also find the content of this book useful.

I have five goals:

- To provide a wider context for the single-purpose tools that are the most common form of knowledge-discovery technology in use today. In particular, I hope that the content of the book will help those who use such tools to see how they fit, or should fit, into larger systems.

- To suggest a better process for integrating knowledge-discovery tools. Most knowledge-discovery tools today are single-purpose, or allow only a few specialized forms of knowledge discovery. However, in an adversarial setting, synergies between tools make the whole much, much more powerful than the sum of its parts – but only if the parts are put together in sensible ways. These arrangements are not always obvious. I have tried to suggest structures for assembling knowledge-discovery tools in force-multiplying ways.

- To urge caution about interpreting the results of knowledge discovery in adversarial settings until their vulnerabilities to manipulation have been fully taken into account. One of the most subtle and surprising features of existing knowledge-discovery technology is how fragile it is in the face of actions by those who want to conceal themselves and their actions. This is not understood widely enough, and leads to an unrealistic reliance on the results of black-box systems.

- To provide a basis for the arguments that need to be made to the general public about the role of knowledge discovery and the data collection associated with it. The dialogue between intelligence and law-enforcement personnel and the wider public has been frustrating on both sides, partly because of differences in views about risks and costs, but partly because the case for widespread data collection and analysis has not been made clearly. Rather there has been a tendency to assume either that widespread data collection is innocuous, or is completely destructive, without a clear presentation of the upsides and downsides – some of which depend on the technologies and how they are used.

- To provide a preview of some of the technologies that are in the lab, that are moving from the research lab into widespread use, how they work, and how they fit into existing approaches to knowledge discovery.

Some of these goals are relevant to those who use knowledge-discovery tools day to day. All of them are relevant to those who are planning the future use of these technologies, in existing domains, and also in new areas where knowledge discovery is not yet common.

This book will also be of use to researchers in artificial intelligence, statistics, information technology, and computing. In these domains it is common to think of knowledge discovery for intelligence and law enforcement as a specialized application of more-or-less mainstream tools and algorithms. It has not been fully appreciated how much the adversarial nature of these settings changes the problems – so that, in fact, little of mainstream knowledge discovery can be safely used in the face of deliberate manipulation. New research that takes this into account is needed, together with assessment of the weaknesses and holes of existing, deployed knowledge-discovery systems.

This book will also be of interest to thoughtful members of the wider public, and especially those who make decisions about public policy towards data collection, surveillance, data analysis, and knowledge discovery, not only in adversarial settings, but also in areas such as customer relationship management, digital government, and social and economic planning. Although these areas are not usually thought of as adversarial, there are always those who try to game the system, and some attention towards this possibility is wise. Many are also concerned about the increased surveillance and data collection carried out by governments as a result of increased Islamic terrorism. It is easy to fall into one of two diametrically opposite errors about this: taking either a utopian view (knowledge discovery will stamp out terrorism as long as we collect enough data and analyze it all well); or a dystopian view (knowledge discovery is the end of privacy and democracy). There are some difficult issues here but, of course, the reality is much more nuanced. The content of this book will help to unpack the black box in which knowledge discovery is often presented in this discussion, and so help to explain the real constraints, and opportunities.

Acknowledgments

I would like to thank a large group of people who read drafts of the manuscript, sometimes several times, and provided extensive feedback which has improved the book immeasurably. They are: Daniel Zeng, James Provost, Clifton Phua, Nikunj Oza, Peter O'Hanlon, Christian Leuprecht, Warwick Graco, James Dutrisac, Antonio Badia, and several intelligence analysts who, unfortunately, must remain nameless. I am also grateful to all of my students – in teaching them, I learn myself; and many of them have directly contributed to my thinking about this area.

I would also like to thank my editor, Randi Cohen, who has helped at every stage, and made the process very smooth.

List of Figures

Chapter 1

Introduction

Developed countries, and increasingly the whole world, are tightly coupled systems of complexity and interconnectedness – a steadily closer approximation to a global village. These rich connections bring many benefits for communications, travel, manufacturing, services, and culture. In particular, there are now unprecedented opportunities for small groups to make an impact on the world because their members can discover each other and work together in ways that were too expensive in a less-coupled world.

The downside of this is that groups whose intentions are malignant, whether criminals, terrorists, or spies, can also make an impact out of all proportion to their size and visibility. The traces that they leave as they plan and execute their actions are difficult to detect. This makes it hard to prosecute them afterwards, and even harder to discover and prevent their actions beforehand.

Large-scale data analysis is the counterweight to the ability of small, *ad hoc* groups to plan and carry out criminal and terrorist actions; in other words, knowledge discovery is one way, perhaps the only way, to bring the symmetry back to the asymmetric situation in which nations find themselves.

Even if this works, and the evidence so far is encouraging that it does, there are a number of difficult issues. Existing legal frameworks are not set up for preventive law enforcement and counterterrorism; there are substantial and difficult issues around widespread data collection and its impact on privacy, the properties of knowledge-discovery techniques and algorithms are not yet well understood, and knowledge discovery raises significant issues of power and corruption.

1.1   What is 'Knowledge Discovery'?

Knowledge discovery is the process of extracting useful knowledge from data. Although this may sound rather complicated, it is actually something that humans are very good at. For example, whenever you notice some object in your field of vision, you have done some knowledge discovery. The actual information that you receive from the outside world arrives in a very low-level form, streams of photons entering your eye and striking your retina. Your retina converts the data from the photons into nerve impulses, losing much of the information along the way, and these nerve impulses travel through a complicated, but by now well-understood, series of specialized regions in your brain. These regions 'recognize' successively more complex features of the scene in front of you, until eventually you 'see' the object.

In much the same way, you can be in a room where many conversations are going on at once, and you will be able to attend to and hear one conversation and make sense of the words. What actually reaches your ears is a single sequence of vibrations in the air, and from this raw data, you extract not just a particular audio subsequence, but also meaningful words.

Another kind of knowledge discovery happens in social situations, where we are adept at figuring out the subtexts in conversations, and aspects of the relationships among the people involved. We receive audible and visual information, and from this we work out higher-level information about the mental states, intentions, and connections of the people involved.

This kind of knowledge discovery can also be carried out by digital systems: devices that capture different kinds of data, and computers executing algorithms that infer knowledge from the data. There are obviously differences between the way humans do knowledge discovery, and the way that digital systems do it – but there are some similarities as well. One theme to which we will return several times is that human and algorithmic skills for knowledge discovery are complementary. Using both humans and computers, it is possible to discover useful knowledge that neither would find well on their own.

1.1.1   Main Forms of Knowledge Discovery

There are four main forms of knowledge discovery, although there are many variants, and ways to combine these basic four. To illustrate them, we will use examples from human life, to emphasize how natural knowledge discovery is as a human activity.

The four mains forms are:

1. **Prediction** – deciding what the outcome or meaning of a particular situation is, by collecting and observing its properties. For example, for many people the weather is a critical factor in their lives, for agriculture, hunting, or travel. Humans have always developed ways to predict the weather, some of them enshrined in doggerel such as "Red sky in the morning, shepherds' warning". Astronomy developed to allow predictions of important agricultural and cultural events such as the annual flooding of the Nile. Hunters needed to develop predictive models of the behavior of their prey, so that animals could be tracked over long distances and times, and attacked in the most appropriate way.

2. **Clustering** – putting objects or situations into groups whose members resemble each other and are usefully different from the members of other groups. For example, animals are clustered based on their properties (for hunting purposes) or their suitability for eating. Plants are clustered based on their suitability for eating or their roles as medicines. Knowing such clusters makes it efficient to decide quickly how to handle a previously unseen situation.

   A special case of clustering is outlier detection, noticing that an object or situation is one that has not previously been allocated to a cluster. Detecting outliers is one way to make sure that full attention is paid when such things are encountered, rather than following a more-or-less automatic process.

3. **Understanding connections** – figuring out how objects, processes, and especially people are connected. In human societies, the ability to see such connections is an important survival trait; whether it is being able to tell which members of the opposite sex are available for marriage, what the dominance hierarchy in a group is, or that these two people are having an affair.

4. **Understanding the internal world of others** – being able to tell what another person is thinking or feeling. This ability is so innate that we would probably not appreciate it fully if we did not have the example of autistic individuals in whom this ability is reduced. In human societies, it is important to be able to answer questions such as: what is this person thinking? how does this person feel towards me? and, is this person telling the truth?

These examples have been deliberately chosen from situations that occur in tribal societies, because humans are well-adapted to such settings. In complex post-industrial societies, these same forms of knowledge discovery still have important roles to play.

1.1.2   The Larger Process

Knowledge discovery is one step in a larger process, which can be usefully divided into three phases. These phases are:

1. **Data collection**. Before any analysis can be done, data must be collected, and put into usable form. As we have seen, in knowledge discovery by humans, the collection phase is largely implemented 'in hardware', although for some of the more social aspects of knowledge discovery, people range from passive to quite active data gatherers (snoops and gossips).

2. **Analysis**. This is the heart of the process, where the knowledge is extracted from the available data. An important part of this stage is evaluating the model that results from the analysis, both on its own terms (does it make sense internally?) and in terms of the situation (is it plausible?).

3. **Decision and Action**. Once the analysis has been done, and a model built from the data, the model can be used to have some effect in the situation. For a predictive model, the action is to make a prediction; for a clustering model, a model of connections, or a model of other people, the result is a deeper understanding of the situation, which can then lead to action.

In human knowledge discovery, much of the data collection and almost all of the analysis is performed below the level of consciousness, some of it in 'hardware', and some of it by unconscious thought processes. This has tended to obscure the difference between collection and analysis because, to us, they seem part of one seamless process.

Of course, humans can reason their way to models from observational data – but doing so consciously does not work nearly so well as when it happens unconsciously. A good example of this is the Watson Selection Task[1]. Given cards with one side colored red and the other side colored green, participants are presented with two red cards labelled, respectively, 16 and 61, and two green cards labelled, respectively, S and E. The task is to turn over the minimum number of cards to test the hypothesis "every card with an odd number on the red side has a vowel on the green side". Most participants find this difficult.

However, if the task is rephrased in a functionally identical way, with the green cards labelled instead "drinks soda" and "drinks beer", and the hypothesis expressed as "people under 18 must drink soda", then most people can complete the task easily. The explanation is that humans have well-developed skills for detecting cheating. The second form of the task allows these skills to be brought to bear, while the first form invokes the parts of our brain that handle purely abstract reasoning.

Human decision-making and action happen much more consciously, except for some of the results of low-level systems such as vision and hearing. For example, a tennis player makes decisions about how to react to a ball crossing the net in a largely unconscious way.

Of course, the entire process is not a one-way system. We are able to adapt all three phases in a goal-driven way. The psychological idea of 'set' shows how we can modulate the data-collection process, even for low-level data. With practice, reactions to particular visual or audible stimuli improve. With training, a musician hears variations in sound that an untrained ear simply cannot perceive, an oenologist can taste aspects of wine that others can not, and so on. At a slightly higher level, if we think about buying a particular car, we will suddenly seem to see cars of that kind much more frequently than before.

Some of the more sophisticated data collection and analysis, for example related to social activities, can be modulated by cultural expectations. This can range from noticing styles of body movement and posture, critical to establish the dominance hierarchy in many cultures at different times, to noticing accents in speech or levels of profanity. As Shaw famously said: "It is impossible for an Englishman to open his mouth without making some other Englishman hate or despise him"[2].

Decisions and actions can range all the way from completely automatic, in the case of reflexes, to completely conscious; and obviously learning how to build good models, and make good decisions based on them, is an important part of education in all cultures.

Although humans are good at some forms of knowledge discovery, they are woefully poor at other kinds. In general, we can predict when humans will be good by considering whether a particular form of knowledge discovery was useful in the setting of small groups of humans living a hunter-gatherer or simple agricultural lifestyle, and whether a high level of skill would benefit both the individual and the group. The examples in the previous subsection were chosen to illustrate this point. Someone who can predict the habits of animals will make a good hunter; someone who can predict the seasonal weather will make a good farmer.

However, when strong knowledge discovery would benefit an individual at the *expense* of the group, we find that humans do not perform particularly well. Deception is a good example. It would be useful for an individual to be able to be deceptive without being detected. However, when experiments involving deception are carried out, we find that individuals are not especially good at being deceptive, nor are individuals especially good at detecting deception. Even when trained police officers are used in experiments, their ability to detect deception is only marginally better than chance (despite a strong and universal conviction that they do, in fact, perform much better than this). There seems to have been a kind of arms race in humans between techniques for being deceptive and techniques for detecting deception that have left us, collectively, in a stalemate.

Other settings where human knowledge discovery is weak are those where either the input data is in a form that our sensory apparatus does not handle well, or the amount of the data is very large. For example, humans do not interpret pages of numbers well, although they may if the data is transformed into some visual form such as a graph. Humans can handle large amounts of data only when it comes directly via our sensory channels; otherwise we have limits on how much we can keep in 'working memory' at a time.

All three phases of knowledge discovery, data collection, analysis, and decision making can also be done using digital collection devices and computer algorithms. However, there are significant differences in what is possible, and how it should be done. Before we explore algorithmic knowledge discovery, though, we must consider how the knowledge-discovery process changes in an adversarial setting.

1.2   What is an Adversarial Setting?

An adversarial setting is one where someone involved is trying to alter the knowledge-discovery process for some reason of their own. Their goal is to create a model that does not accurately reflect the real situation and so, ultimately, to cause different decisions to be made and actions to be taken.

There is no appropriate English word to describe, collectively, those who might be trying to alter a knowledge-discovery process. We will use the term 'adversary' to describe such people. This is not an entirely appropriate term, since it loses the asymmetry between good and bad that turns out to be significant for the analysis, but it is the best term I have been able to come up with.

Most often, the goal of the adversaries is to do one or more of the following: conceal their existence; conceal their properties; conceal their relationships, both to each other and to those around them; and conceal their actions. This kind of directed alteration can take place in a range of settings:

- **International**
  - Intelligence, where the adversaries are spies and agents of other governments;
  - Counterterrorism, where the adversaries are terrorists;

- Defence, where the adversaries are the military forces of other nations, both formal and, increasingly, informal;
- International industrial espionage, where the adversaries are economic agents of other nations;
- Money laundering, where the adversaries are trying to move money illicitly across borders;
- Internet-based crime such as spam, phishing, and denial-of-service attacks, where the adversaries are criminals acting globally.

- **National**

  - Law enforcement, where the adversaries are criminals of all kinds;
  - Tax and benefit fraud, where the adversaries are cheating government programs, either by paying less or by getting more than they should.

- **Organizational**

  - Fraud, especially insurance fraud, where the adversaries are illicitly getting money from an organization;
  - Evading regulations, where the adversaries are organizations that are evading some obligation to their advantage.

- **Intra-Organizational**

  - Fraud, where the adversaries are defrauding their own organization;
  - Misuse of company resources, where the adversaries are using resources to do something that the organization does not intend them to do (for example, running a child pornography ring using organizational computers and network access).

Knowledge discovery is a well-developed field in the intersection of computer science, statistics, and high-performance computing. It is routinely applied in business, for example for customer relationship management; in science, for example for analyzing astrophysical data; and in biomedicine, for example for analyzing the outputs of high-throughput devices such as microarrays. Adversarial settings require some substantial changes to the knowledge-discovery process to respond to the potential for directed alteration and subversion at all three stages of the process.

For human knowledge discovery, the opportunities for subversion are primarily at the data collection, and decision and action phases, partly because we have limited introspective access to the analysis phase and partly because its existence was not fully appreciated until the analogous computing process was developed.

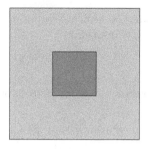 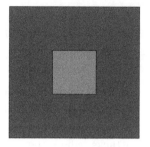

Figure 1.1. *The central squares are the same color.*

For example, the human visual system is easily subverted to see things that are not there, and not to see things that are there. Figure 1.1 shows two large boxes with smaller boxes inside them. The inner boxes are exactly the same shade – but do not look as if they are, because of the differing shades of the surrounding boxes. Optical illusions exploit the idiosyncrasies of the visual system.

These deficiencies of visual processing have been exploited for various good and not-so-good purposes. For example, the builders of the Parthenon carefully altered the shape of the pillars and placed them slightly off-vertical to create the illusion that the structure is taller than it actually is. Camouflage is designed to fool human viewers into failing to detect objects that they would otherwise see well. Makeup is designed to make human faces look different, sometimes better, than they otherwise would. Painting puts blobs of color on canvas in a way that fools us into seeing not just objects, but also depth and perspective. Films display a sequence of still images on a screen, but in a way carefully chosen to induce in us the sense that objects in the images are moving.

Camouflage and disguise are well-understood ways in which the human knowledge-discovery process can be subverted. Data collection via other channels can also be subverted, for example in the various ways that people use to lie or bend the truth (although these are less successful in general).

Drama is a way in which human social knowledge discovery is subverted, although usually with the willing participation of the subverted. When actors are on stage, they work to convey signals, at many different levels, that convey social relationships and emotions that they do not, in fact, have. Bad acting is a failure to carry out this subversion effectively – and when it fails we in the audience suddenly realize that we are sitting in a room watching people on a stage.

The decision-and-action phase of human knowledge discovery is also often subverted, a process that has come to be called, thanks to the hacking community, *social engineering*. Social engineering means playing to human preconceptions about what models mean, to produce a desired decision or action. Some common examples are the ways in which secret information is often obtained – by phoning someone and pretending to be a person who normally has the right to the information. This technique has now migrated to the Internet, where it is known as phishing – emailing or creating a web site that appears to be genuine, and asking people to provide their secret information in the mistaken belief that it is being requested by someone entitled to know it.

The best-selling book, *Breaking the Bank*[3], illustrates the same idea in the context of Las Vegas casinos. A group of highly skilled MIT students developed a team approach to making a lot of money at blackjack. However, to divert any suspicions that might have been aroused, they took great care to look and play the part of typical high-rollers, the kind that casinos welcome because they expect them to lose large amounts. The roles they played made it difficult for casino staff to see, in real time, that they were winning consistently.

In adversarial settings, all three phases must be rethought to take into account the possible presence of manipulation. Provided that the actual analysis is carried out in a secure way, the main opportunity for manipulation is in the data collection – corrupting the data that is used to build models, or the way in which new data is evaluated – and in decision and action – carrying out social engineering. However, an awareness of what kind of analysis is being done and what kinds of models will be built from the data is essential to making these manipulations work.

An adversarial setting in which prediction is used is credit-card fraud detection. The goal here is to predict whether an individual credit-card transaction, or perhaps a series of them, represents fraudulent use of a card (usually because it has been stolen). Factors such as whether the location of use matches the known location of the owner, and whether the purchase is consistent with the type and price of previous purchases, can be used. A more subtle kind of prediction is possible by exploiting awareness of the adversarial nature of this problem, however. When a credit card is stolen, its first use is often to purchase gasoline. The purchase is small enough that, if the card is refused, another form of payment can be used; and if the use triggers an alarm, escape is easy. This suggests that a fraud-detection system should pay more than the usual amount of attention to the transactions that immediately follow the purchase of gasoline, especially when the purchase is at an unusual location. In fact, this rule has already been implemented in some credit-card fraud-detection systems.

Other ways in which data collection can be manipulated apply when the prediction model is based on superficial attributes, rather than those essential to what is being predicted. For example, in several recent terrorist attacks, the participants deliberately acted in a less religious manner, shaved off beards, and used cologne to make themselves look less like the stereotype of a Salafist terrorist. Strategies such as this are also a form of social engineering since, even if a prediction of suspicion were made, their appearance would be sufficiently 'normal' that the prediction might be discounted.

An adversarial setting in which clustering has been used is the study of a criminal conspiracy to fix the prices of large electrical projects in the U.S. in the 1960s. Baker and Faulkner[4] studied the way in which the conspirators were connected to one another, and were able to show that position in the structure could be correlated with, for example, harshness of the sentence eventually given to the participants. (Unfortunately, not the correlation we might have wanted or expected. The leaders of the conspiracy did not receive the longest sentences; the middle-ranked participants did.)

An adversarial setting in which discovering connections is important is money laundering. Drug dealers have a great deal of difficulty accounting for, and so moving, the large amounts of cash that they receive. It is common, therefore, for them to associate with a business, say a pizza restaurant, that does a lot of business in cash. The drug cash can be laundered through the business by, for example, flushing pizza supplies away and treating the drug money as income for the sales of the 'missing' pizzas. To find drug dealers, therefore, one strategy is to look for a characteristic pattern of connections between suspected individuals, largely cash businesses, and other relationships that are more directly related to drugs, such as contacts or telephone calls to countries that supply drugs. Of course, drug dealers try to hide these connections by, for example, using people to move money around in quantities below the (current) $10,000 threshold above which banks must report the transaction. Connections to many such people become part of a pattern that could be searched for.

An adversarial setting in which discovering how others are thinking or feeling is important in kidnapping and other forms of extortion, where insight into the minds of the kidnappers can suggest whether it is reasonable to pay the ransom, and whether extortioners will actually carry out their threat.

One special case of an adversarial setting is quite different, and deserves a fuller discussion. In this case, the adversarial situation is set up because those whom the data describes want more privacy than those doing the modelling are prepared to grant them. They are not really adversaries because they have no malicious intent – they simply do not want to be modelled.

In some situations, this is best resolved by those who want privacy opting out of the process. For example, it is (at the moment) always possible to pay cash and so prevent a business from learning anything about you as a customer. Not only does this prevent their learning your identity, but it also prevents them associating your purchases at different times and in different places to build a model of you, even as an anonymous customer. However, even in this case there are costs as a consumer. Businesses that are able to model their customers are often able to give differential pricing (for example, airline seats) and differential service to good customers. This benefit is not available to those who choose to remain anonymous.

The other approach that people who want privacy take is to pollute the data – taking every opportunity to cause incorrect data to be collected about themselves. This can be a viscerally satisfying response, but it is not clear that it achieves the desired end. By doing so, they fail to get any of the benefits of, for example, being modelled as a desirable customer. In adversarial modelling, their records are likely to make them look like outliers, because they will not fit the 'normal' behavior of most other people, and so they may show up looking like cases of interest when they aren't.

1.3 Algorithmic Knowledge Discovery

So far we have emphasized how humans carry out knowledge discovery, and how the process can be manipulated by those who wish to subvert it. Many aspects of knowledge discovery can also be implemented using digital technology for the collection, and computers and algorithms to carry out the analysis.

The data-collection phase is very naturally handled using technology as, increasingly, transactions are computer-mediated. For example, opinion surveys used to be done by hand, and the results entered into databases later, with the potential for transcription errors. Increasingly, surveys are done on the web, either directly by the respondent or by a telephone marketer as the respondent answers. In cases like this, direct collection of data can dramatically reduce error rates.

The ease with which data can be captured also makes new forms of data capture possible, for example licence plate numbers via roadside cameras; and makes capture of large amounts of data economic, for example closed-circuit television (CCTV) footage. Credit-card and bank-card transactions, telephone call records and content, online web-surfing activity, email messages and their contents, fingerprints, physical location via cell phone or pass scanning at boundaries, commuting patterns via electronic tickets, and travel plans via flight bookings can all be collected straightforwardly.

There are two principal differences between data gathered in a digital, computer-mediated way, and data collected by humans. First, the modalities are different. Most digital data is in forms that humans find difficult to handle and process directly. Even when there is an apparent overlap, the underlying reality is quite different. For example, when CCTV data is collected for human analysis, it is typically displayed in large banks of monitors watched by a human. The watching human is good at detecting suspicious behavior in principle, but in practice is quite likely to miss it because of the difficulty of focusing attention for a long time. On the other hand, it does not matter that the data is large when it is intended for computer analysis – but algorithms are, at present, not nearly sophisticated enough to detect generic 'suspicious behavior'. About the best they can do is detect particular behavior that may be problematic. For example, some transit surveillance systems are able to detect, with high reliability, objects that detach themselves from people, such as backpacks being left behind on platforms. Second, digital data collection usually produces much larger volumes than data intended for human analysis would bother to collect.

In the analysis phase, algorithms are used to extract knowledge from the available data. At first glance, this ability might seem to be hard for computers to reproduce, since it seems to rely on intuition and other skills that humans are good at. And indeed there is a subtle problem with knowledge extraction (in fact, for both humans and algorithms): the problem of induction. How can we reasonably reach a conclusion from a limited set of data? For all of us, the sun has come up every morning that we've been alive. In logic, however, this provides no justification for concluding that the sun will come up tomorrow.

To get around this problem, we must first of all admit that models are not truth or descriptions of truth – rather, they are working hypotheses for which the evidence is good enough that we are willing to act. Hence, we don't party every evening as if it is the last day on earth, because the hypothesis that the sun will come up again tomorrow is one on which we're willing to act.

Computer algorithms for knowledge discovery work by finding hypotheses that are justified, to some extent, by the evidence available in the data. Simply put, they treat the available data as examples and try to find patterns that hold across many examples.

This means that the models that are built will depend on choices that are made about the analysis techniques to apply to the data. There are four different kinds of choices:

1. The choice of the particular model to be built. Different models reflect different assumptions about what kind of qualitative structures and relationships are present in the data.

2. The level of complexity of the model. For each particular model, it is usually possible to choose how complex the model is allowed to be.

3. The choice of algorithm. For a given model of a given complexity, there may be different ways to compute the model.

4. The choice of algorithm parameters. For a given algorithm, there are usually some parameters that need to be set, determining how much work the algorithm will do and so the performance of the resulting model.

The problem with these choices is that there is almost never enough good information about the problem to make them well, at least at the beginning. This chicken-and-egg problem comes up often in knowledge discovery. Usually the best solution is iteration – start with sensible choices based on little information, look at the quality of the resulting model, and use this evaluation to make better choices. This process may need to be repeated a number of times before a high-quality model is obtained. Sometimes it is possible to perform a parameter sweep; take many different combinations of the possible choices and build models for all of them concurrently. However, this is usually feasible only with some of the later, lower-level choices, such as varying algorithm parameters.

The large number of potential models and the problem of induction mean that attention needs to be paid to measuring the quality of models at every stage. The temptation is to get results that seem plausible or interesting and to assume that the technology must have found an underlying truth. Given enough data, there are always patterns present by accident, and the danger is that an analysis algorithm will find these accidental patterns, rather than deeper, but perhaps less obvious, ones.

Algorithmic knowledge discovery tends to be complementary to human knowledge discovery. The kinds of knowledge that humans are good at finding: faces, objects in images, single conversations in noisy rooms, and covert relationships between people are difficult to discover algorithmically. On the other hand, algorithmic discovery is good at finding: predictive patterns and the properties they depend on (where humans tend to be misled by properties they *think* are predictive), deceptive patterns in languages, and models that depend on very large datasets, and datasets that are primarily symbolic.

The third phase is the decision-and-action phase. In mainstream knowledge discovery, it is plausible to allow algorithms to make decisions based on the models they have built. For example, mortgage lenders allow money to be lent based on forms filled out at a web site; and many system tools automatically take action to quarantine files predicted to contain viruses, or spam emails. However, in an adversarial setting, it is almost certainly a bad idea to allow the decision-and-action phase to be driven algorithmically.

If we know that someone is actively trying to subvert the knowledge-discovery process, then we must expect that they will sometimes succeed. Humans may not be good at some aspects of the analysis process, but they are extremely good at 'common sense', a holistic view of a setting. Having humans involved in the final decision and action is a last-ditch protection against the knowledge-discovery system being subverted. At least some knowledge-discovery systems can be reverse engineered, making it possible for adversaries to take precise actions to evade detection, but these actions are often inherently rather odd, and may trigger suspicion by a human overseeing the process.

Of course, the possibility of social engineering must be taken into account, and human decision-making should be based on training, particularly about the algorithmic processes involved so that they have some sense of how subversion might be effective. In a sense, that is one purpose of this book.

1.3.1   What is Different about Adversarial Knowledge Discovery?

We have already indicated that the presence of adversaries requires a different approach to knowledge discovery, even in comparison to mainstream knowledge discovery that is now common in business, science, and engineering. The most important difference, of course, is a sensitivity to the way that the process can be manipulated, both by outsiders and insiders.

We will return to these issues in later chapters, but the main differences in an adversarial setting are:

- Data collection must be controlled so that it is hard for anyone to force particular data into the collection system.

- Data must be protected from alteration once it has been collected, and all access to it should be logged in a write-once (that is, unalterable) way.

- The sensitivity of knowledge-discovery algorithms to the presence of potentially misleading data must be fully appreciated; and algorithms that are easy to mislead may, in the end, be unusable.

- The structured process in which knowledge-discovery algorithms are used should reflect the need to discover adversaries without unduly harassing those who are not.

- The structured process in which knowledge-discovery algorithms are used should take into account the feedback loop between analysts and adversaries, in which adversaries try both to obscure their traces, and to attack vulnerabilities in the knowledge-discovery system.

- The entire analysis process should be transparent to those carrying out the modelling to make it hard for insiders to subvert.

- Access to data should be on a need-to-know basis, with procedures to determine who needs to know and when this should change. Although this is not strictly a requirement for knowledge discovery, without it the data is likely to be heavily polluted even by ordinary people, in their attempts to maintain privacy.

As mainstream knowledge-discovery systems are increasingly used to drive decisions with financial implications, we can expect that more and more systems will become adversarial in nature. When some customers get better service or pricing because of how they are modelled by a knowledge-discovery system, there will be those who will want to try and manipulate the system to their advantage. These requirements will become increasingly necessary in all knowledge-discovery systems.

Knowledge discovery in adversarial settings can take place in two different ways. In traditional law enforcement, the role of knowledge discovery is *retrospective*: when a crime has been committed, an investigation gathers data in a needs-driven way, and both humans and, potentially, algorithmic tools examine this data, looking for patterns that might indicate the perpetrator.

The scope of data that is collected is circumscribed by the crime that is under investigation – data is collected only from and about people in immediate temporal and physical proximity to the crime, expanding outwards to include discoverable connections between them and others. The needs-driven nature of the data collection makes it easy to justify, and there are seldom privacy concerns or complaints about the data collection[5].

Retrospective, investigative, and forensic analysis also take place in other adversarial settings, for example after a terrorist attack or when some corporate malfeasance is uncovered.

However, increasingly knowledge discovery is used in a *prospective* way to try and prevent something bad happening. This is most obvious, of course, in the counterterrorism setting, where the goal of preventing catastrophic attacks trumps even the need to prosecute the perpetrators. However, law enforcement also uses prospective techniques to decide where crime might happen and then to harden these locations or situations to make it less likely. For example, looking at the geographical and temporal location of crimes can be used to schedule police presence to act as a more effective deterrent. Organizations that bear responsibility for the actions of their employees, at least in public opinion if not in law, also try to prevent criminal or even questionable activities from taking place at work or using organizational resources.

When the focus is on prevention, the data collection net must, of necessity, be spread wider. Since potential trouble spots are not known in advance, data about many more things may be required in order to find them. This widespread data collection is much more problematic in terms of its impact on privacy. Society is wrestling with the whole question of prospective knowledge, the costs of its generation, and how it should be used. We will return to this issue in the context of specific knowledge-discovery techniques.

1.4   State of the Art

There are five main areas of application where knowledge discovery is already used, although the extent and sophistication of the tools and techniques in use vary widely. These five areas are discussed below.

Predictive models of risk. Algorithmic models are used to predict the risk posed by a particular object or person in a particular setting, and a decision is made based on this predicted risk. Some examples are:

- Predicting the distribution of crime in time and space, so that personnel levels and patrol patterns can be arranged for best effect, perhaps for maximum deterrence.

- Predicting the likelihood that passengers might want or be planning to carry out a terrorist attack in a transportation setting such as an airport or train station. Airline passenger screening is one well-known example.

- Predicting which people crossing a border should receive significant attention from customs (and other border-control entities).

- Predicting which connection attempts to a computer network are intrusions; for example attempts to break into the system, or carry out a denial-of-service attack.

- Predicting which incoming email messages are spam, and should be sequestered.

These predictive models are built from historical data from which the differences between high- and low-risk objects or people can be inferred.

Predictive models of fraud. This is a special case of the prediction of risk. In many settings, it is important to know whether a particular transaction is ordinary or fraudulent; as before, models for doing such prediction can be learned from historical data. Fraud is believed to account for around 3% of Gross Domestic Product in developed countries, so there are enormous opportunities for economic improvements. By some estimates, each dollar spent looking for fraud produces a return of between $20 and $30. Some examples are:

- Predicting which taxpayers may have filed fraudulent tax forms, and so should be investigated further.

- Predicting patients, doctors, laboratories, pharmacies, or drug companies that may have filed fraudulent claims related to health activities.

- Predicting when a credit-card transaction is fraudulent and should not be authorized.

- Predicting when accounting transactions are fraudulent.

- Predicting a known value, and comparing the prediction and the reported value.

Most fraud prediction does not have to be made in real time (the exceptions being systems such as credit-card fraud detection), so a different level of accuracy is possible. If each potential fraud must be investigated before prosecution, then only the most egregious will typically be pursued. On the other hand, if something is predicted as suspicious but turns out not to be, there is relatively little harm done.

Matching. A class of simple predictive models are those where there is a list of objects or people, and the goal is to match a large set of objects or people to see if any of them appear on the list. In the simplest case, for example a list of names, this matching is simple. However, usually matching requires looking for similarity across a number of dimensions, so the process can become complex. Some examples are:

- Wanted lists and posters generated by law enforcement.

- Licence-plate detection. For example, licence-plate scanning technology is deployed in the U.K. at fixed locations, on police vehicles, and even in aircraft. Each car that passes and is scanned by one of these enhanced cameras has its licence plate compared to a list of plates of interest.

- Face recognition. Although face recognition is a difficult problem, there are many prototype systems that attempt to match faces viewed by television cameras against a list of faces of interest. This is not very reliable in uncontrolled circumstances, where lighting is variable, camera angles are not controlled, and more than one face is visible simultaneously. However, error rates in controlled situations are dropping to usable levels.

Exploring relationships and connections, starting from an object or person of interest. Relationship data expresses the links or connections between people, and between people and objects such as addresses, telephone numbers, bank accounts, cars, flights, and so on. Such data arises from surveillance, from interrogation, and indirectly from other forms of data such as call billing records. In such data, almost all knowledge discovery is done by starting from a known person or object and exploring the neighborhood of that starting point. Some examples are:

- Most criminal investigation. For example, police forces use systems to collect relationship data during complex cases[6]. This data can be used to generate action items, or can be used in an exploratory mode to look at objects and people connected to an object or person of interest.

- Insurance fraud. Such fraud is often detected because those involved in events for which a claim is made turn out to be connected more closely than the laws of chance suggest.

- Money laundering. This is characterized by typical patterns of connections between sources of money, places that are known to turn a blind eye to international banking practices, and middlemen.

- Intelligence and counterterrorism. Understanding the relationships and connections between people of interest can provide insights into targeting, methods of operation, command and control, and recruitment. Intelligence analysts spend a lot of time looking at the connections around persons of interest.

Exploring relationships and connections in an entire structure. In some forms of relationship data, there are no obvious starting points, and ways to analyze the structure as a whole are used to find the interesting regions. Some examples are:

- Telephone fraud. Telephone companies can collect data on call graphs (which numbers call each other). Finding anything interesting in this large structure requires careful analysis – but people who are committing fraud from new telephones tend to call the same set of people that they called from previous telephones, allowing them to be tracked even though they are changing their most obvious feature.

- Intelligence and counterterrorism. It is important to understand the structure within a terrorist or espionage group even before it is possible to identify the most interesting people within it – in fact, this kind of global analysis is one way in which the most interesting people, such as leaders, can be identified.

Selecting data for subsequent human analysis. Although completely automatic knowledge discovery is possible in some settings, there are many others where its most appropriate role is to act as a filter, selecting those people, objects, transactions, or relationships that are apparently of greatest interest – so that a human can subsequently analyze them more deeply. Some examples are:

- Intrusion detection. Although completely automatic intrusion detection systems are used, the more effective ones rank apparent intrusions by their perceived danger, and allow humans to take action based on the ranked list.

- Many organizations are responsible for malfeasance of many kinds by their employees. They may monitor email traffic, and investigate further when emails suggest that something is amiss.

- Most governments intercept message traffic (emails, web browsing, web forums, instant messaging, telephone calls) and analyze the resulting text as part of their intelligence effort. The number of such messages is very large, so automatic techniques are used to select a much, much smaller set for subsequent analysis.

Law enforcement, intelligence, and counterterrorism personnel will have some experience with some of these tools. What may be missing is, first, an awareness of the limitations of each family of tools; and, second, an awareness of what other tools are possible, and how the components of a set of tools can complement each other to allow more sophisticated knowledge discovery. Understanding the limitations of a tool or technique is best done by understanding how it works, at least at the right level of abstraction. Understanding how tools can work together is best done by seeing what other tools can do, and the synergies that can be created.

Notes

[1] You can try this test at http://www.philosophersnet.com/games/logic_task.htm.

[2] In the Preface to *Pygmalion* (1916).

[3] B. Mezrich, *Bringing Down the House: How Six Students Took Vegas for Millions*, Arrow Books, 2002 and now adapted into a film, *21*.

[4] W.E. Baker and R.B. Faulkner, "The social organization of conspiracy: Illegal networks in the heavy electrical equipment industry", *American Sociological Review*, 58:837–860, December 1993, studied the way in which conspirators in price fixing of large electrical projects were connected to one another.

[5] Note, however, in historical detective fiction, which reflects the views of the times, how often members of the upper class assumed that they were above suspicion, and so should not be questioned when a crime occurred in their vicinity. Clearly, our attitude to criminal investigation has been learned.

[6] The HOLMES system collects relationship data during complex cases. It records all entities mentioned during witness statements and officer reports, and draws connections between them. These connections can be explicitly

explored, asking questions such as "who else has lived at this address?" or "have these two people ever called the same phone number?".

Chapter 2

Data

Good knowledge discovery relies on the properties and the quality of the data from which it is derived. In this chapter, we consider the different kinds of data that are collected, and how this influences the kinds of knowledge that can be discovered from them. We also consider the channels by which data is collected, and how these channels impose their own constraints on the data. In adversarial settings, one way to manipulate or subvert discovered knowledge is to change the way in which data is collected, or alter it after collection, so we will also consider how data is protected, and how its quality can be assessed. Finally, there is a considerable debate going on about the relationship between knowledge discovery and privacy. As a foundation for this debate, we will also consider how much data is required for effective knowledge discovery.

2.1 Kinds of Data

Data collected for knowledge discovery is usually very large, partly because many of the collection channels are automatic. The number of people who deal with a government or large corporation is in the millions, in some cases hundreds of millions. The number of transactions about which data is recorded is much larger: there are several billion telephone calls made in the U.S. each day, hundreds of millions of credit-card transactions, and billions of web page views. Although data can be collected in many different forms, it is worth looking more closely at a few of the more common kinds of data.

2.1.1   Data about Objects

The most common kind of data consists of a list of records, each of which describes the properties of some object. Often this object is a person; and the properties are things like age, income, height, ethnicity, or address. Another common possibility is that the object is a transaction; and the properties are things like date and time, amount of money involved, how the transaction was paid for, and so on.

In the simplest case, all records have values for the same set of properties, and these properties are called the *attributes* of the record. The list of records forms a table or matrix, with one row for each record, and one column for each attribute. We call this form of data *attributed data*.

It may also be the case that different records have different numbers of properties. For example, the record describing what each customer at a store has purchased will have some properties common to all records, for example time and total amount spent, but different properties describing the objects purchased, since one customer may have purchased just one thing while another may have purchased many. In this case, the list of records is not easy to represent as a table, which makes it significantly harder to work with.

Attributed data about people is gathered by most organizations: retail stores to keep track of their customers' shopping habits or credit standing, charities for mailing lists, governments for tax purposes, and telephone companies for billing. Such information is also gathered at a higher level, for example by credit-rating companies, frequent-flyer programs, and their off-shoot loyalty programs, producing large, detailed records about the financial properties of individual's lives.

Attributed data about transactions is gathered, largely automatically, whenever people are involved in transactions. For example, every credit-card purchase, every bank transaction, every telephone call, and every web page download generates a transaction record. Many transactions are also generated without any direct human involvement, as computers talk to one another, and to sensors.

2.1.2   Low-Level Data

A second kind of data is that where each individual attribute value makes little sense by itself, but a large collection of attribute values makes sense *in a particular arrangement*. The most important example of this is image data, where the individual attributes are pixels. Such data arises from pictures, and video, especially video from closed-circuit television (CCTV). Audio data is also of this form.

Another variant of this kind of data is data collected by sensors. For example, a chemical or nuclear plant may be instrumented with a large number of sensors that gather data about temperatures, pressures, and concentrations. Making sense of this data requires an awareness of how the different values *fit together*, as well as what the values are.

Low-level data is most often gathered automatically. It also tends to be very large. Often, for example in video, each individual record (one image) is not as useful as a set of related records.

Low-level data can often be directly analyzed by humans, provided it can be made to match our normal modes of sensing. Humans can usually recognize what objects are in an image, a task that is still difficult to do algorithmically. However, while humans are good at dealing with a single record of this form, they perform less well when there are many records. For example, humans watching banks of closed-circuit television feeds soon start to miss potentially important activities that are plainly visible.

Similarly humans are able to understand the audio obtained by intercepting telephone calls, but the sheer number of such calls makes it impossible for humans to be the primary means of finding suspicious activity this way.

2.1.3   Data about Connections

A third kind of data is data that describes the properties of the *connections* or *relationships* between objects, rather than properties of the objects themselves. Such data is naturally represented as a *graph*, with nodes corresponding to the objects, and edges representing the connections among objects. The edges may have attributes associated with them as well.

In such data, it is the shape of the graph, rather than individual nodes or edges, that contains most of the information. Often the nodes represent individuals, and the connections between them represent relationships such as: "is a relative of", "meets with", "knows", or "communicates to". The connection can be symmetric (if I meet with you, then you also meet with me), or asymmetric (if I communicate to you, you don't necessarily communicate to me, and may not even know who I am).

Connection data is what results from conventional surveillance, watching a group of people, their movements, and their communications. Connection data can also be extracted from many kinds of attributed data by looking for records in which the values of particular attributes match, or almost match. For example, given transaction data about telephone calls, it is straightforward to construct a call graph by extracting the calling and called numbers from each transaction record. Given a dataset of names and addresses, it is possible to extract geographical neighbors by looking at house numbers,

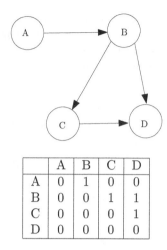

	A	B	C	D
A	0	1	0	0
B	0	0	1	1
C	0	0	0	1
D	0	0	0	0

Figure 2.1. *Connection graph and adjacency matrix.*

street names, and postal/zip codes. Also, from transaction data such as birth certificates it is possible to extract family trees, a special form of connection data.

Connection data can be represented as a list of node-node records, but it is often useful to represent it is an *adjacency matrix*. Such a matrix has one row and one column for each node, and its ijth entry is 0 if node i is not connected to node j; otherwise, it contains a value that represents the properties of the connection. If the only property of interest is that node i is connected to node j, then a 1 might be used, and the adjacency matrix will be a binary matrix. The value might also be a positive integer representing the importance or weight of the connection, or the *affinity* between node i and node j.

Figure 2.1 shows a small set of connection data, showing the connections between four nodes as directed arrows. The resulting adjacency matrix is also shown. Notice that, because the connections are directional (A connects to B, but B does not connect to A) the resulting matrix is not symmetric. By convention, each node does not connect to itself, so the diagonal of the matrix is all zeros.

2.1.4 Textual Data

A fourth kind of data is textual data. Such data arises naturally whenever people write, and it can also be transcribed fairly easily from speech and audio. Text can come from books and articles, letters, statements, email, blogs, web pages, and instant messaging; as well as from speeches and telephone calls.

Text in its raw form (certain words in a particular order) is, of course, something that humans are good at extracting knowledge from. Algorithms have difficulty extracting knowledge, in textual content, with the same ease as humans, but it turns out that there are complementary forms of knowledge that can be extracted algorithmically.

It is also useful to convert text into other representations, for example, the frequency of use of each word in each document. This representation is not a natural one for humans but it makes some interesting algorithmic analysis possible.

A variant of textual data is called *semi-structured data*. This is the kind of data that is created whenever you fill in a form: some parts look like ordinary attributes and take on values from a fixed set, while other parts look like freeform text.

Whenever text is formatted to create a particular appearance, the way in which it is arranged can sometimes convey extra information, making it semi-structured in a different way. For example, HTML, the markup language used to create web pages, describes each element of a page in terms of what it is, and the decision about how to display it is made independently and later. A string can be tagged as a second-level heading, and different browsers may make different choices about which fonts at what sizes should be used to display the string. Hence, although the author's *intention* is to say something about how the string should look, the tagging also says something about what the string *means*. This extra information can be exploited during analysis.

2.1.5 Spatial Data

In some settings, spatial information is critical to make sense of the knowledge implicit in the data. This kind of data is a bit like low-level data and a bit like connection data.

For example, data collected about crimes committed may contain the location of each crime as one of the attributes. Treating this attribute as important, including the implicit spatial information that comes from geography, and plotting the locations may make it clear that there are clusters of certain kinds of crimes in certain locations. In the same way, the locations of meetings or places of residence may contain information that is not easy to see without including the spatial aspect of the data.

Biosurveillance data also has a strong spatial component. For example, outbreaks of infectious diseases and food poisoning can be detected by noticing the geographical distribution of cases[1].

2.2   Data That Changes

All of the kinds of data we have discussed can also change over time, and
it is important to be able to handle this property as part of the knowledge-
discovery process as well. There are two qualitatively different ways in which
changes in the data can be significant.

2.2.1   Slow Changes in the Underlying Situation

Data is often treated as if it describes an underlying situation that is static.
This is almost never a realistic assumption, partly because humans vary in
their behavior on a short time scale. For example, the population of criminals
in a particular area might contain a subset of regulars, but there is also likely
to be a population of transients – as a result, the profile of crime in that area
will change from week to week, and possibly even more frequently.

Modelling any significant situation should include a mechanism to update the discovered knowledge. The obvious way to do this is to continue
to collect new data and incorporate this data into the model at appropriate
intervals.

The complicating factor is that, almost certainly, older data should be
removed or discounted from the modelling process, since it describes a reality
that is no longer true. Because data is so large, it is usually not realistic
to store it indefinitely, so the older data may not still be available. Even
if it were, many knowledge-discovery techniques are not able to remove the
effects of older data from the model – although many *incremental* knowledge-
discovery algorithms are known, very few *decremental* algorithms are known.
It is also often not clear how much to discount older data. In other words,
determining the rate at which older data becomes stale may itself be a difficult
problem. The simplest solution may, in the end, be to repeat the knowledge-
discovery process at regular intervals in a zero-base way, starting from the
most recently collected data.

2.2.2   Change is the Important Property

In other settings, it may be changes in the underlying data itself that are the
critical signal that needs to be extracted.

The most obvious example is when the data comes from a set of sensors.
If temperature sensors are placed in a building and their readings are collected
periodically, it is a sudden change in the reading of one or more of them
that should cause the fire alarm to be set off. In this case, the extracted
knowledge is not important in itself, but acts as a baseline to which newer

data is compared to detect a significant change. It is a change in the discovered knowledge that is critical, not the knowledge itself.

Detecting change is not necessarily a trivial process. For example, consider tsunami detection, and suppose that there are sensors that measure seismic activity, depth of the water, and overpressure at the ocean bottom. A change in any single one of these sensors does not usually signal a tsunami – rather it is a set of coordinated changes in the correct pattern that is the signal that must be detected. So discovering knowledge from the incoming sensor data is a non-trivial task. Also, measurements such as water height change with the tides in a regular way, and these changes are not interesting for tsunami detection. So the processing of the signals from these sensors must discount changes at one rate, while paying particular attention to changes at another (much faster) rate.

Another situation where a change is the critical signal is the increase or decrease in 'chatter' among members of terrorist groups, which may signal an imminent attack. This change can be noticed even when the content of the communication is inaccessible, perhaps because the communications are encrypted. Again, though, deciding that there is an increase or decrease in chatter may need to take into account other reasons for increased or decreased communication, such as day of the week, season, and religious or social events.

2.2.3   Stream Data

Another aspect of data that is relevant is how much there is and how fast it is collected and arrives for analysis. Stream data might be of any of the kinds described above; its special property is that it arrives so fast that it cannot be stored for analysis for more than a very short time interval.

For such data, analysis is limited to examining each piece of the data once, and having a limited amount of time to do whatever processing is required for that piece of data. Data may even arrive so quickly that some records might have to be discarded without analysis.

Examples of such data are data from traffic sensors on highways, radar returns from aircraft, or video from CCTV cameras.

2.3   Fusion of Different Kinds of Data

Data about the 'same thing', that is the same person, or the same transaction, may be collected in different places, via different channels, and in different forms. To understand what is really happening in the most sophisticated and deepest way, all of the information about a single 'thing' must be put together so that its relevance can be assessed. This is called *data fusion*.

Even data that is of the same form, for example attributed data, can still be collected from different places. For example, a customer may interact with a retail store via its bricks-and-mortar store, via its website, and via a toll-free telephone number. If the store wants to model this customer's buying behavior, it needs to realize that these interactions are all with the same customer, and fuse the information about the different interactions into a single view of what this customer is like.

In a more complex setting, an intelligence analyst may need to realize that an image captured by a CCTV camera, a photo on a visa application, and an airline reservation are all part of travel by one individual.

Fusing data is critical to discovering knowledge; separate analysis from each of the different pieces of data, even with the most sophisticated tools, will miss some aspects. This is why the metaphor of "connecting the dots" has become so ubiquitous in discussions of counterterrorism.

The most obvious way to connect different data about the 'same thing', perhaps a person or a transaction, is to use a *key*. A key is an attribute that is associated with the same object in the different contexts where data is collected. For example, common keys associated with people are customer numbers, transaction numbers, or credit card numbers. Using such numbers, a customer's different interactions with a store can all be associated with the customer.

Names are another common form of key, but names have serious drawbacks, both in common use and in algorithmic analysis of data. First, names are not unique, so it is relatively easy to associate, incorrectly, information about several people, thinking it is about one person.

Second, it is socially acceptable to vary the name one goes by in multiple ways, and so the form that is captured with data at different times and different contexts can vary. This is the converse of the previous problem – now data that really is about one person looks like it is about more than one. 'Jonathan Paul Smith' may legitimately go by 'Jon Smith', 'John Smith', 'Jon P. Smith', 'J.P. Smith', or 'J. Paul Smith' and this makes reconciling these keys very difficult.

Third, those who wish to conceal their identity can exploit this looseness in the use of names to deliberately create keys that are hard to reconcile by mixing up their given names, using spelling variants, and so on. These can be characterized as genuine mistakes if the issue is ever raised, so there is little risk to doing this. Chen's research group at the University of Arizona found that 35% of gang identity records and 55% of narcotic identity records were incorrect versions of others, caused by a combination of apparently deliberate alteration and clerical errors.

Fourth, the rules for transliterating names from one language to another are often quite loose, which means that names can be further obfuscated by applying different rules in different settings. There are at least fifteen acceptable ways to render the name Mohammed in English, and at least four to render the name Zhou. When an intermediate language can plausibly be used, the number of possibilities increases even further. The same human propensities to transcribe digits in numbers also allow those who wish to conceal their identities to 'accidentally' transcribe digits in their Social Security Numbers, telephone numbers, and addresses.

This lack of good keys for people explains the interest in biometrics. A *biometric* is a key that is somehow fundamentally associated with a particular person, and so can allow data about them to be accessed from multiple repositories, and to be fused reliably into a single descriptive record for analysis.

The oldest biometric system was the Bertillon system of measurement of parts of the body, the first rigorous method of identifying criminals. This was replaced by fingerprinting, which was the standard biometric for a century, and is now being replaced by DNA. Other common biometrics are iris characteristics, hand characteristics, ear characteristics, and behavioral properties such as voice or typing rhythm.

The two critical properties of a useful biometric in this context is that it should be digital, and that it should be stable and unforgeable. A picture in a passport is an example of a non-digital biometric. It allows a border official to establish, fairly reliably, that the passport document belongs to the person who presents it, but it cannot be used to access further information about that person. Passports that include a digital biometric such as a digitized photo, or a digitized fingerprint associate the document with the person presenting it, but also allow other data to be associated with that person using the digital biometric as a key.

Unfortunately, many digital biometrics are either unstable or are relatively easy to forge. For example, voices change over time, especially with illness, so voice recognition is problematic as a biometric. The weaknesses of fingerprints have been known for a long time – Austin Freeman published a detective novel in 1907[2] that hinged on the creation of a false fingerprint using technology readily available at the time. Today's fingerprint readers can be easily spoofed, sometimes simply by pressing down on a sheet of plastic wrap over the reader, causing them to resense the previous finger impression. Even iris biometrics can be easily fooled by the printed image of someone else's iris.

Although keys are helpful to fusing data collected via different channels and in different forms, it is also possible to fuse data that does not contain keys, using extra knowledge about the domain. For example, AOL released anonymized logs of web searches by its customers. Despite the fact that no user-identifying information was included, at least some of the users could be identified by people who knew them, solely based on the content of the searches. The fine details of census data are not made public for similar reasons; whenever the number of people matching a particular combination of criteria is small enough, it becomes possible to identify them, even without explicit identifying data. Marketing data at the individual zip-code level is available for the U.S., and families with unusual makeups, for example with six children, can easily be identified in such data.

It is also possible that features of the data themselves act as keys, unsuspected by those about whom the data is collected. These features can be summarized as *style*. As we shall see, authorship of anonymous documents can sometimes be determined simply from the differences in the use of words and punctuation from one author to another. Poker players are familiar with *tells* that act as keys in particular kinds of observational data.

2.4   How is Data Collected?

In the previous section, we have implied that data can be collected in many forms and in different ways. We now set out to illustrate some of those ways, and discuss how the channels by which we get data affect the data and what can be done with it.

It is helpful to distinguish the channels by which data is gathered by the nature of the collection interface. There are four distinct possibilities.

2.4.1   Transaction Endpoints

Transaction endpoints collect data because of a specific interaction whose properties are recorded. The most obvious example is a credit-card purchase in a store. The use of the credit card allows the creation of a record that associates the purchaser, the store, the product or service purchased, and the cost.

The data captured is fairly reliable, since the transaction will not go through without some validation that the credit card's owner exists and is solvent. The store has no reason to deceive about its identity or the cost since it loses financially if it does. The only real opportunity for manipulating the data is to alter the identification of the product or service purchased.

Transaction endpoints collect data explicitly, and with the consent of the parties to the transaction. Data is collected as a side-effect of a necessary, although voluntary, action.

2.4.2   Interaction Endpoints

Interaction endpoints collect data because of some incidental interaction. The obvious example is where a cell phone informs the local cell tower of its presence whenever it is turned on, regardless of whether calls are made or received. This interaction creates records that can be used to locate the cell phone (and by implication its owner) without the owner necessarily being aware that data is being collected.

Data is gathered as a side-effect of some other property, in this case wanting to have a cell phone turned on. The use of cookies by Internet browsers is another example of how data about a person can be collected without the person's awareness and without any necessary benefit to the person. The gathering of data is voluntary in the sense that a person has to do something to enable its collection, but it is possible, perhaps common, for the person to be unaware of the data collection. As technology becomes more sophisticated, people may become less aware of incidental data collection. For example, RFIDs are tags that respond with a unique identifier when queried by a low-power radio transmitter. Someone may wear or carry one without being aware of it, allowing anyone sufficiently close to accurately identify the RFID, and so by implication some of the person's properties[3].

The weakness of such data is that, precisely because the data is collected as a side-effect, it is not reliable. If someone goes out and leaves their cell phone turned on at home, then it is impossible to gather the data about their travel patterns. In other words, the key for such data is not a biometric but a form of key that is much more loosely associated with the person. Of course, this also makes it possible for the data to be manipulated deliberately to subvert subsequent analysis.

2.4.3 Observation Endpoints

Observation endpoints collect data without the cooperation, and perhaps without the knowledge, of the person concerned. The most obvious is closed-circuit television surveillance. Even in jurisdictions where such observation must be signposted, it is often impossible to tell whether it is actually happening at any given moment because cameras are frequently enclosed in dark glass hemispheres.

Such data collection is implicit and involuntary. However, as a result it is hard to generate keys for the collected data since the people involved do not provide them. At present, therefore, the data collected in these settings is of limited usefulness[4]. Some of the research aimed at automatic face recognition is an attempt to generate automatic biometric keys from video data.

2.4.4 Human Data Collection

Of course, data in any form can be collected by some non-technical means and made available digitally using data entry. However, the costs of doing this mean that such data is usually small in comparison to automatically collected data. Human data entry has error rates much higher than most forms of automatic data collection, so this limits the usefulness of data collected in this way as well.

2.4.5   Reasons for Data Collection

Two other issues related to data are worth mentioning. Some data for analysis is collected more or less as a side-effect of whatever an organization normally does. In fact, this is how knowledge discovery began – organizations collected transaction data automatically, and they began to think that there was some potential benefit in analyzing this historical data for patterns relevant to their businesses. This has become so important that data is now often collected with the explicit goal of discovering knowledge from it. In this setting, the data is usually collected without any preconceived ideas of what might be interesting about it, or where the most interesting knowledge might be found.

In contrast, some data is collected for an explicit purpose, and that purpose guides the kind and amount of data that is collected. In other words, the properties of a particular model guide the data collection, and the data is supposed to support the correctness or appropriateness of the model.

An example may make the difference clearer. The city of London collects a congestion charge for vehicles that enter the center of the city each day, using cameras to read licence-plate numbers for the purpose of identifying the vehicles[5]. This data can be used, say as part of a criminal investigation, to show that a particular car passed a particular point at a particular time, but the data was collected anyway, regardless of whether information about that car was asked for. In contrast, if a particular car is involved in a hit-and-run accident at a particular place and time, police officers will try to find someone who saw the car there at the right time. This data collection is *a posteriori*, and driven by a specific need for a small amount of data.

This example highlights one of the important trade-offs in data collection. To validate a particular hypothesis, only a small amount of data is needed, but there are so many plausible hypotheses that this is useful only for after-the-fact and forensic determination of some event or incident. In situations where there is a need to induce a likely hypothesis, such as that the risk of terrorist attack at this time and place is high, very large amounts of data must be collected. After a crime has been committed, the investigating officers need to ask only a few people for alibis. To be able to generate these alibis ahead of time for all but the guilty party would require much more data.

The second issue is whether the data will be collected from specialized channels of high-quality data, or from much broader channels, where the quality of the data is probably not as good. Intelligence analysts face this dichotomy all the time: they have access to sources with particular, secret information; but the same conclusions could often be reached by sophisticated analysis of information in the public domain. For example, the Able Danger Defense Intelligence group is alleged to have identified four of the September 11th hijackers from publicly available data, although the data used was of terabyte scale.

2.5   Can Data Be Trusted?

In most commercial and scientific settings, the problems of data unreliability come primarily from measurement errors and corruption in transmission. In adversarial settings, it becomes much more important to be aware of, and control, the ways in which data is collected, stored, and moved. The opportunities for manipulating data can be divided into these phases:

- Before the data is collected;

- At the point of data capture;

- Between data capture and analysis;

and the kinds of alterations to the data that can occur can also be divided up into:

- Naturally occurring errors;

- Deliberate introduction of errors that can be disowned;

- Deliberate introduction of errors that cannot be disowned.

Before data is collected, naturally occurring errors are things like wear and tear on a magnetic stripe causing it to read incorrectly, or poor connections to a video camera causing the picture to blur. Deliberate errors that can be disowned are things like growing a moustache to make facial recognition more difficult; able to be disowned because people grow moustaches for all sorts of innocent reasons. Another example in this category is applying mud judiciously to a vehicle licence plate so that it cannot be read by cameras, or so that it will be misread. Deliberate errors that cannot be disowned are attempts to change the collected data that would themselves be suspicious if noticed. These include things like wearing a rubber mask, a favorite tactic in *Mission Impossible*, or changing the figures on a licence plate with tape or paint.

At the point of capture, naturally occurring errors are often those introduced by humans recording and transcribing the data. These can be helped along by choosing names that are hard to spell or numbers that are easy to muddle, and by 'helping' the person capturing the information by reading information to them, but incorrectly. Deliberate errors that can be disowned are things like using a slightly different form of name, or switching two digits of an address, zip or postal code, telephone number, or other identification number. These errors can be disowned because ordinary people who are not trying to manipulate the collected data also make them, so they do not necessarily signal intent to corrupt the data. Pretending to be less sober than one actually is during interrogation is another tactic of this sort. Deliberate errors that cannot be disowned include things like giving a false name, or completely wrong address, telephone number, or other identification number.

The kind of endpoint used is relevant here. There tends to be more confidence that data is collected accurately when the data collection is implicit, perhaps supported by the belief that those who are unaware of the data collection are thereby unable to manipulate it. This, of course, is exactly wrong – those with the most to hide are also most likely to be aware of implicit data collection, and so to try and manipulate it. Explicit endpoints tend to incorporate automatic checking of data because of the possibility of innocent errors. It was much easier to use an altered credit card when a printed slip was produced from it, than it is now, when the card is read automatically and checked in real time against a database.

A more subtle form of manipulation is to create data that is more likely than usual to be selected for analysis. In many settings, the total amount of possible data is so large that good models can be built from a sample of the data. A particular data record may be manipulated to look more interesting than usual in the hope that it will be selected for model building. For example, records representing large amounts of money or large-profit items are more likely to be selected if a store is trying to build a model of its good customers.

The third opportunity for manipulating data is between the point where it is collected and the point where it is analyzed. The threat here is from insiders who have access to the data, and may be motivated to manipulate it, either on their own behalf or at the behest of some outside party. For example, in the Canadian province of Ontario, lottery retailers obtained winning tickets by telling their owners that they did not win, and retrieving the tickets for their own use. This was detected only by comparing the expected winnings of lottery-ticket sellers to their actual winnings and noticing the large discrepancy.

The best defence against manipulation between collection and analysis is to maintain complete and unforgeable logs of access to the collected data, and separate those with access to these logs from those with access to the data.

2.5.1   The Problem of Noise

In adversarial situations, the data collected has potentially been manipulated. It is also important to be aware that collected data is almost never just the result of a single activity that we might want to model. Data is always a snapshot of a complex physical world, and overlapping human actions and motivations. The activities that we are not interested in but that are reflected in the data are called *noise*.

In the simplest case, noise is present in data because of physical overlap of multiple factors, either in the real world or in the collection device. For example, a temperature sensor will produce, over time, a reading that varies slightly, even if the space in which it is located is at a 'constant' temperature. This can be because of slight variations in the movement of air around it, or because of the inherent noise of the electronics from which it is built. In the analysis of data from an array of such sensors, for example in a fire-alarm system, we need to remain aware of this potential variability and build some flexibility into our model. The data we collect is the sum of two processes happening in the real world: the presence or absence of a fire, and the inherent small variation in temperature readings.

Consider a system in a large store that checks end-of-shift total takings in cash registers against the total sales that each cash register processes. It would not be sensible to charge any person whose cash balance was less than total sales with theft – it is understood that the amount in the cash register at the end of a shift is the result of two independent processes: collecting money for sales, and mistakes in making change. Modelling this situation without allowing for the human error process that it captures produces unusable models. (In fact, in this setting, the signal that a person is pilfering from the cash register is that their cash balance is always either correct or over, since they perceive having a negative balance as potentially causing suspicion – a good example of the misjudged response often exhibited by adversaries.)

What might be considered noise in one setting can be signal in another. For example, gathering sales information by totalling sales through cash registers, and by periodic stock taking will produce slightly different answers because of shoplifting. If the goal is to model the success of a sales campaign, this difference might be considered noise. If the goal is to measure shoplifting, then it is the signal of interest.

2.6   How Much Data?

The remaining issue is how much data is needed to extract useful knowledge about a given situation. This issue usually leads to a tug of war between those who value privacy above all else, and want to limit data collection to the minimum possible, and those who are convinced that more is better, and want to collect as much data as possible. Is it possible to say anything technical about how much data is required to get good results?

There are two ways in which more data could be gathered. The first is to gather more *records*; the second is to gather more *attributes*.

In general, the quality of a model built from data increases with the amount of data on which it is based, although most of the improvement comes from the early records. Even a small amount of data, of the order of, say, fifty records can provide a good approximation in many circumstances. Diminishing returns set in after that so that the ten-thousandth record provides much less useful information for building the model than the tenth does. However, data corresponding to adversaries is typically quite rare, so that a very large amount of data might need to be collected in order to get a reasonable number of examples of one part of the structure of the model. As we shall see, in an adversarial setting, many of the models are actually models of normality, and it becomes easier to see the traces of adversaries as the representation of normality becomes clearer.

On the other hand, increasing the number of records used to build models has costs. Collection and storage are not free, and the algorithms used to build models are often of quadratic complexity (that is, their cost increases as the square of the number of records). Doubling the number of records analyzed therefore increases the cost of building the model fourfold. Collecting more records also requires greater intrusion into the lives of ordinary and innocent people, which they rightly resent. We will return to this issue in more detail later.

Increasing the number of attributes associated with each record will improve the quality of the resulting models only if the extra attributes are discriminatory for the differences between ordinary records and records associated with adversaries. Unfortunately, there is usually no way to know what such attributes will be beforehand, so there is a tendency to collect anything that might be useful, and then use attribute-selection techniques (discussed later) to discard those that turn out not to be discriminatory. Human guesswork about which attributes are best to use is not very trustworthy – our intuitions about this turn out often to be quite poor. So the bottom line is that there are both good reasons to collect many attributes, and a natural tendency to think that more is better.

On the other hand, useless attributes have a significant effect both on the complexity of model building, so that it takes longer, and on the quality of the resulting models. For example, if two attributes measure the same underlying phenomenon, but in slightly different ways, then some model-building techniques will produce a model that spends much of its structure accounting for the slight differences between the two attributes. Collecting useless attributes also adds to the intrusiveness of data collection in the same way that collecting extra records does.

One of the most difficult issues is what to do if the relevance of a particular attribute changes over time. A useful attribute may eventually become less useful (perhaps, in an adversarial setting, because the adversaries learn that it is relevant and work harder to make their values for it more innocuous). Similarly, a less-useful attribute may, over time, become more useful. It may be necessary to continue to collect a larger set of attributes than those that are actually used simply so that these questions can be revisited regularly.

2.6.1   Data Interoperability

When data is collected and analyzed within a single organization, the process can be arranged so that data formats are compatible from stage to stage. However, it is often the case that data is handled by more than one organization. For example, the data collection may be contracted out to an intermediary; or several organizations may want to pool their data for analysis. In such situations, there are always complexities arising from incompatible data formats, records collected using slightly different criteria, attributes collected by one organization and not by the other, and different conventions or criteria for labelling records. These issues, although conceptually straightforward, can be of great practical difficulty. It is not uncommon for the majority of the resources and time to be spent on getting the data to a state in which it can be used as input to an analysis process.

Data ownership is another difficult issue. By definition, it is hard to know how much knowledge can be extracted from a particular dataset until knowledge discovery has been done. As a result, organization are reluctant to allow others access to their data since it represents a potential valuable resource. However, because they cannot estimate the value of this resource, a kind of paralysis sets in, and it is always the safer decision to keep the data than to share it.

It is also important to keep track of the *metadata* associated with a dataset. For example, consider a dataset built from consumer surveys, in which individuals go out and ask questions of 'the man in the street'. Suppose one of these individuals decides to stay home and make up answers rather than actually ask the questions. When the data from all of the collectors are aggregated, and knowledge discovery is carried out, it will probably become obvious that some of the data has been fabricated. If the names of the collectors have not been kept associated with the records of the surveys they carried out, it is not possible to track the fabricated data back to the person who fabricated it, and so it becomes much more problematic to remove those records from the dataset. Potentially, the fabrication throws more of the data into question than if the metadata were available.

Especially in adversarial settings, some records will be detected as potentially anomalous. Before any conclusion is drawn from this, it is a good idea to track back the data that seems anomalous, and to check the metadata to see if there is any obvious reason why the apparent conclusion should be suspect. For example, was it all collected via one channel, on one particular day, or in one particular location?

2.6.2   Domain Knowledge

Domain knowledge is a completely different kind of knowledge from that discovered in datasets, and refers to the background information about the problem setting that is known by those familiar with it. For example, law-enforcement personnel know many of the standard tricks used by criminals; and fraud, money-laundering investigators, and auditors know many of the standard techniques that are used for profit and for concealment.

Domain knowledge plays a role in two ways. First, it can be used at the beginning of the knowledge-discovery process to provide information about what is likely and unlikely, and what kinds of results would be interesting and useful in that domain. Domain knowledge can also be used to constrain the kinds of models that it makes sense to build, both by providing estimates of how complex such models need to be, and providing hints about how to set parameters.

Second, domain knowledge is useful after the knowledge-discovery process to evaluate the results. For example, a domain expert may have a strong sense of whether a particular model is plausible or not.

In some settings, for example knowledge discovery in biomedical applications, domain experts are critical to good modelling. Living cells are so complex that there are many, many possible models of their activity, and a domain expert can prune the potential set of models before they are constructed, and assess the plausibility of models after they are constructed.

Adversarial settings are at the other end of a continuum. Although domain knowledge can be useful, it also carries substantial risks. The reason is that adversaries are actively trying to evade detection, and one way to do so is to exploit the blind spots of domain experts. In other words, adversaries, by definition, are trying to do the unexpected, so approaches that try to exploit expectations become more vulnerable by doing so.

The bottom line is that, in adversarial settings, domain knowledge can be useful, but it needs always to be treated with caution.

Notes

[1] In one of the earliest examples, John Snow realized that cholera cases in an area of London clustered around one particular water pump. The handle was removed, effectively ending the outbreak. See `www.ph.ucla.edu/epi/snow.html` for further details.

[2] *R. Austin Freeman,* The Red Thumb Mark *(1907).*

[3] It was briefly suggested that RFIDs should be used to replace dog tags for soldiers in combat, until it was pointed out that the ability to identify the proximity of a soldier from a particular country could be used in unfortunate ways.

[4] Recent data from the U.K. suggested that fewer than 3% of prosecutions made use of CCTV footage, despite its ubiquitous presence in the U.K., primarily because those appearing in the images could not be reliably identified.

[5] Details about the London congestion charge and how it is enforced using licence-plate cameras can be found at `www.cclondon.com`.

Chapter 3
High-Level Principles

In this chapter, we address the big-picture issues for knowledge discovery in adversarial settings. We first consider what sort of traces or signals adversaries are likely to leave in data. Several aspects are different from conventional knowledge discovery: adversaries are rare to begin with; they are actively trying to hide and, worse still, to manipulate the process; there is often a need, or at least a desire, for prevention rather than prosecution; and there is almost never a clearly defined, agreed-upon, or even knowable form in which the traces might come.

Knowledge discovery is only part of a larger situation (organizational, national, international) for dealing with adversaries and their actions, in which many non-technical factors play important roles. In this chapter, we also address some of these issues, in particular the larger process of sensemaking, the way in which worldviews themselves create blind spots with which technology cannot help, and the complex and difficult issues that arise in trying to do widespread data collection and still maintain privacy.

3.1 What to Look for

Knowledge discovery for counterterrorism and law enforcement aims to detect the traces of adversaries in various forms of data. But what do these traces look like? And how should we think about the problem of finding them?

A first approach to this might be to think about what it is that adversaries do in particular settings, try to deduce what kinds of traces these patterns of thinking, communicating, and acting might leave in data, and then set out to look for these expected traces. This plan would guide the kind and amount of data to be collected, and what our knowledge-discovery tools would look for in the data, once collected.

This approach is the norm in law enforcement, after a crime has been committed. The details of the crime guide, in a general way, what kind of investigation is done. Evidence is collected from the crime scene; this evidence, together with answers to the classic questions of means, motive, and opportunity focuses the investigation on certain people; and data is collected about these people, for example their locations at the time of the crime, and whether or not they have benefited. Analysis of this data, in a successful investigation, eventually suggests the overwhelmingly likelihood that one or more specific people committed the crime. Knowledge-discovery techniques can assist this conventional form of criminal investigation, especially when the number of suspects is large, and the interactions and possibilities are complex.

In counterterrorism, and to a certain extent in law enforcement, there is a trend towards prevention. This can range from the straightforward, such as modelling the density of crimes so as to allocate resources geographically in an appropriate way, to complex, such as trying to prevent the transport and use of a weapon of mass destruction. However, across this entire range, the idea of prevention introduces difficult problems: the lack of a clear legal framework and consistent public opinion about whether or when this is a good idea; concerns about the need to collect data in advance of the commission of a crime and the impact this has on privacy and the presumption of innocence; concerns that the ability to prevent actions that have only been contemplated gives governments undue power to squash, or at least chill, dissent; and concerns that prevention is too hit-and-miss, and so too costly for the benefits it might provide. The force of these problems varies from setting to setting, becoming most difficult when large-scale data collection and analysis are carried out in the interests of national security.

Knowledge discovery for preventive analysis is quite a different problem from the more conventional use of knowledge discovery for investigation. In the conventional setting, the crime itself creates the context for the data collection and data analysis. The set of people to be investigated are those known to be connected to the crime, perhaps because they were in the vicinity at the appropriate times; and the objects to be investigated fit within a window of time and geography. Although some, usually most, of these people are innocent, it is understood and accepted that some level of undeserved suspicion falls on them temporarily.

In a preventive framework, there are two broad strategies. The first is to consider patterns that are characteristic of the actions to be prevented. Historical data can be examined to discover such characteristics. Actions can then be taken to watch for these patterns, or to block their occurrences, and so to prevent fresh crimes. This can take the form of explicit prevention, for example restraining orders or the U.K.'s antisocial behavior orders, which assume that a record of past behavior by individuals justifies curtailing their future actions. This can also take the form of implicit prevention, such as increasing police patrols in places where certain crimes are predicted to be more likely to take place.

This pattern-based use of knowledge discovery is based on data collected as the result of previous criminal activity. This use is found objectionable by some, but on the basis that past behavior is not necessarily predictive of future behavior, rather than on the basis of the data collection and analysis itself. In other words, the objection is to the use made of the knowledge, rather than the knowledge discovery itself.

The second strategy is used when historical patterns are not strong enough to provide information about likely future actions, and so not useful or reliable for prevention. This is often the case in counterterrorism, where adversaries try to design attacks that evade existing defences, these defences themselves being based on previous attacks. Pattern-based use of knowledge discovery is of limited usefulness in this case. The possible cost of failing to prevent an attack is high so, unsurprisingly, attempts have been made to extend knowledge-discovery techniques to this more-difficult prevention scenario.

The challenge is *how* to replace the pattern-based knowledge discovery. Patterns can no longer be derived using historical data that describes the adversaries and their actions because, by definition, the adversaries do not look like adversaries by the standards of previous patterns. Instead, we need to collect data about a large number of people and objects about whom we have no *a priori* suspicion, hoping to find the more tenuous signals of potential adversary activity within them. It is this wide collection of data about people who are, of course, overwhelmingly *not* adversaries that many people find objectionable.

However, these objections are, to some extent, based on a misconception about the purpose and use of wide data collection. There are two reasons why such data collection is unavoidable. First, the data corresponding to the adversaries cannot be preferentially collected since we do not know which it is until after the analysis. Second, the presence of data about many, many normal individuals and their actions provides a background of normality, against which the actions of adversaries are thrown into starker relief, making them easier to discover.

Figure 3.1 shows a small example of this. On the left-hand side, it is not obvious that the point labelled with a circle is different from the points labelled with crosses. When many other points of the kind labelled with crosses are added, it becomes much easier to tell. In other words, it is easier to recognize a record as definitively belonging to an adversary when there are many records of ordinary people available. Of course, normality itself

Figure 3.1. *Detecting an unusual object is much easier when many normal objects are present.*

may have plenty of internal structure, but normality is always common so it remains easy to distinguish the two cases.

It is plausible, in most settings, that normal individuals, transactions, and behaviors will be common; or, to put it another way, the traces of adversaries are rare in data. This provides a starting point for knowledge discovery. The first stage of knowledge discovery is to separate the data into two categories: normal and abnormal. In a sense, this is easy – any structure in the data that occurs many times can be assumed to be normal, can be eliminated, and plays no further role in the analysis. The situation is similar to a police officer standing by the side of a road with a radar gun. Every passing car is subject to 'groundless suspicion' as it is 'inspected' by the radar beam. However, the goal of the process is to *eliminate* cars travelling below the speed limit. In fact, radar guns are normally set to signal the police officer only when a car is detected travelling at excessive speed. The comparison would be even more apt if radar guns were designed to detect only cars moving much faster than the average speed of traffic – for then the returns from most cars would not simply be ignored but would determine what 'the average speed of traffic' means at this moment in time.

Once normal data has been identified and removed, what remains is the data corresponding to abnormal structure. This does not, of course, correspond exactly to the traces of adversaries; but we might plausibly expect that the traces of the adversaries will be contained within it.

It might be argued that there is no such thing as normal, and that what seems to be normal is just the effect of averaging over a large number of different behaviors or actions. There is some truth to this; this small-scale clustering of people with similar properties is the explanation for the long tail phenomenon[1] – the fact that less-popular objects such as books, CDs, DVDs, and so on do not sell at high rates, but they all do sell. The long tail suggests that there is a continuum of similarity, starting at one end with a liking for 'hits' that define similarity for large groups of people; moving down through niches of various kinds, to small groups whose similarities are defined through a liking for distinctly minority tastes. If this is the case, then there is really no such thing as abnormality; just normality within smaller and smaller subgroups.

However, it is important to distinguish two different environments. In the world of *taste*, each person is free to be as much of an individual as he or she wants to be, and there are no (or few) global constraints to cause clumping of similarity. In other words, in such environments, small groups with similar tastes, perhaps along only a few dimensions, are the norm. Larger groups emerge in the overlap of these individual tastes, probably helped on by advertising and opportunity. However, there are other environments where the similarities and differences among people are constantly, if subtly, constrained by social processes. As humans, there are many ways of thinking and behaving that we are not free to choose, because we live embedded in a society that constrains our choices. In such an environment, there will be much more obvious clumping of the data, and so an obvious meaning for normality. As a result, those who live outside the mainstream of society, for whatever reason, will be visibly abnormal. Because it will not always be obvious which of these different environments is dominant in a particular dataset, and because there are, in any case, many, many different possible groupings, it is better to think of the goal of analysis as *ranking* records according to their normality/abnormality rather than trying to discover a hard boundary between the two properties.

Having identified a (large) set of records as describing normal structure, and discarding them from further consideration, we have reduced the problem to distinguishing between data that is abnormal simply because it is unusual, and data that is abnormal because it reflects some form of malfeasance. Can we expect to distinguish these two cases?

Part of the answer comes from thinking about what normality means. Data that describes something normal or ordinary should look normal or ordinary no matter what kind of analysis is applied. Analysis might look at the data based on properties of an individual data record itself, based on how its properties compare with the properties of other similar data records, or based on much more global properties such as how it connects or relates to other data.

For example, consider data about telephone calls made from a residential phone. The analysis could consider simply how many calls are made each day. The call record might be considered normal if the number of calls is between 0 and 15. At a slightly more abstract level, the distribution of the times that calls are made could be calculated, and the call record considered normal if all of the calls were between 7 a.m. and 11 p.m., with peaks between 3:30 p.m. and 9 p.m. At an even more abstract level, the set of other numbers called could be considered, as well as whether or not any of the phones with these other numbers called one another. Now it is less intuitively obvious what the normal pattern should be, but it is certainly possible to work it out from call data. The point is that anyone using a residential phone in an ordinary way is overwhelmingly likely to produce usage data that looks normal, no matter what kind of analysis is used, and at what level of abstraction. That is what *normal* means.

Someone whose phone usage is simply unusual, is likely to appear abnormal according to one or more of these measures, but is unlikely to appear abnormal to others. For example, suppose the phone belongs to an insomniac. The distribution of times at which calls are made will probably look unusual (although even here, it is not possible to call many other people in the middle of the night even if awake), but the total number of calls made, and the connection pattern among the phones called will probably not be unusual.

An adversary, on the other hand, tends to create unusual data records whenever they are associated with the particular criminal task in which he is involved. He will, of course, try as much as possible to present a normal facade, no matter what data is collected. However, it becomes more and more difficult to make this facade work at all levels of abstraction and from all directions. For example, a member of a terrorist group may make fewer phone calls than average, and they may be of shorter duration because of concerns about interception. The set of numbers called may call each other much more often than the typical pattern.

Detection of the abnormal becomes easier when some of the data properties result from aspects that are emergent, that is which arise not simply from the actions of individuals as individuals, but from collective actions, not all of which can be controlled by any one person. For example, members of a terrorist group may each make a typical number of calls, at typical times of day, but may be detected because all of their calls are to one another, whereas ordinary people call their friends, but occasionally other people too.

Emergent properties are the most robust because they are the hardest to manipulate. However, they absolutely require the collection of large amounts of data so that the essence of emergent normality can be inferred.

The other fact that makes data belonging to adversaries distinguishable from data belonging to unusual but ordinary people is that adversaries must take into account that knowledge-discovery technology will be used against them. Of course, because the technology is relatively new and some adversaries are amateurs, this will not always be the case. However, in general it is plausible to assume that they know that analysis of their data is possible. As a consequence, they are forced to take steps to alter their data, to the extent that they can, to try and make themselves look more normal. They may also take steps to alter their data to exploit weaknesses of the knowledge-discovery systems being used against them.

This concealment and manipulation is difficult for three main reasons.

First, the requirements of whatever illicit activity they are doing forces data values that are exceptional, unless the data collection is very poor. Second, it is often hard to decide, reliably, what normal data looks like to try and simulate it. Third, consciously trying to *construct* normal data that is usually generated subconsciously produces data that is detectably unusual. In other words, the attempt to produce normal data often ends up producing even more unusual data, making the gap between normal and abnormal even wider than it was to begin with.

These difficulties provide an opportunity for knowledge discovery – create systems that are tuned to look for the signals of concealment and manipulation, and arrange systems so that they elicit reaction from adversaries as much as possible. In other words, knowledge-discovery systems should use the equivalent of a big sign saying "Knowledge Discovery in Use", and then include analysis that looks explicitly for reaction to the sign.

Unusual structure in emergent properties tends to be even more marked when a *group* of adversaries is acting together, which is usually the case. Such a group has two commonalities: a shared need to act in ways that further their illicit activity, and a shared need to evade detection. This tends to create not only a reaction, as described above, but a *correlated* reaction. Unusual, correlated data is a strong signal for adversaries because other kinds of correlation tend to be common and so seen as normal. On the other hand, abnormal, eccentric data tends to be uncorrelated.

So, in summary, the best overall strategy for detecting adversaries in data when the goal is to prevent their activity rather than to prosecute them afterwards is to look, first, for abnormality. This requires a multifaceted examination of the data at different levels of abstraction, and from different perspective and scales. Normal data, by definition, should seem normal from all directions. Unusual but innocuous data should look normal by most measures. Data corresponding to adversaries should look abnormal by several measures, especially those that are hardest to manipulate, usually those that depend least on the values in particular data records, and most on properties that records share (correlations or connections).

Of course, this approach is not able to discover a lone-wolf adversary, who does not associate with anyone else, because he will be indistinguishable from an eccentric. Fortunately, most illicit activities require some kind of support from others, and so some interactions.

It is also important that the analysis technology is hard to reverse engineer in the sense that it is hard, preferably impossible, to determine how to construct data that will be considered innocuous. The best way to do this is to ensure that the way data is categorized depends on global properties of all of the data considered, not just on properties of individual data records. Again, the role of normal data is important in creating this global backdrop.

3.2   Subverting Knowledge Discovery

Apart from the properties of the data describing adversaries, we must also consider how they may actively try to subvert the knowledge-discovery process. To consider this, it is helpful to divide the entire knowledge-discovery process into three stages:

1. The data-collection phase;

2. The analysis phase;

3. The decision phase.

Although most manipulation (except insider attacks) requires doing something different at the time that the data is collected, a manipulation may target any of these three stages, depending on how much knowledge adversaries have of the way in which each stage works.

3.2.1   Subverting the Data-Collection Phase

The easiest opportunity for subverting the knowledge-discovery process is at the beginning, targeting the data-collection phase directly. Whenever data is collected in an explicit way, it is possible for those about whom the data is collected to gain some understanding of the process. With this understanding, they are often able to take steps to change the collected data in ways useful to them.

This is not quite as easy as it seems, because many collection channels have some robustness built into them. This robustness is not usually there to prevent explicit manipulation of the collected data, but because of the natural human tendency to make mistakes. However, this robustness does provide some resistance to manipulation. For example, credit-card numbers have check digits appended to them primarily because, originally, credit-card numbers were copied by hand, and people tend to mistype a digit or reverse a pair of digits. The check digit protects against this kind of mistake, but also has the largely unintended benefit of protecting against trivially fabricating credit-card numbers.

The two strongest ways to subvert collection are, first, to avoid collection at all, and second, to change the keys associated with the collected data so that it is no longer associated with the appropriate person or transaction. Of course, this assumes that it is obvious that data is being captured, as it is when an explicit transaction takes place.

Avoiding collection altogether can be done only in certain limited situations. For example, by noting the field of view of surveillance cameras, an individual can take care not to be seen by them. Avoiding data collection is not usually possible, though, because the situation requires *some* data to be associated with every transaction. For example, passing through a transit turnstile requires some payment action by everyone who passes through, and evasion attracts attention. In some situations, avoiding collection can be done by creating a partial record, for which the key(s) are useless. For example, walking past a surveillance camera with a hat pulled down and a collar turned up can make the captured image useless, but of course this works only if dressing this way is plausible in the situation – this approach does not work in Hawaii. Even here, it is hard to conceal height, weight, gait, and other information that could potentially be identifying.

Changing the key that is associated with the captured data is often a better tactic. For example, when passing a surveillance camera, a disguise means that a person's image is captured, but it cannot be associated with the right key, that person's normal appearance, so it is of limited usefulness. Identity theft has, in part, become such big business because stolen identity records allow those who wish to prevent capture of data about themselves to do so by appearing to be somebody else. The stolen driver's licenses, passports, and other identity documents can be used at places where transactions force *some* data to be captured, but make it seem as if the transaction belongs to somebody else.

Subversion of the collection stage is harder when the capture is done more implicitly. Those under surveillance may not realize that data about them is being captured. For example, it may not be obvious that a live cell phone (and sometimes even one that is turned off) is in contact with the nearest cell tower so that it can deliver incoming calls. As a side-effect, the approximate location of the cell phone is constantly available to the owner of the cell tower – the particular tower and, with some technologies, the direction from the tower. Technologies for car licence-plate scanning are another non-obvious form of data capture, and now support a thriving stolen licence-plate business in the U.K.[2]

3.2.2 Subverting the Analysis Phase

Subversion to influence the analysis stage of surveillance requires a more sophisticated understanding of knowledge discovery, and is more the focus of this book. Understanding the role that data values play in building models of what is happening in the real world provides opportunities to build blind spots into models, spots in which adversaries can hide. We will return to this in the following chapters for different kinds of analysis technologies.

3.2.3 Subverting the Decision-and-Action Phase

Data can also be subverted so as to alter the decision and action phases of surveillance. For example, a terrorist might change his name to Smith in the hope that the selection of a record with this name as a potential terrorist would make it seem as if the analysis were flawed. There are also many opportunities to influence the decision-and-action phase using social engineering, that is exploiting assumptions about the problem setting which are not valid, or not completely valid, in practice. For example, recall the card-counting students in the book *Bringing Down the House*[3], who relied on playing parts that were carefully designed to match casino expectations of high rollers. It is also well-understood that many security measures, such as passwords, can be subverted by social-engineering measures such as phoning and pretending to have lost the password, or claiming that it needs to be updated, and getting the owner to reveal it. Phishing uses social engineering to convince people to reveal information via email or web sites using the same general approach.

3.2.4 The Difficulty of Fabricating Data

As discussed above, adversaries are forced to produce data that is different from the data belonging to normal people for two reasons. The first is that they are forced to do particular things by the nature of their illicit activities, and the essentials of these forced actions are usually obvious to those looking for them. For example, criminals must indulge in criminal acts, and terrorists must plan and carry out attacks. These actions must leave *some* traces if the appropriate data is being collected. Because these actions are different from the actions of normal people, the traces must themselves be different. As long as sufficiently large quantities of data are collected, there must be some differences between the records of adversaries and the records of normal people. The question is: are these differences large enough to be detected against a background of the huge variation among normal people?

The second reason that the data associated with adversaries is different from that of normal people is that they, unless very unsophisticated, are aware of the fact that the data will be analyzed and cannot afford to ignore this. Adversaries actively want to conceal themselves in the data. In other words, aware of possible data analysis, they do not want to appear as straightforward and obvious outliers, exposed by some simple analysis of the data. They may be expected, therefore, to pay some attention to altering the data collected about them so as to make it seem more normal. They may attempt to make the values of the attributes fall as close as possible to a normal range. This suggests that obvious outliers in data are more likely to be the result of ordinary eccentricity than the presence of adversaries. Adversaries may also want to manipulate the knowledge-discovery process, so they may choose data values that have the greatest impact on the models built from collected data. Overall, we expect that the data associated with adversaries can be found on the 'fringes' of normal data – not quite normal, but not obviously abnormal either.

However, even with this goal of looking (almost) normal, deciding on an appropriate strategy is not trivial. First of all, it may be quite difficult to know what normal values for attributes are. For a single attribute it is probably possible to work out normal *ranges* for the values it takes. It is much harder to select normal ranges for several attributes at once so that their correlations seem normal. For example, suppose that you want to create a fictitious height and weight for yourself, quite different from your actual properties – if you are tall, become short; if you are short, become tall. Now what is a reasonable weight to associate with your new chosen height? Most people will have difficulty coming up with a plausible value, let alone the most common one. This is also the reason that those who check ages, for example in bars where there is a minimum drinking age, ask people what year they were born. A person with genuine identity documents of course knows what year they were born; someone who has borrowed someone else's identity documents may have to stop and think, even though age and year of birth are tightly connected.

Even when the normal range of an attribute is known, it is not entirely straightforward to select a normal value from this range. For example, it is well known that, when people make up numbers, the distribution of the digits that they choose is different from the distribution of digits in numbers that were not made up[4]. This insight has been used to flag tax returns for further analysis, and can also be used to suggest when accounting books have been altered. Customs officers are trained that, when pressure is put on normal people who are not smuggling, they get angry very quickly. A smuggler, knowing this fact, will still have trouble deciding how quickly to get angry in order to seem normal.

The values of some attributes also reflect associations between the person or transaction involved and other people or transactions. This makes their values hard to choose since the choice in one record may not 'connect' properly with the values in other records. For example, if someone masquerading as a person from a different culture is asked how many friends they have, it may be difficult for them to come up with a plausible, let alone typical, answer, especially on the spur of the moment.

Thus, although adversaries want to alter the data that is collected about them, this is actually much harder than it seems.

A more difficult problem faced by adversaries, and a great opportunity for knowledge discovery, lies in the fact that humans intrinsically have difficulty in presenting a false front to the world. Human minds can be modelled as two pieces, a conscious mind and a subconscious mind[5]. Although the conscious mind can be controlled, it is much, much harder to control the subconscious mind.

Humans are quite poor at presenting a different appearance from the underlying reality. Those who are able to do this well are called actors, and are often very highly paid for the skill. A play can be completely ruined by a poor actor who allows the audience to realize that the action is being carried out by ordinary people, on a wooden platform, at the front of a large room.

Not only are humans intrinsically poor at presenting a different appearance from the underlying reality – their attempts to do so may actually *create* a dissonance; and the harder they try, the worse the dissonance becomes. This seems to arise from the attempt of the conscious mind to overcontrol the subconscious mind, and can lead to signals that are visible in data collected about the person or their actions. One small example of this is called, by psychologists, purpose tremor. This describes the problem that we have carrying out, consciously, actions that we normally do unconsciously, for example inserting a key into a keyhole, or hitting the ball in some sport[6].

Dissonance provides an opportunity for knowledge discovery. In many situations normal people allow data to be collected in routine ways about which they hardly think; adversaries can never afford to be so cavalier about data collected about them. Increasing the apparent significance of the data collected can cause them to react more strongly. Thinking more carefully about the values collected will almost certainly lead to values that are more artificial, and so more unusual, than they would otherwise have been.

The bottom line is that the differences between data about normal people or transactions, and data arising from the actions of adversaries will tend to be small, because the adversaries are working hard to make sure that this is true. One way to amplify this difference is to look for a threefold distinction: the difference due to illicit action, the difference due to concealment and self-consciousness, because of dissonance, and the difference due to manipulation of the process. The second and third differences may often be easier to detect than the first.

The other critical property of adversaries is that they are rare. This means that, in collected data, only a few records will be the result of illicit activities. This creates problems for knowledge discovery which, in mainstream settings, is tuned for problems where there are more or less equal numbers of records of each kind.

One way to think about the adversarial setting is that the data is describing two different situations at once: normality and illicit activity. Any knowledge-discovery technique is trying to build a model that fits the data well, that explains the situation as appropriately as possible. Conventional knowledge discovery is prone either to making this model fit too well, and so ignoring the small amount of data about illicit activity; or to building a model of a hybrid situation, which is neither normality nor illicit activity. This is a perfectly reasonable strategy when anomalies in the data are perhaps due to noise, but an Achilles Heel in an adversarial setting.

3.3 Effects of Technology Properties

It is also important to consider how the limitations of technology interact with their use in an adversarial setting.

The first observation is that standard knowledge-discovery techniques are relatively easy to manipulate. On the whole, the algorithms that are used for knowledge discovery assume that the data is in a trustworthy form. This creates an opportunity for changing the data in ways that change the models built by the knowledge-discovery process. Not much attention has been paid to this possibility. In later chapters, we explore how different knowledge-discovery techniques are susceptible to subversion of their outputs by careful manipulation of their input data. This creates places in the data (worse still, knowable places) where certain data records will be treated in particular ways, providing hiding places for adversaries.

Algorithmic knowledge-discovery tools are good at extracting knowledge from large, complex datasets that are in forms that humans find difficult. As such, they can find structures in data that would be hard to find in other ways. In particular, they are good at situations where assessment of risk is a critical factor. Humans are notoriously poor at estimating risks, particularly when the risks are in the middle range. This, of course, is partly why humans behave in ways that are not predicted by the theories of mainstream economics, which assume completely rational behavior. Assessment of risk is therefore an area where knowledge discovery can complement human skills effectively. However, algorithmic knowledge discovery is not well suited to making decisions or taking actions without some human input. In general, it is a good idea to leave decisions with consequences to humans to make. This is partly because humans usually have a much wider picture of the situation and can bring contextual knowledge to bear in a way that is difficult for computer systems. The weakness of requiring humans to make decisions is that they are vulnerable to social engineering. In some commercial applications, for example deciding whether or not to grant a mortgage, entirely automatic systems have been built. In an adversarial setting, this is a dangerous approach.

One of the mistakes in applying algorithmic knowledge discovery to adversarial settings is to imagine that the correct way to formulate the problem is that of directly predicting the form of action (crime, fraud, attack) that might be employed. So, for example, people sometimes imagine that counterterrorism knowledge discovery can be used to predict attacks – either the location of attacks, or the mode by which an attack might take place. Similarly, a law-enforcement organization might imagine that knowledge discovery can be useful to predict either the kinds of crime which are likely to happen in the future, particular crimes, and even who is going to commit them (the premise of the film *Minority Report*). This is not something that the technology is capable of doing at present, and probably not for the foreseeable future.

The problem is that there are far too many possibilities for future illicit activities. An approach which requires the knowledge-discovery technology to somehow consider all of these possibilities and make predictions about them is destined to fail. This is all the more true because the adversaries are actively trying to find opportunities or holes in the system that they are subverting. By definition, these holes are not obvious to those in the defending position, or else they would have already plugged them in some way.

A more productive role for knowledge-discovery technologies is the assessment of risk of particular kinds of illicit behavior that have already been established. However, this is still a relatively weak approach since the number of opportunities that have been considered will always be a small fraction of those that are available or possible.

A better approach overall is to use knowledge-discovery techniques to look for anomalies in the dataset. Of course, many things that appear anomalous are, in fact, completely normal or innocent. However, it is plausible that anything that appears in the dataset many times is representative of some normal activity or action. Therefore those things which represent illicit activities might be expected to be found among those things that are relatively rare in the dataset. As discussed previously, they are unlikely to be found as extreme outliers, but rather to be found in the margins of the dataset.

Hence pattern-based approaches to looking for illicit activity will always be limited. There are some situations where the way in which illicit activity is reflected in the data is well understood, and where it is difficult for adversaries to avoid leaving these kinds of traces in data. In these situations pattern-based knowledge discovery can be useful. However, in situations where the illicit activity may come in many possible forms, pattern-based knowledge discovery is risky. On the other hand, it is usually straightforward to understand and build a model of normality. Applying such a model to a dataset selects those parts of the data that deserve further scrutiny – those parts that do not fit the model of normality. It is in these parts that traces of illicit activity are most likely to be found. Given the large size of real-world datasets, a good model for normality is more important and useful than a good model for illicit behavior. In other words, to look for a needle in a haystack, a good model for hay is more important than a good model for needles. Finding a small pile of non-hay quickly, by discarding all of the hay, makes it straightforward to look for needles, but also all sorts of other things not normally found in haystacks.

And we don't need to know what these other things are in order to find them efficiently.

Naively, knowledge-discovery systems are often conceived of as a single, monolithic black box. Data is fed into this black box, and useful, actionable knowledge comes out of the other end. Such a view is too simplistic. Technologies for knowledge discovery are not powerful enough to work in this way. Even if they were, it is not obvious that this would be a good way to deploy them. In fact, it is usually better to conceive of the knowledge-discovery process as a multi-faceted process, in which each facet is itself a sequence, involving multiple stages. Each facet examines the data from a different perspective; and each facet and each stage learn properties about the data that can be used to help in other parts of the analysis. In other words, knowledge discovery is a defence in depth – an adversary record has to pass every stage in every facet to avoid detection.

There are many advantages to a multi-faceted, staged approach. In general, using a staged approach allows a better set of decisions to be made about each record, since early decisions about which records are of little interest can be used to reduce the number of remaining records. More resources and attention can be spent on those records that seem most likely to contain useful knowledge.

There are also some administrative benefits. For example, as data passes from one stage to another, there is an opportunity to exercise oversight on the properties of that data, based on the results of the preceding analysis.

Knowledge discovery is also full of chicken-and-egg problems. Many techniques require some parameters to be set, but the analyst does not usually know enough to set these parameters in an optimal, or even principled, way. As a result, the process is necessarily iterative. An initial model can be built using simple and naive assumptions about parameters. Looking at the results of this model can provide enough information to make better choices and a revised model can be built with the new parameters. This process can be repeated as necessary.

An ideal knowledge-discovery process therefore examines data from multiple perspectives, using a sequence of analysis techniques within each one, and iterating as necessary to use information being learned to refine the analysis process.

It is also important to remain aware that the real-world situations that knowledge discovery is modelling change, and sometimes on quite a short time scale. People change rapidly, and so the signature of normal activity reflected in data will change over time. There is a need to repeat the knowledge-discovery process on newly collected data regularly to reflect the changing external environment. This is made easier by the use of a staged process as well.

Some of the power of knowledge discovery comes from putting together data from a number of different sources. We will discuss some of the mechanisms and issues with doing this in the next chapter. However, it is as well to remember that what kinds of data will be put together and how they are kept up to date depends, to some extent, on the hypotheses about what might be found in the data.

3.4   Sensemaking and Situational Awareness

Knowledge discovery is one part of larger systems designed for law enforcement, crime prevention, intelligence, or counterterrorism. One way to understand this larger framework, and the role of knowledge discovery within it is *sensemaking*.

Sensemaking helps an analyst build a mental model of an entire threat situation, in a sufficiently deep way not only to understand the interactions and drivers of the system at a particular moment in time, but also how the system might evolve, or be driven, either by the analyst or by the adversaries. In military settings, sensemaking is very close to *situational awareness*.

One significant system for sensemaking is Cynefin[7], a system developed by Snowden. It characterizes systems as being of five kinds:

- *Known* systems in which the relationships between cause and effect are straightforward, well-understood, and widely agreed upon. Engineering, as taught to undergraduates, is a known system.

- *Knowable or complicated* systems in which the relationship between cause and effect requires significant investigation, but can be worked out with enough time and effort. Engineering, as used in the real world, is a knowable system.

- *Complex* systems in which the relationship between cause and effect emerges from the interactions of large numbers of autonomous agents who are mutually adapting. In these systems, only local connections between cause and effect can be discovered, and primarily by *noticing* rather than by *investigation*. In other words, planned probing of the system is unlikely to lead to understanding, but some understanding can be gleaned by considering the evolution of the system in its normal state. The Law of Unintended Consequences is the most important model of how such systems work. Much of politics and economics addressed complex systems.

- *Chaotic* systems in which the relationship between cause and effect is too complex or transitory to establish.

- *Disordered* systems where there is no (apparent) relationship between cause and effect.

Understanding these possibilities helps to put adversarial knowledge discovery in context. Mainstream knowledge discovery tends to assume systems that are in the knowable, perhaps even the known, space.

Adversarial knowledge discovery, though, should always be considered as taking place in the complex space, or possibly even in the chaotic space. In these settings it is always the case that some part of the state is concealed, and that some of the drivers are invisible. Furthermore, some of the agents are not only acting strongly in their own interest, at odds with the interests of wider society, but also explicitly acting to increase the level of confusion. Such systems will tend to teeter on the edge of chaos, at least at certain critical times.

There are significant dangers in trying to treat complex or chaotic systems as if they are knowable or known. A compelling example used by Kurtz and Snowden is of West Point graduates who were asked to manage a kindergarten. They tried to plan this task using rational design principles, that is treating the system as known, or at least knowable. The result was disastrous. Some thinking and observation of teachers afterwards helped them to see that what succeeds in this kind of environment is to stabilize desirable patterns and destabilize undesirable patterns. In other words, a kindergarten is a complex system, and does not respond well to attempts to manipulate it as if it were a known system.

In another example, a group of Marines were taken to the New York Mercantile Exchange, where they used the trading simulators, in competition with a group of traders. Unsurprisingly, the traders won. However, when the traders came to the Marine base and played war games against the marines, the traders won again. The traders were accustomed to seeing opportunities and acting on them, while the Marines were trained in a rational model of planning and action.

Treating adversarial situations as knowable is a common mental error, even in situations where it is obviously dangerous. For example, the U.S. Army's Counterinsurgency strategy manual (U.A. Army Field Manual FM3-24 Counterinsurgency) contains language like this: "The underlying premise is this: when participants achieve a level of understanding such that the situation no longer appears complex, they can exercise logic and intuition effectively." (and more in the same vein in sections 4.2 to 4.13). The use of the word "complex" here is not, of course, in the Cynefin sense, but the framing is consistent with an assumption that counterinsurgencies can be made knowable.

There is a temptation to treat problems of criminal investigation, prevention, and counterterrorism as if they were systems in the known space.

Especially tempting is to see knowledge discovery as a tool for making knowable systems more known. The risks of doing this have been well-described, for counterterrorism, in a set of thoughtful papers by French and Niculae[8], Bellavita[9], and Lazaroff and Snowden[10]. In particular, Bellavita makes the point that the purpose of knowledge-management technologies is not to drive the process towards the known.

3.4.1   Worldviews

Another reason for some of the difficult problems that have arisen using knowledge-discovery technology, particularly in counterterrorism, is that most law-enforcement, intelligence, and counterterrorism personnel, policies, and systems are modernist in their philosophy about the basic problem and how it should be addressed. Modernism has its roots in the Enlightenment, and makes a number of relevant assumptions. The first is rationality, that the way to make decisions, argue about best courses of action, and reach agreements is by reasoned discussion. Different people may start from different axioms, but even this can be explored by discussion. Modernism also makes an implicit assumption that humankind is making progress in a positive direction, and that there are mechanisms that can produce overall improvement in people, organizations, and cultures.

Modernism makes it hard to understand the motivations and actions of people with a different worldview, all the more so if analysts are not explicitly aware of their own worldview. Modernism tends to lead people to make statements such as "Sensible people can't possibly believe X".

There are three particularly relevant alternate worldviews of which analysts should be aware:

- Postmodernism. This worldview has been described as characterized by "incredulity towards metanarratives"[11], that is a general view that all discussions and arguments are, at bottom, attempts to impose some form of hegemony, that is power without force.

  The difference between this worldview and the modernist one is at the heart of much of the otherwise puzzling resistance of many in the general public to widespread data collection in the service of counterterrorism and the war on terror. Those who work in counterterrorism, and many in government, see it as a truism that widespread data collection and knowledge discovery are obvious defences against a major terrorist threat, whose benefits clearly outweigh their drawbacks. They often fail to understand why these ideas, seemingly so obvious, are received with such resistance. Failing to understand that the problem is one of differing worldviews, analysts and policy makers try to deploy better arguments – making the situation worse. To a postmodernist, better, more forceful, and slicker arguments are just more evidence supporting their view that the real purpose is about imposing more order or grabbing more power. Law enforcement faces something of the same problem, but the issues are longer-standing, so that people have become accustomed to the intrusiveness and power of law enforcement[12].

- Anarchy. This worldview is one of those held by a variety of adversaries, especially terrorists. Anarchists view all government as unnecessary at best, and evil at worst; they often believe that removing government power will, as it were automatically, lead to the creation of a perfect society. There are anarchists in developed democracies, but they are more common and more radicalized in countries whose governments are repressive and/or incompetent. Salafist Islamic militancy, although couched in religious terms, has an anarchist component to it.

  The problem with anarchy as a worldview is that it leads to a mission that is purely destructive – tear down the existing structures to 'free' the new structures to arise. As a result, there are few strategic goals and almost no tactical ones, except destruction. Understanding how such groups work, and what they might do next is difficult because, in a sense, they do not know either. Anarchists were active in the period before the First World War in most of Europe, and no effective strategy for containing them, let alone defeating them, was ever developed. They, the countries they opposed, and their goals were swept away in the carnage of that war.

- Religious. The worldviews held because of religious belief are reasonably consistent and logical, given the assumptions on which they are based. Hence, unlike anarchy, it is possible to work out what the strategic goals of a group espousing such a worldview might be, and so work out points of leverage. However, although modernism has its roots in the Christian belief that the universe is consistent and understandable, most modernists now do not hold significant religious beliefs. The risk is that modernists think, implicitly, that those who hold a religious worldview do not *really* believe it. They are therefore inclined to see religious worldviews always as either a facade or a means to power. They fail to fully take into account that some people *really do believe* in the religious worldview that they claim; and so miss clear signals about possible strategic actions, and also opportunities for exerting leverage.

The other risk of modernism is that it has a weak or non-existent concept of evil; 'bad' things happen because their perpetrators are misguided in some way. Either they have failed to understand their options rationally, or the 'system' has provided them with distorted incentives. This means, in many settings, a chronic underestimation of the energy and resources that adversaries are prepared to expend. This can be seen most clearly in the almost complete incomprehension of suicide bombers by Western democracies.

3.5   Taking Account of the Adversarial Setting over Time

Knowledge discovery in adversarial settings is a kind of arms race, with adversaries adapting to the knowledge-discovery tools deployed against them. Of course, in some settings it will be difficult for them to do this – because they do not know enough to work out which tools are being used or how they work; or because they do not know enough about what data is being collected, in particular what data is being collected about *other* people. It is tempting to rely on 'security by obscurity' and try to keep secret the entire knowledge-discovery process. This is a dangerous strategy – adversaries are not necessarily stupid and are certainly motivated to work out new ways of concealment. It is better to build a process guaranteed to be effective even if adversaries know something about how it works, rather than one that relies on secrecy to be effective.

One of the most obvious examples of this arms race is in the detection of email spam. Spam-detection technology develops rapidly, but the techniques used by spammers to get their emails delivered to human recipients also continue to develop, with considerable ingenuity on both sides. This is also an extremely open race. Both sides can clearly see what the other is doing, since new examples of spam are always available for inspection, and spam-detection tools can always be purchased by spammers to reverse engineer.

Given that adversaries will respond to analysis and knowledge discovery, it is important to adjust both the knowledge-discovery models and the process to counter such responses. In fact, this kind of adjustment has to be done anyway, because ordinary people, as individuals and as groups, change fairly rapidly, so models need to be updated to reflect these changes in the background of normality. In other words, there are two underlying trends in any situation that need to be accounted for in the knowledge-discovery process: slow but large-scale changes in the behavior of ordinary people, and fast, small-scale changes in the behavior of adversaries (or at least their apparent behavior) designed to affect the process.

This implies that whatever models are used for knowledge discovery need to be rebuilt periodically using the same construction process – sometimes the process itself will also have to be rethought. This requires collecting new data that reflects the changing real-world environment, looking at how it differs from earlier data, and using it to build new models.

This raises several important questions. The first is how to judge the rate at which the real world is changing, and so how the newly collected data and the previous data should be used to build new models. In the simplest view, fresh models should be built from new data. This, of course, works but may need large amounts of new data. If the underlying changes are small or slow, it may be more reasonable to collect less new data, and build models from a mixture of the older data and the new data. Unfortunately, it is difficult to know in advance what the right solution to this problem is. It may be necessary to try several alternatives as a way of understanding how big the issue of change really is.

Rebuilding models from fresh data also carries a non-trivial risk. When an initial model is built, the adversaries do not necessarily know that it is happening and data about them can be captured and used in the model without any chance for them to alter it deliberately. However, if new models are built periodically using fresh data, then adversaries can try to influence the model by manipulating the data that is collected and used to build them. On the face of it, the data from a small number of adversaries should never be frequent enough to influence a model, but, as we shall see, they have two opportunities: they can create data that is interesting enough that it is likely to play a role in any model; and some models are, in fact, easily manipulated in critical ways by just a few well-chosen pieces of data.

In summary, periodical updating of knowledge-discovery models is often necessary because the real-world situation that is being modelled changes. This process needs to be done with caution, both to accurately reflect the changes, and to prevent the models from being indirectly manipulated via the data used to build them.

3.6 Does This Book Help Adversaries?

The answer to this question at its simplest is: Yes. Adversaries can learn a lot about how knowledge discovery works, and plausible ways in which it can be used against them. However, there are several reasons why the content of this book, and other books like it, should be widely available. The first reason is that those who use the technologies described can do so much more effectively if they understand more about how these technologies work and, in particular, where they are weak, how they can be manipulated, and when the results should be taken with a grain of salt. Especially as some adversary activities have major consequences, there is a great deal of ongoing work developing and installing sophisticated knowledge-discovery tools and systems, and it is important to be aware of whether these are likely to work well, and how they should be fitted together to make the best overall systems. Many users of these technologies will have experience with one, or a few, technologies and may have their appetites whetted for other possibilities.

Second, researchers and developers of knowledge-discovery algorithms and technologies need to understand that the possibility of malicious alteration of parts of the data, of the tools themselves, or of the results of the knowledge discovery completely changes the problem. New approaches that use more-robust algorithms, processes that are resistant to tampering and manipulation, and training about interpretation, decision-making and action are all urgently needed.

Third, there is a pressing need for the wider public, and particularly governments and lawmakers to understand the costs and benefits of large-scale knowledge discovery. In most countries, the legal frameworks needed for widespread data collection, and for proactive and preventive action based on discovered knowledge fit poorly with the wider framework of criminal justice. Attempts to solve some of the poorest fits using legislation have not been successful, either as pieces of legal technology or as laws that have the agreement of the governed. There are many complex issues here, and the widest and best-informed discussion possible is needed to address them.

Fortunately, as we shall see, many of the techniques described in this book cannot be successfully exploited, even if they are completely understood. We will argue repeatedly that the best techniques are those that rely on discovering potentially suspicious traces by comparing them to the much-larger quantity of normal activity, rather than by evaluating each individual fact or record independently. Such comparisons prevent the knowledge-discovery algorithms from being reverse engineered in a useful way, and so prevent adversaries from being able to construct behaviors, actions, or profiles that will enable them to evade detection, even when they understand the algorithms that will analyze their data. (Ironically, given the opposition to widespread data collection, it is the presence of large amounts of data about normal people and normal activities that prevents this reverse engineering.)

Some techniques actually work better when adversaries not only know about them, but change to try and manipulate them or evade detection. These changes in response to actual or apparent detection may actually differentiate them more clearly.

3.7   What about Privacy?

The most difficult issue in knowledge discovery is privacy, all the more so as there is a trend from *reactive* knowledge discovery, after a crime has been committed, to *proactive* knowledge discovery, aimed at preventing or mitigating crimes, and more importantly terrorist attacks, before they happen.

Part of the problem is understanding what is meant by privacy. At one end of the spectrum, some people view privacy as a human right, while at the other people view privacy as unachievable in a networked and computerized world[13]. To further complicate the issue, privacy as a practical matter really existed only during the last hundred years or so – before that everyone in each community had a good idea of what everyone else was doing. Those who were poor lived cheek by jowl, and those who were better off had servants who acted as surveillance and dissemination combined. Only in the last hundred years have human beings ever been alone for significant amounts of time.

I suggest that privacy can really be understood only as privacy with respect to some other party. It makes sense to think about how much privacy each person might want from their government, from businesses with which they interact, from their social community, and from their family; much more sense than to think of privacy as a global property. And considering these other parties makes it possible to see more clearly what the underlying issues might be that drive the demand for privacy.

In the case of governments, the primary underlying concern is the asymmetry of power that exists in the relationship between an individual and a government. For most people, changing governments means emigration, which is difficult at best and impossible for most people most of the time. The relationship is therefore a critical one, and privacy is an important part of maintaining some leverage in it. This applies to the political dimension: in democracies, the other way of changing governments is to vote them out, something that most governments resist to the extent they can. Widespread invasions of privacy, such as surveillance, are seen by some as exerting a 'chilling effect' on political discussion, even though the fabric of modern democracy could not function without government knowledge of its citizens (validating identity, and managing revenue, for example).

In the case of businesses, common attitudes to privacy are much less demanding. Even businesses have been surprised at how willing people are to reveal details about themselves, in return for quite small economic benefits. It is not yet clear whether this represents a clear-headed assessment of the benefits against the costs – the advantage to the customer is usually better service and sometimes a better price – or whether it represents ignorance about the implications. In other words, people may not care that businesses build detailed models of them, or they may not really know. The contrasting attitudes to privacy with respect to governments and to businesses are striking, considering that businesses also have a great deal of power. Although there are apparent choices between businesses, in fact geography often limits choices of, for example, supermarkets; and the vast scope of multinationals limits choices in particular markets.

In the case of social groups, expectations of privacy are almost completely determined by culture. Mainstream Western culture assumes high levels of privacy within social groups, but this is, as noted above, a relatively new development. In village life, there is little privacy. In most other cultures, there is little or no privacy within a social group.

Within families, expectations of privacy vary, and probably derive mostly from expectations of the relevant social groups. Some families share everything, at least until the children are teenagers; others maintain quite high levels of privacy between family members.

Knowledge discovery does require data on which to work; and it is important to have data about normal people, transactions, and activities to act as a backdrop against which adversaries can be more easily seen. This data can and should be collected only with the informed consent of those whom the data describes. This requires a full discussion of the needs and issues. Attempts at this discussion so far have been muddled. This is partly because of differences in worldviews, as described in Section 3.4.1. But the biggest problem has been the lack of *clear* explanations of the motivations, both in social terms, and in technical terms. In social terms, the change from reactive to proactive knowledge discovery is a major change in the balance between government power and individual freedom of action, one that can be justified in some situations such as terrorism where the consequences of failing to prevent an attack can be large. However, this change cannot also be justified in more ordinary situations, and advocates have failed to clearly point to the boundary between the two kinds of situations. There is widespread fear of a 'slippery slope' of knowledge discovery, justified by counterterrorism, then applied to stifle political dissent, then to crime prevention, and then to social infringements. In technical terms, advocates have failed to understand, and so to explain, the needs for widespread data collection, but also what use is then made of the data. The fact that data collection is widely equated with suspicion is a clear illustration of this ineffective communication.

Notes

[1] The long tail phenomenon is explained in detail in C. Anderson, *The Long Tail: Why the Future of Business is Selling Less of More*, Hyperion, 2006.

[2] For example, some examples of how popular car cloning is can be found at `www.bbc.co.uk/insideout/westmidlands/series7/car_cloning.shtml`.

[3] B. Mezrich, *Bringing Down the House: How Six Students Took Vegas for Millions*, Arrow Books, 2002.

[4] This is known as Benford's Law, although it was originally discovered by Simon Newcomb, in the context of physical constants. Pietronero *et al.* (L. Pietronero, E. Tosattib, V. Tosattib and A. Vespignani, "Explaining the uneven distribution of numbers in nature: the laws of Benford and Zipf", *Physica A: Statistical Mechanics and its Applications*, 1–2:297–304, 2001) show that the distribution of digits arises when the underlying process changes in a multiplicative way, that is fluctuating by percentages up and down, rather

than additively. Hence we probably have inflation to thank for the fact that Benford's Law applies to the numbers on tax returns. Many complex systems, both natural and human have this multiplicative nature, so we can expect to see Benford-type digit distributions in many contexts. This result is also related to Zipf's Law, which explains how, among other things, word frequencies are distributed in natural languages. Underlying both is the idea of a power law distribution, which we will also return to in later chapters.

[5]Not in a Freudian sense, but simply as a functional view of how minds seem to work.

[6]Stephen Potter, in his book *Oneupmanship*, gives many examples of how to defeat an opponent by making a normally unconscious behavior conscious. For example, he suggests that a winning tennis strategy is to ask one's opponent whether he or she breathes in or out while throwing the ball up to serve.

[7]The paper C.F. Kurtz and D.J. Snowden, "The new dynamics of strategy: Sense-making in a complex and complicated world", *IBM Systems Journal*, 42(3):462–483, 2003, gives a good general explanation of the approach. The paper M. Lazaroff and D. Snowden, *Anticipatory Models for Counterterrorism*, in: R.L. Popp and J. Yen, (eds.), *Emergent Information Technologies and Enabling Policies for Counter-terrorism*, chapter 3, pp. 51–73. IEEE Press Series on Computational Intelligence, 2006, illustrates its application to the domain of counterterrorism.

[8]S. French and C. Niculae, "Believe in the model: Mishandle the emergency", *Journal of Homeland Security and Emergency Management*, 2(1):1–16, 2005.

[9]C. Bellavita, "Changing homeland security: Shape patterns not programs", *Homeland Security Affairs*, II(3):1–21, 2006.

[10]M. Lazaroff and D. Snowden, *Anticipatory Models for Counter-terrorism*, in: R.L. Popp and J. Yen, (eds.), *Emergent Information Technologies and Enabling Policies for Counter-terrorism*, chapter 3, pp. 51–73. IEEE Press Series on Computational Intelligence, 2006.

[11]By Lyotard, in his book J.-F. Lyotard, *The Post-Modern Condition: A Report on Knowledge*, volume 10 by *Theory and History of Literature*, University of Minnesota Press, 1984.

[12]However, the problem is not as settled as it might seem. The issue of ticketing drivers for speeding is contentious in most countries. Often, there is at least an implicit sense that police ought to 'play fair' in detecting speeding, for example by allowing radar detectors, and disallowing automatic speed cameras. Any proposal to change the rules about how speeding is detected provokes a firestorm of protest.

[13] As Scott McNealy famously said: "You have zero privacy anyway. Get over it." (SUN Press Conference, January 1999, reported in *Wired*, www.wired.com/politics/law/news/1999/01/17538).

Chapter 4

Looking for Risk –
Prediction and Anomaly
Detection

Prediction is the process of estimating some property of new records, using a model learned or derived from data for which the property is already known. In essence, prediction says something about the future, based on the past.

In this chapter, we consider how prediction can be used as a tool to fight against crime, fraud, and terrorism. There are many misconceptions about how this kind of knowledge discovery can be applied, fuelled by films such as *Minority Report* in which police arrest people for crimes that they have not yet decided to commit. This scenario is not in the least plausible, but issues about the extent to which prediction has a role to play in preventing crimes and attacks are subtle and need a full discussion.

4.1 Goals

4.1.1 Misconceptions

There is a great deal of confusion about the goals of predictive technologies in adversarial situations, partly because of a tendency to ascribe more power to such technologies than they have. Media coverage creates the impression that knowledge discovery is able to:

- predict individual criminal acts, in advance, with such accuracy that preemption is the only reasonable course,

- by using a single, monolithic predictor built from vast amounts of data, collected from all aspects of life.

This scenario is pure fiction. Several authors have written critiques of knowledge discovery as if this scenario was not only realistic, but very close to realization, but these critiques amount to attacking a straw man.

4.1.2   The Problem of Human Variability

There are several obvious reasons why a scenario in which knowledge discovery is used to predict detailed criminal behavior is impossible. First, the future is not predictable, even in principle. Computer scientists know that even simple clockwork mechanisms, called Turing Machines, have aspects of their future behavior that cannot be predicted, even in principle.

Prediction technologies are estimates of likely future regularities based on observed regularities in the past. This model applies only in a very weak way to systems in which humans make decisions. Whether or not one believes in free will, as an observed fact humans are deeply unpredictable. Someone may show all of the signs of setting out to perform some act, but draw back at the last minute for reasons that are not apparent from the outside. Humans are deeply stateful, and this internal state is not accessible, perhaps not even in principle.

4.1.3   The Problem of Computational Difficulty

This level of prediction is also impractical, even as an approximation. It would require inconceivably large amounts of data. Our understanding of technology does not even begin to approximate this task. We would not be able to estimate the reliability of the predictions well enough anyway – testing relies on statistically similar data, but today's data is always going to be different from tomorrow's and yesterday's.

Even after a crime has taken place, the role of knowledge discovery is not to detect who the criminal is, so much as to guide the investigation in plausible, or perhaps probable, directions.

4.1.4   The Problem of Rarity

If we assume that records in a dataset are of two kinds: those that describe normal and unusual activities, and those that describe the activities of adversaries, then there are actually four different cases:

1. Records that are good and are labelled as good. In most adversarial settings, these are the vast majority of the records.

2. Records that are good but are labelled as bad. If the data collection and modelling process has been done well, records like this should be extremely rare. They create a problem because the people associated with these records potentially face consequences as a result of the labelling; but they will usually make a fuss as a result, so such records attract attention, and the labelling can be fixed.

3. Records that are bad and are labelled as bad. These records are the most useful in the dataset, but they are typically rare, and this creates problems for prediction.

4. Records that are bad but are labelled as good – data about adversaries that has not been detected as such. These records are the most problematic of the four kinds because they confuse the placement of the boundary that should separate the two kinds of records. Furthermore, those associated with such records have no incentive to report the (undeserved positive) consequences of the misprediction, so it is hard to correct the dataset. Such records often arise as the result of victimless crimes; if the labels are corrected at all, it is often much later when the bad activity is discovered. Although we would like to believe that the number of such records is small, the number is both unknown and often, in practice, unknowable with any confidence.

The rarity of records labelled as bad makes it hard to model them, and so to distinguish the boundary between them and the records associated with normal behavior. Sometimes, the bad records are replicated before processing to balance the two classes of records more closely – for some algorithms, this will produce better performance.

It is tempting to think that the pool of examples of criminal behavior can be expanded by including artificial records that encode patterns of typical adversary actions. There are two problems with this idea. The first is that it is inherently difficult to understand how to generalize a criminal action, that is which features are intrinsic to the criminality, and which were simply one-offs for each example. The second is that, in an adversarial setting, adversaries are always trying to find new forms of criminality to avoid detection, and so there will always be new, never-before-considered patterns that *should* trigger detection, but will not. The difficulty with using known patterns is that it leads to fighting the last war.

There is also the problem caused by the nonzero error rate of any prediction technology. If a prediction system existed that correctly predicted a potential criminal action 99.999% of the time, it still makes mistakes one time in one hundred thousand, or ten times in a million. Given a large population, this is a large number of mistakes, with the associated costs in investigation time and resources, and annoyance or worse to those falsely accused.

4.1.5   The Problem of Justifiable Preemption

Much of the legal system in Western countries assumes that the role of government is to protect citizens from one another, but only when the citizens who are victims invoke this role. Otherwise, governments should leave citizens alone to live their lives. As a consequence, there are many customs and rights of citizens not to be arbitrarily investigated. For example, in common-law legal systems, people have the right to be treated as innocent until proven guilty.

However, this picture is overly simplistic. There are already a wide range of situations in which investigation takes place either without particularized suspicion, or before a crime has actually taken place. These situations include those where:

- There is no investigation without probable cause. Particularized suspicion against some individual(s) is required, and a warrant that requires some form of judicial authority must first be obtained. For example, searching of private property or tapping telephone communication is normally this kind of situation.

- A mild suggestion of a probable cause leads immediately to further investigation. For example, a "Terry stop"[1] in the U.S.A. allows a police officer to conduct a limited search (a "pat down") of an individual, and areas within that person's control, for a weapon. The officer must have a suspicion that the person is armed and dangerous, and has been or *is about to* engage in a criminal act. Furthermore, the officer may seize any contraband discovered during the search provided that it is obvious what the contraband is. As part of a Terry stop, an officer is entitled to ask the person to identify him- or herself.

   The significance of a Terry stop is that it already contains a preemptive component. In the original case, an officer had observed several men walking back and forth looking into a particular store window, and suspected that they were about to rob it. When they met another man, he stopped them and patted them down, discovering two guns in the process. The court held that the officer was justified in both his intrusion and search in the circumstances, although *no crime had taken place*.

- There is widespread (that is, nonparticularized) investigation without reasonable cause with the goal of altering the environment. For example, analysis of crime statistics with the goal of redistributing police patrol routes comes under this heading. In general, this kind of analysis seems to cause few concerns, even though it usually requires collecting and fusing large amounts of data from different sources.

- There is widespread investigation without reasonable cause with the goal of selecting some individuals for further investigation. This sounds alarming, but is actually common. Some examples are: traffic radar speed traps, digit analysis in accounts, income-tax return profiling, medical-fraud analysis, stock and security fraud analysis, searching for money laundering, spam filtering, intrusion detection in networks, and car licence-plate scanning. Many governments also intercept electronic communications (usually excluding their own citizens), and some organizations monitor the email, and perhaps other online activities, of their employees.

  This is obviously a wide spectrum of different situations, and some people find some of them problematic. However, it is striking that those that tend to be found most problematic are those that are most recent (for example, licence-plate scanning), which suggests that expectations and views about the legitimacy of widespread investigation without cause are constantly changing.

- There is investigation, after a crime has occurred, with attention focused on certain individuals with motives and/or opportunities, but no other *a priori* grounds for suspicion. This kind of investigation is widely accepted (although perhaps not by those who actually find themselves under investigation), even though the targets of investigation include many people for whom probable cause is small.

The most contentious issue in relation to knowledge discovery is the use of widespread data collection as part of the defence against terrorism. This could be seen as a larger version of the kind of widespread analysis that already takes place in situations where adversary action is expected, for example fraud and money laundering. On the other hand, the special role of governments as the investigating agency, and the secrecy about the detailed process, suggest that it is substantially different and new. Social attitudes and legal frameworks are still developing in this area, with a rush to allow more intrusive data collection and analysis in the wake of each attack or thwarted attack, followed by a gradual rebellion against it as time passes and no attacks take place. It would be better to address these complex issues in a more measured way, taking a strategic view. The potentialities and limitations of the technology involved are an important part of this discussion.

4.1.6   The Problem of Hindsight Bias

It is hard to assess the performance of a knowledge-discovery system in an adversarial setting objectively. When the system fails to detect some bad activity, and that activity comes to light in some other way, it is tempting to portray this as a failure of the system. This fails to fully account for the difference that hindsight makes.

Hindsight makes bad activities seem more inevitable or obvious than they actually were. As humans, we fill in gaps so well that sometimes we fail to notice that the gaps are there. What seems like a solid chain of evidence leading to some conclusion after the fact is often much more tenuous before the fact. This is the reason why magicians are so reluctant to show how tricks are done – they seem so obvious once the mechanism is revealed.

Hindsight also fails to notice how many different ways a chain of reasoning could have been expanded in the forward direction. These (as it turns out) false branches are not even visible when looking back along the chain of reasoning.

4.1.7   What are the Real Goals?

Prediction technologies in adversarial settings will use data in which the interesting cases are usually rare; data that describes, directly or indirectly, the actions of humans who are internally extremely variable; and models whose error rates are not negligible. What can such technologies be used for? The answer is that, on the whole, they should be used as inputs to human decision-making, rather than driving decisions directly. In other words, rather than predicting criminal or terrorist actions, they should be thought of as predicting the *risk* of such actions. Furthermore, they should not be thought of as predicting yes or no answers, but rather values that indicate the degree of risk. Used in this way, predictors can be valuable tools.

The ways in which risk prediction can be used depend on the balance between the reliability of the prediction and the consequences of an incorrect prediction. There are four different situations where a different balance suggests a way of exploiting the prediction.

- **Using risk to make an immediate decision**. In situations where the consequences of an incorrect prediction are small and there is enough data from previous adversary action to build a robust predictor, it may be reasonable to use the prediction to make a decision without human intervention. An example is credit-card fraud detection. A credit-card transaction can be refused automatically using a prediction system because there have been enough previous examples of fraudulent card use that the traces it creates are well understood; and the consequences to the customer if the transaction is not in fact fraudulent are quite small (a telephone call). The consequences of not refusing a transaction that is fraudulent are more significant, so fraud-prediction models are constantly being improved, but credit-card companies are willing to take some losses as a cost of doing business.

- **Using risk to deploy resources for deterrence.** If the consequences of an incorrect prediction are larger, or the data on which it is based do not contain enough examples of the pattern of concern, predictions can still be used to guide the deployment of resources. For example, police forces improve their crime rates by deploying police presence preferentially to locations and at times where it is more likely that crimes will occur. These times and locations can be predicted, approximately, from statistics about previous crimes. The prediction is not that a *particular* crime will occur at this time and place, but that the probability of a class of crimes is higher at this time and place than at other times and places. Weak predictions can be tolerated because they still produce an improved outcome – but better predictions would obviously be better.

- **Using risk to direct resources for investigation.** If the consequences of an incorrect prediction are even larger, or examples in the data are even less frequent, prediction can be used to guide subsequent investigation. For example, if witnesses to a hit-and-run see a licence-plate number, they do not have to be very certain of the number to justify a search of registration records[2]. In the same way, a prediction about some criminal activity does not have to be guaranteed to be correct to justify further investigation.

Some of the most successful uses of predictive knowledge discovery have been in the area of fraud. Such systems do not predict that records A, M, and X, say, are fraudulent. Rather they predict that A, M, and X have a significant risk or probability of being fraudulent. Since, often, there are not enough resources to investigate every possible instance of fraud, it is particularly useful if such models rank the records in order of 'suspicion' so that the most likely cases can be investigated first, and the others as resources permit. This approach is used in insurance fraud, medical fraud, and tax fraud. The same general approach is used to investigate money laundering.

Predictive models can also suggest (and rank) possible leads to follow in a criminal investigation, that is who, on the face of it, is the most 'suspicious'. The same issues come up in intelligence, where there are many possible people, actions, and connections, and it is helpful to be able to rank them by risk so as to allocate investigative resources in the best way.

- **Using risk to predict crimes and attacks.** Finally, there are some situations where the available data is not useful enough to make robust predictions. This is usually because the situation of interest is rare, or the adversaries are especially motivated to avoid discovery.

If the consequences of a wrong prediction are small, it may still be reasonable to act on the predictions, at least in a limited way. For example, it is possible to build a predictive model of likely terrorist targets, but it is doubtful that such a model would be highly accurate. Nevertheless, using its predictions for target hardening would be worthwhile.

In situations where the consequences of an incorrect prediction are large, it is also worth acting on weak predictions, because failing to act may be disastrous. The obvious case here is a terrorist attack using weapons of mass destruction. Even a poor prediction needs to be acted upon to the extent that resources allow.

A number of critiques of predictive knowledge discovery for counter-terrorism have been published, especially during the furore about the naively named Total Information Awareness Program in the U.S. For example, the U.S. Public Policy Committee of the Association for Computing Machinery, in testimony to the Senate Committee on Armed Services[3], argued that plausible error rates are necessarily so large that they would lead to large numbers of innocent people being falsely accused. Schneier[4] has written extensively about the inappropriateness of using data-mining technology as a tool in the fight against terrorism. He also makes the point that the error rates will never be small enough not to trigger a flood of false alarms, and that almost all of the investigative and reactive effort will be diverted to handle these false alarms. This is an important point, but Schneier, and the ACM commit-tee assume that 99.999% accuracies are unattainably remote, despite the fact that defect rates well below this are commonplace in many industrial settings, not by some kind of magic but by working at the process to reduce defects. They also assume, less explicitly, that predictions will be implemented by a single, monolithic process, with simple yes/no predictions. Neither of these assumptions is valid, so the criticisms are not compelling with respect to state-of-the-art knowledge discovery[5].

Jonas and Harper[6] have also written on this issue, again making the point about the accuracy required for prediction to be useful. However, they also make the important point that knowledge discovery based on patterns is ineffective, at least for counterterrorism, although it is widely used in criminal investigation and, to a lesser extent, in crime prevention. There are very few examples of terrorist attacks (relatively speaking) and so very few sources of patterns. Furthermore, terrorists are less likely to repeat patterns they have already used (although it is worth noting how stable the patterns used by burglars, serial killers, and espionage agents tend to be, and al Qaeda has shown a fixation with aircraft). They argue that the logical conclusion, and the one we use in what follows, is that threats should be sought in the anomalies in data. However, they object to this on two grounds: that everyone is an anomaly, and that a fear of being considered anomalous tends to drive people to increased conformity. It is certainly the case that, in a small to moderate number of people, everyone looks like an anomaly – people are very different. But as the number of people being considered increases, the overall variability does not continue to increase – because no matter how unusual someone is there tend to be more and more people like that person, as the sample population gets bigger. Humans are incredibly variable, but we are also social creatures, and our social interactions balance out our variability in predictable ways. Criminals and terrorists, because they are, to some extent, outside of society, live with a different balance, and so exhibit discernible characteristics, especially against a background of normality.

4.2 Outline of Prediction Technology

Given a never-before-seen record, the goal of prediction is to predict the value of one of its attributes, given values for the others. The attribute to be predicted is called the *target attribute*. The target attribute can take a finite number of values, for example 'low risk' or 'high risk', in which case the target attribute is sometimes called the *class label*, since it allocates the new record to a class. In this case, prediction is called *classification*. Alternatively, the target attribute can take on an infinite number of values, for example a risk score between 0 and 1. In this case, prediction is called *regression*. Regression is more useful than classification in adversarial settings because it automatically provides a way to rank records by their predicted values.

Some prediction technologies predict not only the value of the target attribute, but also an associated confidence in that prediction, usually expressed as a probability.

Introductions to basic knowledge-discovery technologies can be found in books by Tan, Steinbach and Kumar[7], Kantardzic[8], and Dunham[9].

4.2.1 Building Predictors

To build a model that will accurately predict the value of the target attribute of new records, data for which the correct predictions are already known must be available. Usually, the correct predictions are known because the data is historical, and so the relationship between the ordinary attributes and the target attributes has become known. For example, to predict how powerful a hurricane will become, data on previous hurricanes at a similar stage of development can be labelled with their eventual power to create the necessary data. The data used to train a model is called the *training data*.

Various techniques, discussed in detail in Section 4.4, are known for building predictive models. Each technique makes different assumptions about the possible relationships and the complexity of the dependence between the ordinary attributes and the target attribute.

Once a model has been built using any one of these techniques, it is wise to assess its performance before deploying it for use. The most important performance measure for a predictive model is its *prediction accuracy*, the percentage of the time that it makes the correct prediction on never-before-seen records. Since we do not necessarily know what the correct prediction should be for new, never-before-seen records, we need another way to estimate prediction accuracy. The conventional way to do so is to withhold some of the available labelled data from the training phase, and present it to the constructed model as if it were new data (with the target attribute values removed, obviously). The model then makes predictions about these records. We have the correct labels to which these predictions can be compared, and so we can compute how well the predictor is performing. The withheld data used to do this is called the *test data*.

In situations where data is in short supply, withholding records to be used as test data may deprive the model of significant information. One strategy for measuring whether or not this is important is called *cross validation*. The labelled dataset is partitioned into a training and test dataset in a number of different, random ways. A different model is built from each of these training sets and tested using the matching test set. The resulting set of prediction accuracies gives an indication of how robust the *particular kind* of predictor is for this data. It does not, of course, provide any extra information about how good each of the individual predictors is.

If, say, ten different partitions of the dataset are used, then this is called 10-way cross validation. If the average prediction error across the ten predictors is large, this signals that the particular prediction technique is too weak for the prediction problem it is attempting to solve. A large variation in the test prediction accuracies may also suggest that records in the data are quite different from one another, so that more training data may be required.

A better way to generate training and test data is called *out of bag sampling*. Suppose that the entire available data contains n records. Build a training set by sampling randomly from the available records until a set of size n has been chosen, replacing each record in the dataset before drawing the next. As a result, some records may be chosen for the training set more than once. After this process has been used to build a training set, there will be some records that were never chosen, on average about $n/3$ of them. These records become the test set.

In general, a predictor built from such training data will be slightly better than one built from a subset of the original dataset – the training data set seems larger because of the repetitions, and is more representative of the scenario from which the original data was taken. For example, if the original data contains some records that are quite similar to each other, then this will be reflected, in a slightly enhanced way, in the training data. Furthermore, the statistical errors in the measured prediction error on the test data behave as if the test data was of size n, instead of size $n/3$ – in other words, the confidence intervals on the error are smaller. The prediction error determined in this way provides information about how well the chosen kind of prediction technology works on the data, but it also provides information about how well a particular predictor is working.

If the testing procedure suggests that the prediction performance is adequate, then the model can be deployed, that is used to predict the target attribute of genuinely new records.

4.2.2 Attributes

We have already seen that the target attribute can take on either a finite set of values, or an infinite set of values. The same is true of the ordinary attributes. A *categorical* attribute is one whose values are chosen from a finite set with no additional structure or relationships. For example, the attribute 'Credit Card' might have values chosen from the set {Mastercard, Visa, American Express}. An *ordinal* attribute is one whose values are chosen from a finite set, but a set whose members have some kind of ordering relationship among them. For example, an attribute 'Life Stage' might have values chosen from the set {Child, Adolescent, Adult, Senior}, and there is some implicit ordering on the values. For example, 'Child' is closer to 'Adolescent' than to 'Senior'. A *numeric* attribute is one that can take on an infinite number of values from a set with some implicit ordering. For example, an attribute 'Income' might have values ranging from 0 to several billion. Some numeric attributes could also be represented as ordinal. For example, an attribute 'Age' takes values from 0 to about 120, with an obvious ordering, and could be represented using an ordinal attribute as long as non-integer ages are not important.

One of the most difficult attributes to represent are ordinal attributes where the implicit relationship is cyclic. For example, the days of the week are obviously representable using an ordinal attribute with values {Monday, Tuesday, ..., Sunday}. Most of the implicit relationships are captured, for example Tuesday is closer to Wednesday than Friday. However, Sunday is close to Monday in reality, but far away in the representation. Dealing with this problem requires mapping the ordinal attribute to something that better captures the real relationships. For example, the days of the week could be mapped to equally spaced points on the circumference of a circle, and the coordinates of these points used as two new, numeric attributes.

4.2.3 Missing Values

In real-world situations, it can happen that some attribute values of some records are not present in the collected data, and this can spoil the modelling process. How serious a problem this is depends on *why* particular values are missing.

The simplest case to deal with is when the values are missing at random, that is as if someone had rolled some dice for every attribute value, and removed it from the data with some fixed probability. In this case, it may be possible to compensate for the missing data, either by replacing it in some sensible way, or because the modelling technique is able to take its absence into account.

However, data that is missing from a dataset is almost always missing for a reason. For example, if data is collected by asking people questions, say a telephone survey, then they are more likely to refuse to answer sensitive and personal questions than more routine questions. So the answers will be disproportionately missing for some of the questions. This is much more difficult to deal with during modelling.

4.2.4   Reasons for a Prediction

An important distinction between different kinds of predictors is whether they provide, or can provide, reasons in support of their predictions. A predictor that provides reasons is called *transparent*. People find such predictors more comfortable to use because their predictions are explained. This can be significant when the prediction seems counter-intuitive, and so can make the process more resistant to social engineering. However, this is something of an illusion, because a prediction is not necessarily more accurate simply because the prediction technology is able to provide an explanation for it. Predictors that provide only a prediction, without giving reasons to support it are called *opaque*. Unfortunately, with our current state of knowledge, the strongest predictors are also opaque.

4.2.5   Prediction Errors

We have already discussed how prediction accuracy can be a measure of the quality of a predictor. In many situations, it is important not just to know how many prediction errors there are, but how they are distributed. For example, if we are predicting the risk of some phenomenon, a prediction that a record is high-risk when it is not is quite different from a prediction that a record is low-risk when it is not. The cost of errors is not symmetric.

Predicting that a record is high-risk when it isn't is called a *false positive*. False positives are not usually a fundamental problem, since it is often possible to repeat the analysis of the case represented by the record. For example, if the record comes from a medical test, then the test that produced it can be repeated. If the record comes from the scan of a piece of luggage, then the luggage can be rescanned. The problem with false positives is a more pragmatic one – when the rate of false positives is high, a lot of extra time

Predicted to be Actually is	Class A	Class B	Class C
Class A	310	41	12
Class B	38	292	8
Class C	15	14	270

Figure 4.1. *Confusion matrix for a three-class prediction problem.*

and work is spent retesting. Those using the predictor lose confidence in its predictions, and may even cease to use it.

Predicting that a record is low-risk when it isn't is called a *false negative*. False negatives create a much more important problem because, typically, no further action is taken. For example, if a medical test comes back negative, the test is not repeated and the patient may not be properly diagnosed until much later. If a piece of luggage contains a weapon that is not detected, the luggage will not be rescanned and so the weapon will never be detected.

Both false positives and false negatives reduce the performance of a prediction system but for different reasons. Most predictors can be tuned to decrease the rate of one, at the expense of increasing the rate of the other. Finding the best trade-off can be addressed using techniques such as the area under an ROC (Receiver Operating Characteristic) curve, but is often better addressed by using more powerful models or using multiple models together. Notice that which errors are false positives and which are false negatives depends on some intuition about which target attribute value is 'good' and which is 'bad'. Often the target that is 'bad' is also one that is relatively rare.

The distribution of a predictor's errors is often summarized using a *confusion matrix*, which displays, in a tabular way, the number or percentage of cases that fall into the available possibilities. For example, Figure 4.1 shows a confusion matrix for a particular model, trained on 1000 examples, and with three possible values of the target attribute (Class A, Class B, and Class C). The numbers on the diagonal show how many cases have been correctly classified into each class; the off-diagonal elements show how many cases have been incorrectly classified.

In this confusion matrix, we see that the predictions are mostly accurate – the sum of the diagonal elements is 872, so the overall prediction accuracy is 87.2%. Classes A and B are hard to differentiate, which can be seen from the substantial number of off-diagonal elements in the top-middle and left-middle squares. Class C is relatively well distinguished from both Classes A and B.

In many, perhaps most, real-world situations, it is difficult to know where the boundary between classes should be placed. Even for simple prediction problems such as to whom mortgages should be granted, choosing a different boundary can increase returns at the expense of increased risk of default, or *vice versa*. There is seldom enough information to decide, from first principles, where the boundary should be.

4.2.6   Reasons for Errors

In mainstream knowledge discovery, a particular prediction technique is chosen so that its expressiveness and power match the complexity of the problem domain; its parameters are then chosen so as to minimize mistakes caused by noise in the data.

The first choice requires a model that is forced to generalize from the data it sees, so that it avoids overfitting; and that has enough complexity that it can match the complexities of the boundaries between classes. The second choice is typically captured by some form of objective function that measures how poorly the predictor is working. The goal is to minimize this objective function within the framework of the model's complexity.

The discussion in the previous section assumed that only a count of the number of errors (mispredictions) was of interest. However, in practice, objective functions penalize both the number of errors and their magnitudes. In fact, for sound statistical reasons, it is plausible to penalize errors using squares of magnitudes – think of fitting a straight line to a set of two-dimensional data.

In an adversarial situation, both of these choices are problematic. First, it is plausible to regard the real-world situation being modelled as a combination or mixture of a system that captures normality, and one that captures the bad behavior being searched for. These are, potentially at least, completely different kinds of systems, so it is not obvious what the complexity of the combined system is. It does not seem plausible to assume that the combined system is normality plus a few percent of something different. Second, given that manipulation of data is a possibility, attention should be paid to how the model is penalized for incorrect modelling, since some of this may have been induced directly. In particular, penalizing misprediction of outlying records makes the model a hostage to such records.

4.2.7   Ranking

One way to address the problem of boundary placement is to use iteration: choose a boundary, see how the predictor performs with that boundary, then adjust the predictor's parameters to move the boundary, and so alter the predictor's performance as desired. A better way is to recast the problem as one of *ranking* the objects from best, with respect to the property of interest, to worst. The property of interest is whatever the boundary was dividing. For example, in the mortgage case, the ranking is from most mortgage-worthy to least mortgage-worthy. An alternate ranking is to order applicants by the predicted amount of mortgage they are eligible for – those who would have been denied a mortgage by a boundary predictor are now predicted to be allowed a very small, perhaps zero mortgage.

The advantage of ranking over using an explicit boundary is that many boundaries can be created from the ranking, by deciding where to place a cutoff in the ranking. The ranking itself provides extra information that makes it easier to see where reasonable places for a boundary might be; and different values of the boundary can be tried without having to rebuild the predictor each time. For new data records, the prediction places it somewhere in the existing ranking, and this position, as well as the density or sparsity of other records around it, provides a rich picture of the significance of the new record. For example, a new record can be far from the boundary, or close to it; and it can be in the middle of a group of similar records, or very different from records seen so far. This information is not nearly so visible in a classifier.

When the dataset contains records that describe the properties and actions of adversaries, we expect that such records will be infrequent, and it will be hard to learn their characteristics. Furthermore, there is no reason to expect that the records associated with adversaries will all be somehow similar. What we can do with data in which most of the records describe normal people or normal activities, is to build a model that ranks records by normality.

In this ranking by normality, we can now pay particular attention to those records that are ranked at the lower end. Here we expect to find records corresponding to all kinds of *abnormality*. Most of them will be completely innocuous – there are many unusual but perfectly natural people or actions in the world. However, we can reasonably expect that the records corresponding to adversaries and their actions will *also* be in this part of the ranking.

A boundary inserted into this ranking might retain many ordinary records along with those of the adversaries, but it will also allow many ordinary records (the most 'normal' ones) to be discarded. The overall problem has now been simplified. The remaining records can now be examined using the same or a different technique, with the same attributes or perhaps some new ones. In the new data, the number of adversary records is a larger fraction of the total, and so finding them will be slightly easier than it was in the original data. If only 1 record in 1 million is an adversary record in the original data, but we discard 90% of the records in each round (which assumes that our model of normality is such that 10% of all records are classified as abnormal), then after two rounds of analysis, the adversary records are now 1 in 10,000. Low error rates are now practical as well.

The choice of boundary at each stage must be made so that no adversary record is ever classified as normal. If this causes many other records to be kept for the next stage, then the number of stages may need to be increased, but the adversary record will eventually be in data small enough for its presence to become obvious.

The use of multiple stages, each one reducing the data remaining in consideration, has a number of other practical benefits. First, most records receive only a cursory analysis and are discarded in the early stages, reducing the impact, or the perceived impact, on most people.

Second, being selected for a subsequent stage is a weak kind of probable cause, and so can justify the release of new attributes for the remaining records. This means that only a smaller set of attributes has to be collected or exposed to the early-stage predictors, further reducing the privacy impact of analysis.

Third, the boundaries between stages are an ideal point for procedural, and perhaps even judicial, oversight of the entire process.

4.2.8   Prediction with an Associated Confidence

Predictors that predict the target attribute, together with an associated confidence, have some of the advantages of ranking. Roughly speaking, records can be divided into: confidently predicted to be normal (and so safe to ignore), weakly predicted to be normal (pass to a subsequent stage), weakly predicted to be abnormal (pass to a subsequent stage), and confidently predicted to be abnormal (act on the prediction). The precise choice of the boundary does not matter so much, because any records that fall close to the boundary, on either side, will receive further scrutiny. Furthermore, the amount of scrutiny, and so the cost, can be matched to the likelihood of significance.

4.3   Concealment Opportunities

Prediction can be subverted by an insider who manipulates the collected data, the algorithms used to build predictors, or the results before they can be used. In most adversarial situations, this possibility is well-understood, and processes are in place to prevent insider attacks.

However, adversaries have an alternate way of subverting prediction, by altering the data that is collected, especially the data that is used to build the models. Although all of these attacks depend on manipulating the way in which data is captured (or not), it is helpful to divide possible techniques into three kinds, depending on which phase of the overall process they target:

- The first is to attack the data-capture phase, preventing data being captured at all or changing the data so that the resulting record cannot be associated to the person or action it belongs to. Even if the record is predicted to be high-risk, there is no consequence for the person who actually generated it, because it appears to be about someone else.

  When the data capture is human-mediated, or when it is digitally collected but without checks, there are many ways to alter the data to make it unusable: reverse adjacent figures, use name variants, or simply make up content (a common practice with web forms). Some data collection that might be expected to be robust is actually unchecked: for example, iris scanners are easily fooled by a printed iris held behind a card with an appropriately sized hole in it, so a free-standing iris detector is easily manipulated (whereas CCTV surveillance of an iris detector would prevent the most egregious spoofing, at least).

  When the collected data is checked at collection time, the easiest way to change the data is to simulate someone else, or someone else's data. This can be done by complete or partial identity theft, by disguise (to fool cameras), or by changing one's voice.

  Altering the collected data in this way is the weakest attack – it does not allow the prediction process to be manipulated; all it does is to pollute the collected data so that particular records cannot be selected, or correctly identified if they are.

- If the prediction technology being used is understood by adversaries, especially if the particular form is known, then much stronger attacks are possible. In fact, many prediction techniques are remarkably fragile with respect to direct manipulation of the training data. This level of attack involves introducing particular data into the prediction system, not with the goal of changing the outcome for these records, but to create holes or blind spots for other data, causing them to be wrongly predicted.

  These attacks are of two kinds. Red-team attacks introduce data records that describe adversaries and their actions, but that are labelled as low-risk. They create a shelter for similar adversary records that are then more likely to be classified as low-risk. Blue-team attacks introduce records that have typical low-risk attribute values, but that are labelled as describing adversaries or their actions. They create shelters somewhere else in the data space for adversary records to be misclassified as low-risk, by causing the boundary between the two kinds of records to move.

  Obviously, this kind of attack requires a substantial level of sophistication in understanding how the prediction technology works.

- A third form of attack is *social engineering*, that is manipulating the data collected in such a way that the prediction technique makes correct predictions, but the predictions are discounted when it comes to making decisions or taking action based on them. The goal is to discredit the predictions by making it seem as if they must have been caused by design failures in the technology or errors in the algorithms, that is, to make them seem like false positives.

This attack does not require the same level of understanding of the knowledge-discovery techniques. Instead it requires a deep understanding of human psychology and, in particular, the psychology of those who will be making the ultimate decisions about whether or not to act on predictions. It can be applied in a tactical way by manipulating the data collected, but it is worth remembering that it can also be applied strategically by trying to create a misleading impression of who the adversaries are and what they are like.

4.4   Technologies

We now review some of the prediction technologies that are available. All of these techniques can be used in adversarial settings, but usually require sophisticated use, in particular using more than one technique, and arranging their use in carefully thought-out ways.

4.4.1   Decision Trees

Perhaps the simplest predictor is the decision tree[10], familiar from the game of Twenty Questions. A decision tree is a tree whose internal nodes each contain a test, usually applied to a single attribute, and whose leaf nodes are labelled with one of the possible target attribute values (class labels). A new record is classified by starting at the root, applying the test found there to the record, and then moving down the tree to one of its subtrees based on the result of the test. This process is then repeated at the root of the subtree, until the record arrives at a leaf. The target attribute value associated with the leaf becomes the prediction for the record. The target attribute must necessarily be categorical or ordinal. In general, there will be more than one leaf corresponding to each target class label. In other words, there is usually more than one way for a record to be classified into any particular class.

Figure 4.2 shows a small example decision tree. Given a new record, the value for attribute a_1 is examined; if it less than 15 the record passes down to the left-hand subtree, otherwise it passes down to the right-hand subtree. The left-hand subtree is a leaf, so the record is immediately classified as belonging to Class 1. The right-hand subtree examines the value of attribute a_3. If it is greater than 12, the record passes down to the left-hand subtree where it is

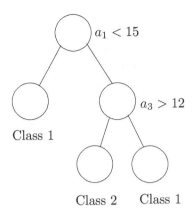

Figure 4.2. *An example of a decision tree.*

classified as belonging to Class 2. If it is less than or equal to 12, the record passes down to the right-hand subtree where it is classified as belonging to Class 1.

If the test at an internal node involves a categorical or ordinal attribute, then there is one subtree associated with each possible value that the attribute can take. If the attribute is numeric, the test is usually an inequality on the attribute value, and there are only two subtrees, one for when the inequality is satisfied and the other for when it is not.

A decision tree is a transparent predictor, since the path that each record takes on its way to a leaf corresponds to a set of tests that must all be satisfied by the record. The conjunction of these tests is a kind of rule that explains why the record was classified as it was. A decision tree makes a prediction, but with no indication of its confidence in its prediction.

Using a decision tree is straightforward and intuitive, but building one is more difficult. Given some training data, the first choice is what test to place at the root. This requires selecting the attribute (and if it is numeric, the attribute *value*) that best discriminates among the classes. For example, if we are trying to predict the safety characteristics of cars, their colors are probably not very predictive, whereas the presence or absence of airbags probably is.

The choice of the best, or most discriminating, attribute can be made formal in terms of measures such as *information gain, information gain ratio,* or *Gini index* that can be computed for each of the available attributes[11]. Once these measures have been computed, the attribute with the best score is chosen, and the corresponding test calculated and inserted in the tree. The training data is then divided based upon which case of the test each record satisfies, and the process is repeated, with a subset of the training data, at the root of each subtree.

The creation of new subtrees stops when the records remaining in the training data at a particular node are all (or mostly) of one class. The current node is then made into a leaf and labelled with the dominant class present in the training data that reached it[12].

Decision trees are somewhat brittle – if slightly different training data are used, then the entire structure of the tree may change, although its prediction accuracy will tend to remain about the same. Hence, although rules justifying its predictions can be extracted, these rules do not necessarily describe deep reasons that lie behind the predictions.

This brittleness also makes it straightforward to subvert decision trees, with some access to the training data. The tests created at nodes close to the leaves rely on relatively small numbers of training-data records, so the insertion of even a single deceptive record, carefully designed, can alter the structure of a subtree and make it possible to misclassify other, new records in predictable ways[13].

We assume that an attack intended to subvert a predictor is made by causing records to be inserted into the training data. However, it is not plausible to assume that the attacker has access to the rest of the training data, nor that the attacker knows, in detail, the algorithm used to build the predictor. In the case of decision trees, this means that the attacker does not know the internal structure of the tree.

However, it is plausible that an attacker can have access to data that is similar to that used to build the predictor since such data is not usually well-protected, and much of its structure could often be roughly inferred anyway. Call this the *attacker training data*.

There are two different kinds of records that could be inserted into the training data. A *red-team attack* tries to insert records whose attributes are typically red but that are labelled blue (normal). For example, in passenger screening, a red-team attack is when a passenger meeting many criteria for being a terrorist behaves like a normal passenger. A *blue-team attack* tries to insert records whose attributes are typically blue but are labelled red (that is, that should be classified as 'bad'). In passenger screening, a blue-team attack is when a passenger looks innocuous but does something to attract suspicion.

Both forms of attack can be used to subvert decision trees. A blue-team attack is typically more expensive, since getting the record inserted into the training data may require the individual whom the record describes to be captured (in order to be convincing that the record should be labelled red).

The basic strategy is quite simple: match an existing record in the training data with one or more similar records labelled with the opposite class label. However, it will be difficult to do such a matching using all of the attributes, for this would suggest that none of the attributes have much predictive power. Rather, it is better to match the values of some of the attributes and set the others to neutral values.

The question then becomes: which attributes are the best to try to match, and how can the attacker tell? This is where the attacker training data comes in. The attacker can mimic likely decision trees that will be grown using this data and can get some estimate of the predictive power of each attribute (using information gain, gini index, or one of the other standard measures).

Perhaps a little surprisingly, the best attributes to choose are those with low to moderate predictive power. Attributes with high predictive power will tend to generate tests close to the root of the tree. Subverting the boundaries of these tests requires many inserted records because the fraction of the training data used to build them is still large. On the other hand, attributes with very little or no predictive power will not be tested in the decision tree at all. Attributes whose predictive power is modest tend to appear in the decision tree close to the leaves, and this is the ideal place to manipulate the tree's structure. The size of the training data used to decide on the best attribute and best test at such nodes is quite small, so even a single inserted record can have a substantial influence[14].

A blue-team attack is straightforward. To hide a particular red record, construct blue-labelled records that have attribute values similar to it for the attributes chosen for manipulation, but make sure that the attribute values for the other, important attributes are typical of the blue class. This makes it likely that, when the tree is built from the data with the inserted record, it will look much as it would have without that record, except that a few nodes close to the leaves will classify the inserted records *and the red record chosen for concealment* as blue. Even a single, carefully chosen inserted blue record can be sufficient to conceal a red-labelled record.

A red-team attack can be used to change the attribute tested at levels close to the leaves from one that would properly discriminate red from blue for one that does not discriminate as well. This requires finding an attribute that has very little predictive power, and that does not discriminate well between red and blue records in the ordinary data, and increasing its predictive power by inserting a red record (or perhaps several) that looks very different from blue records in the value of this attribute. The effect is to make this attribute seem to have greater predictive power, forcing it to be chosen as an attribute to be tested in the tree, and exploiting the fact that it does not correctly classify some existing red records. This attack does not work for an attribute that is already tested in the tree, since inserting more extreme red attribute values does not move the decision boundary, the value against which the attribute is tested.

The need to update predictors to respond to changing situations means that there are repeated opportunities for this kind of attack by manipulating the training data. The danger for knowledge discovery is that the kind of records that these attacks insert are, in some sense, particularly interesting since they (by design) violate the structure implied by the existing model. The temptation is for the model builder to choose them preferentially because of their apparent interest, playing into the hands of the attacker.

Decision trees are classifiers, since the predictions associated with each leaf are for a particular class. Regression using decision trees is sometimes discussed in the literature, but what is meant is the prediction of a finite set of numerical values at the leaves. The main difference from classification is that the class labels are inherently meaningful, and do not necessarily have to be decided in advance. Decision trees do not do true regression, and so cannot do ranking very well.

4.4.2   Ensembles of Predictors

An interesting question with a surprising answer is: how does the quality of a predictor improve as it is allowed to see more data records? In other words, suppose we built a predictor from the first 10 training records, then from the first 20 records, and so on, and then measured the prediction accuracy of each of these predictors and compared them. Intuitively, we might expect that accuracy increases with the number of training records seen, perhaps linearly. In fact, the accuracy increases very rapidly with the first few records and then flattens off as further records are seen. As few as 40 or 50 records can produce a predictor whose accuracy is 80% or more of what a predictor trained on a very large number of records will achieve.

At first glance, this might seem to suggest that only a few records should ever be used for training, and the rest discarded. However, if we took a subset of the previous training records and built a sequence of predictors using them, then we would observe the same rapid increase in prediction accuracy, but the curve would flatten at a much lower level.

How can this be explained? A simple example might help. Suppose that we want to learn the difference between birds and animals[15], and the training data begins with records like this: sparrow(bird), rhino(animal), robin(bird), hippo(animal), ... The first record is always useful because it tells us something we didn't know before. In this case, so is the second, and having seen these two records we might hypothesize that the difference between birds and animals depends on size, or flying, or number of legs but probably not on color – sparrows and rhinos are both brown. The third example, robin, however, is not nearly so useful because it tells us nothing new for or against our hypotheses. The fourth example is also not very useful because it gives us no new evidence for or against our current set of hypotheses.

However, suppose the next example record in the training set is: ostrich(bird). This record is much more useful to us, because it suggests that our hypothesis that size is a distinguishing feature is probably not correct. Likewise, a record kangaroo(animal) is useful because it calls into question our hypothesis that number of legs is an important attribute.

From this example, we can see that some training records are more useful than others, because they falsify some of our candidate hypotheses. However, the property of being useful depends on the context: what records have already been seen and taken into account by the predictive model. Now the behavior of the prediction accuracy as a function of records seen can be explained. Early records are almost all useful because they are unlikely to resemble each other and so help the model to explore the space of possible attributes and see how the classes depend on them. However, the rate at which new records are useful drops off because records are increasingly similar to records that have already been seen. Of course, new and useful records continue to occur but with decreasing frequency, so the increase in prediction accuracy slows down.

However, if we started with a sample of, say, half of the original records, then the model increases its prediction accuracy in a very similar way at the beginning. However, the number of useful records left after this initial phase is much smaller than before, so the final prediction accuracy will still be lower. In other words, the prediction accuracy achieved after long training depends on the total number of useful records seen, but useful records always appear disproportionately at the beginning of any training data, because the property of being useful depends on what records have been seen already.

It turns out that there is a way to exploit the fact that most improvement in prediction accuracy comes from the early records used for training, and that is to build ensembles of predictors instead of a single, monolithic one.

Suppose that we observe that the steepest part of the curve of increasing prediction accuracy as a function of records seen lies between 1 and r records. Choose a sample of r records from the training data and build a predictor from this sample. The accuracy of this predictor will probably only be 80% of the accuracy of the single monolithic predictor, but it can be built quickly and cheaply, and is sometimes also smaller than the predictor built from the entire training data. This predictor has been built effectively because a large fraction of the records it sees are useful because they come from novel regions of the data space.

Now choose another sample of r records (with replacement, so it may contain some of the same records that were used to build the first predictor). Build another predictor from this sample.

Continue to build predictors from samples of the training data until there are a fairly large number of them, say m. Each of the predictors, individually, is not as good a predictor as the monolithic one built from all of the training data.

The ensemble of predictors is used together in the following way: given a new record, ask each of the predictors to make a prediction and take the plurality of their votes to be the global prediction.

An ensemble predictor works well in two different ways. First, it uses the training records in an effective way, because in each subset more of the records are novel. Second, the global vote will almost certainly have a higher prediction accuracy than that of a monolithic predictor built from all of the training data.

The reason that the ensemble performs better than a monolithic predictor is that the individual predictors make mistakes on different records. For any given record, although some of the individual predictors may make the wrong prediction, it is likely that most will make the correct prediction. In technical terms, the ensemble cancels the variance of the individual predictors caused by the fact that they were trained on different samples of the dataset.

Technically, the individual training datasets are supposed to be independent samples with replacement from the entire training dataset for this ensemble approach to work. In practice, ensembles work well even if the data is created in less-careful ways. For example, simply partitioning the whole training dataset and learning predictors from the pieces tends to work well. The reason is probably that most practical datasets contain a great deal of repetition – many copies of almost identical records. This flexibility makes it easy to implement ensemble construction in parallel.

The process of building ensembles described above is called *bagging*[16]. A more sophisticated process called *boosting*[17] or *arcing*[18] can also be used, especially for datasets where the boundary between the classes is difficult.

In boosting, each record in the whole training dataset is labelled with a selection probability. Initially, this selection probability is uniform across the records, set to $1/n$ if there are n records.

The first training dataset is selected by drawing examples from the whole training dataset using the selection probabilities, with replacement, so a record may be selected more than once (in this first round this corresponds to selecting them uniformly randomly). A predictor is built from this training dataset.

Now the newly built predictor is applied to the whole training dataset. Those records that it classifies correctly have their selection probabilities decreased, and those that it classifies incorrectly have their selection probabilities increased (and a normalization is applied so that all of the selection probabilities continue to sum to 1).

A new training dataset is now drawn from the training data using the altered selection probabilities, so that examples that were hard for the first predictor to get right are disproportionately present in the new training dataset. A predictor is built from this training dataset as before.

Now either the ensemble of the two predictors or just the newly built one is applied to the whole training dataset, and the records that are misclassified have their selection probabilities increased and those that are classified correctly have their selection probabilities decreased.

A third training dataset is now chosen based on the altered selection probabilities, and a third predictor is built. This process continues until the desired number of predictors has been built. Predictors built later in the sequence can be thought of as experts, focusing more and more of their attention on the difficult cases, while still generally getting the easy cases right.

For new records, the ensemble of predictors each produces its own class prediction and the plurality of the votes for a class becomes the global prediction, just as in bagging.

Although boosting looks as if it contains a sequential dependency, it can also be applied to data whose records have been partitioned into different subsets. Hence a parallel version of the algorithm is possible[19].

Both bagging and boosting can be used for regression if the individual predictors produce numerical outputs. All that is required is to *average* the predictions of each individual predictor, rather than using voting.

The ensemble idea can also be used when the individual predictors are of different kinds, that is each based on a different model and construction algorithm. In this case, the effect of the ensemble is to cancel the *bias* introduced by making a choice of a particular predictor with particular complexity.

Ensembles are resistant to manipulation by altering the training data, for two reasons. First, an added record, or even a small set of added records, does not necessarily appear in the training data subset used to build each component of the ensemble, so some component predictors will not be affected by the manipulation. Second, even when an added record is included in the training data, the other records that are part of the same training subset are not predictable, so the effect of the added record is harder to determine. As a result it is hard to create records that will change the decision boundary, let alone in a controlled and predictable way.

The number of votes for the most-common target class can be used as a surrogate for the confidence of the ensemble in its prediction. If there are 30 predictors in the ensemble and two target classes, then a 28 to 2 prediction for target class A is much more confident than a 16 to 14 prediction for target class A, even though the ensemble prediction is the same in both cases.

This idea can also be used to allow ranking, even if the component predictors are only classifiers. Instead of treating the number of predictors that vote for the winning class as a confidence, treat it as an indication of how strongly the record belongs to that class. For example, suppose that an ensemble uses 100 decision trees as the base classifiers, and there are three target classes. For each record, we can count the number of votes for the winning class, and treat this as a score for ranking. This score is really measuring how *difficult* it is to classify the record in its class, since an easy-to-classify example will presumably be classified correctly by almost all of the decision trees, while a difficult one may generate disagreement among the classifiers. However, difficulty of classification is often a reasonable surrogate for being an unrepresentative member of a class, and therefore one that should be ranked low. Since ensembles often have many component classifiers, this ranking can be done in a fine-grained way.

The idea of an ensemble of attributes works even if the division of the training data is not by record, but by attribute. Dividing data up so that some subset of the attributes of all of the records is in one subset, and another subset of the attributes in another subset, and so on would be an odd thing to do deliberately – but real-world data is often collected this way. If data is collected via different channels, then some data about each person or object may be collected in one place, and other data about the same people or objects in another place. Of course, this data could be collected together in one place and a model built from it there. However, it is sometimes useful to be able to build a predictor *without* gathering the data – the owner of each piece can then contribute to the global model without violating the privacy associated with the individual data.

It is not at all obvious that a plausible predictor can be built when each training data subset knows only some aspects of each record. The reason that this usually works is because of the Naive Bayes Assumption. This assumption, which has been used to simplify complex calculations of probabilities, assumes that attributes are independent when, usually, they are not and correlation information is crucial. It has been shown that the effect of making this rather strong assumption is that the probabilities of assigning records to each class will be wrong, but these probabilities will still be ordered correctly by magnitude. In other words, if the appropriate probability of assigning a given record to Class A is 75%, to Class B is 20%, and to Class C is 5%, then a predictor that makes the Naive Bayes Assumption may generate probabilities 60% for Class A, 30% for Class B, and 10% for Class C, but choosing the highest-probability class as the global prediction still gives the correct answer. When an ensemble of predictors is built from data partitioned by attribute, the collective vote of the ensemble will probably distort the probabilities for each target class, but taking the class with the plurality of votes will still tend to produce the correct answer.

Ensembles are important tools because of the difficult political and practical issues raised by the large number of organization with overlapping, and sometimes competing, interests in law enforcement and intelligence. The success of ensemble predictors shows that silos are not necessarily bad for the quality of predictions – they can improve predictions by cancelling out the variance in the data that each organization collects, and can prevent the groupthink that can pervade a single organization.

The fact that each predictor encapsulates the content of a particular subset of the data, but does not reveal the data directly, can improve the overall quality of predictions by encouraging some stakeholders to participate who would not otherwise wish to or be able to. For example, some jurisdictions have privacy legislation that prevents them from sharing data at the level of individual records. The ability to nevertheless contribute to a global predictor using a local predictor makes it possible to use this data without compromising individual privacy. This is helpful between countries, but also between companies, particularly those who are competitors, enabling them to learn knowledge such as typical rates of fraud, and whether they are individually being attacked or victimized by the same adversaries.

There are other lessons from ensembles that are useful for understanding how to combine knowledge from different organizations. Having each organization provide ranking information rather than simply prediction provides a better basis for combining knowledge, but if this is not possible, then simple voting schemes can also be helpful, provided that there are enough different votes.

Special ways to combine predictions may be appropriate when the aim is to predict rare situations. Ensembles provide a smooth and continuous way to balance false positives and false negatives by varying the number of votes needed for a prediction to win. For example, the false positive rate can be reduced by changing the criterion for a particular class to be the global winner from simply a plurality of the vote to a percentage of the vote, say 80%. Similarly, the false negative rate can be reduced by changing the criterion for a particular class to be the global winner down to 20%. If the consequences of getting a prediction wrong are great, say missing a potential dirty-bomb attack, then it may be appropriate to act if *any* member of the ensemble predicts the possibility of such an attack.

4.4.3 Random Forests

Random Forests is an algorithm that builds predictors with the simplicity of decision trees, and the power of ensembles[20]. A random forest is an ensemble of specially built decision tress, built as follows:

1. The available data is divided into a training dataset and a test dataset using the sampling-with-replacement strategy. The chosen records form the training dataset, and those that were never chosen become the test set.

2. A decision tree is grown from the data, but with the following modification. At each internal node, a subset of size $Mtry$ of the attributes is randomly chosen, and then the ordinary node test-selection procedure followed on this subset of the attributes.

   Because of the availability of a test set, the performance of the tree being built can be measured at any time. The growth of this particular tree may be terminated in the usual way, when each of its subtrees has been replaced entirely by leaves, when it attains sufficient prediction accuracy, or some combination of these stopping criteria.

3. The process is repeated to select another out-of-bag sample of the data and to build another tree. This stops when a prespecified number of trees have been built.

The construction process produces a better set of trees than simply repeating the ordinary decision-tree construction would do. Each attribute used for a test at an internal node has been selected in a doubly contextualized way. First, it is considered based on some subset of the records, selected for the tree in which it appears. Second, it is considered in comparison to some other $Mtry -1$ attributes for this particular internal node.

The random forest is deployed in the usual ensemble way, with the prediction of the forest being the plurality of the votes of the individual trees for the target class (or the average for regression).

Random forests are one of the strongest known prediction technologies, especially for multiclass problems (where there are more than two target classes).

Like all ensemble techniques, random forests are opaque, since it rapidly becomes difficult to see why several hundred trees have produced the global prediction they have. It is hard to subvert them by manipulating training data, since both attributes and records are selected at random during the construction of each tree. It is hard, therefore, to control what happens in one tree, let alone in an ensemble of many.

Because random forests are ensembles of specially built decision trees, they have all of the benefits that come from that. In particular, random forests can be used for ranking, especially as they usually involve many hundreds of component trees. As with any ensemble, the number of votes for the predicted target can be used as a surrogate for the ensemble's confidence in its prediction.

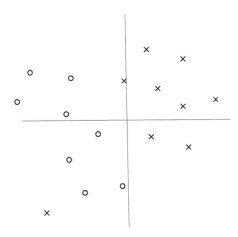

Figure 4.3. *Two-attribute data with two classes.*

4.4.4 Support Vector Machines

Support Vector Machines (SVMs)[21] are strong two-class predictors, able to implement regression and classification. To get some intuition about how they work, consider the dataset shown in Figure 4.3.

The records in this dataset have two ordinary attributes, and the values of these attributes have been used as coordinates to plot points corresponding to each record. Each point has been labelled depending on the target class to which it belongs, crosses for one class and circles for the other. It is clear that the two classes can be separated from each other in space; in fact they are so distinct that they can be separated linearly, that is by inserting a straight line between them. The question is: which straight line is the best? This straight line corresponds to the prediction model: given a new record, we can plot it in space, and classify it in the cross target class if it is on one side of the line, or in the circle target class if it is on the other.

For the training data, it is not obvious what would make one line better than another, provided that points of each class stay on different sides of the line. However, it matters a good deal for classifying new records, some of which might lie in the currently empty space between the two kinds of symbols.

It turns out, and this is the intuition behind Support Vector Machines, that the best way to choose this boundary line is to consider the thickest block that can be inserted between the points of the two classes, and then take the centerline of this block as the actual boundary. This is shown in Figure 4.4.

In general, only a few of the points actually touch the block, and so only these few points determine the block's position. The other points are

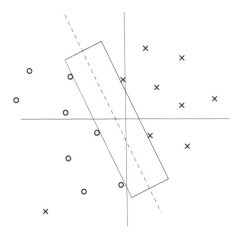

Figure 4.4. *The thickest block that fits between the two classes; its center line is the boundary.*

irrelevant so far as determining where the best boundary goes. These points that touch are called the *support vectors*, after which the technique is named. We can see that it must be the case that not all records are equal when it comes to classification – some, those whose points are support vectors, are much more informative about the difference between the classes.

This intuition extends to higher dimensions, that is to datasets with more than two attributes. The separation of the two classes now becomes a hyperplane, but the same idea continues to work.

The algorithm for computing the best separating hyperplane is only of quadratic complexity in the number of records in the training set (that is, it grows as n^2 if the number of records is n), so it is reasonably fast in practice. Intuitively, the algorithm works like a kind of tug of war between the support vectors on one side and the support vectors on the other, so that the separating hyperplane ends up in an equilibrium position.

When a new record is presented to the classifier, its classification depends on which side of the separating line it falls. It turns out that this is equivalent to determining the net pull on the new record from all of the support vectors.

The distance of a new record from the boundary can be regarded as a kind of surrogate for the confidence of the prediction, although this distance really measures how easy the record is to classify. Hence a large value plausibly does correspond to high confidence, but a small value is only a low-confidence prediction.

Of course, it may happen that points from the two classes overlap so that there is no clear space between them in which to insert a block. More work is required, but the same approach can be extended by imagining the block to be made of foam, allowing some points to be inside the block, but charging a substantial penalty for any such points. The further the point is inside the block, the larger the penalty.

This does not significantly complicate the algorithms, so this extension comes at little cost. Of course, it introduces an extra parameter whose value must be set, the penalty to be paid for each point inside the block. Setting this penalty high makes the separating plane fit well with the data, but the position of the hyperplane may be substantially moved by only one or two points in the training data. Having a smaller penalty reduces the global quality of the fit, but also reduces the impact of a few unusual points.

Often the boundary between two classes is a difficult and convoluted surface, making it hard to build a compact predictor to describe it. Support vector machines provide a way to avoid this difficulty. The original data records are mapped into a higher-dimensional space by creating new attributes as combinations of the existing ones. Although this higher-dimensional space is harder to work in, if this mapping is done carefully the boundary between the two classes may be much simpler, ideally expressible in a linear form as a hyperplane.

Figure 4.5 shows an example. The points in one class are drawn as crosses, and the points in the other as circles. In 2-dimensional space, the boundary between the two classes is some form of ellipse. Now if we create a third attribute by squaring each of the initial two attributes and adding them together, the points farthest from the origin in two dimensions are also highest up in the third dimension. So we get a 3-dimensional space in which the points of the two classes can be separated by a plane, roughly perpendicular to the new, third axis.

Although it seems as if creating all these new attributes and increasing the dimensionality carries a significant performance penalty, the special structure of the calculations used in an SVM actually allow these to be largely avoided, as long as a carefully chosen mapping, called a *kernel*, is used. All of the calculations involving data records occur in inner products, and the effect of an inner product of two points in the higher-dimensional space can be obtained by doing a different calculation using only the values of the original attributes. This is known as the 'kernel trick'.

Support Vector Machines are vulnerable to attacks that insert new records into the training data. Recall that a red-team attack inserts a record labelled blue but that is more typical of the red class, and a blue-team attack inserts a record labelled red that is more typical of the blue class[22].

The strategy behind both kinds of attacks is that a record from the training data that is slightly on the 'wrong' side of the true class boundary causes the learned boundary to rotate slightly to compensate. This rotation opens

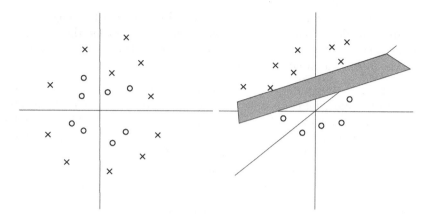

Figure 4.5. *Points from two classes in 2-dimensional space separated by an elliptical boundary can be separated by a plane when they are mapped into three dimensions.*

up a segment that can conceal a potentially large number of other records. This weakness arises because the position of the boundary depends only on the support vectors, and these are typically a small subset of the training data. Even a single inserted record, if it can be made to be a support vector, can effect a substantial change. Making a record into a support vector is straight-forward, by arranging to place it close to the likely boundary. An attacker can not, in general, know where the actual boundary is; but it is plausible that an attacker has access to similar data and can build an approximation to the real model. Only an approximate knowledge of the boundary is required for this attack to succeed.

For example, a blue-team attack inserts a red-labelled record that is slightly on the blue side of where the boundary really should be, given the ordinary training data. This makes it likely to become a support vector for the red side of the boundary.

The probable position of the boundary can be determined from the at-tacker training data. The effect of the added red-labelled record is to create a region on the opposite side of the data where other records would have been classified as red, but will now be classified as blue. The further the inserted record is from the rest of the data, the greater its influence on the position of the boundary will be, but this also increases the risk that it will be seen as anomalous and discarded.

Figure 4.6 shows a blue-team attack in the 2-dimensional example data. An extra data record has been added. It is a typical blue record (shown by a circle), but it is labelled as red. As a result, the boundary has changed so that it falls on the red (cross) side of the boundary. The change in the boundary

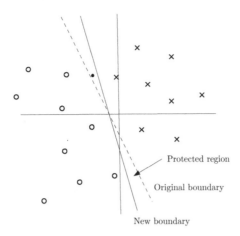

Figure 4.6. *An SVM blue-team attack. Circles are red records, crosses are blue records. The marked circle is labelled red but has typical blue attribute values. The boundary moves to create a protected region in which records that should be labelled red will be labelled blue.*

creates a region on the opposite side where other records that would previously have been classified as red will now be classified as blue.

The red-team attack works in a similar way. An inserted blue-labelled record with typical red attribute values is positioned so that it is just on the red side of where the true boundary should be, making it likely to be a support vector for the blue side of the boundary. This has the effect of pushing the boundary slightly towards the red records in the area near the inserted record, and opens up a segment in which records that would previously have been predicted as red will now be predicted as blue.

Figure 4.7 shows the matching red-team attack. Here the extra data record is a typical red record (shown by a cross), but it has been labelled as blue. Again the boundary changes to place it on the red side. As a result, a region is created near it where other records that would previously have been classified as red will now be classified as blue. Both attacks have a similar effect on the boundary.

SVMs can be used in ensembles, where they are more resistant to manipulation. For example, adding a record to data used to train an ensemble of SVMs will cause the decision boundaries to rotate slightly for those data subsets in which the added records appears. However, the decision boundary will not be quite the same as the boundary built from the entire training data, so the region this opens up for potential concealment is hard to determine. For those data subsets in which the added record does not appear, the boundary will still be different, although more similar, to the boundary learned from the entire training data. Because of voting, regions protected in different SVMs

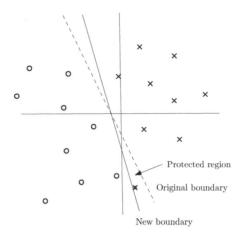

Figure 4.7. *An SVM red-team attack. Circles are red records, crosses are blue records. The marked circle is labelled blue but has typical red attribute values. The boundary moves to create a protected region in which records that should be labelled red will be labelled blue.*

will not necessarily be the same, so it is difficult to guess a region that is protected in enough of the manipulated SVMs to successfully win a vote across all of them.

Although Support Vector Machines are powerful classifiers, they have significant vulnerabilities to manipulation that must be taken into account when they are used in adversarial settings.

SVMs are classifiers, but the distance from the boundary can be used as a kind of ranking. This is meaningful, since the support vectors are the points that are most similar to points of the other class (except for points that actually lie inside the block between the classes from which the boundary is derived). Points that are not support vectors are increasingly dissimilar to points in the other class as their distance from the boundary increases.

In problems where there are more than two target classes, SVMs can still be used, but they have to be used in a kind of ensemble. There are two ways to do this. SVMs can be trained for every pair of classes; or SVMs can be trained for each class against the rest. The second is probably slightly more common. New records are evaluated by all of the SVMs and the global prediction made on the basis of each individual SVM's prediction. In the one-versus-the-rest case, it becomes possible to fail to classify a record because all predictors claim it is not in their class. More typically, a record is classified in one target class by one predictor and in the 'rest' by all of the others. The construction and use of multiple predictors make this an expensive option.

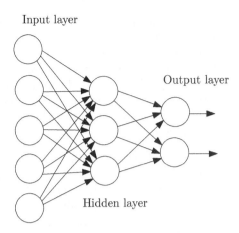

Figure 4.8. *A neural network with 5 inputs, predicting 2 classes.*

4.4.5 Neural Networks

Neural networks[23] are predictors based loosely on neurons and the way they are connected in brains. Given a dataset with m attributes, predicting membership of k classes, a typical neural network is shown in Figure 4.8, for the case $m = 5$ and $k = 2$.

The neural network consists of three layers: the input layer on the left, the middle or hidden layer, and then the output layer. The output of each of the neurons in the first two layers is connected to the inputs of *all* of the neurons in the next layer. Each connecting edge has an associated weight.

The input-layer neurons each replicate their input to all of the neurons in the next (hidden) layer. The neurons in the other layers compute the weighted sum of each of their inputs, apply some thresholding function to it, usually a nonlinear function, and then transmit the result downstream.

A neural network is used as a predictor by inputting each attribute value of a new record to the input neurons, and observing the values produced by the output-layer neurons. The neuron corresponding to the predicted class outputs the value 1, while the other neurons output the value 0. It is also straightforward to allow the output values to represent probabilities that a given record belongs to each class, in which case some or all of the outputs could be nonzero, and the neuron with the largest output value would be the prediction of the target class.

Neural networks are trained using an algorithm called *backpropagation*[24]. The weights on each of the edges are initialized to small random values. Each record of the training data is presented to the input nodes, and the corresponding values are propagated through the network to the outputs. The actual output produced by the neural network is compared to the desired output. The difference is used to modify the weights of each of the internal edges by making small changes to them in such a way that, if the same record were immediately presented to the network again, the actual prediction would be closer to the desired one. This is done by propagating the difference back across the output-layer neurons, creating a difference between the actual and desired outputs of the hidden-layer neurons, which in turn leads to an adjustment of their input weights[25].

The next record is presented to the network, and another round of weight adjustment takes place. This is repeated for the entire training dataset. However, effective training requires that the neural network see every example in the training data many times, so the entire training process is repeated, often after rearranging the order of the records. Typical training may require using the training set hundreds of times, making neural-network training expensive.

Neural networks have two advantages that can cancel out the high cost of training them. First, their use of nonlinear internal elements means that they are good at modelling complex boundaries between classes. Second, since each hidden-layer neuron sees the values of all of the attributes, neural networks are able to use all available correlation information in the training data.

Neural networks are opaque predictors. The reason why the network makes the predictions it does are implicit in the weights, but there are many weights and it is usually hard to understand their significance. The exception is that weights that are zero, or very close to zero, reveal results that do *not* depend on earlier values, for example particular inputs.

Neural network outputs can be configured in a number of useful ways. For a k-class problem, the simplest output configuration is a single output node corresponding to each class, with an output of 1 for the correct class, and output 0 for the others. This is easily extended by allowing the outputs to be real values between 0 and 1 representing the confidence of the prediction of each class. For example, in a two-class problem, the prediction (0.98, 0.02) is a confident prediction for class 1, while (0.55,0.45) is a much less confident prediction for class 1. Neural networks can also be configured with a single real-valued output neuron representing the rank of each input record according to some score function.

Neural networks are hard to manipulate. The general strategy of creating a red-team attack by adding records to the training data with typical red-team attribute values but labelled as blue, and creating a blue-team attack by adding records with typical blue-team attribute values but labelled as red, is possible, but it is hard to construct such examples and be sure that they will work. The difficulty is that neural networks have access to the correlations among attributes. Artificial records must therefore not only have the right individual attribute values to create the desired impression, but they must also have the right correlation structure. This is difficult to estimate from the attacker's training data and may be impossible – it may not be possible to look truly blue without being blue and *vice versa.*

4.4.6 Rules

Rules are statements of the form: if attribute i has value v, and attribute j has value w, then the class label is A. In other words, their general form is

$$predicate\ on\ the\ attribute\ values \rightarrow prediction$$

The number of attributes considered on the left-hand side, and what kind of predicates are possible are completely arbitrary but, in practice, left-hand sides are usually equalities or inequalities on a small number of attributes. Rules can either be definite, so that if the left-hand side was satisfied, the right-hand side must have been true in all the examples used for training; or rules may have an associated *confidence*, so that if a left-hand side was satisfied, then the right-hand side was true with some *probability* in the examples used for training.

A rule can be thought of as a description of a local regularity that is present in the data: for *this* small set of attributes (and therefore for a small number of dimensions), if *this* property is present then the class attribute can be predicted to have *this* value. Usually, it takes many rules to adequately explain a whole dataset.

Rules are very intuitive for humans since we seem to use them ourselves as shortcuts to avoid detailed thinking each time we encounter a common situation. However, as humans, we seem to apply rules in a contextualized way that conceals some of the problems that appear when using them as a predictive model.

The most difficult problem is what to do when the left-hand side of more than one rule is satisfied by a new record, and the right-hand side predictions for the class label are different. This problem happens to humans too, and is arguably the source of much confused thought and action. Metarules such as preferring the rule that has the shortest left-hand side are possible, but it hard to argue that this is always the best strategy.

The problem of how to handle overlap also causes difficulties for building the rules in the first place. There are two basic strategies for rule building: starting from left-hand sides, or starting from right-hand sides[26].

Starting from left-hand sides means finding a set of training records with the same (range of) values for one attribute, say a_1, and mostly the same class label, say c. Some rule systems require that *all* of the records should be in the same class; others that only a fraction of them must be, in which case each rule has an associated confidence reflecting this. This set produces a rule of the form $a_1 \rightarrow c$ with high confidence. Now we try to expand the left-hand side by seeing if there is a large subset of the records explained by the current rule that also shares the same (range of) values for another attribute, say a_3. If so, this rule can be extended to one of the form a_1 *and* $a_3 \rightarrow c$, probably with slightly lower confidence. Expansion of the left-hand side continues until the confidence becomes too low to be useful.

Starting from the right-hand side means considering all of those records that are labelled with, say, class c, and then looking within those records for the largest set of attributes with the same (range of) values. This set defines a rule. This is then repeated for the next class label, and so on.

The simplest way to avoid multiple rules that can be satisfied by the same record is to remove training examples from the training dataset as soon as a rule that explains them has been created. However, this makes the rule set extremely sensitive to the order in which the rules are created. For example, a strong relationship between a certain configuration of attribute values and a class may not be noticed because the examples that would generate it have all been explained by other, less significant, rules before the strong rule could be considered.

If examples that already have explanations are not removed from the training dataset, then the set of rules will be redundant in the sense that each training record will potentially have been explained by more than one rule. It is possible to perform a rule-pruning phase after all of the rules have been generated. Weak rules that explain only examples that are entirely explained by other rules are removed from the set.

Although rules are an attractive technology, since they offer a reason for every prediction they make, they are also quite weak, since the prediction is based on 'local' properties of each record. Rules are unable to take into account larger-scale properties, such as the correlation among attributes, that are often important in complex real-world settings.

Rules are conceptually easy to subvert. To prevent a rule being learned, training data must be added that reduces the confidence of that rule below whatever threshold is required. To insert a desired rule, training data providing instances of the rule must be added. However, confidences are based on frequencies of occurrence and co-occurrence of attribute values, so large numbers of training records need to be added to have the desired result. This makes the manipulation difficult in practice.

Because rules describe only a local property of records, they cannot be used for ranking.

4.4.7 Attribute Selection

Most datasets used for knowledge discovery have been collected primarily for some other purpose, at least in part. As a result, the available attributes are not necessarily those best suited to the prediction task. Significant attributes may not have been collected, perhaps because of expense or perceived intrusiveness. It is also common to have, in the data, attributes that are not significant or relevant. Such attributes have been collected for whatever the primary purpose of the data collection was. Alternatively, there is often a temptation to gather attributes 'just in case' since it is rarely clear, in advance, which attributes are actually most significant.

Attribute-selection algorithms try to choose the attributes that are likely to be most useful before a predictor is built from the data. There are two reasons for this: a dataset with fewer attributes is easier to work with and building the predictor will take less time and resources; and some predictor-building techniques can be misled by irrelevant or almost-duplicate attributes, and so the quality of the predictor can be degraded.

Choosing good attributes is a chicken-and-egg problem – it is hard to tell how useful an attribute will be from first principles, without building a predictor. Statistical properties of attributes are not very helpful in deciding whether they have predictive power. For example, an attribute whose values are constant across all records clearly has little predictive power, but one whose values follow some more interesting distribution may either be highly predictive or simply be random, and it is hard to tell the difference.

Correlation information is slightly more useful, but not as much as one might think, because transitivity is not well-behaved with respect to correlation. Two attributes that are both highly correlated with the target class may be either highly correlated with one another, or hardly correlated at all. If attribute a_i is highly correlated with a_j, and a_j is highly correlated with a_k, then a_i is not necessarily highly correlated with a_k. An attribute that is hardly correlated with the other attributes, or even with the class label, may be random noise that should be discarded, but it may also be useful because its slight correlations with many other attributes increases each of their predictive power. A group of attributes that are very highly correlated with each other could be reduced to single representative member, but it is hard to know which representative is the best one to keep.

One approach to attribute selection is to use a simple and cheap predictor as a way of gauging attribute usefulness. The idea is to train a simple predictor repeatedly, using subsets of the attributes, and either score each attribute's quality by the average predictive accuracy of the predictors in which it participates, or by how often it is retained in the model. For example, an attribute with little predictive power may not appear in the tests at any internal node in a decision tree.

A set of attributes has many subsets, so it is not practical to try all of them. A number of simple strategies are commonly used to decide which subsets of attributes will be considered. For example, forward attribute selection starts with a single attribute, then adds a second attribute, then a third, and so on. Backward attribute selection starts with the full set of attributes, discards one, then another, and so on. Choosing random subsets of the attributes is also plausible.

Another approach is to build a simple predictor on the full set of attributes, and then permute the values in each column of the training dataset randomly and build a new predictor from the full set of attributes each time. If an attribute is important in building a good predictor, randomizing its values by permuting its column should produce a predictor whose accuracy is noticeably diminished. On the other hand, if the attribute is not very important, a predictor built from a randomized version of its column should have similar accuracy to the original predictor. The difference in predictive accuracy is an indication of importance – the greater the change, the more important the attribute.

The weakness of these strategies is that the way in which the attribute-selecting predictor uses attributes may not match well with the way that the eventual predictor will use them. For example, decision trees are not good at exploiting correlation among attributes while neural networks are extremely good. Using a decision tree to select attributes may discard information that the neural network could have exploited. (Neural networks are too expensive to build to make good attribute-selection tools.)

The random-forests prediction technique has two built-in ways to estimate attribute importance. The first is based on how often each attribute is selected, from the randomly chosen subset of attributes, to be the one used for the split at each internal node of a tree; that is how much the gini index, which measures the discriminatory power of the chosen attribute, increases when the split is implemented. Because many trees are built, many internal-node choices are made, so there are many chances to evaluate each attribute, and in the context of different sets of fellow attributes.

Random forests also provides an alternate measure of attribute importance. For any ensemble, the entries in each column of the training or test set are randomly permuted, and the effect on prediction accuracy measured. If an attribute is critically important, then the data with that attribute's values permuted should produce much lower accuracy than the dataset arranged normally. On the other hand, if the attribute has little predictive power, then permuting its values should not change the prediction accuracy very much. The difference between the prediction accuracy on normal and permuted data estimates the attribute importance.

Both of these approaches can be very helpful in eliminating attributes that are irrelevant or lack predictive power, without having to build many different versions of the predictor.

Domain knowledge can also be used for attribute selection with the proviso that, in adversarial settings, experts do not necessarily understand the situation as well as they might think they do; and their knowledge can potentially be exploited by adversaries.

4.4.8 Distributed Prediction

Ensemble prediction techniques can be naturally extended to the situation where the rows of a dataset are spread across a number of geographical locations. Rather than collect all of the data into a dataset at a single location, predictive models can be built locally from each of the pieces of the dataset. These local predictors can be used for new records by collecting them or redistributing them, and applying them collectively to new records.

There are a number of reasons why data might be collected in this distributed way. Even within a single organization, there are typically different channels by which data is gathered: web sites, stores, call centers, and so on. Different organizations might wish to model their entire industry. Different governments might want to develop global models of criminals or terrorists. There are often practical problems with collecting the data into a single monolithic dataset.

This distributed form of predictor building has a number of advantages. First, raw data does not have to be moved from the locations where it was collected to a central location. This collection both uses resources and takes time. Second, less storage for the data is needed, and it can be arranged in shallower hierarchies, which has substantial performance implications for the model building. Third, and most importantly, each location does not have to make its raw data visible to other locations, enabling it to provide greater privacy for the records. The local predictors encapsulate the properties of the local data, to be sure, but the properties of individual records are effectively hidden. This also makes it possible to model the properties of data that cannot be collected into a single dataset, perhaps because of different privacy legislation regimes.

4.4.9 Symbiotic Prediction

Algorithms are effective with data that is large and numeric; humans are effective with data that is visual or language-based. Symbiotic prediction uses a tight coupling of predictive algorithms and human feedback to produce a model that is better than either could produce by itself.

The process starts with building a predictive model from training data, using a technique that provides confidences as well as predictions. When the predictive model is deployed, new records whose predictions have high confidence are handled entirely by the model. Predictions with low confidence are shown to a human, together with the associated confidences for each possible class, and the human provides the final classification. In some situations, it may also be appropriate to keep these records for updating or training a revised model.

This approach works best when data is hard for algorithms to classify well, but relatively easy for humans. An example is the CAVIAR system[27], which attempts to identify the species of flowers from images. When the system is not confident about a prediction, it displays examples of the three most likely species, and allows the user to input the best answer. Those cases which the technology finds easy are predicted well; those cases that are referred to a human are also predicted well because the human is choosing from a small set of possible target classes rather than all of them. The overall result is high prediction accuracy with little demand on the human involved.

A similar approach has been taken by the MINDS intrusion detection system[28]. Intrusion detection is a difficult prediction problem because most intrusions are different from what has been seen before, but so is most normal traffic! The MINDS system predicts and acts to block intrusions that are like those it has seen before, but displays traffic about which it is not sure to a human analyst, ranked by the system's estimate of how likely it is to be an attack. The analyst can then label new traffic as either innocuous or an attack, and this information is used to update the automatic part of the model.

Again, caution is needed so that humans do not label records as innocuous just because they do not fit some preconceived view of what bad records should look like.

4.5   Tactics and Process

The discussion of the properties of predictive technologies suggests some ways to combine prediction technologies to address the difficult problems of extremely large datasets, patterns that may be quite rare, and the need to attain very low (preferably zero) false-positive rates. There are three important parts to this process.

The first is to spend some time tuning each particular predictive technology. This is unavoidable because the best way to find the boundary or ranking of interest is almost never obvious from the raw data alone. Each technology has some parameters that need to be set; it is never clear how

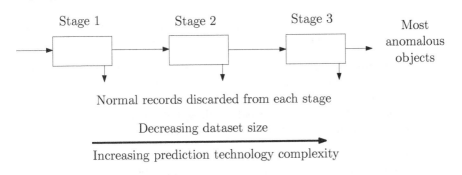

Figure 4.9. *Stages of prediction.*

to set these parameters to their optimal values; so training and testing are critical to making sure that each predictor is working as well as it can.

The second is to arrange prediction into a sequence, as shown in Figure 4.9. The figure shows three stages, with the amount of data passing from stage to stage decreasing steadily. Each of the stages might be a simple predictor, or a complex predictor, for example an ensemble of some kind.

If each stage is a ranking predictor, then it is straightforward to compose them in this way. Each stage produces a ranked list of the records that it is given. An appropriate boundary is then applied to separate the records into those that will be discarded, and will not flow on to subsequent stages, and those that will be kept and will flow on to subsequent stages. The boundary should be chosen in a way that reflects the costs of false positives versus false negatives. For example, in terrorist or medical-test settings, the cost of false negatives is high, so it is reasonable to place the boundary so that the false negative rate is (close to) zero. This, of course, means that the false positive rate is higher, so a greater fraction of records are retained for subsequent analysis. In other settings, for example fraud detection, it may be known that there are resources to investigate only a small number of potential frauds, so there is little point in retaining records whose chances of reaching the threshold for investigation are small.

The remaining potential problem is the presence of bad records that have been mislabelled as good (usually because the relevant bad actions have not yet been discovered). As we commented earlier, such records can be common in datasets describing victimless crimes, since it often takes a long time for the crime to be noticed, and the corresponding record relabelled. We might expect these records to resemble known bad records, but it is impossible to distinguish them from false positives. However, we can make some progress by observing that, in a ranked set of values, the density of examples should vary. Unusual records are also rare, so the density of records at that end of the ranking should be low. Once we reach normal records, the density should increase rapidly. Placing the boundary just at the point where the density increases rapidly is likely to place most bad but mislabelled records on the 'bad' side of the boundary, and so keep them for subsequent analysis.

The second-stage predictor now works with data in which the proportion of bad records is much higher than in the original data (depending on the boundary chosen after the first stage). This makes this predictor's task easier because the two classes are better balanced, and also because the dataset size is smaller, so that more resources can be spent considering each record.

After the data passes through the second-stage predictor, a decision about where to place the boundary can be made, discarding some records that are no longer of interest, and passing some records on to the third stage. This prediction and selection process can be extended to subsequent stages. At each stage, the pool of remaining records is increasingly likely to contain the bad records.

Although it is conceivable that the same prediction technology be used at each stage of this pipeline, it is more sensible to use cheap technologies in the early stages, and more expensive technologies at the later stages. In a sense, it does not matter if the early stages do not provide a sophisticated ranking, as long as many records can be safely discarded. As the data passes through the stages, the number of records remaining decreases, making it sensible to apply more sophisticated analysis to the remaining records. It is possible to add the rankings of previous stages as attributes before building the subsequent downstream predictors, making them into metapredictors.

At the end of the pipeline of stages, the number of records should be small enough to use human judgement to make sure that the records really do seem to be bad (bearing in mind the possibility of social engineering), and to decide what actions and consequences will follow from their selection.

There is a considerable amount of extra information available for each record as a result of its passage through the various stages. For example, each record's rank according to each of the predictors is known, and this may be indicative of whether it represents a true or a false positive.

This kind of staged detection process is a cost-effective way of deploying prediction technologies. It also has other benefits. In particular, the boundaries between the stages provide a natural place for several interesting things to happen. First, extra attributes can be added to the remaining records. This provides a way to mitigate the 'fishing expedition' nature of using large datasets that many people find objectionable. Only when some level of reasonable suspicion exists for records, evidenced by their selection by the predictors in the preceding stages, are more-sensitive attributes collected or made available. This more closely mimics the way in which criminal investigation proceeds: when a crime occurs, those with a motive or an opportunity are asked to account for themselves, but such data is not required from everyone in the vicinity. As the investigation proceeds, more details are demanded, but from a smaller set of people.

Second, the boundaries between stages provide a place for oversight, whether procedural or judicial. This might require demonstrating that an appropriate boundary has been chosen, or limiting access to the remaining records to only some analysts, or other kinds of controls to protect privacy and due process. Such properties are also enhanced by strong control over access to data and rankings, for example using unalterable logs of actions.

Staged prediction systems also have another big advantage over monolithic ones. The difference between records representing the bad activity being predicted and normal records is often very small, and correspondingly hard to detect. With a staged detection system, it does not matter much if the character or technology of the early stages is publicly known, as long as the precise details of its operation are not known. In fact, it can be a positive advantage. Adversaries who become aware of the early-stage prediction technology have to take it into account in the records they generate, and so in the way they behave, since otherwise they risk being detected in an embarrassingly simple way. On the other hand, normal people are likely either not to know about the prediction system or to care, and so do not change their behavior, and so their records.

The reaction by the adversaries typically creates a greater difference between their records and normal records than the original difference. This is because, knowing that they must change their records, but not knowing exactly how to do so, and how much change is enough, they are almost inevitably forced to overreact. The later stages of the prediction system, in effect, learn to distinguish *reaction* (concealment) from normality.

For this to work it is crucial that the exact details of the early-stage predictors are not public. The difficulty is that adversaries can learn something of the operation of *any* prediction technology by probing, creating records and seeing how they are classified. For example, airline passenger screening can be probed by sending team members travelling, without doing or carrying anything incriminating, and seeing which ones are subject to enhanced security, or even denied travel. This eventually reveals a lot about how the predictions are being made. Worse still, it enables a team to be chosen with high probability that they will not be detected simply by removing from the possible team anyone who attracts attention when travelling. This has been called the Carnival Booth strategy[29].

To counter this, it is a good idea to include a small element of randomness in the choice of each decision boundary, so that a record that falls on one side of the boundary today *may* fall on the other side tomorrow. This dramatically reduces the confidence that adversaries can have in information that they obtain using probing. Knowing that a team member was not selected

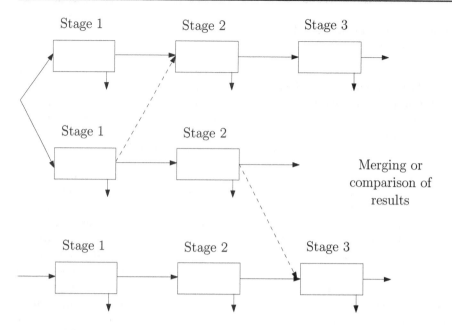

Figure 4.10. *Multifaceted prediction combining a number of predictor sequences. The results of any predictor can become extra input to another predictor (as indicated by the dashed lines).*

for enhanced security today is no guarantee that they will not be selected tomorrow, when they may be on a mission.

The third part of the overall process is to use more than one sequence of predictors to analyze data. There are several reasons to do this. The first is that different families of prediction technologies can be used in each sequence, perhaps looking at the data at different levels of abstraction. This helps to prevent blind spots that a particular sequence of predictors might have. The second is that it brings some of the advantages of ensemble approaches: the different sequences have different biases and variances; they may also work with different records about the same people or transactions, collected via different channels or by different agencies. Different sequences provide a way to avoid groupthink, and to allow different datasets to be exploited without all of their data being collected in one single repository, with the associated risks to privacy and insider manipulation.

Figure 4.10 shows a combination of sequenced predictors combined into a multifaceted prediction system. The rankings, and potentially other information, about records can be passed from one sequence to another if this seems useful, or can be kept within a single sequence.

4.6   Extending the Process

So far we have discussed prediction as if it were a static problem, with well-defined classes that do not change over time. There are two reasons why almost all prediction models in adversarial settings need to be rebuilt period-ically:

- Humans are extremely variable, so the background of normality against which adversaries are being sought may change. If the amount of data about normal individuals or actions is large, this effect may be small, but it is nevertheless a good idea to consider regularly how large it is.

- In an adversarial setting, adversaries learn from what works and what doesn't and so, in part, how knowledge discovery is being used against them. This will cause them to adapt their behavior, to try and avoid being detected, and so try to move across the predictor's decision bound-ary. They may not know enough about the process to do this with preci-sion, but they will nevertheless tend to change. Rebuilding the predictor at least checks on this behavior, and can prevent them from escaping detection. As an added bonus, learning how their data is changing pro-vides some insight into the evasive strategies they are attempting.

So there are good reasons to rebuild prediction models from time to time. However, there are also two downsides to such rebuilding. The first, and most obvious, is that there are costs involved. Some new data must be retained to use as training data for the new model. Second, the continual selection of new training data provides opportunities for manipulation using the red-team and blue-team attacks described earlier.

Ensemble predictors have particularly attractive properties for retrain-ing. For example, rather than building all of the component predictors at once, a new one can be built periodically until the desired number have been built. Of course, this means that initial predictions may be weak because they rely on a small ensemble. However, responding to changes in the data is now straightforward. Once in a while a new component predictor is built, and the oldest of the existing component predictors is discarded. The ensemble as a whole tracks changes in the underlying data as long as these do not happen too rapidly.

The same basic idea can be used in a slightly different way. First, build a complete set of component predictors in the usual way. Now, as the ensemble is used to predict new records, each predictor can keep track of how often its prediction agrees with the global prediction of the ensemble. When it is time to update the ensemble, the predictor with the worst track record is discarded, and replaced by a newly built one. This approach has the added advantage that the rate of change in the underlying data can be estimated by tracking the average agreement of individual predictors with the global prediction, and noticing when it drops.

In the scenario described above, there is slow drift in the behavior of the normal population and perhaps a slightly faster drift in the behavior of the population of adversaries. Rebuilding the predictor reflects the changing boundary between these two groups and their actions over time, but the rate of change is expected to be quite slow.

In some settings, it is the change in the underlying data that is the signal of interest. For example, syndromic surveillance systems look at the rates of emergency-room visits and doctor visits with certain constellations of symptoms, trying to predict an outbreak of disease, either natural or contrived. In this situation it is the stability of the model itself and its decision boundary that is of primary interest, rather than the use of the boundary for prediction.

4.7 Special Case: Looking for Matches

So far, we have considered settings in which there is training data available from all classes. A special case, which we now consider, is when there is data from only one of the classes. The problem becomes to build a predictor that classifies records as in that class, or not in that class, without any opinion about what other class they might potentially be in.

There are two cases: when the one class for which we have data is the class representing the adversaries, and when the one class represents normal cases. We consider the first possibility first.

The simplest version of this setting is where we have a finite list of 'bad' things, perhaps of adversaries, and we want to determine whether each new record corresponds to one of these 'bad' things. In other words, the problem is *matching*. One obvious example is the 'no-fly' lists that many countries maintain to limit terrorist's opportunities to travel. Each potential traveller's attributes, usually just a name, are checked against the list, and a classification, "on the list" or "not on the list", is produced.

Such models are not very effective, since it is easy to acquire a false identity if all that is required is a verifiable name, and there have often been problems with the way in which such lists are constructed.

A more interesting case, that comes up repeatedly in law enforcement as well as intelligence and counterterrorism, is when the list is a list of photos of adversaries. The problem of matching now becomes more difficult. The traditional approach to matching involved people looking through books of photos, exploiting human abilities to recognize faces well despite variation in age, superficial features, camera angle, and lighting.

Automating such matching required learning a prediction model every bit as difficult as any we have talked about. However, the model needs to learn the faces of only the adversaries. Much progress has been made on this problem, although some care needs to be taken to make sure that the uses of such systems are congruent with their error characteristics[30]. Collecting images in a wholesale way in public places and then attempting to see if any of them match with those on some wanted list is unlikely to work well because the error rates cannot plausibly be made low enough to avoid finding a possible match every few minutes. In contrast, deciding whether a given small set of facial images contains someone on a wanted list, or matching one small set of faces against another, is practical because the final determination can be left to a human. The primary role of the automated part of such a system is to reduce the number of plausible possibilities.

One important role for biometric identifiers is to make matching systems easier. Rather than having to learn a difficult model of individual characteristics, the problem reduces to matching against a list of biometric values. This simple presentation of the use of biometric identifiers conceals some awkwardness. First, a digitized photo is a biometric that can be used, by a human, to match a passport with an individual, but each person can have many different digitized photos of themselves, and so this is less useful as a way to match them against a list. Here the problem is that each person can have more than one biometric identifier of a particular kind. The converse problem also exists: more than one person can have the same biometric identifier. For example, DNA biometrics are based on the structure of a small set of sites. Although the chance of two people having the same structure is low, false matches *can* occur in a world whose population is more than six billion.

Avoiding detection by matching systems is relatively easy because it is usually obvious what attributes will be used, and these can then be altered as appropriate. Historically, disguise has been used to alter appearance and avoid face detection. Most other biometric systems are easily spoofed. An amusing discussion of how this was done for a wide variety of devices can be found at: www.heise.de/ct/english/02/11/114/. The interesting question here is whether it is possible to alter attributes, for example by disguise, in a way that fools both a biometric matching system *and* human observers. For example, a large ginger beard and an eye patch may fool a face-recognition system but it tends to backfire by attracting attention from police and others.

4.8   Special Case: Looking for Outliers

The second case of prediction from examples of only one class is when the known class represents ordinary or normal records. In some settings, a useful way to predict the activities of adversaries, at least in part, is simply to detect those records that are not typical. This is not the same as the matching case in the previous section, because normality is too broad a concept to be captured as a list.

This case is very common, because it is usually hard, or perhaps impossible, to get examples of records from the other class(es). Even if we can, they are often very sparse representatives of those classes; also, of course, they represent actions or states that are constantly being changed as adversaries find new ways to exploit the system.

Although ranking allows outliers to be detected, the ranking predictors we have discussed so far all require training data from at least two classes, and so we cannot build a ranking predictor if we only have data from one class.

In general, techniques that make weak assumptions about the data are to be preferred since, with records of only one class available, we know less about the structure of the data.

There are four approaches to detecting outliers using one-class prediction, although there is substantial overlap of ideas among them:

- **Boundary methods**. The idea is to wrap some form of boundary around the records from the known class, and predict that new records that fall outside the boundary are from the other class, that is, are outliers.

- **Distribution methods**. This assumes that ordinary records are arranged as they are because of some underlying distributions of their attribute values. New records that are sufficiently unusual with respect to these distributions are predicted to be outliers.

- **Density methods.** Here the assumption is that records in the known class are similar to each other. New records are outliers if they are not similar (enough) to the training records.

- **Reconstruction methods**. If the way in which records or regions of records are generated is known, then it can be modelled. New records that cannot be reconstructed by this model are classified as outliers.

We will postpone the discussion of density and reconstruction methods to the next chapter.

To use a boundary method, we must take the existing training records and find a way to wrap them with a boundary. Since the available records are a sample of some larger universe of normal records, we do not want to wrap the existing records exactly, but rather wrap them loosely enough that new, normal records will fall within the boundary and so be predicted as normal. In other words, the boundary needs to generalize the properties of

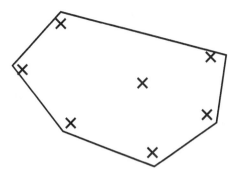

Figure 4.11. *Wrapping a set of points corresponding to normal records in a convex hull.*

the training objects. The problem is that we have no outlier records to use in the test data, so the entire test data consists of normal records. A boundary will always look better the larger the volume it encloses. Clearly we need to use a quality function that tries both to reduce the test error and the total volume enclosed.

The kind of boundary to use depends on our understanding of what the normal data is like. If the normal objects have the property that other, new, normal objects are likely to have attribute values in between the attribute values visible in the training objects, while outliers will not, then we can wrap the training objects in a *convex hull*. This is shown in Figure 4.11.

If the boundary is not expected to have smooth faces like a convex hull, then Support Vector Machines can be adapted to the one-class problem[31]. In the simplest case, we use a radial basis function which wraps the training data in a rough ellipse, providing a different kind of generalization than a convex hull. However, the ability of SVMs to create such an elliptical boundary in a higher-dimensional space makes much more interesting boundaries possible. If the training data is mapped to a higher-dimensional space, and the records wrapped by a radial basis function in the higher-dimensional space, the effective boundary in the space of the original attributes can be quite 'crinkly' and so can wrap the training data points quite tightly, while still providing some generalization. This is shown in Figure 4.12, where the ellipse is shown as a solid line, and a boundary that is elliptical in a higher-dimensional space is shown as a dashed line.

So far we have assumed that the region occupied by the normal records is a single contiguous region and, of course, this need not be so. The convex hull approach can be adapted to this case by using more than one convex hull, one to wrap each contiguous set of records, but it is harder to adapt the SVM approach.

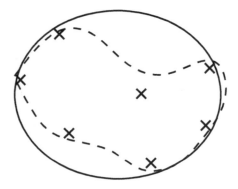

Figure 4.12. *Wrapping a set of points corresponding to normal records with a radial basis function (solid line), and a projection into low dimension of a high-dimensional radial basis function (dashed line).*

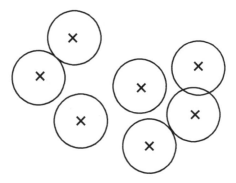

Figure 4.13. *Wrapping a set of points corresponding to normal records with equal-sized balls.*

An alternative is to cover the region containing the normal records with a large number of basic building blocks, rather than trying to wrap it in one, or a few, large shapes. The *k-centers* approach covers the training data with equal-radius spheres, using as few as possible. New records that fall within a ball are predicted as normal, while those that fall outside any ball are predicted as outliers. This is shown in Figure 4.13.

To use the distribution method, we must assume that the normal data are generated by some statistical distribution. The simplest example would be to assume that the attribute values are generated using a Gaussian or normal distribution. Such a distribution has a standard deviation that measures how likely it is that some value generated from the distribution is far from the mean. We can decide on some threshold, say 6 standard deviations, and predict that any value further than this from the mean represents an outlier.

Because records have many attributes, the decision about how to combine unusual values for each attribute into a decision about how unusual the
record is as a whole requires some care, and the theory to do this is well-
known[32]. However, the situation may be more difficult in an adversarial
setting, since the outliers will be trying, as much as they can, not to appear
as outliers. Potentially this means that some attribute values will be in normal ranges, creating the impression that the record is more normal than it
actually is. One possible solution is to perform the test using several random
subsets of the attributes. Normal records should always appear normal, but
outlier records may be revealed as outliers when subsets of the attributes that
exclude those with normal range values happen to be chosen.

Again we have implicitly assumed that the normal records were explained by a single distribution, but is also possible to use a mixture of distributions as the model for normal records.

From one point of view, a distributional model is a kind of density
model, in which the density is assumed to decrease in a predictable way with
increasing distance from the mean of the distribution. Most density-based,
one-class predictors, however, assume that densities vary in much more local
ways.

4.9 Special Case: Frequency Ranking

When attributes can be real-valued, there are an infinite number of possible
records. However, there are some situations where the number of distinct
records is finite (although it may be very large), and there is a need to assess
new records according to some frequency-based criterion. For example, a
record that has appeared frequently has already been assessed multiple times,
and presumably been categorized as innocuous, and so it can be categorized
as innocuous again with little risk. In fact, any record that has been seen
before is presumptively likely to be innocuous, since it will have already been
assessed completely.

We have already argued that normality is common, so being able to
detect records that are common in a fast and inexpensive way can be a useful
early-stage predictor.

In the discussion that follows, we assume that each record consists of
a single value, representing its properties. It may be necessary to reduce a
multiple-attribute record to such a single value using a hash function. Sometimes it is enough to use only the key field from each record as the value.

4.9.1　Frequent Records

We first consider the problem of detecting whether a new record is a frequently seen one. A model of frequent records can be built from training data, simply by counting frequencies; but a more interesting model can be developed incrementally as new records are observed. This means that a most-frequent records list, sometimes called a *hotlist*, can be built and maintained without the need for an initial building phase.

We assume that there is a fixed-size window in which information about the frequently seen records will be kept, in the form of record-count pairs. This window is much smaller than the space that would be required to accumulate a frequency histogram for all of the records. The following pseudocode[33] maintains a *counting sample*:

$\tau := 1$
for all t in the dataset
　　if t already in the window
　　　　increment its count
　　else
　　　　add t to the window with prob $1/\tau$
　　if window overflows
　　　　$\tau' := \tau \times$ factor
　　　　for each s in the window
　　　　　　flip a biased coin, decrementing the count on each
　　　　　　tails, until a head is flipped.
　　$\tau := \tau'$

Each record is checked against the current window. If it is already present, its count is incremented. If not, it is added to the window with a probability that decreases as pressure on the window increases. If the window overflows (as it soon will in typical data), the threshold for entry is increased, and the counts of records already present are adjusted to become what they would have been if the new threshold had been used from the start.

The counts in a counting sample are underestimates of the actual frequency of occurrence, since some early occurrences have been missed because the test for addition to the window is probabilistic. More accurate counts can be computed by adding a compensation factor ($\approx 0.418\tau - 1$) to each count. Any record that occurs with frequency greater than or equal to τ is expected to be in the sample.

This approach can be extended to include all records whose frequency exceeds some predefined support, by allowing the window to expand as needed, while still maintaining the desired frequency property.

If the most-frequent q records are desired, the window size is set to q – and with high probability, these records and their frequencies will be in the window after all records have been seen.

4.9.2 Records Seen Before

If the problem is to determine whether a new record has *ever* been seen before, rather than determining its frequency, then we can use a different approach. It is possible, of course, simply to keep a sorted list of the record values seen so far, and search the list for a match for each new record. However, the search time is logarithmic in the number of records previously seen, so the time for the check increases, and the amount of storage required becomes prohibitive when there are a large number of different values.

A better approach is to use a *Bloom filter*. A Bloom filter consists of a large array of bits, initialized to zeros, and a set of k hash functions, each of which maps record values to position in the bit array.

Two operations can be applied to a Bloom filter:

1. **Check** whether a record has already been seen. This is done by applying the hash functions to the record value, and examining each position in the array to which the value maps. If any of these positions contains a 0, predict that the record is new; if all contain a 1, predict that the record has been seen before.

2. **Add** a record to the filter. The hash functions are applied to the record value, and the positions in the array to which it maps are all set to 1.

Checking a Bloom filter can produce a false positive, that is, it can report that a record has been seen before when, in fact, it has not. This happens when all of the array positions to which the value maps have already been set to 1s as the result of the addition of several other records to the filter. Checking cannot produce a false negative.

Bloom filters also do not allow records to be deleted. It is never safe to delete 1s in particular positions since they may be there as the result of the addition of records other than the one being deleted. Bloom filters are fast, both to check and to add to, and require less space than storing the entire list of records seen.

In an adversarial setting, a Bloom filter can be used as an early-stage check of whether a record has been seen before. A record that has never been seen is subjected to a full analysis, using other predictors. If, in the end, it is classified as innocuous, it can be added to the Bloom filter. When the same record is seen again, the Bloom filter detects this, and the rest of the analysis can be skipped.

Of course, false positives from the Bloom filter cause problems for this approach, since this would clear occasional records that are actually bad. One way to deal with this is to replace the single bits at each location by small counters, say counting from 0 to 3 (and so using two bits rather than one).

There are two different ways to increase the counters associated with these modified Bloom filters. The first is to treat the k locations as a k-place ternary counter; the other is to treat it as a set of unary counters. In both cases, when a record is added for the first time, every location is set to 1.

In the first case, when a record is added for the second and subsequent time, the low-order location is incremented by 1, with the usual carry to the next lowest location if the low-order location was already set to 3, and so on. If $k = 10$ a record has to be seen 10,000 (3^{10}) times before all of the counter locations reach 3. (Of course, if the low-order location of one counter combination is, by chance, a higher-order location of another counter combination, the virtual counter may increment much faster than this.)

In the second case, when a record is added for the second and subsequent time, any one of the locations is incremented by 1. If $k = 10$, a record has to be seen 30 times before all of the counter locations reach 3.

Of course, both of these counter values are *overestimates* of the number of times a record has been seen, so this must be taken into account when deciding how to act on counter values.

These counters can be used to estimate when a record is frequent, to decide whether it needs to be fully processed or not. If the virtual counter value, is small, a record should be treated as suspicious. The exact threshold, together with the collision probability, can be used to reduce the probability of clearing a bad record by accident to acceptable levels.

4.9.3   Records Similar to Those Seen Before

Bloom filters can be extended to detect occurrences of records that have values similar to those already seen. This is done using *locality-sensitive hash functions*, which have the property that similar input values map to the same position(s) in the bit array.

Using these extended Bloom filters, we can maintain a list of innocuous record values, and detect new records that are close to or similar to these innocuous records. As long as the similarity measurement is precise enough, new never-before-seen records can still be classified as innocuous using only the Bloom filter check.

4.9.4   Records with Some Other Frequency

The hotlist technique can keep track of records that have occurred frequently in the dataset, but cannot be extended to keep track of records with other frequencies. For example, we may want to notice the second occurrence of a record that is rare. In other settings, we may be interested in records whose frequency is moderate.

Bloom filters where each location holds a counter provide an alternate way to detect high-frequency records. Using either way of incrementing the virtual counters, frequent records drive the counters to high values. In fact, the value of the counter provides an (over)estimate of the frequency of the corresponding record.

Frequencies in particular ranges can be estimated using counter-based Bloom filters by periodically setting the count in a random location back to 1. (It should not be set to 0 because this would create false negatives.) When a record is checked, 1s in all of its locations indicate that it has been seen before, but is rare. A record that has 3s in all of its location is extremely common. Records with intermediate frequencies have intermediate counts.

Resetting counters can be done on the basis of time, in which case frequency estimates are estimates of frequency in time; or on the basis of records added, in which case frequency estimates are estimates of frequency density in the stream of records.

4.10   Special Case: Discrepancy Detection

Another way to use prediction that applies only in adversarial settings is to predict an attribute whose value is already known. For example, a taxpayer's gross income could be predicted from other data on a tax return; or a doctor's total income could be predicted from patient numbers and types. For ordinary records, the prediction should agree (roughly) with the actual value; if it does not, this is taken as a sign of a potential problem. Those records with the greatest discrepancies can then be investigated further.

Discrepancy analysis is a way of assessing the internal consistency of the values of the attributes of each record. Normal, innocuous records should exhibit broad regularities for this consistency, which can be learned by a predictor. Records associated with adversaries should show greater discrepancies.

Any of the prediction technologies we have described could be used for this task. However, irrelevant attributes inherently have less consistency among themselves and with significant attributes – as an extreme example, an attribute whose values are random is only consistent with other attribute values by accident. Hence, it is important to apply discrepancy detection using only attributes that are known to be significant. Techniques that are good at selecting attributes are to be preferred – for example, random forests.

Notes

[1] Terry vs. Ohio, 392 U.S. 1, (1968).

[2] And note that looking at the registration records of cars with similar licence-plate numbers is not taken to mean that their owners are subjected to unwarranted search or suspicion. They are, arguably failing to be presumed innocent until proven guilty.

[3] usacm.org/usacm/Letters/tia_final.html.

[4] B. Schneier, *Why Data Mining Won't Stop Terror*, in: *Wired*, 2006.

[5] See T.E. Senator, *Multi-Stage Classification*, in: *Proceedings of the Fifth IEEE International Conference on Data Mining*, pp. 386–393, 2005 and D. Jensen, M. Rattigan and H. Blau, *Information awareness: A prospective technical assessment*, in: *Proceedings of the 9th ACM SIGKDD International Conference on Knowledge Discovery and Data Mining*, 2003 for detailed counter-arguments.

[6] J. Jonas and J. Harper, "Effective counterterrorism and the limited role of predictive data mining", *Policy Analysis*, 584:1–12, 2006.

[7] P.-N. Tan, M. Steinbach and V. Kumar, *Introduction to Data Mining*, Addison-Wesley, 2006.

[8] M. Kantardzic, *Data Mining: Concepts, Models, Methods, and Algorithms*, Wiley-IEEE Press, 2002.

[9] M. Dunham, *Data Mining Introductory and Advanced Topics*, Prentice Hall, 2003.

[10] Decision trees were invented independently by Ross Quinlan, a computer scientist: J.R. Quinlan, *C4.5: Programs for Machine Learning*, Morgan-Kaufmann, 1993, and by Leo Breiman, a statistician: L. Breiman, J.H. Friedman, R.A. Olshen and C.J. Stone, *Classification and Regression Trees*, Chapman and Hall, New York, 1984, who called them Classification and Regression Trees (CART).

[11] Historically, information gain and information gain ratio have been associated with decision trees, and Gini index with Classification and Regression Trees. In practice, there seems to be little difference in performance between these two kinds of measures of discriminatory power. Information gain ratio performs better in situations where there are many possible values for an attribute.

[12]There are many possible extensions and alterations to this basic algorithm, and an extensive literature, in which further details can be found.

[13]J.G. Dutrisac and D.B. Skillicorn, *Subverting Prediction in Adversarial Settings*, in: *2008 IEEE Intelligence and Security Informatics*, pp. 19–24, 2008.

[14]J. Dutrisac, "Counter-Surveillance in an Algorithmic World", Master's Thesis, School of Computing, Queen's University, 2007.

[15]Technically birds are animals too, but there isn't a good collective noun for what ordinary people think of as animals.

[16]L. Breiman, "Bagging predictors", *Machine Learning*, 24:123–140, 1996.

[17]Y. Freund and R. Schapire, *Experiments with a New Boosting Algorithm*, in: *Proceedings of the 13th International Conference on Machine Learning*, pp. 148–156, 1996.

[18]L. Breiman, "Arcing classifiers", *Annals of Statistics*, 26(3):801–849, 1998.

[19]For example, C. Yu and D.B. Skillicorn, "Parallelizing boosting and bagging", Technical Report 2001–442, Queen's University Department of Computing and Information Science Technical Report, February 2001; A. Lazarevic and Z. Obradovic, *The Distributed Boosting Algorithm*, in: *KDD2001*, pp. 311–316, August 2001; and A. Lazarevic and Z. Obradovic, "Boosting algorithms for parallel and distributed learning", *Distributed and Parallel Databases, Special Issue on Parallel and Distributed Data Mining*, 11(2):203–229, 2002.

[20]L. Breiman, "Random forests–random features", Technical Report 567, Department of Statistics, University of California, Berkeley, September 1999.

[21]Good introductions are C.J.C. Burges, "A tutorial on support vector machines for pattern recognition", *Data Mining and Knowledge Discovery*, 2:121–167, 1998 and N. Cristianini and J. Shawe-Taylor, *An Introduction to Support Vector Machines and Other Kernel-Based Learning Methods*, Cambridge University Press, 2000.

[22]J.G. Dutrisac and D.B. Skillicorn, *Subverting Prediction in Adversarial Settings*, in: *2008 IEEE Intelligence and Security Informatics*, pp. 19–24, 2008.

[23]See C. Bishop, *Neural Networks for Pattern Recognition*, Oxford University Press, 1995 for a more detailed introduction.

[24]There are also many other training techniques that have been considered in the literature but backpropagation is by far the most common.

[25]The actual adjustment of weights is done by considering the output, for a fixed input example, to be a function of the set of weights. The particular

output observed corresponds to a single point on this surface. The slope at this point is computed, and the weights are adjusted to make a small step up or down in this space, depending on whether the actual output was too small or too large. There are a number of refinements that guide how large a step should be taken (the learning rate) and how much the direction of the step should depend on the directions of previous steps (the momentum).

[26]Examples of rule-construction systems that start from right-hand sides are *association rules*: R. Agrawal, T. Imielinski and A.N. Swami, *Mining Association Rules between Sets of Items in Large Databases*, in: P. Buneman and S. Jajodia, (eds.), *Proceedings of the 1993 ACM SIGMOD International Conference on Management of Data*, pp. 207–216, Washington, D.C., 1993; and k Disjunctive Normal Form (kDNF) L.G. Valiant, "A theory of the learnable", *Communications of the ACM*, 27(11):1134–1142, November 1984. An example of a rule-construction system that starts from left-hand sides is CN2: P. Clark and T. Niblett, "The CN2 induction algorithm", *Machine Learning*, 3(4):261–283, 1989.

[27]A. Evans, J. Sikorski, P. Thomas, S-H. Cha, C. Tappert, G. Zou, A. Gattani and G. Nagy, *Computer Assisted Visual Interactive Recognition (CAVIAR) Technology*, in: *2005 IEEE International Conference on Electro-Information Technology, Lincoln, NE*, 2005.

[28]www.cs.umn.edu/research/MINDS/.

[29]S. Chakrabarti and A. Strauss, "Carnival booth: An algorithm for defeating the computer-assisted passenger screening system", Course Paper, MIT 6.806: Law and Ethics on the Electronic Frontier, www.swiss.ai.mit.edu/6805/student-papers/spring02-papers/caps.htm, 2002.

[30]In 2006 state-of-the-art false-reject rates, when false-accept rates were set to 1 in 1000, were about 1 in 100 for face recognition and iris recognition. For face recognition, the false-reject rate goes up to around 1 in 10 when the lighting is uncontrolled (www.frvt.org). Fingerprints are significantly more accurate. The false-reject rate of the best single-finger tests is about 1 in 200 for false-accept rates at 1 in 1000 (fpvte.nist.gov). To put this in context, Heathrow airport sees 185,000 passengers per day.

[31]See, for example, D.M.J. Tax, *One Class Classification*, PhD Thesis, Technical University Delft, 2000.

[32]The Bonferroni correction, which will be described in any introductory statistics book.

[33]P.B. Gibbons and Y. Matias, *New Sampling-Based Summary Statistics for Improving Approximate Query Answers*, in: *Proceedings of ACM Conference on the Management of Data*, pp. 331–342, 1998.

Chapter 5

Looking for Similarity – Clustering

Clustering is primarily a way of exploring data. Its goal is understanding, rather than direct decision making. Given a set of records, a cluster is a subset of the records that are similar to each other, with respect to some reasonable measure of what similarity means, and not so similar to the rest of the records. We can learn from clustering at two levels. First, the large-scale structure, how many clusters there are, what shapes they form, where they are located, and the voids in between them provide information about the problem domain. Second, the locations and shapes of each individual cluster provide information about those records that are placed in it, from which we can infer an underlying reason *why* these records are similar. At the heart of clustering are both similarity and dissimilarity. For example, retail stores often cluster their customers and try to learn what kind of customer each cluster represents. This can be used to influence the design and layout of stores, the kind of merchandise stocked, and even the opening hours. At the global level, a clustering can show where clusters are *not* – which may represent an opportunity for a new product or service.

In adversarial settings, one of the important goals of clustering is to find adversaries or their actions without needing any preconceptions of what they might be like. If we assume that the records associated with them must, at some level, be different from those of ordinary people or actions; and that their records will tend to resemble each other because of their related illicit activity, then we expect that they will reveal themselves as a (small) cluster that is separate from the typically larger clusters representing normal activity. Thus clustering helps to avoid the need for deciding on predefined patterns that we expect the adversaries to use.

Clustering naturally leads to prediction. Once a cluster has been found, its properties can be explored and predictors built to predict new records that resemble the records in the cluster.

The key decision required for clustering is the definition of what it means for two records to be similar. This depends, of course, on the values of the attributes in each record, but there are many ways to measure the significance of similarities or differences in value for each attribute, and how these attribute-based similarities and differences should be combined to give record-based similarities and differences.

After this decision has been made, the second key decision is what it means to be a cluster. This is one of those decisions where we know it when we see it, but it is hard to turn intuition into a concrete algorithm. There are two interrelated issues: what shape does a cluster have to have; and how do you tell where the boundary or edge of each cluster lies, that is, when does a record lie outside a cluster? Different answers to these questions define the different forms of clustering discussed in this chapter.

5.1   Goals

It is somewhat surprising that, when a set of records is evaluated with regard to their similarity, clusters emerge at all and, in fact, this does not always happen. However, humans are social creatures and we tend to come up with similar approaches to the issues we face, and similar solutions to problems. Social structures develop to reflect common ways of doing things, but once they exist, they reinforce those common ways and keep them stable. Television programs start on the hour and half hour, although there is no intrinsic reason why starting on the quarter hours would be worse. Most people get up between 6 and 8:30 in the morning and go to bed between 10 and midnight. These social patterns play through into data collected about many different aspects of our lives, so that data tends to form well-defined clusters, even though people are, at a fine-grained level, extremely variable. In domains that are less driven by the larger social fabric, clustering is not so clear-cut. For example, data about music, film, or book preferences exhibits some clustered structure (bestsellers, genres such as mystery, science fiction, or fantasy) but the records form much more diffuse clouds. For almost any conceivable collection of interests there will be someone with those interests. This is, of course, why web services such as Ebay, iTunes, and Amazon do so well – the so-called *long tail* phenomenon[1], which means that even the rarest films, songs, and books are almost certainly purchased by someone every month.

In the world of data collected about people, their actions, and their tastes, what can we expect about the records of adversaries? The illicit activities in which they engage will tend to force attribute values that are unusual. On the other hand, they will try, as much as possible, to look and act like everyone else. The net result is that the records that describe them will be found at or just outside the margins of clusters representing normal actions and appearances. This creates a challenging problem because the dissimilarity between a cluster of adversaries and another cluster may be very small. This may make detecting that such adversary clusters are present in a clustering difficult, and why the problem is deciding where the boundary of a cluster lies is so important.

The goals of clustering in an adversarial setting include:

- Finding unusual, interesting, or suspicious groups. Adversaries are expected to form a group because of their related illicit activities; these groups are expected to be small compared to the groups associated with normal activities; but these groups are probably quite similar (that is, close) to the larger normal groups because adversaries are trying not to stand out.

- Finding outliers, that is, records not in any cluster. Some adversaries may be lone wolves, or playing some special role in illicit activity that makes their records different from normal records, but also different from the other members of an adversary group. It is useful to find such records for their own sake, but they may also provide hints about what other adversary activity might look like, since their collaborators may appear to be within ordinary clusters, but close to the outlying record.

- Finding the properties of a group that is discovered as a cluster. Once a cluster of adversaries has been identified, the underlying reasons, that is, the attribute values, that distinguish it from other, normal clusters, are themselves of interest. These values may provide hints about the characteristics of the group, their mission or intent, or their methodology.

- Finding and understanding clusters that are surprising either by their existence, location in the space of attributes, or density. All small clusters in a large enough dataset are, in some sense, surprising, but, in an adversarial setting, all such clusters need investigation because they may signal something unusual that is happening. For example, in demographic data such clusters may signal the presence of an unusual disease cluster, a rather special adversarial setting.

- Finding clusters in time and space. Another special form of clustering is where attributes related to time and space are present. Clustering based on these often-implicit attributes may reveal patterns that would otherwise not be noticed.

- Understanding homogeneities and inhomogeneities of behavior. If clustering in data about human behavior is always a little surprising, but tends to arise from social norms, data in which clustering seems either especially strong or unusually weak may allow deeper insight into the extent to which social pressures are at work, and so into microcultural differences. For example, changes in the extent to which a civilian population is willing to implicitly support insurgents or terrorists may show up as changes in the inhomogeneity of data.

- Finding nearest neighbors without finding clusters. In situations where there is no strong clustering, because human variability dominates social norms, it may still be interesting to explore the local structure around records (people, activities) of interest. This idea underlies recent research on social search, collaborative filtering, and tagging, in which information from similar objects is used to improve some task.

Clusters from records describing normal behavior are qualitatively different from those of adversaries. Normal clusters tend to be large, because there are many more normal records in most datasets. Normal records also tend to be similar to other normal records in many different ways – so the structure of normality may not be just large clusters, but large clusters that are themselves close, even overlapping, with each other.

5.2   Outline of Clustering Technology

Before it makes sense to talk about how to cluster records, we must define some kind of measure of similarity – what it means for two records to be alike, and what it means for them to be different. This turns out to be quite difficult, because the 'right' way to measure similarity depends very strongly on the problem domain – and even then there are technical difficulties[2].

Consider a very simple case where we have records about people, and for each person, we have an attribute describing their height (in inches) and their age (in years). Suppose that we have three records:

	Height	Age
Person 1	70	35
Person 2	71	35
Person 3	70	36

Which person is more similar to Person 1 – Person 2 or Person 3? The issue of how to measure similarity first of all means deciding how to interpret differences in a value of a single attribute, then deciding how to weight differences in different attributes relative to each other, and then deciding how to combine these differences into an overall difference (or, inversely, similarity).

For an individual attribute, we could decide that two records with exactly the same value are similar, but if they have different values then they are dissimilar, regardless of the magnitude of the difference. Some examples are gender, or credit card, which are naturally categorical, but age could also be treated this way. Alternatively, we could decide that differences in value increase in significance in a linear way, so that the significance of a difference in value of 2 is twice the significance of a difference of 1. For example, this seems natural for attributes such as height or income, but not for age where the difference between 17 and 18 is much more significant than the difference between 37 and 38. We could also decide that differences in value increase in significance quadratically so a difference in value of 2 is four times as significant as a difference of 1. For example, the amount of education a person has affects their income in a non-linear way. It is often hard to make a convincing argument that one of these possibilities is more appropriate than another.

When the significance of differences in the values of two attributes is to be assessed, the issue of the units in which they are measured becomes critical. Consider the three records in the original table. Because of the way height and age have been measured, Person 2 is 1 unit different from Person 1 in height, and Person 3 is 1 unit different from Person 1 in age. However, if the attributes had been collected in units of feet and months, respectively, then the records would look like:

	Height	Age
Person 1	5.833	420
Person 2	5.916	420
Person 3	5.833	432

and the difference in ages suddenly seems much more significant than the difference in heights. The units in which measurements are collected are often arbitrary, especially with respect to one another, so comparisons are often difficult to get right.

One standard approach is to normalize all of the attribute values so that they have roughly comparable magnitude. One way to do this is to subtract the mean value of an attribute from all of the values of that attribute. This produces values for every attribute that are centered around zero.

However, different attributes will still have different ranges: some may go from -5 to $+5$ while others go from -100 to $+100$. These ranges can be made more comparable by dividing the values in each column by the standard deviation of that column. This scales them so that about two-thirds of the values lie in the range from -1 to $+1$, depending on the precise distribution of values. This method of scaling is called converting to *z-scores*.

For example, subtracting the means from each column of the original table gives these values:

	Height	Age
Person 1	−0.3	−0.3
Person 2	+0.6	−0.3
Person 3	−0.3	+0.6

and there is no need for further scaling. On the other hand, subtracting the mean from each column using the data in feet and months gives

	Height	Age
Person 1	−0.028	+4
Person 2	+0.056	+4
Person 3	−0.028	−8

so the magnitudes of the two attributes still seem quite different. When the standard deviations are used, the data becomes

	Height	Age
Person 1	−1	+1
Person 2	+2	+1
Person 3	−1	−2

and a much more plausible view of the relative significance of the attributes results.

Once different attributes have been scaled to comparable magnitudes, there remains the issue of how to combine the differences in different attributes into a global measure of similarity or dissimilarity.

The first issue is how to *align* the directions of increasing magnitude of attributes in a meaningful way. The measurement of heights and ages might correlate in a positive way, especially in the age range 1–25. However, if it happened that ages were recorded in the opposite direction, as the number of years left to reach 100, then height and age would correlate in a negative way. This changes the way distances based on geometry, and on correlation, behave, especially when other attributes are involved. Unfortunately, it often requires deep understanding of the application domain to know which direction is most meaningful for each attribute.

The second issue is how to *accumulate* the dissimilarities of the individual attributes. They could simply be summed, giving a measure often called the Manhattan distance. Another intuitive similarity measure is to exploit geometric intuition. If each attribute is considered as defining an axis, and the value of each attribute as defining a position on that axis, then each record naturally defines a point in space spanned by the axes. The difference between two records is the distance between their points. In this space, Euclidean distance corresponds to weighting differences within a single attribute so that significance increases quadratically, and combining individual attribute differences using the square root of the sum. Geometry suggests that this is a very natural measure of similarity, but it does emphasize large differences in a single attribute over small differences in a number of attributes. For example, in the following data:

	A1	A2	A3
Record 1	1	1	1
Record 2	2	2	2
Record 3	1	1	4

Record 2 is Euclidean distance $\sqrt{3} \approx 1.7$ from Record 1, while Record 3 is Euclidean distance 3, showing how single-attribute differences have more impact.

When the attributes have categorical values, or nominal values that are not easily mapped into numeric ones, measuring similarity becomes more difficult. Single-attribute similarity based on equality or non-equality is possible, but the geometric intuition is lost.

Clustering algorithms all work by allocating records to clusters in such a way that the similarity within each cluster is high, and the similarity between each pair of clusters is low. Of course, measuring similarity between clusters is not necessarily trivial, although, in a geometric representation, the distance between the midpoint of each cluster, its centroid, is a natural dissimilarity measure.

One of the difficulties in using a geometric intuition and Euclidean distance as a dissimilarity measure is that datasets with many attributes correspond to spaces of high dimension. A dataset with m attributes has records that correspond to points in m-dimensional space. In high-dimensional space, distances are not well-behaved. For example, suppose that each numeric attribute can take on three values: large and negative, close to zero, or large and positive. Suppose that the attribute values are uniformly randomly distributed in each of these three intervals. Then the probability that a random record with m attributes will be close to the origin is $1/3^m$, which is very small. Two records will be close only if their attribute values *all* fall into the same intervals, and the probability of this happening is, again, $1/3^m$. In other words, in high-dimensional spaces, randomly scattered points tend to lie in a higher-dimensional sphere, far from the origin and far from each other as well. Of course, the points from a dataset will not be randomly scattered, but the distance to their nearest and farthest neighbor may not be very different.

Digital data collection can sometimes generate data that appears to be of much higher dimensional than it really is. This happens when, for example, several attributes are actually measuring the same underlying reality and so are highly correlated. Each of the 'repeated' attributes adds an apparent dimension to the space without adding a dimension to the part of the space occupied by the data points. Sometimes the apparent dimensionality of the data is enormously larger than its real dimensionality. For example, an image of a three-dimensional object may be captured using the values for thousands of attributes, the color values and intensities of pixels, but the object in the image is still three-dimensional underneath.

Unlike prediction, where the available data must be divided into a training dataset and a test dataset, clustering algorithms can use all of the available data. Of course, such data is not labelled with a class attribute.

For prediction, the existence of a test set allows the performance of any predictor to be measured. For clustering, there is no access to the 'right' answer, so other kinds of assessments must be made. Various metrics have been proposed; most based on some combination of ensuring that the intra-cluster similarity is high and the inter-cluster similarity is low, but none is completely satisfactory.

5.3   Concealment Opportunities

As we did for prediction, we can categorize the concealment opportunities according to the phase of the process that they target: data collection, analysis, or decision and action.

The most obvious form of concealment is to prevent a record being captured in the first place. For prediction, if a data record must be captured, because the capture mechanism is unavoidable, or because it would be obvious that a record should have been captured and was not, a good concealment strategy is to alter the key attribute(s). For clustering, there is no particular key attribute, so any attributes could be altered, but the best strategy is to alter those that will make the record seem most like a member of some large, presumptively innocuous cluster. Appropriate estimates for which attributes to alter and in which direction can be made by collecting attacker data, and looking at the clusters in it. Sometimes there may already be some sense of where the obvious clusters will be, so it will be obvious what kind of alterations will make a given record seem more innocuous. For example, people often manipulate their home address in order to make it look as if they live in a better neighborhood than they do – the 10021 zip code in New York is known to be desirable[3].

Another possible way to conceal a cluster that is already quite similar to a larger innocuous cluster is to add extra records that 'bridge' the two clusters. These new records have some of the characteristics of the clusters on both sides, and so make it harder to see that there is actually a gap between the clusters. They also make it harder to understand the clusters themselves. This can be a low-cost way for adversaries to hide their cluster because the new records can be created at little cost – the corresponding records can be almost completely ordinary, as long as they have a few attributes that are just a little more dissimilar than usual from the norm of the larger cluster, in a carefully-chosen direction. We will see that many clustering algorithms can be misled by the presence of only a few records, provided their properties have been carefully chosen.

The third way to conceal the existence of a cluster of adversaries is to use social engineering. Rather than try to hide the existence of the cluster, the goal here is to come up with a convincing, but innocuous, explanation for the cluster's existence. The essence of this approach is to have a convincing cover story for the revealed similarities between records. For example, a terrorist group can masquerade as a group pursuing some kind of hobby.

Each of the technologies used for clustering makes different assumptions about what clusters look like, and what the relationships among them should be, so each creates specialized opportunities for manipulation as well.

5.4 Technologies

Clustering algorithms can be divided into four main kinds, depending on how they view what it means for records to form a cluster (which depends also on how they view similarity). The four approaches are:

1. **Distance-based clustering**: records belong to the same cluster when they are sufficiently close together using some distance measure that represents similarity.

2. **Density-based clustering**: records belong in the same cluster when they have enough neighbors who are close enough to them using some distance measure that represents similarity.

3. **Distribution-based clustering**: records belong to a cluster when their positions agree well with the positions expected from some multivariate distribution function.

4. **Decomposition-based clustering**: records belong to a cluster when the clusters can be fitted together using particular structural rules.

These different families of clustering algorithms will produce different clusters from the same dataset. Deciding which is best in a particular setting usually requires some knowledge of the domain, and of the properties of algorithms that are used.

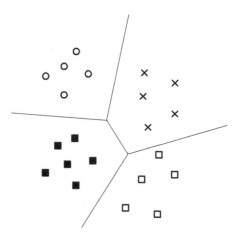

Figure 5.1. *The clusters from a distance-based clustering have straight-line (hyperplane) boundaries.*

5.4.1 Distance-Based Clustering

Distance-based clustering algorithms define clusters by their centers, usually centroids, and allocate the point corresponding to each record to its nearest cluster center. The clustering therefore divides up the high-dimensional space into regions that look like soap bubbles packed together, with (hyper)planes between each region.

The best-known, and simplest, algorithm for distance-based clustering is k-means[4]. The algorithm is initialized by choosing k initial cluster centers. Each of the points corresponding to data records is allocated to its nearest cluster center. The centroid of the set of points allocated to each cluster is then computed, and this becomes the new cluster center. Moving the cluster center in this way can change the allocation of points to clusters, so this allocation is recomputed, a new cluster center computed as the centroid of the newly allocated points, and the process repeated until the allocation of points to clusters no longer changes.

The algorithm usually converges in a few (tens of) iterations. It has two weaknesses. Like many clustering algorithms, it requires the analyst to decide how many clusters are present in the data, and it performs badly if the initial cluster centers are poorly chosen.

Analysts seldom have a robust or principled way to assess how many clusters 'should' be present in a dataset. This is especially problematic in an adversarial setting, where a group of adversaries is likely to try and ensure that their cluster, to the extent that they form one, either overlaps with or is close to another cluster. Increasing the number of expected clusters may

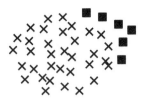

Figure 5.2. *Convexity makes it hard to detect a small cluster wrapped around a larger one.*

tease out such hidden clusters, but it may also make it hard to be sure about the presence and structure of more mainstream clusters.

It is possible to do a parameter sweep, and run the algorithm repeatedly with increasing values of k, looking for a maximum in some cluster-quality measure. This is difficult in an adversarial setting, since the quality measure difference between the k clustering that fails to see a small cluster of adversaries, and the $k + 1$ clustering that does see the cluster, may be very small.

The problem of initializing cluster centers has been well studied. In general, initial centers should be far from each other, and close to concentrations of dataset points. One way to ensure this is to choose points from the dataset to be initial cluster centers. Choosing a larger number of random points from the dataset, and then selecting the k initial centers from among them can also work well. It is also common to rerun the algorithm with different initial centers and see whether the clusters discovered are essentially the same.

The k-means algorithm is usually implemented using Euclidean distance, but it works for any similarity measure that is a metric, so it can be extended to a wide variety of settings. However, it will not handle data with categorical attributes unless they can be sensibly mapped to numeric values.

The vulnerabilities of distance-based clustering come from the relatively simple way in which judgements of membership in clusters are made, and the fact that every point is allocated to *some* cluster.

A point, or group of points, that is close to a larger cluster is almost certain to be allocated to it because the distances of its members from the cluster centroid are not much larger than the distances of the points actually in the cluster. The convexity assumption about the shape of clusters means that if the small cluster can be 'wrapped' around the larger cluster, even slightly, it is virtually impossible for the two clusters to be separated by the k-means algorithm. This situation is shown in two dimensions in Figure 5.2.

The other weakness is that every single point is allocated to some cluster. This makes it difficult to notice points that are outliers, far from any other

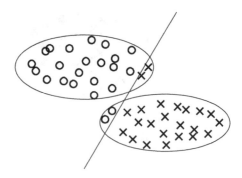

Figure 5.3. *A situation in which a distance-based clusterer will perform poorly.*

points. Visualizations will not necessarily show such points clearly, and their effect on the average distance from the centroid of their cluster may not be large either if the cluster contains many points.

5.4.2 Density-Based Clustering

Density-based clustering assumes that membership in a cluster depends on being close enough to sufficiently many other members of the cluster. This circular definition can nevertheless be used to find good clusterings. In distance-based clustering, clusters occupy convex regions of a geometric space. Density-based clusterings can discover clusters that are more spider-like, with points extending outwards in arms from the more-central region of a cluster. Figure 5.3 shows a situation in which a distance-based clusterer will find a poor clustering, while a density-based clusterer will do much better. The straight line shows the boundary where the points on each side are nearest to the centroid of other such points. This boundary produces the clustering implied by the crosses and circles. However, it is clear that this is not a good clustering for these points – the one implied by the ellipses is much better. A density-based clusterer does not make this mistake, because it is able to allocate records based on what their neighborhood is like.

A typical density-based clusterer like DBScan[5] selects a point from the dataset at random, and then tries to find a complete set of its neighbors using a set of rules about what being a neighbor means. Close neighbors are those points within some small distance, say ε. The neighbors of these neighboring points are then examined, and those within the same small distance are also considered to be in the same cluster. However, some refinement is usually required so that second-level neighbors must be neighbors of at least some chosen number of first-level neighbors. This avoids clusters that grow too far along thin chains of close points, which tends to lead to 'stringy' clusters. If there are enough points reachable from the initially chosen point to qualify as a cluster, these points are removed from further consideration and labelled as a cluster. Another random point is chosen as the seed of a new cluster, and this process continues until no further clusters can be found. Not all points in the dataset will necessarily be allocated to clusters. This happens when the neighborhoods of such points are quite empty, so that it is arguably appropriate to consider them as outliers.

One of the big advantages of density-based clustering algorithms is that the number of clusters is not a user input – an advantage because the user often does not have a good intuition about how many clusters are present. However, the user instead has to provide an estimate for the crucial distance, ε, used to count how close another point must be to be a neighbor. This may be also be difficult to estimate well. It should be chosen to be smaller than the difference between normal records and suspicious records. This difference is probably knowable for some attributes, but hard to know for others, and depends on how many attributes there are in total, which may change if attribute selection is used.

Density-based clusterers have both strengths and weaknesses in adversarial settings. Their strength is that points that are dissimilar to all other points are detectable because they fail to be clustered (whereas a distance-based clusterer will allocate them to the nearest cluster regardless). This makes them useful for detecting individuals, and perhaps small groups, that are significantly different from every other record in the dataset. However, sophisticated adversaries will try hard not to look like outsiders, and density-based clusterers make it easy for them to conceal their existence by attaching themselves to some other group via a small bridge of points. For example, it may be worth including some members in the group whose only role is to form such a bridge by generating more or less normal attribute values, but with a slight bias towards the values that the active members of the group are forced to have. These inactive members cause the 'normal' cluster to bulge towards the adversary group, making it harder to separate the two clusters, or even to realize that there are two clusters. For a distance-based clustering algorithm, a bridge may require enough extra points to cause the centroid of the 'normal' group to move, but a density-based clustering algorithm is fooled using only enough points to ensure that each has sufficient neighbors.

5.4.3 Distribution-Based Clustering

Distribution-based clustering assumes that clusters represent the visible signs of some underlying process at work in the world about which the data has been collected. Clusters should therefore have shapes and properties that reflect the distribution(s) characteristic of that process. For example, if each cluster reflects the same underlying activity by many people, or many basically similar transactions, then the points corresponding to each record should be normally distributed around some center, so a Gaussian distribution is appropriate to fit to the cluster.

In a distance-based or a density-based clustering, boundaries between clusters are hard – a point is either in this cluster or in that cluster. Distribution-based clustering allows membership to be a softer decision – a point is in this cluster with probability p_1, this cluster with probability p_2, and so on. This reflects the fact that most probability distributions do not have edges, so even a point far from the mean of the distribution has a small, but non-zero probability of being generated by it.

If we want to fit a set of distributions to given data, we have two kinds of unknowns: the properties of the distributions and the (soft) allocations of points to distributions. The way in which these unknowns are computed is *Expectation-Maximization* (EM)[6], a technique that iterates setting values for the two kinds of unknowns in a way that maximizes the likelihood of the entire clustering. In a way, it is reminiscent of the two phases of k-means.

Given a number of distributions with known shapes, and known parameters (for example, means and variances for Gaussians), the expected likelihood of the observed data being generated from those distributions is calculated. This is the Expectation step. Initially, these parameters can be estimated in some simple way, perhaps from basic statistics of the dataset.

In the Maximization step, new estimates for the parameters are calculated by maximizing the likelihood function.

The expectation step is now repeated using these values for the estimates, which then allows the maximization step to be repeated. This process continues until the parameters cease to change. The resulting parameters define the clusters discovered from the data, and the probability of membership of each record in each cluster can be computed. Because the algorithm works by assuming that the distribution parameters are missing values to be estimated, the approach extends smoothly to *other* missing values, such as the values of particular attributes for some records. Hence it is appropriate to use when some attribute values failed to be collected. It can also be used, although in an expensive way, to check on the validity of suspicious attributes. Such attributes can be deleted from the dataset, the algorithm used to estimate them, and the estimated values compared with the observed ones. If the values are plausible, given the entire remainder of the data, then the values are probably reliable. If there is a large discrepancy, the values may have been manipulated.

Expectation-Maximization requires the analyst to choose the number of clusters expected in the data. However, because it looks for clusters that conform to specific shapes, it is less likely to be misled by random groupings of points, and so a parameter-sweep approach can be effective. The analyst must also define the probability distributions to be used, and this can be hard for previously unstudied data. In fact, most implementations assume that the distributions are Gaussian, which is often plausible but should be explicitly considered when choosing to use this approach.

Expectation-Maximization is vulnerable to attack by inserting carefully chosen points into the data[7]. Suppose that the data consists of one 'normal' cluster and a (typically much smaller) cluster of adversaries. The separation between the clusters will probably be quite small. Inserting points that are far away from the clusters at both ends of a line passing through the centers of the clusters might be expected to make the two clusters look like one. In fact, it does even worse – EM thinks that the data contains two clusters with approximately the same centroids; but with very different variances, one small, including the two original clusters, and one very wide. The adversary cluster may actually help to suggest the presence of the wide cluster. The presence of other clusters does not spoil this ability for manipulation of the clustering. This vulnerability to manipulation by adding only a few extra records is a major weakness of the EM clustering algorithm.

This is illustrated in Figure 5.4. Here the normal cluster is in light gray, and the adversary cluster in dark gray. Adding just a few extra points, indicated by crosses, causes EM to discover two clusters, one smaller one indicated by the dashed region, that includes both real clusters, and a much larger one indicated by the dotted region that 'explains' the extra points.

5.4.4   Decomposition-Based Clustering

Decomposition-based clustering regards the dataset records as rows of a matrix whose columns correspond to the attributes. Several matrix decompositions are known; each decomposes the dataset matrix into a product of simpler matrices from which group structures can be extracted. Different choices of matrix decompositions correspond to different assumptions about the necessary structure of a set of points that would make them a good cluster.

The best-known matrix decomposition clustering technique is *singular value decomposition* (SVD)[8]. Given a dataset with n rows and m columns (that is, an $n \times m$ matrix), each row is interpreted as the coordinates of a point in m-dimensional space, relative to the usual set of orthogonal coordinate axes. The SVD transformation finds a new set of orthogonal axes in such a way that the greatest amount of variation in the dataset lies along the first new axis, the second greatest amount of variation along the second axis, and so on. The main benefit of this transformation for clustering is that the decomposition also computes the amount of variation along each of the axes. When this variation is small in some directions, the corresponding dimensions can be ignored. This avoids many of the difficulties of working in high-dimensional spaces when the data is actually of much lower dimension.

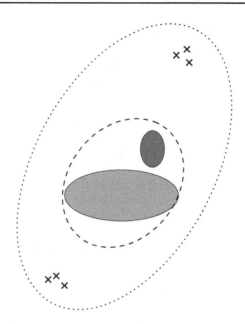

Figure 5.4. *Adding only a few extra points, carefully located, fools EM into thinking there are two clusters (dashed and dotted), one of which contains both the normal and adversary clusters (shaded).*

Formally, a singular value decomposition of an $n \times m$ matrix A (where $n \geq m$) expresses it as a product

$$A = U S V'$$

where the dash indicates matrix transpose, U is an $n \times m$ matrix with orthogonal columns, S is an $m \times m$ diagonal matrix of non-increasing entries called *singular values*, and V is an $m \times m$ matrix with orthogonal columns. The rows of U are coordinates for the corresponding records in the transformed space, the diagonal entries of S give the relative importance of each dimension in the transformed space, and the rows of V' are the new axes.

If the singular values are sufficiently small beyond diagonal position, say $k + 1$, then the right-hand side matrices can be truncate, so that U is $n \times k$, S is $k \times k$, and V is $m \times k$, and the equality above becomes an approximate equality. This truncated right-hand side is a faithful approximation of the data in a space of dimension k. Because the attributes of most real-world datasets are at least partially correlated, it is not unusual to reduce the dimensionality of a dataset to the square root of its apparent dimensionality.

In the lower-dimensional space, a number of partitioning strategies can be used to find clusters. For example, k-means can be applied to the (shortened) rows of the U matrix with the expectation that it will be easier to find the real clusters present in a space of the right dimensionality. (The necessary distance computations are cheaper too.) Alternatively, the values of the first column of the U matrix can be sorted into increasing numeric order. In the best case, this sorted list consists of regions of similar value, separated by sudden jumps or increases in value. These jumps suggest boundaries between clusters, while the regions of similar value suggest records that belong in the same cluster. Alternatively, the points in the transformed space can be regarded as vectors and clustered based on the angles between them. This is a particularly good strategy for data where many of the attribute values are zero, and the presence of non-zero values is more significant than their magnitudes.

Singular value decomposition is, underneath, quite similar to fitting Gaussians to the data. An alternative in situations where clusters are likely to have shapes that are far from Gaussian is *Independent Component Analysis* (ICA)[9]. ICA finds components that are statistically independent, a stronger property than the orthogonality of SVD. It was developed for applications such as extracting one audio signal from many, when the combined signal is captured in several different places. This has important applications in, for example, sonar.

An Independent Component Analysis expresses an $n \times m$ data matrix A as the product of two matrices:

$$A = C\,F$$

where F captures the underlying statistically independent structures present in the data, and C explains how these have been mixed together to produce the observed data. For example, if microphones are placed in a room in which several conversations are taking place, A represents the signals received by the microphones, F the signals corresponding to what each speaker is saying, and C describes, for each microphone, the way in which each conversation is mixed to produce the signal received by that microphone. The mixing might depend on how far each microphone is from each speaker, and the way the surfaces in the room absorb and reflect sound waves. Notice, once again, that there are two kinds of unknowns: those related to the properties of the hypothetical generating structures, and those relating to how the observed data is connected to these generating structures. This intuition can be used to compute several matrix decompositions using alternating procedures such as conjugate gradient minimization.

The rows of C correspond to the records in the dataset. Although these rows are not coordinates, because the rows of F are not orthogonal and so cannot play the role of axes, it often works to assume that they are. Some care is needed: two rows of C that have similar entries may not in fact be similar, but rows that have dissimilar entries must be dissimilar underneath.

Applying k-means to the rows of C can still be used, with some care, as a clustering technique.

Unfortunately, there is no necessary, or even reproducible, ordering of the columns of C, so the important structure in the data is not necessarily associated with particular columns, as it is for SVD. The product of the ith column of C and the ith row of F is an $n \times m$ matrix called the ith component of the decomposition of A. The magnitude of the entries of this matrix can be some indication of the importance of the ith column of C relative to C's other columns[10].

Several other matrix decompositions, for example *Semi-Discrete Decomposition* (SDD) (see Section 5.4.4), and *Non-Negative Matrix Factorization* (NNMF), have also been used extensively for knowledge discovery.

Adversarial manipulation of an SVD decomposition can be done by exploiting the fact that SVD looks for variation in the data. The same kind of manipulation that misleads EM will also mislead SVD. If there is a large cluster, and a reasonably close, smaller cluster whose existence is to be hidden, then adding only a few new records suffices to make the two clusters look like one. The new records must be carefully chosen as before: form the line through the centroids of the two clusters, and place one or two new records far away from the two clusters in each direction along this line, as shown in Figure 5.4. This attack also causes Semi-Discrete Decomposition to classify each of the added records as a small cluster, and merges the two larger clusters into a single one.

This attack is quite strong, but it fails if the clustering is inspected visually in an appropriate rendering, since the original clusters are still visibly separated. The two new records are also so unusual that outlier detection techniques may classify them as suspicious.

5.4.5   Hierarchical Clustering

All of the existing clustering techniques we have discussed so far are called *partitional* clusterings, because they define a single set of clusters, into which all or most records are placed. An alternative is hierarchical clustering[11], which generates clustering at all levels of resolution.

The simplest and most common form of hierarchical clustering is agglomerative. Initially, each record is considered as its own cluster of size 1. In the first step, the two most similar records (clusters) are aggregated into a single cluster of size 2. In each subsequent step, the two most similar clusters are aggregated to form a larger cluster. The process is complete when all of the records have been aggregated into a single cluster.

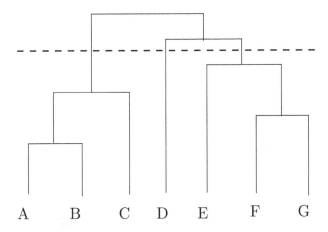

Figure 5.5. *An example of a dendrogram.*

The record of the order in which the clusters were joined together provides a view of the similarity structure that can be examined at any chosen scale. This structure is called a *dendrogram* – an example is shown in Figure 5.5. Objects A and B are most similar in the dataset, and so they are made into a cluster first. Then objects F and G are next most similar, so they are joined into a cluster. On the third step, the cluster containing A and B is joined to object C to create a larger cluster, and so on. Drawing a horizontal line at any level defines a clustering. The dashed line shown in the figure divides the objects into three clusters: A, B, and C; D by itself; and E, F, and G.

Just as for partitional clustering, a measure of the similarity between pairs of records needs to be defined. However, hierarchical clustering also requires a way of deciding how similar two *clusters* are, since most stages of the process require aggregating two clusters rather than two records. This is not entirely straightforward.

One measure of cluster similarity is the minimum distance between the clusters, that is, the minimum distance between pairs of records, one from each of the clusters. This is plausible, but tends to create 'stringy' clusters, rather than compact ones, since two clusters will be joined based on how close to each other their nearest faces are, regardless of what shape each cluster has. This cluster similarity is called *single link*.

An alternative measure of cluster similarity is to use the distance between the *furthest* edges of the two clusters. This is the minimum of the maximum distance between pairs, one from each cluster. This measure tends to create convex, roughly spherical, clusters. This cluster similarity is called *complete link*.

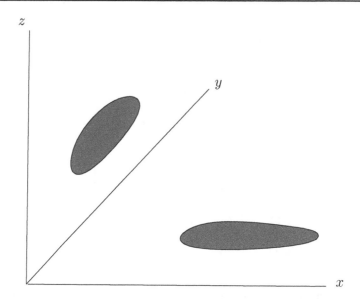

Figure 5.6. *Two two-dimensional clusters in three-dimensional space.*

There are many other cluster similarity measures that have been suggested, of varying complexity. The decision about which to use is difficult and requires a significant understanding of the data; different choices produce very different clusterings.

Once a dendrogram has been constructed, there is then the question of how to interpret it, that is, at what resolution to consider the clusters it defines. While partitional clusterings require a difficult choice of the number of expected clusters, hierarchical clusterings have the opposite problem: *any* number of clusters up to the number of objects can be selected. There is often no better reason to choose the 'right' number of clusters than in the partitional case. Of course, outlying clusters are visible in a dendrogram as a set of records or small clusters that are aggregated only late in the process.

5.4.6   Biclustering

It often happens, in real-world datasets, that different clusters have structures that depend on the values of *different* sets of attributes. Even in a two-cluster dataset, one cluster may be associated with a high value for an attribute, but records of the other cluster may not necessarily have low values for that same attribute – they may have a wide range of values for that attribute. This situation is shown in three dimensions in Figure 5.6.

The leftmost cluster in this figure is associated with values close to zero for the attribute plotted on the x-axis, but many different values of the at-

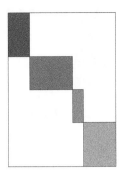

Figure 5.7. *If biclusters are present, there must be a way to sort the rows and columns to produce a structure like this, where each gray region holds entries with similar magnitudes.*

tributes plotted on the y- and z-axes. The rightmost cluster is associated with values close to zero for the attribute associated with the attribute plotted on the z-axis, but many different values of the attributes plotted on the x- and y-axis. The first attribute is predictive for the leftmost cluster, while the third attribute is predictive for the rightmost cluster.

The previous discussion of clustering, therefore, has been a bit of a simplification, since it implicitly assumed that attributes were either useful or not useful. For example, in computing distances, all attributes have equal weight in the distance computation. The reality is that some attributes are useful *for some clusters* but not so useful for others.

In this common situation, it is better to think of the problem as finding *biclusters* – clusters that describe similarities among a *subset* of the records based on similarities among a *subset* of the attributes. Although biclustering has received most attention in the context of biomedical data, many, perhaps most, datasets contain biclusters rather than simple clusters.

In their simplest form, the presence of biclusters means that there is some way of sorting the rows and columns of the dataset to produce blocks of similar values, as shown in Figure 5.7. Each block corresponds to a cluster, but a cluster that is associated with some of the objects, and also with some of the attributes. Of course, we do not know, in advance, how to do this sorting.

A more realistic form of biclustering is shown in Figure 5.8, where the biclusters overlap, both for objects and for attributes. As before, there is some (unknown) way of sorting the rows and columns to produce blocks of similar entries, but any particular record (row) or attribute (column) is associated with more than one of the biclusters.

There are several algorithmic approaches to finding biclusters. The sim-

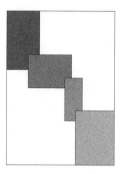

Figure 5.8. *Biclusters often overlap for both records and attributes.*

plest tries to find regions of the dataset matrix with entries of similar values, either using a divide-and-conquer approach or greedily. For example, the dataset can be sorted into descending order based on the row and column means, making it likely that a good bicluster can be found near the top left-hand corner of the matrix. A good split point for the first column is the row that minimizes the variance of the entries above it in the column. A good split point for the first row is the column that minimizes the variance of the entries before it in the row. These two split points define a bicluster in the top left-hand corner, which can either be taken as the first bicluster, or the process can be repeated using the second column and second row to select a smaller top left-hand corner block. The entire process can then be repeated on the remaining matrix, or the remaining matrix and the strips below and to the right of the chosen block. Many variations of this technique have been tried.

Ordinary clustering algorithms can be used in an alternating way as biclustering algorithms too. A first attempt to cluster the rows (records) produces tentative cluster labels. The clustering algorithm can then be used on the transposed dataset, where the objects are treated as the attributes, and the tentative class labels for the objects are treated as extra record attributes. This provides a tentative clustering of the attributes. The clustering of the records can then be improved using the new information about the clustering of the attributes, and so on.

A higher-level approach to biclustering is the *Semi-Discrete Decomposition* (SDD)[12]. This is a matrix decomposition, superficially looking like an SVD, which decomposes a data matrix A, of size $n \times m$, into a product

$$A = XDY$$

where D is a diagonal $k \times k$ matrix, X is an $n \times k$ matrix, and Y is a $k \times m$ matrix. The entries of X and Y are from the set $\{-1, 0, +1\}$, and k is not necessarily bounded above by n or m.

An SDD can be understood as describing the entries of A as the sum of a set of stencils, describing locations in the matrix, and magnitudes. The product of a column of X, a diagonal entry of D, and a row of Y is an $n \times m$ matrix, just like A. It typically has entries only in some locations, and the magnitudes of the entries are either $+d$ or $-d$, where d is the entry from D. In other words it describes a bicluster, a subset of the rows and columns of A with equal values d, except that some values have positive sign and some have negative sign. A is the pointwise sum of all of these bicluster matrices, so the decomposition gives a biclustering for the data. A particular entry in A might appear as a sum of entries from different bicluster matrices, so biclusters are allowed to overlap in both rows and columns.

For example, suppose that we are given a data matrix

$$A = \begin{bmatrix} 1 & 2 & 1 & 2 \\ 1 & 2 & 1 & 2 \\ 2 & 4 & 4 & 1 \\ 2 & 4 & 4 & 1 \end{bmatrix}$$

in which there are some very obvious biclusters. The Semi-Discrete Decomposition produced is

$$\begin{bmatrix} 1 & 2 & 1 & 2 \\ 1 & 2 & 1 & 2 \\ 2 & 4 & 4 & 1 \\ 2 & 4 & 4 & 1 \end{bmatrix} = \begin{bmatrix} 0 & 1 & 0 & 1 & 0 \\ 0 & 1 & 0 & 1 & 0 \\ 1 & 0 & 1 & 0 & 1 \\ 1 & 0 & 1 & 0 & 1 \end{bmatrix} \begin{bmatrix} 4 & 0 & 0 & 0 & 0 \\ 0 & 2 & 0 & 0 & 0 \\ 0 & 0 & 2 & 0 & 0 \\ 0 & 0 & 0 & 1 & 0 \\ 0 & 0 & 0 & 0 & 1 \end{bmatrix} \begin{bmatrix} 0 & 1 & 1 & 0 \\ 0 & 1 & 0 & 1 \\ 1 & 0 & 0 & 0 \\ 1 & 0 & 1 & 0 \\ 0 & 0 & 0 & 1 \end{bmatrix}$$

The product of the first column of X and the first row of Y produces the matrix that describes the stencil, or footprint of the first bicluster, namely

$$\begin{bmatrix} 0 & 0 & 0 & 0 \\ 0 & 0 & 0 & 0 \\ 0 & 1 & 1 & 0 \\ 0 & 1 & 1 & 0 \end{bmatrix}$$

and the magnitude of the corresponding diagonal element of D (4) gives the average magnitude of the entries.

The clusters produced by ordinary clustering algorithms are often actually biclusters. This can be detected by taking the rows of the data matrix corresponding to each cluster and looking at the magnitudes of the attributes associated only with those rows. Attributes (columns) with small variances are those that are associated with each cluster to form a bicluster. The advantage of using a biclustering algorithm is that similarity among attributes will be used explicitly to help select good clusters, but it can still be useful to notice biclusters that are produced from ordinary clustering algorithms.

5.4.7　Clusters and Prediction

In any dataset, it is always possible that some of the records are mislabelled. This is a particular problem in adversarial settings where, inevitably, some of the adversary activity has not been detected. As a result, some records that should be labelled as bad are not.

Clustering can sometimes help with this problem. Intuitively, mislabelled records should resemble records from the class they really belong to. Given a labelled dataset, we can cluster it, ignoring the class label. The resulting clustering can then have its points labelled with the class labels. Even by inspection using some visualization, it may become obvious that some records have been mislabelled.

More algorithmically, a suitably small threshold can be chosen, and the neighbors of each record (those closer than the threshold) examined. These records should all (or mostly) have the same class label. Records for which this is not true are candidates for having been wrongly labelled. It is also plausible to cluster the entire dataset, and then each of the classes independently. A record that is not an outlier in the global clustering but is an outlier in one of the single-class clusterings is also a candidate for having been wrongly labelled.

5.4.8　Symbiotic Clustering

Because humans are good at dealing with visual data, visualizations of clusterings provide an opportunity for human feedback. Attempts to hide clusters can be frustrated by using SVD and visualizing the result, making it obvious that what appears to be a single cluster to an algorithm is probably two. SVD is particularly useful because its faithful projection into a small number of dimensions makes it possible to visualize data that would otherwise be difficult. Human interaction can also be used to judge whether an algorithm's suggestion that certain records are outliers is justified.

A more complex way to use human skills to improve clustering is to provide a small amount of extra information. One common form for this is to indicate that two records *must* be in the same cluster, or that two records *cannot* be in the same cluster. Obviously, there is usually too much data for a human to provide this information for very many pairs of records – but just a small amount of information like this can dramatically improve clustering. This approach of providing extra information about just a few records is called *semisupervised clustering*[13].

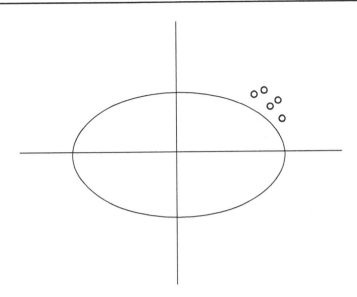

Figure 5.9. *Unusual attribute values for multiple attributes drive points into the 'corners' of the data.*

5.5 Tactics and Process

In general, clusters that are close to larger clusters, and not too obviously different, are hard to detect. By the nature of the problem, clustering algorithms never have access to the 'right' answer, so detection of a suspicious cluster can be based only on an accumulation of subtle signs. We can design a process to help extract these signs, but that is about the best that can be done.

We expect that genuine clusters in the data should be robust and so should appear much the same using different clustering techniques. This is obviously not the case using algorithms that look for qualitatively different clusters but, even here, we expect to see some agreement. An obvious step is to use multiple clustering technologies and see what the differences are between the clusterings that they each discover. Small differences in places where there is otherwise broad agreement may indicate records that should be investigated further.

Equally obviously, attributes that are hard to manipulate are to be preferred. The more difficult an attribute is to manipulate, the more likely it is that the records of adversaries will have slightly unusual values. In data made up mostly of such attributes, we expect that the anomalous records, and clusters made up of them, are likely to be found in the corners of the dataset, as shown in Figure 5.9.

Another approach is to use randomization to select either random records, or random attributes. For dense clusters, random selection of records may thin out the boundary regions of the cluster while still making it clear that it is a cluster. If there are records identified as suspicious, these should be left in the dataset in the hope of seeing a clearer separation between them and their neighboring clusters. Random selection of attributes, or perhaps random projection can help to make the gap between a small cluster and the larger one it is clinging to more visible.

It is always a good idea, even for techniques that automatically identify the number of clusters present, to increase the number of clusters by one, and see where the extra cluster lies. If the initial clustering was a good one, it is typically quite hard to extract a new cluster – and the new one is likely to be obtained by breaking an existing cluster into two large pieces. If this subdivision leaves one large coherent piece, and a much smaller, peripheral piece, this suggests that the smaller piece may be of interest as a missed, or concealed cluster.

5.6   Special Case – Looking for Outliers Revisited

In the previous chapter, we discussed the problem of finding outliers in data where we had training data from only one class. We can now frame that problem as one of finding a clustering of the training data, and then predicting records that do not fall within any cluster to be outliers.

Two approaches, density-based methods and reconstruction methods, can be better explained now that clustering has been discussed. All of the clustering techniques we have presented can be adapted for outlier detection, but some are more sensible than others. For example, k-means partitions the space spanned by the attributes, so every record belongs to some cluster – but every cluster has a centroid, so it is plausible to compute the distance of each record to the centroid of its cluster and predict that it is an outlier if this distance is sufficiently large, perhaps larger than a third of the average distance of this centroid to its nearest neighboring centroid.

Density-based clustering techniques, of course, automatically provide a way to detect outliers – they are the records that are not assigned to any cluster. A number of definitions of density are possible.

A density-based model can be used even without actually constructing a clustering in the following way. Given a new record, compute the distance to its nearest neighbor in the training data (the normal records). Then compute the distance of this neighbor to *its* nearest neighbor, and compute the ratio of these two numbers. If this ratio is sufficiently large, predict that the new point is an outlier. This allows for varying density in different regions of the

Input layer

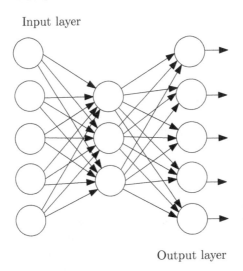

Output layer

Figure 5.10. *An auto-associative neural network tries to reproduce its inputs on its outputs.*

normal points, so that the density of points can peter out at different rates in different directions and still make effective predictions about new objects that are outliers.

Another approach to outlier detection is *reconstruction modelling*. The essential idea is that the model of the one normal class encodes membership in terms of how to *build* its members. This hypothetical construction process is applied to new records. Those that turn out to be hard to build are classified as outliers. We will explore two quite different implementations of this idea.

The first is to use *autoassociative neural networks*. We have seen how neural networks can be used as predictors. Here we build a different kind of neural network, using the same basic neurons, but arranging them in a network with the same number of output nodes as input nodes, and with the number of neurons in the middle, hidden layer much smaller than the number of inputs (number of attributes).

Figure 5.10 shows a small example of an autoassociative neural network, with five input attributes, and so five outputs. Each of the edges between nodes has an associated weight, randomly initialized.

The autoassociative network is trained by presenting each training example to the inputs, allowing the values to propagate through the network using thresholded weighted sums as usual, and producing outputs corresponding to each attribute. The goal is to reproduce the input attribute values on the outputs. This is not trivial because of the narrow hidden layer which forces the network to encode, somehow, the latent structure of the training examples.

The output will usually not match the desired output (a copy of the input) so the difference can be used to alter the weights in the network using the same backpropagation algorithm used for predictive neural networks. As before, the training data must be passed through the network many times before it becomes fully trained.

When the network is deployed, new records (that is, their attributes) are fed through the network. For records that resemble those in the training data, the normal records, the network should be able to produce a reasonable approximation to its input on its outputs because it has learned the deep, underlying structure of normality. If the new record is an outlier, the reconstruction is likely to be poor because the network does not know how to represent its structure in a compact way that can pass through the narrowest layer. The difference between input and output becomes a measure of how unexpected or unusual each new record is.

A second approach is to use singular value decomposition as a way to detect outliers. We have seen that, in many real-world datasets, the dimensionality of the data is much smaller than it appears. If we take a matrix of training examples that actually occupy a space of dimension, say, k then the rows of the matrix product US will have small values in all of the columns $k+1$ to m. Given an SVD $A = USV'$, new records have size $1 \times m$ and can be mapped into the space spanned by V'. Rearranging the equation gives $U = AVS^{-1}$, so a record that looks like a row of A can be mapped into a record that looks like a row of U by multiplying it by VS^{-1}. For records that resemble the training data, this mapping produces records that also have small values in columns $k+1$ to m. However, records that are not like those in the training set are likely not to lie within the k-dimensional space of the normal objects, and so will have large values in some of the columns $k+1$ to m. This can be used to classify them as outliers.

Notes

[1]C. Anderson, *The Long Tail: Why the Future of Business is Selling Less of More*, Hyperion, 2006.

[2]Further details of clustering techniques can be found in P.-N. Tan, M. Steinbach and V. Kumar, *Introduction to Data Mining*, Addison-Wesley, 2006; M. Kantardzic, *Data Mining: Concepts, Models, Methods, and Algorithms*, Wiley-IEEE Press, 2002; and M. Dunham, *Data Mining Introductory and Advanced Topics*, Prentice Hall, 2003.

[3]To the extent that there has been an outcry among its residents because it is being broken up, since some of them will now be in a new, less-desirable zip code.

[4]J.B. MacQueen, *Some Methods for Classification and Analysis of Multivariate Observations*, in: *Proceedings of 5th Berkeley Symposium on Mathematical Statistics and Probability*, volume 1, pp. 281–297. University of California Press, 1967.

[5]M. Ester, H.-P. Kriegel, J. Sander and X. Xu, *A Density-Based Algorithm for Discovering Clusters in Large Spatial Databases with Noise*, in: *2nd International Conference on Knowledge Discovery and Data Mining (KDD'96)*, Portland, Oregon, 1996. AAAI Press.

[6]A.P. Dempster, N.M. Laird and D.B. Rubin, "Maximum likelihood from incomplete data via the EM algorithm", *Journal of the Royal Statistical Society, Series B*, 39:138, 1977.

[7]J. Dutrisac, "Counter-Surveillance in an Algorithmic World", Master's Thesis, School of Computing, Queen's University, 2007.

[8]Fur further details see D.B. Skillicorn, *Understanding Complex Datasets: Data Mining with Matrix Decompositions*, CRC Press, 2007. SVD is also related to Principal Component Analysis (PCA).

[9]See A. Hyvärinen, "Survey on independent component analysis", *Neural Computing Surveys*, 2:94–128, 1999 for an accessible introduction.

[10]An example of the use of ICA for clustering can be found in F.R. Bach and M.I. Jordan, "Finding Clusters in Independent Component Analysis", Technical Report UCB/CSD-02-1209, Computer Science Division, University of California, Berkeley, 2002.

[11]S.C. Johnson, "Hierarchical clustering schemes", *Psychometrika*, 2:241–254, 1967.

[12]See D.P. O'Leary and S. Peleg, "Digital image compression by outer product expansion", *IEEE Transactions on Communications*, 31:441–444, 1983; G. Kolda and D.P. O'Leary, "A semi-discrete matrix decomposition for latent semantic indexing in information retrieval", *ACM Transactions on Information Systems*, 16:322–346, 1998; and T.G. Kolda and D.P. O'Leary, "Computation and uses of the semidiscrete matrix decomposition", *ACM Transactions on Information Processing*, 1999 for the basic details of SDD, and S. McConnell and D.B. Skillicorn, *SemiDiscrete Decomposition: A Bump Hunting Technique*, in: *Australasian Data Mining Workshop*, pp. 75–82, December 2002 for an example of its use to find biclusters.

[13]A short survey is N. Grira, M. Crucianu and N. Boujemaa, "Unsupervised and semi-supervised clustering: A brief survey", satoh-lab.ex.nii.ac.jp/users/grira/papers/BriefSurveyClustering.pdf, 2005.

Chapter 6

Looking Inside Groups – Relationship Discovery

So far, knowledge-discovery techniques have focused on individual records. There are, of course, implicit connections between records that are exploited for clustering, but these connections are derived from common or similar values of some of the attributes. We now turn to the situation where there are explicit connections between records, and the properties of these connections are more significant than the properties of the individual records themselves.

In this situation, the records often describe individuals, and the explicit connections describe some kind of relationship or affinity between them. Such connections sometimes arise as the result of explicit decisions, for example, because of functional relationships between the individuals, such as working on a project together. Connections between people also arise for other, more implicit reasons. We are social creatures and so we create connections that, one by one, appear almost accidental, for example by hitting it off with someone else in a social setting. When the total effects of such person-to-person connections are considered at a larger scale, they reveal deeper and more interesting properties about cultures and subcultures. Individuals also create connections because of their qualities as individuals, for example their personalities, and these can reveal their individual properties in ways that are hard for them to conceal or fake.

Relationships contain richer and deeper information than simply the data associated with each individual. This information is even more valuable in adversarial settings because some of it arises without much conscious awareness by the individuals concerned. Just as a fish is not aware of water, people tend not to be aware of the social and personal pressures that lead them to connect to other people. Such connections can therefore be especially revealing.

Relationship data can be analyzed at different levels and different kinds of knowledge extracted. At the simplest level, the links between pairs of individuals tell us something that might not be obvious just from their attribute values. The structure of the connections between a small set of individuals provides more information, from which more abstract knowledge can be extracted. Finally, the global structure of relationships in an entire social group allows a global kind of knowledge to be extracted.

6.1   Goals

The goals of knowledge discovery from relationship data can be separated into two:

- **Selecting** interesting regions from data about a large set of relationships;

- **Analyzing** the information found in an entire graph; or a region selected as interesting.

Relationship data that is collected about a large number of individuals or objects will usually contain much that is not of interest, especially in an adversarial setting. Finding those regions in the data where further analysis will be productive is an important, but difficult, step.

Analysis of the entire structure or possibly a selected substructure can take a number of forms. These include:

- Finding how well-connected each individual is. The position of each individual and how well that individual is connected to others by connections of high affinity reveal a lot about power or importance, and how it is distributed among the people involved. Often there is considerable disparity between the graph of actual connections and the 'official' graph, for example, represented by an organizational chart.

- Finding how easily information can flow around the structure, assuming that edges with high affinity are ones along which information flows easily. For example, friends tell each other things, sometimes even when they shouldn't. Although this is related to how well-connected each individual is, importance and power are not necessarily distributed in the same way as usefulness as a conduit of information. Anecdotally, in many business organizations, information flow happens via secretaries or via the smokers who congregate outside to smoke. These connections also tend not to reflect 'official' connection structures.

- Finding the most important individuals in the structure. Again this is related to how well-connected an individual is, but the most important people are not always the best connected, or even the most central, especially in an adversarial setting, where there are advantages to being difficult to locate.

- Finding regions of the graph structure that correspond to known patterns, to unusual local structure, or to local anomalies. Often, a property typical of adversaries is reflected in a particular pattern of connections, whether it is the pattern typical of drug dealing or money laundering, or the cell structure meant to make it hard to destroy an insurgent group. Such a pattern may be found by searching for it explicitly in the structure, or it may be found because it is rare, and so unusual or anomalous.

- Discovering how new individuals are added to the structure over time. Recruitment, reorganization, or getting new equipment can all change an existing structure. Understanding how the structure changes as the set of nodes changes can reveal approaches and attitudes to change.

- Finding nodes that are, in some sense, equivalent. In many contexts, individuals who disappear and reappear can be detected because they make connections with the same individuals in each incarnation. For example, cell phones stolen by the same person can be identified because the set of numbers they call stays the same.

- Finding clusters in the graph structure. Clustering plays the same role in relationship data that it does in attributed data, finding groups of individuals who are similar, and distinct from other groups. The problem is different because the relationship between local distance and global distance in attributed data is straightforward, but the relationship between local affinity and global affinity in relationship data is much more complex.

- Improving prediction for individuals using the extra information about affinity. Especially in situations where one of the target classes is rare, prediction accuracy can be improved by using the fact that the objects in the rare class are likely to be connected to each other directly or to be near-neighbors in the graph.

The kinds of knowledge extracted from graph data are similar to those that can be found using prediction and clustering, but new, more interesting, and more complex forms of knowledge can also be found.

6.2 Outline of Relationship-Discovery Technology

The data on which relationship discovery is based consists of nodes, usually representing individuals but sometimes records of other kinds, and edges be-

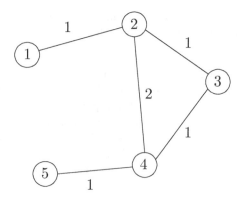

Figure 6.1. *A small example graph.*

tween them. There may be attributes associated with each node, and there are usually attributes associated with the edges.

In the simplest case, nodes are just labelled with identifiers, and edges have an associated numeric value, an edge weight. These edge weights describe the *affinities* between the nodes that they join. Usually a larger weight indicates a greater affinity. For example, an edge weight might record how many times two individuals have met, or how many times they have communicated, or the closeness of their blood ties.

Figure 6.1 shows a small graph. The most basic properties of a graph are how many nodes it contains, and how many edges exist between pairs of nodes. If the number of nodes is n, then the number of edges must, of course, be no larger than n^2, but is usually much smaller in practice. In other words, most pairs of nodes are not directly connected. The example graph has 5 nodes and 5 edges. The *degree* of a node is the number of edges to which it is connected.

We may also be interested in how far apart a pair of nodes are in the graph. This can be measured in two ways. The first is simply to count the number of edges that separate two nodes along the shortest path between them. The second is to take into account the affinities of the edges, so that the calculated distance represents a meaningful affinity between the two nodes, the appropriate affinity that would exist if there were a direct edge between them. If an edge weight represents an affinity, then its reciprocal represents a distance, and distances along paths can simply be added. So the overall affinity along a path whose individual steps are labelled $a_1, a_2, \ldots$ is the value a satisfying

$$\frac{1}{a} = \frac{1}{a_1} + \frac{1}{a_2} + \ldots$$

As we shall see later, even this slightly complicated way of measuring affinities

$$\begin{bmatrix} 0 & 1 & 0 & 0 & 0 \\ 1 & 0 & 1 & 2 & 0 \\ 0 & 1 & 0 & 1 & 0 \\ 0 & 2 & 1 & 0 & 1 \\ 0 & 0 & 0 & 1 & 0 \end{bmatrix}$$

Figure 6.2. *Adjacency matrix for the example graph.*

over greater distances is not completely adequate. In the example graph, the affinity between nodes 1 and 4 is 2/3 since $1 + \frac{1}{2} = 3/2$, and the affinity between nodes 1 and 3 is 1/2 since $1 + 1 = 2$. Hence node 1 is more like node 3 than node 4, which seems intuitively right for this graph.

The *diameter* of the graph is the maximum length of the shortest paths between all pairs of nodes, and measures a more-global property of the graph. Diameters are usually considered only for the case where each edge has equal weight, but the concept could easily be generalized to use the long-distance affinity above. The simple (unweighted) diameter of the example graph is 3, the distance between node 1 and node 5.

Although we will not consider this case much, it is also possible for the edges to be directed, that is to pass in only one direction from one node to another; and more complex definitions of what it means to be an edge can also be made.

Graphs are more complicated to work with than attributed data. It is easy to draw a picture of a graph, at least of a simple graph, but this representation is not easy to calculate with. Instead, a graph is often represented using an *adjacency matrix*. If the graph has n nodes, then its adjacency matrix has n rows and n columns, and its ijth entry records the weight on the edge joining node i to node j. If the edges are undirected, then the matrix is symmetric, that is, the ijth and jith entries must be the same. Usually, the iith (diagonal) entries are set to zero, although it is sometimes useful to consider each node to be connected to itself by a weighted edge as well.

The adjacency matrix for the example graph is shown in Figure 6.2. Because the edges are non-directional, the adjacency matrix is symmetric and the diagonal entries are all zeros. The number of non-zero entries in each row or column shows the degree of the corresponding node.

Knowledge can be extracted from graph data at different scales. It may be useful to know properties of the set of individual nodes: for example, how many other nodes each one is connected to. More generally, we may want to identify those nodes that are unusual in the set – they may represent people with unusual connections to others, perhaps because they are in a leadership role in a criminal group.

At a slightly larger scale we may be interested in the neighborhood of each node, for example properties such as how many of a node's neighbors are connected to each other. Sets of nodes that are richly connected among themselves typically represent some kind of community.

At a larger scale still, we may want to learn if there are regions of the graph that exhibit an unusual structure, that is some combination of nodes and edges that is of special significance, or that does not occur anywhere else in the graph.

Finally, we may want to be able to divide up the entire graph into pieces that represent plausible clusters, well-connected within themselves, but sparsely connected to other clusters.

6.2.1   Real-World Graphs

Most real-world graphs have a much smaller diameter, the distance across the graph, than we might intuitively expect, given the number of nodes and the density of edges. Even random graphs are like this. In contrast, graphs that have been constructed in a regular way, such as lattices, have diameters that grow quite quickly as a function of the number of nodes. For example, a lattice of 100 nodes arranged in a 10×10 grid has a diameter of 18 (to get from one corner to the opposite corner).

The diameter of *any* graph can be dramatically reduced by adding just a few new edges. Watts and Strogatz[1] showed how to add edges to a lattice to reduce its diameter to logarithmic in the number of nodes. Bokhari and Raza[2] gave a general construction that reduces the diameter of *any* graph to logarithmic adding at most one new edge at each node, fewer new edges than required by the Watts-Strogatz construction. So, in a sense, it is not surprising that random graphs have small diameters. For the 100-node lattice, adding such edges would reduce the diameter from 18 to 7.

Many real-world graphs have even smaller diameters, diameters that grow only as fast as $\log \log n$ for a graph with n nodes. This diameter can be treated as constant for practical purposes – for a graph with 1 million nodes, the diameter would be only 4.

The reason why both real-world and random graphs have such small diameters is because the distribution of the node degrees, the number of edges connected to each of the nodes, is very skewed. A few nodes have very high degree, fewer nodes have medium degree, and most nodes have quite low degree. The probability that a node has k neighbors is proportional to $1/k^{\gamma}$, where γ captures the precise shape of the frequency decrease and lies between 2 and 3 for many real-world networks. This relationship is called a *power law*. However, the high-degree nodes, although rare, turn out to be frequent enough to create short paths between all pairs of other nodes.

Milgram[3] carried out an experiment that showed that, in the U.S. in the Sixties, it was possible to find connections between any two people using a path of no more than six steps; an observation that has come to be called "six degrees of separation". This is surprising because most people know at most a few hundred people and, worse still, the people they know tend to be geographically quite concentrated. This finding has been replicated for the whole world, and for the Internet, although the path lengths required are perhaps longer[4].

The intuitive reason why these continent-spanning and world-spanning paths are so unexpectedly short is that local, highly-connected regions tend to be connected to each other by infrequent, long-distance links that act as bridges between the local regions. Although these bridges are rare, they are enough to create short paths across the whole graph. This property is a consequence of the distribution of node degrees: nodes with large degrees act as connectors for many subgraphs and allow many different parts of the graph to be reached in only a few steps.

This is often called the *small world* property of a graph – although the neighborhood of most nodes consists of a small richly interconnected set of other nodes, the entire world is reachable via a few longer connections. For example, a short path from anyone in the U.S. to anyone in Britain can probably be based on the path: – Congressperson – President – Queen – Member of Parliament – . People like presidents and royalty have connections not just to a few more people than most, but to orders of magnitude more people than most.

This property of short paths travelling via a few well-connected nodes typically repeats at all levels of granularity in graphs. For example, short paths between people in a single town are probably based on passing through a mayor or a school principal. Each region of a graph looks like a miniature version of the whole graph. Graphs with power-law degree distributions are often called *scale free* for this reason.

One way to build scale-free networks that seems to have some explanatory power is *preferential attachment*. This is a model of how a network grows, and postulates that a new link attaches to a node with a probability that depends on that node's current degree – popular nodes, in the sense of having many attached edges already, become even more popular. Using this growth rule produces networks that do seem to mimic the structure of observed real-world networks. And this kind of pattern of growth is also plausible, at least in some settings. For example, the probability that someone will create a link to a web site is likely to be greater if it is a useful site; which means that there are probably already a lot of links to it from other places. A person with many friends is introduced to more people, and so has more chances to make new friends.

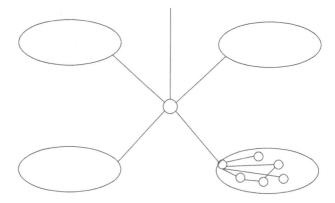

Figure 6.3. *High-degree nodes connecting mostly to low-degree nodes.*

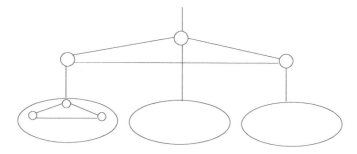

Figure 6.4. *High-degree nodes connecting mostly to high-degree nodes.*

However, there is an important distinction between two kinds of scale-free graphs. In both kinds of graphs, local regions of the graph are connected together by high-degree nodes, but the two kinds differ in how these high-degree nodes are themselves connected.

The first possibility is shown in Figure 6.3. Here the high-degree nodes connect mainly to the low-degree nodes in each region, with only a small number of connections 'upwards' in the network. The network is a bit like a tree of subnetworks, and the long-distance paths involve going 'up' in the tree and then 'down' again. The scale-free nature of the graph means that this picture of the connections applies at all scales, that is to any local region as well. In this graph, a high-degree node is likely to be connected mostly to low-degree nodes.

The second possibility is shown in Figure 6.4. Here the high-degree nodes connect primarily to other high-degree nodes. Again, the scale-free nature of the graph means that the picture looks the same for any local region as well. In this graph, nodes are mostly connected to nodes with about the same degree as themselves: high-degree nodes to high-degree nodes; low-degree nodes to other low-degree nodes. Presidents and royalty are well-connected to each other, but there is no super-president who knows qualitatively more people and so can act as another level of connector.

Both versions can be constructed by preferential attachment. Technical networks tend to be of the first kind; for example, the Internet is connected (roughly) by a hierarchy of gateways, most web sites have links to a relatively small number of sites that are pointed to by many, many sites. Human networks, on the other hand, tend to be of the second kind. For example, popular people tend to have friends who are also popular, researchers work with people who are about as productive as they are, and so on. Preferential attachment is only part of the explanation for why real-world graphs look the way they do.

Understanding what real-world networks are like is a prerequisite for understanding what features of networks are unlikely or anomalous, and therefore probably of interest in an adversarial setting.

6.2.2   Selection in Graphs

These general properties suggest the background of normality that might be expected in graph data about people or their activities. We now consider what might change in an adversarial setting.

There are two kinds of knowledge discovery using graph data. One possibility is that the graph data has been collected about a large number of people or objects, and the primary goal is to find the part of the graph that describes the connections among adversaries and their activities. In other words, the focus is on *selection* of part of the graph.

The other possibility is that the graph data describes only the adversaries and their activities, and we want to extract knowledge about them from the entire data. The first possibility could, of course, lead to the second.

For selection, the goal might be to look for known patterns associated with actions that adversaries do. For example, dealing drugs also requires a related way to launder the money that is paid for the drugs. A drug dealer is someone who not only has connections to a supply of drugs, but also has connections to a mechanism, such as a cash business, for laundering the money. Knowing this pattern, examples may be searched for in the graph data. In graph data about telephone numbers called, each phone tends to call a small set of numbers frequently. If another phone also calls this same small set of numbers, it is likely that its owner is either the same person or someone closely associated with them.

However, as we observed for prediction, it is hard to think of all possible patterns that might be of interest, and new variations are being developed constantly. The other way to think about selection is to look for any substructure in the graph that is unusual. The logic is this: any structure that reflects the behavior or actions of ordinary people will be repeated many times in the graph data. Those structures that are rare in the data therefore represent behavior or actions that are not common. The abnormal or suspicious behaviors of adversaries will not be the only cause of these uncommon patterns; other unusual actions of behaviors will also create uncommon patterns. But the uncommon patterns are a small part of the entire graph data, and the adversary behavior is likely to be within this small part. It is more cost-effective overall to select such parts of a graph and apply some deeper analysis to these parts.

So we have two broad strategies for selecting the interesting part of a graph dataset and focusing attention upon it: look for parts of the graph that match a known set of patterns, or look for parts of the graph that have unusual structure of any kind.

6.2.3   Analysis of Graphs

The second problem is when we have graph data that is entirely about the behavior, actions, or relationships of adversaries. Such data might result from selection; it might come from surveillance of the adversaries, or from accessing their communications (see Chapters 7 and 8). Some of the analysis that is possible for such data includes:

- Selecting substructures, perhaps individual nodes, of particular interest;

- Analyzing the global structure of the graph;

- Analyzing the neighborhood of single nodes of the graph;

- Deciding whether subsets of the nodes in fact represent the same entity; and

- Ranking the nodes (and possibly the edges) in a way that reflects their importance;

Substructures of the graph are potentially interesting for the same reason as before: they may be instances of a known pattern whose meaning is already understood, or we may want to find the most unusual substructures present. For example, an unusual substructure might represent a specialized subgroup or the staff around a leader.

The global structure of the graph data may shed light on the way command and control work in the group, or how information is communicated. For example, the cells that have carried out al Qaeda attacks match very closely with tightly connected regions in the graph of family relationships and personal history, indicating that al Qaeda relies on personal ties, rather than functional expertise, to build its cells[5]. The global structure may also reveal how information passes through the group; how recruits enter the group and what their trajectory is like as they gain experience; and where the opportunities for maximal disruption are to be found.

The neighborhood of a particular node can often be revealing. It is usually impractical to examine the neighborhoods of all nodes, so selecting the ones of potential interest is non-trivial. For example, insurance fraud can sometimes be detected by examining the connections of the claimant. In a car accident, it is suspicious if the two drivers are related to each other, and this may be discovered, even if their overt details are all different, by following chains based on current and previous addresses, names on current and previous policies, and the like.

A related issue is whether multiple nodes in the graph represent different individuals or not. There are many innocent reasons why data about the same person or object might appear in the data as more than one node: typographical errors, normal variation in usages such as names, and differences in data collection via different channels. However, those who are trying to conceal themselves and their actions are likely to manipulate these possibilities to create multiple nodes as often as possible. This blurs or obscures relationships that might otherwise be easy to see in the data.

Finally, we might want to rank the nodes (and possibly the edges) in some order of importance, and focus attention on the most important nodes. This is how, for example, Google sorts search results into an order where the most important pages are presented first – by using the graph structure of the web to create an importance ordering of the nodes (pages).

6.3 Concealment Opportunities

Given the kinds of analysis described above, what opportunities are available to conceal or mislead by altering the collection of graph data? These can be categorized as follows:

- **Hide nodes.** The best way to prevent a particular node, whether it represents a person or some other object, from being analyzed is to prevent it and its associated attributes from being visible in the first place.

- **Hide connections.** Whether or not data about a node is collected, analysis can be hampered by hiding some or all of the connections to it. This distorts the neighborhood around the node, and prevents many techniques from learning much about it. Some care is required not to overdo hiding connections, given that node data has been captured. For example, a node with no connections will be extremely unusual, and so will attract attention rather than avoiding it.

- **Prevent collection or force miscollection.** If nodes or edges are necessarily visible, the next strategy is to try to prevent their collection; or, if this is not practical, cause them to be collected wrongly. This may involve changing some of the attribute values associated with the node or edge. We have discussed ways to do this in Chapter 4.

These three strategies make it hard to use pattern matching to select interesting parts of large graph data, because some of the nodes and/or edges that the pattern is looking for are missing, or their attributes do not match what is expected. There is some risk that selection by looking for unusual substructures will focus attention on places where nodes or edges are missing, or attribute values have been changed, because it has made this region somehow different from the rest of the graph.

- **Steal identities.** When each node represents a person, it may be hard to prevent data about the node being collected because it will be obvious that *someone* is present or active. It may be easier to allow the node's data to be collected, but under a false identity so that it does not reveal anything about the actual person. Even if the connections of the node are revealing, they point to the wrong person.

  Identity theft prevents selection of substructures because the neighborhood of the node seems completely normal. It *is* the neighborhood of a normal node, at least for a while until the new user of the identity starts to act in a different way. This strategy is therefore a powerful one for concealment, which explains why identity theft is such a large criminal business.

- **Create false identities.** At one time, this option was far easier than stealing an existing identity. However, increasingly it is hard to fabricate an identity for two reasons. First, the guarantee of an identity used to exist in governments, for example because of birth certificates and so on, and in other institutions such as the church, for example because of baptismal certificates which can be used as identity documents in some countries. However, identities today are also validated for many by their presence on the Internet, via web pages that they have created, and which are archived at random intervals by, for example, the Way-Back Engine. Such identities are hard to forge (even for governments, making espionage more difficult). Second, making a false identity fit into the graph of relationships is increasingly difficult, since some of the pieces are beyond the control of the forger. For example, even if identity documents can be created, it is not possible to create tax returns going back a number of years, credit records, travel records, educational records, and all the traces left in data by living a life.

The previous manipulations hide structures that are local to one or a few nodes. However, analysis of more global properties is also possible, and so we must also consider manipulations that will alter such global properties.

- **Create indirect paths for direct ones.** One important part of global structure is the length of paths between nodes. The length of the path between two nodes is a measure of how closely related the two nodes are; and these paths together define properties such as the diameter. A strategy to confuse this structure is to change path lengths. This can be done by adding extra edges to make nodes appear closer than they actually are. However, it is more likely that adversaries will want to appear more separated than they actually are. This can be done by hiding edges, as described above, but it can also be done by creating other nodes whose main purpose is to lengthen the paths. If A wants to conceal his connection to B, an extra node X can be created, with A connected to X and X connected to B. This technique has a long history in espionage with the use of cutouts, letter drops, and so on playing the role of the extra nodes. Communications can be passed through accommodation addresses or their electronic equivalent, free email addresses. The common interests of two organizations can be concealed by building a network of shell companies and ownership to make it seem that they are at arms length, when they are not.

- **Create multiple nodes for single ones.** It is also possible to create multiple nodes that all represent the same person, rather than extra 'dummy' nodes as in the previous point. The attributes of these multiple nodes are subsets of the attributes of the actual person or object. By smearing the attributes across multiple nodes, it becomes hard to decide whether or not they represent that same person or object; and much harder to work out the structure of the local neighborhood. For example, a person can use more than one cell phone, can use more than one email address, can use pseudonyms or aliases, or, in the extreme, can create multiple identities.

All of these strategies aim to confuse the structure implicit in graph data. Of course, all of the techniques discussed in previous chapters for altering the values of attributes associated with nodes and edges can also be applied.

On the other hand, there are structural features, particular arrangements of nodes and edges, that we might expect to find associated with groups of adversaries that will be difficult, perhaps impossible, for them to conceal. Such groups need to be able to communicate with each other in a robust way.

They also need to ensure that the loss of a node (either to interception or arrest, depending on the situation) does not destroy the group. These two requirements are difficult to achieve together, and force certain kinds of structures. One common example is the use of cells, each one tightly connected internally, but connected to the others via very few edges. As we have seen, scale-free networks do not look like this, but instead are characterized by some highly connected nodes. Such nodes would be disastrous from a security point of view, since deletion of that node would destroy or disconnect a large number of other nodes. So it is unlikely that the structures constructed by adversaries will resemble the structures that arise from preferential attachment. Cell structures are incompatible with the typical structure of scale-free networks, and so may be detectable as anomalies within such networks[6].

Scale-free networks usually acquire the long-distance edges that connect different subgroups of the nodes because they have evolved over time. Someone in *this* subgroup knows someone in *that* subgroup far away because at one time they lived in the same place, and one or both of them have moved. Or perhaps they met at some third place such as a work-related conference, or a vacation. The connections associated with a criminal or terrorist group are likely to have been constructed for a particular purpose rather than developing over time, and so are likely to be characteristically different. Terrorists tend not to meet other people because their children play sports together or because they went on holiday to the same place, and so often they will not be as well-connected to the larger social network of a location as ordinary people are.

6.4   Technologies

Graph data are inherently difficult to work with, but they are also rich in possibilities for analysis. Here we look at the major families of analysis technologies that have been applied to graph data. We have suggested that the analysis task comes in two forms: selection of graph regions of interest; or analysis of the detailed properties of a graph or graph region. Some of these technologies are obviously aimed at one or other of these problems, but a number can be applied to both – graphs are so complicated that most kinds of analysis require some further focusing on particular parts of the structure[7].

6.4.1   Social Network Analysis

Social Network Analysis (SNA)[8] is an approach to graph data in which the nodes represent individuals, and the edges represent connections, relationships, between them. A basic assumption of the approach is that such graphs reflect the behavior of both individuals, and of larger social groups. Understanding the structure of the graph necessarily reveals the underlying structures and relationships among the people concerned. Social network analysis developed as a replacement for and extension to earlier models of social anthropology in which people were seen as primarily members of a single group. Social network analysis turns away from this view, regarding people as simultaneous participants in many different aggregations, some of which look like groups in the usual sense, but some of which are tenuous and geographically dispersed as well.

The edges in such a structure can represent many different kinds of connections. They may represent relationships, based on blood, on friendship, on power, in mutual interest, or on compulsion. They may also represent connections based on information flow[9]. Understanding such connections provides information about how and why individuals learn, decide, and act; and so information about groups in an emergent sense.

Social network analysis tends to focus on measures associated with each node of a graph, each measure condensing information from the structure of the graph to information about each individual. It is therefore aimed at understanding the entire graph, node by node.

For example, *betweenness* measures the extent to which each node (each individual) lies between other individuals in the network, both those to which it is directly connected, and indirectly connected. An individual who is the only connection between two different communities has high betweenness; an individual who connects people who have many other ways of reaching each other has low betweenness.

Another measure, *closeness*, is a measure of how close each individual is to the other individuals, based on (possibly weighted) path length. It is the reciprocal of the shortest path length between an individual and all of the other nodes of the graph.

Both betweenness and closeness capture some idea of how important each node (individual) is to the network, but in a different way. If the edges reflect information flow among individuals, then betweenness captures how critical a node is to the overall information flow, while closeness captures how important a node is to *fast* information flow.

Measures such as *density* can be applied to a network at different scales: the local density of edges around each node, up to the ratio of the total number of edges to the number of nodes. The greater the density of a graph, the harder it is to disrupt by removing nodes or edges, and the faster information can be communicated.

Another useful set of measures are those that capture the diameter of the graph. For example, a *path length* can be defined for pairs of nodes. The maximum, minimum, and average of the path lengths over all pairs of nodes capture something useful about the global structure of the graph.

Radiality measures how quickly the number of nodes reachable from an individual node increases with the number of steps outward from that node in the network. This is obviously related to the degree, the number of edges attached to each node, but also captures how often the increasing region around a node reaches previously unreached nodes. This property says something about how fast information or influence can spread out from each node.

Theories of human socialization, and the observed properties of human networks, such as their scale-free characteristics and the tendency of high-degree nodes to connect to other high-degree nodes provide expectations about the values of these social network measures. Nodes for which the values are unexpected become targets for deeper analysis.

Most technologies for computing social network measures were developed for what are now considered quite small networks; so some caution is needed when using older software packages that compute these measures[10].

6.4.2 Visualization

As humans, we are extremely good at detecting patterns in data presented to us visually. Finding ways to display graph data visually allows us to exploit this strength.

The problem is that the devices used to render graphs visually are either two-dimensional (screens) or three-dimensional (visualization rooms or virtual reality glasses), but the graph data itself may not be easy to flatten into two or three dimensions. Clever graph-drawing algorithms can be used to render the graph data in the best possible way. However, this might, in the end, not be very good.

The inherent dimensionality of the graph structure might be much greater than two or three. Flattening it into a few dimensions requires shortening some edges and stretching others, distorting the affinity relationship among the nodes. It is also likely that some parts of the graph will be hidden 'behind' other parts of it, and that the flattening will place some nodes and edges so close together that it is hard to resolve their details. There is no straightforward flattening of a graph that will display it in a way that makes its important structure obvious.

As a result, the ability of a human analyst to extract knowledge from graph data depends on how it has been rendered, and is therefore limited by the cleverness of the rendering algorithm in deciding how to place the nodes and edges. Most graph-drawing technology has focused on renderings that reveal as much structure as possible, especially symmetries. In an adversarial setting, it is not clear that the same goals for the drawing algorithm are appropriate. It might be more useful to render the most unusual aspects of the graph in the most obvious way, leaving the repetitious structures to be fitted in wherever they can be – the reverse of what happens today.

Many visualization systems have been developed, several of them targeted for adversarial knowledge discovery. They are, however, expensive both in terms of the analysis required and the infrastructure required to use them.

Visualization has, of course, always been an important part of knowledge discovery. Visualization tools and systems should always aim for synergy with human analysis skills across three dimensions:

- Visualization should play to human strengths in perception, for example by using colors so that differences in human perception of hue match the underlying differences in the values being displayed. Our understanding of how the human visual system works has grown rapidly in the past two decades, so there is a great opportunity to incorporate what has been learned into the design of knowledge-discovery tools.

- System response times should correspond to the scale of human expectations and exploratory thinking. In visualization, more than in most knowledge-discovery areas, the process is an interactive, real-time one, with an analyst developing a hypothesis from some initial rendering of the data, and educing data to support this hypothesis in a more and more focused way. Part of this process is new renderings of the current form of the data. For humans to follow trains of thought, it is critically important that the tools involved respond at speeds that match. If the responses are too fast, the analyst may feel led or pressured by the data, rather than taking the time to consider each display; if the responses are too slow, the analyst may become distracted by other trains of thought.

- The affordance of the tools should match the kinds of exploration that an analyst wishes to do, given the type of data available. In some situations, this may be refinement of data and its rendering; in others, it may be operations as simple as rotation of the rendering, zooming in to a particular region, or changing a color coding.

The (U.S.) National Visual Analytics Center has published a research agenda which discusses these properties in much greater detail[11].

Visualization can be broadly divided into two kinds. The first involves two orthogonal sets of properties: relationships and intensities. For example, a graph of relationships can be rendered in a way that shows the local affinities among the nodes, with position and distance conveying one kind of property; and the color of nodes displaying another kind of orthogonal property.

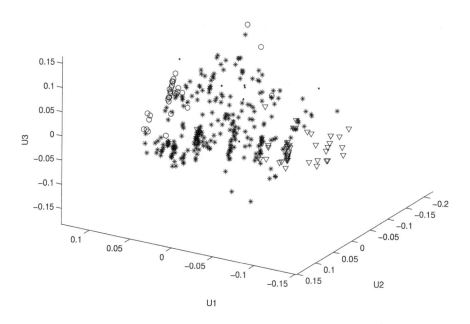

Figure 6.5. *Al Qaeda members, positions according to demographic properties and relationships; symbol coding by inferred educational level; then by inferred national origin.*

For example, Figure 6.5 shows a set of people who have been involved with al Qaeda, each point corresponding to a person (the same plot with names attached is shown in Figure 6.6 for those who are interested in particular people)[12]. The position of each point represents both similarities between attributes, such as age, education, and religious background; and explicit connections among members, such as being related or being friends. This plot therefore provides an accurate picture of the group. It is clear that there are some subclusters, associated with particular subgroups with the same national origin and, as a result, usually involved in the same attacks. However, overall the group is quite homogeneous. The symbol coding comes from an unsupervised clustering of the data on a different basis. The symbols · and ○ represent members with substantial educational attainment; the symbol square represents moderate educational achievement; and the triangle represents low educational achievement. There are some members, towards the left-hand end of the cluster with substantial education, in some cases even graduate degrees. Towards the right-hand end of the cluster, there are other members with very little education. Within each group, the different symbols represent national origin.

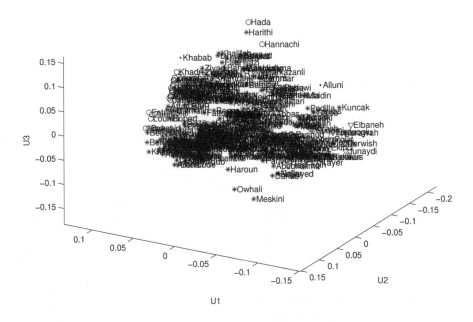

Figure 6.6. *The same plot, with names of al Qaeda members.*

The second kind of visualization involves only one kind of property, for example relationships or attribute values, but in situations where there are so many objects (records or points) that they cannot all be displayed at once equally. Visualization in this setting tends either to provide different layers of abstraction, or to provide some form of fisheye representation.

The different layers of abstraction view is familiar from digital displays of maps, which provide a map and perhaps an associated satellite image at some initial resolution. The user can then zoom in to whatever the finest resolution available is, or zoom out to get a wider, contextualized view.

There are two limitations with this approach. The first is that zooming in loses context; you can't maintain a sense of the wider context. The second is that, at any given level of abstraction, the rendering provides no hint of where it might be interesting to zoom in. This does not matter if the areas of interest are already known, but does not support exploratory analysis very well.

Fisheye representations try to address the first problem, by making it possible to zoom in a way that preserves some context. Typically, the content that is the current user focus is rendered in detail, and the detail decreases the further away from the focus it is. This does not, of course, help with finding an initial area of interest, but once such an area is identified, it provides a useful way to explore the area and its context.

An example of such a tool aimed at graph data is the Inxight Startree[13], which renders hierarchies on a hyperbolic plane that is then mapped to a circular display. The upper levels of the hierarchy tend to be placed near the center of the circle, while the leaves are placed around the diameter, occupying a segment related to how important they are. Users can interactively alter their focus, either by clicking on the rendering of an object, or by dragging one to a different location.

The big, mostly unexplored, problems with visualization technologies are that they overemphasize regularities and symmetries, both because this is a practical way to provide good (and aesthetically pleasing) renderings and because these regularities are often the properties of interest in graphs; and the technologies do not assume any adversary content in the data being rendered. Both of these are major drawbacks for applications in adversarial domains. In many, perhaps most, adversarial settings, it is the anomalous regions of the data that are of greatest interest, but a rendering algorithm is likely to push these off into corners where they are hard to notice. There has also not been, as far as I know, any study of how hard it is to manipulate data in order to mislead a visualization tool in a way that conceals particular structure.

6.4.3   Pattern Matching/Information Retrieval

Another approach is to treat the graph data as a repository against which queries can be executed. A query looks like a fragment of graph data: a set of nodes, and edges between them, and perhaps values or wildcards for some of the attributes of the nodes and edges. The search returns all the regions in the graph data that match the query subgraph.

Conventional information retrieval regards the data to be searched as a string, or possibly a table in a database. However, it has been obvious for a long time that documents, and many other data types as well, have a natural hierarchical structure; and queries that are aware of this structure are much more expressive. For example, it is useful to be able to search in a document for a paragraph containing word A, inside a section whose heading contains word B.

The most general hierarchical description of documents in common use is XML. Two main approaches to querying XML data have been followed. The first is to use special-purpose query languages such as XSLT and XPath[14], which play the same role for hierarchical data that SQL plays for databases. The second is to integrate XML query functionality into conventional programming languages, for example XJ, XQuery, $C\omega$, and CDuce[15]. Each of these languages is rather limited in its ability to express XML queries. Some can only express queries in which the components are above and below each other in the hierarchy (XJ, XQuery); others can express queries in which the components are siblings (CDuce); but it is hard to get the full range of expressiveness and still preserve the programming language's type system[16]. Conceptual graphs have been developed to represent the relationship between different parts of text in a typed way, and to allow queries to mention not just the content, but also the typed relationships to be matched[17]. They resemble XML query languages, but with more emphasis on the types of the edges, and with a limited ability to capture directed, acyclic graphs rather than simply trees.

Hierarchies are a limited form of graph, although still very important. There have also been several attempts to define graph query languages that can be used for graphs that are not also trees, that is, which contain cycles. We review three different approaches:

1. The SUBDUE graph analysis system is primarily an unsupervised system which tries to find interesting substructures within a graph. It works by conducting a search for common patterns, in much the same way as a rule-based system would try to find rules – growing subgraphs from initial single nodes in all possible ways. Each substructure is assigned a quality based on minimum description length measure, that is, how much space (in bits) is required to represent the entire graph using a coding of the subgraph as a building block. As a result, substructures are considered interesting if they occur often throughout the graph. Applications include finding common subcircuits in integrated circuits, and finding common motifs in protein structures[18].

   SUBDUE has also been used in a supervised mode, where it is given a positive graph and a negative graph, and tries to identify subgraphs that are interesting, in the sense of the previous paragraph, in the positive graph but that do not appear in the negative graph. In other words, it identifies common substructures that appear in one graph, but not in the other.

   Heuristics are used throughout the implementation of SUBDUE to keep the running time polynomial, but it is still an expensive approach to the problem. The need for approximate matching was fully realized by the designers, and so some variability in subgraphs is allowed, but handling this increases the execution time.

   The unsupervised mode is perhaps not very useful in adversarial settings, since the structures of greatest interest will be rare rather than common. The supervised mode is perhaps more useful – using a graph known to be completely normal as the negative graph might make it easier to discover abnormalities in another graph.

2. QGRAPH is a true graph query and update language[19]. A user can issue a query in the form of a subgraph, or a schematic for a subgraph, and the matching subgraphs within the structure will be returned. It is also possible to express a substitution to be made for the queried subgraphs, allowing a graph to be transformed. There is no explicit support for approximate matching, but some of the expressiveness features of queries can achieve similar results, for example, asking for one or more of a particular kind of edge, and for ranges for set-valued attributes.

   QGRAPH can obviously be useful in an adversarial setting when it is known what the subgraph structure associated with adversaries or their actions looks like. However, as we have suggested, this is not always easy to discover, and runs the risk of missing subgraphs whose existence was not suspected.

3. Concept chain graphs[20] are graphs derived from a corpus of documents, showing connections between concepts that are mentioned in different documents. These graphs are built by extracting concepts from each document (using techniques we will discuss in Chapter 7), and connecting documents either when they mention the same concept, or when the concepts are connected via some ontology. Concept chain graphs can be queried either using textual queries asking for the best chain connecting concept A and concept B (together with the textual context justifying each link), or by providing a subgraph query and retrieving all examples of it from the corpus.

   Concept chain graphs are obviously useful ways to extract deep information from text; and could be generalized to other forms of graph data.

Inductive Logic Programming (ILP) was developed as a way to analyze logical relationship data[21]. However, the underlying algorithm is designed to cover or explain an entire graph in terms of a set of smaller templates, and so the approach can be adapted as a way to analyze arbitrary graph data. In ILP applications, interesting results are usually subgraphs that have explanatory power, that is, their instances cover or explain a large part of the graph. In adversarial settings, it may be those subgraphs that explain only small parts of the graph that are actually most interesting[22]. In other words, the subgraphs that have explanatory power are explaining normality, a useful result in itself, leaving those parts of the graph that are somehow anomalous unexplained, as candidates for further investigation.

Telephone call graphs are an interesting special case, first because the information they contain is useful in many different settings, and second because of the challenge they pose because of their size and rate of change. Cortes and Pregibon[23] designed a new way of representing telephone call-graph data to make it easier to query them to find common calling patterns. Instead of preserving the call graph as a graph, they instead turn it into a list, with each row corresponding to a single telephone number. The contents of the row is a list of a subset of the edges incident with that node.

There are two issues in choosing the subset to retain. The first is to handle the rapidly changing data. They do this by weighting each edge by the number of times it has been used, and then joining the most recent day's data to a downweighted version of all of the previous data. The ratio of the relative weight of the historical data can be adjusted to reflect the time period of most interest; for example, in looking for cell-phone fraud, the calling pattern of a new phone needs to be matched against the calling pattern of an older phone over the previous week or two, not over the past year. They also truncate the list associated with each phone at a predefined frequency level, so only the most common calls are reflected in the data.

This 'flattened' form of the graph data makes certain kinds of queries easy to make. For example, it is straightforward to test how much overlap there is in the set of numbers called by a specified set of telephones.

This approach was used successfully to address a number of kinds of telephone fraud, particularly stealing cell-phone service. There are some issues, however, in using it for investigating more sophisticated adversary use of the telephone system. For example, truncating call lists at a given frequency removes rare calls from the data, but it may actually be these rare calls that are the most interesting.

Graph information-retrieval approaches are vulnerable to manipulation because they are looking for particular configurations of nodes and edges, and their associated values; anything that manages to omit one of these pieces can prevent an entire matching subgraph from being detected. They are therefore, in a sense, quite fragile. Probabilistic extensions can probably help, but the problem of graph information retrieval is already so difficult that it may be some time before such extensions can be useful.

6.4.4 Single-Node Exploration

There are many systems that allow exploration in graph data, provided that a starting point is known. For example, there are often certain people known to be of interest, and exploring the graph starting from the nodes that represent these people is a productive way to learn more about the graph. In social-network data, this exploration allows their immediate social circle to be discovered. This can reveal aspects of their lifestyle, for example how many of their social circle are geographically close or remote; how large their social circle is; what the power structure around them is, for example, are their immediate associates of roughly the same power and ability, much greater or much less? Are they in a 'line' or a 'staff' role?

Another application is discovering how far apart the nodes corresponding to two individuals are. Graphs representing the relationships among people tend to have small-world structure, so the expected path length between two randomly chosen people is known. If the measured path length disagrees with this expectation, it may signal useful information or, at least, grounds for further investigation. There are two cases: the nodes corresponding to the two individuals are closer than they 'should be', or they are farther apart than they 'should be'.

The first case occurs when some apparently random circumstance associates two people, and the question is whether it is as random as it appears. For example, insurance fraud is often carried out by collusion: one person steals something or causes an accident, allowing the other person to make an insurance claim. Searching relationship data outwards from the person who makes the claim, for example by following connections based on addresses, telephone numbers, postal or zip codes, or explicit relationships, should not normally reach the other individuals involved in the claim too quickly. If it does, this is a strong signal for fraud. The same approach can be used to evaluate whether two people who appear to meet accidentally are actually meeting with intent.

The second case, when the distance is greater than expected, occurs when a close relationship is expected, but does not appear in the data. This can happen, of course, because some part of the data was not collected, but it may also have happened because of a deliberate attempt to obscure the relationship.

Both cases illustrate the most important limitations of this approach: there must be some reason to choose a starting point, because graphs are typically too big to make starting from every node plausible; and there must be some expectation about the expected or right distance between pairs (or larger sets) of nodes.

Systems such as Netmap[24] and i2[25] are only a couple of literally hundreds of tools that support an analyst in this kind of exploration. These tools are interactive, not automatic. An analyst has to choose a starting point, look at the rendering of the neighborhood of that starting point, and then decide how to expand the search outwards.

Large criminal investigations also rely on similar tools. For example, the Holmes[26] system collects data, both structured and free text, from reports generated during a criminal investigation, and constructs connections between the entities mentioned in them. The system allows the relationships between entities to be explored from any starting point, as well as allowing searches on any text. It can be used to generate investigative actions, as well as to check whether any non-obvious connections have been missed.

Single-node exploration can be manipulated in three ways. Two of them are obvious: omitting paths so that nodes that are actually connected appear not to be; and inserting paths so that nodes that are really unconnected seem to be connected, either diverting suspicion to others or attempting to social engineer the expected path lengths. The third manipulation is more subtle: try to replace the true single node representing an individual by a constellation of nodes whose relationship to the true node is ambiguous. This has the effect of lengthening all of the paths that should pass through the true node, but also increases the uncertainty the analyst has about whether any particular node really corresponds to the person being considered. In other words, smearing the content associated with an individual across several nodes is both a piece of technical engineering to disrupt path lengths, and a piece of social engineering to make sure that the analyst remains overtly aware that nodes do not necessarily exactly correspond to individuals.

Techniques for making the first two manipulations are, by now, obvious – either avoid the (correct) capture of data about particular nodes, or cause false node data to be captured. The third manipulation exploits the human tendency to describe the same things in different ways at different times. We have already alluded to the fact that criminals use this tendency to make sure that details on arrest records and the like are hard to match with other records; by using variant names, and making 'mistakes' such as reversing digits in phone numbers and addresses. Because ordinary people do this innocently, it is hard to force the collection of accurate data. The result is that a set of relationship data can contain records of the form:

John Smith, 123 Main St., Somewhere, 34567, (555) 123 4567
John Q. Smith, 213 Main St., Somewhere, 23657, (555) 123 4576
J. Quincy Smith, Sumwhere, 123 4567

Human inspection might suggest that these records all describe the same person, but even for humans there are going to be some borderline cases. Trying to make these decisions algorithmically is difficult.

The state of the art in handling this issue is the Entity Analytics tool suite from IBM[27]. These tools take an agnostic approach to identity, maintaining different nodes whenever it is not certain that two individuals are the same person, but able to collapse them conceptually during particular kinds of analysis. As new data becomes available about particular nodes, the new data is used to reevaluate the neighborhood of the nodes to see whether decisions about identity can now be refined. They also have the ability to use anonymized forms of identity so that graph data from multiple sources can be analyzed together without violating the privacy of each source.

6.4.5   Unusual-Region Detection

So far, we have considered the neighborhood of a node in terms of the paths that emanate from it, and the nodes that are encountered along these paths. We can also consider the region around a particular node, not only the nodes that are encountered by expanding radially from the starting point, but also the connections among these nodes that we encounter. We have already seen this idea briefly in the social-network measure of *radiality* which measures how often nodes that are encountered in the growing region around a starting node are genuinely new nodes, and how often they have already been seen. We want to be able to answer not only questions such as "how big is the set of people within two steps of a particular person?" but also "how many of these people *also know each other*?". Answers to such questions distinguish the cliquiness of the neighborhoods around particular individuals. Someone who has fifty acquaintances who are mostly unknown to each other is a connector, and very different from a person who has fifty acquaintances who all know each other as well, and so who is a member of a very tightly connected group. As we commented before, the standard cell organization, designed to make it hard to discover members of an underground group is characterized by tighter coupling than usual of immediate connections (the members of the cell), but looser coupling than usual at the next level out. This pattern may be detectable by considering regions.

One successful approach to unusual-region detection is the use of *scan statistics*. Scan statistics are primarily used to estimate the density of points of interest within different regions of space, so that regions with an unusual density can be selected. This idea has been extended to graphs, requiring a modified definition of what local regions are, say all of the edges and nodes within k steps of a given node. A relevant property can be defined on such regions, say the number of edges, or the density of edges, or something like that. The expected value for the property is known, either using an assumption about what normal parts of the graph data are like, using one of the preferential-attachment models, or using knowledge of normal behavior in the problem domain. The value of the property can then be computed for every region of the graph, and regions for which the value is unexpectedly large (or small) can be flagged[28].

The scan statistic can also be normalized for scale, so that the probability of its value exceeding a given threshold is significant, no matter where it occurs. For example, if the scan statistic is the number of steps in the graph required to find a neighborhood that contains at least ten distinct other nodes, then normalization by the degree of the region's central node may be appropriate.

It is difficult to manipulate data to affect scan statistics, because it requires understanding exactly what statistic is being measured and, because the values of the scan statistic are defined over regions, it is hard for an individual to manipulate all of the nodes in a region. Even if the region corresponds to the entire criminal or terrorist group, it is still risky to try to manipulate the data that is captured, because it is hard to judge or guess what a normal region looks like. (This does indicate why it is usually a good idea to use a statistic defined on regions of at least two different sizes, however.)

6.4.6 Ranking on Graphs

Often affinity between graph nodes is a local indication of some more global property that may be of interest, for example power or importance. In such situations it is possible to rank the nodes of the graph according to this emergent property. This provides an alternative approach to social-network properties, but also discovers other kinds of emergent properties that are not usually considered in social-network settings. For example, the approach we are about to describe is used by Google to rank web pages by importance[29]. In the Web, a link to a page is considered an implicit vote for that page's importance.

Suppose we have a graph with weighted edges, and we let each node begin with an equal share of the desired global property. For concreteness, let us assume that the property is importance in the graph. In the first round, each node exports its importance to its neighbors in proportion to the edge weights of each of its edges. In other words, if it has three edges attached, with edge weights 2, 3, and 5, then $2 + 3 + 5 = 10$ so $2/10$ of the importance is exported to the node at the other end of the first edge, $3/10$ to the node at the other end of the second edge, and $5/10$ to the node at the other end of the third edge.

Although importance flows in both directions along each edge, after the first round each node ends up with a different amount of importance – the amount it exported along each edge is not necessarily the same as the amount that came back along that edge, because this amount depends on the degree of the node at the *other* end of each edge.

The process is now repeated for a second round, then for a third round, and so on. With a few mild conditions on the structure of the graph, this process reaches a steady state where the amount of importance at each node stays fixed. The nodes of the graph can then be ranked by how much importance they have accumulated when the process stabilizes. The final, stable distribution of importance reflects something deep about the global structure of the graph.

This stable allocation of importance to the nodes of the graph is actually another way of thinking about an eigenvector of the adjacency matrix, A, that describes the graph, in fact the principal eigenvector. An eigenvector is a vector v with the property that:

$$Av = \lambda v$$

where λ is a constant. From the point of view of importance, λ describes an increase or decrease in the total importance in the graph, but we care only about the relative amount of importance at each node. The power algorithm for computing the principal eigenvector corresponds exactly to the importance-passing algorithm described above: start with a vector of all 1s, multiply the vector by the matrix, divide each entry in the new vector by the sum of the entries (which removes the cumulative effect of the λs), and repeat until the vector does not change any further.

Although this technique is usually initialized so that every node begins with the same importance, it can also be used in a more directed way. The power method for calculating the principal eigenvector guarantees that the eventual distribution of importance to nodes converges to the true importance implied by the global graph structure. However, the rate at which this happens varies, and can be exploited to explore a particular region of the graph. If all the importance is initially allocated to one node, then the stable distribution after a few multiplications describes the global affinity of all of the other nodes to the starting node. If the node is not particularly unusual, the importance will quickly spread out through the whole graph. However, if the node is a member of a well-connected subgroup of nodes, who are not necessarily obviously connected only to each other, then the importance value will spread out in a much more limited way in the first few iterations. Seeing which other nodes acquire significant importance after a few rounds is a way of discovering a group of nodes connected to the initial node and to each other that might be hard to see in other ways. Used in this way, the algorithm can be thought of as propagating *suspicion*, rather than importance, around the graph.

The way in which emergent properties such as importance are distributed across the nodes depends, in detail, on the connection structure of the graph. As a result, it is extremely hard to manipulate a graph or a small piece of a graph, to create a particular outcome, except for a few obvious exceptions. Many people would like their web pages to be ranked higher by search engines. The Google PageRank algorithm[30] uses this importance redistribution approach (with some extra complexities) to decide how to rank pages. It is reasonably resistant to manipulation because the way to improve the score of a particular page is to get other pages to create links to it. Doing this requires actions by *other* people. Unfortunately, it is possible to create link farms, collections of pages that point to each other and to pages that want to increase their rank, and this *does* increase the importance allocated to such pages.

In an adversarial setting, two things are different. First, nodes typically want to *decrease* their importance, making themselves harder to notice.

Second, the links are (almost always) bidirectional, so importance cannot be decreased simply by creating large numbers of outgoing edges and letting importance drain away. The best way not to seem particularly important is to have the same neighborhood structure as many other nodes, but it is not necessarily easy to discover what this is, and may not be easy to construct even if it is known. Also, since the way importance accumulates depends on both local and global properties of the graph, small local anomalies, caused because adversary nodes are somehow different, show up in an unpredictable way in importance scores. In the worst case, a local anomaly may be amplified in a node's importance score, making it unusually high or low and so drawing attention to it. Manipulation in the presence of such subtle properties is difficult.

6.4.7   Graph Clustering

Another common operation that can sensibly be applied to graph data is clustering. The space inhabited by a graph looks, at first glance, to be rather like the geometric space that is used in several clustering algorithms, but there are actually substantial differences.

First, in a geometric space such as those used in clustering attributed data (Chapter 5), the distance between any two objects depends only on properties of the two objects, which is reflected in where they are placed in the space. It is independent of whatever other objects might be present. However, in a graph space the distance between any two objects depends on the lengths of all of the possible paths between them, which is turn depends on the properties of *all* of the other objects that appear along those paths. Looking at it another way, adding a single new object in a geometric space does not change the relationships between the existing objects – but it potentially changes *all* the relationships between the existing objects in a graph space.

This point conceals another much more critical decision, and that is how to extend local affinity, which is defined only for connected pairs of objects, to longer-range affinity between objects that are not directly connected. There is no necessarily correct answer here – it depends on the situation that the graph data is modelling.

For example, we could simply consider the affinity between two objects with only an indirect connection to be the greatest affinity between them along any path that connects them. We used this model in the example graph in Section 6.2. This makes sense if the affinities represent inverse delays or some other property that adds linearly, and where only the shortest path between two nodes is important. However, there are other kinds of affinities where it is necessary to consider not only the 'lengths' of the paths, but *how many* different paths there are. For example, capturing the *influence* one node has on another obviously depends on how far apart they are in the graph, but also on how many different paths there are between them, since influence could travel via all of these paths and have a cumulative effect. Properties like this require a different, more complex, extension of local affinity to global affinity.

The second difference between a geometric space and a graph space is that they are 'inside-out' with respect to one another. Consider a graph with a star shape: one central node connected to each of the other nodes, with the other nodes connected only to the center. From a graph point of view, the center node should clearly be thought of as central. However, its row in the adjacency matrix is filled with non-zero entries, so in a geometric space its position will be far from the origin, with the points corresponding to the other nodes much closer to the origin. Although there is an obvious correspondence between the two views, a twist is required to map one to the other.

Finding clusters in graph data is, in a sense, just the same problem as finding clusters in attributed data. We want to find regions of the graph with high local and global affinity between the nodes within each cluster; and low global affinity for the edges between the clusters. However, global affinity is an emergent property from the local affinities, so it is hard to find such clusters directly. Algorithms based on finding good edges to cut are possible, but it turns out that the best approach is to *embed* the graph in geometric space, and these use geometric-clustering techniques. This corresponds to finding good edge cuts, but is easier both to carry out and to understand as a geometric operation.

An appropriate embedding will be one that takes into account the extension of local affinity to global affinity, and also the necessary inside-out transformation from graph space to geometric space. In a good embedding we need two properties. The first is that the points corresponding to nodes will be placed in geometric space so that nodes connected to each other by high-affinity edges will be close together; and nodes that are not directly connected to each other but that have high global affinity will also be placed close together. The second is that nodes that are well-connected will be placed close to the origin; and nodes that are peripheral in the graph will be placed far from the origin.

In most situations, the best starting place for an embedding of a graph is the *walk Laplacian*. This matrix, W, is obtained from the adjacency matrix by a kind of normalization. Given an adjacency matrix, the off-diagonal entries are negated, the diagonal is filled in using the (weighted) degree, and each row is divided by the (weighted) degree. Figure 6.7 shows the walk Laplacian matrix for the small example from Figure 6.2.

The embedding of the graph into a geometric space is done by computing a singular value decomposition, or eigendecomposition of the walk Laplacian. We will assume an SVD (introduced in Section 5.4.4) to avoid introducing

$$
\begin{bmatrix}
1 & -1 & 0 & 0 & 0 \\
-0.25 & 1 & -0.25 & -0.5 & 0 \\
0 & -0.5 & 1 & -0.5 & 0 \\
0 & -0.5 & -0.25 & 1 & -0.25 \\
0 & 0 & 0 & -1 & 1
\end{bmatrix}
$$

Figure 6.7. *Walk Laplacian of matrix from Figure 6.2 on page 161.*

a new decomposition, and because the singular values are necessarily in decreasing order.

We have a decomposition:

$$W = U S V'$$

where the product US, which is $n \times n$, is the new representation of the graph. Each row can now be interpreted as attributed data, really a position in space, associated with each of the n nodes.

The matrix W is actually of rank at most $n-1$, since if we know the connections for the first $n-1$ nodes, then we know all the connections for the last node as well. Hence only the first $n-1$ columns of US are meaningful, that is, we have embedded the graph in a geometric space of dimension $n-1$. Each row of this matrix is the coordinates of the corresponding graph node in the geometric space. This embedding preserves the local (explicit) and global (implicit) affinities of the nodes in the original graph. It also places highly connected nodes close to the origin, and sparsely connected nodes far from the origin; in other words, it implements the required 'twist'.

Partitioning the geometric space into which the graph has been embedded, for example using a hyperplane, corresponds to finding a normalized cut in the graph. A normalized cut is a good one when it divides the graph into two pieces that are balanced in terms of the number of nodes in each, and the sum of the edge weights in each piece, and this is usually an appropriate way to cluster in most datasets[31].

Just as before, with an SVD, we can truncate the US matrix product to some k columns, and this corresponds to embedding the graph in a geometric space of dimension k in a faithful way. In geometric terms, this can be understood as removing some structure that perhaps reflects noise. In terms of the original graph, this corresponds to removing edges whose presence is least consistent with the affinity structure of the entire graph.

There is one problem that affects all analysis techniques that depend on modelling the way emergent properties flow around graphs. Adding a node that is connected to every other node collapses almost all of the connection structure, since the shortest path between any two nodes is almost certainly the one via the added node. This is, of course, an extreme case, but highly connected nodes like this do exist in real-world datasets. For example, suppose we examine travel patterns of employees because we suspect that a group of them have been meeting secretly off-site or have been meeting with a competitor. If the data includes their travel to their normal workplace, then any more-subtle connections will be overwhelmed by the fact that all employees travel to the same site. Extremely popular films, books, or television shows cause the same problems for systems that try to analyze the buying habits and preferences of consumers. If someone walks down the street greeting everyone they meet, it is much harder to tell whether they have made a covert information transfer.

Adding this kind of data does not cause the same problems in attributed data, because adding a new record does not change the distances between the existing records.

Because highly connected nodes like this do occur in the real world, adversaries can create (or become) such nodes to make themselves harder to detect without necessarily attracting suspicion. For example, if an adversary group wants to make their existence as a group hard to detect in email communication patterns, their members could try to become responsible for sending out large mailings to many people. This creates a structure around them that makes it hard to see the smaller-scale structure of their illicit communication.

There are two ways to address this problem. The first is to remove high-degree nodes from the data before analysis. Although this is conceptually straightforward, it is practically difficult to decide how high is too high – the risk is that too much structure will be removed.

The second way to deal with the problem is to use a better embedding. This can be done by using the embedding described above, but then projecting, in the $(n-1)$-dimensional space, the points onto the unit sphere centered at the origin. The angles between the vectors from the origin to each point on the surface of the unit sphere can then be used as a measure of their affinity – the smaller the angle, the more similar they are [32]. The problem node can be projected only in one direction onto the unit sphere, so the structure around the other nodes projected in roughly the same direction can still be distorted, but the structure of nodes projected in other directions is less distorted, so more subtle relationships can be detected among them. An alternative is to use a different form of embedding based on the pseudoinverse of the Laplacian[33] or minimum rank perturbation theory.

6.4.8 Edge Prediction

Once graph data has been embedded in a geometric space, it becomes possible to ask how close two nodes are, even when they are not directly connected. In other words, we can go from the local affinity of connected nodes, to the global affinity of all nodes, and so back to an estimate of the local affinity of two unconnected nodes[34].

Two unconnected nodes that appear to have a strong local affinity, that is, which are close together in an embedding, suggest that some relationship exists between them – a missing edge that is somehow likely to exist to be consistent with the entire rest of the graph. This might be a covert relationship that the nodes are trying to hide, or a relationship that exists but failed to be captured in the dataset. Another possibility is that it is a relationship that could plausibly exist, but doesn't exist yet. For example, in a graph of collaboration between researchers, such missing edges suggest people who should, or might soon, work together.

Embedding is a way of discovering latent relationships in graph data, relationships that are implicit in the connections and affinities in the entire remainder of the graph. This has two advantages: those who wish to conceal relationships may not realize that the relationships are in fact detectable; and, even if they realize this, it is hard to understand how to reverse engineer the explicit connections so as to hide the implicit ones.

Any graph can be enhanced by adding in some set of predicted edges, and then repeating any of the analyses we have discussed in this chapter. For example, this will improve pattern matching, since edges that were missing, perhaps uncollected, will have been added using edge prediction.

6.4.9 Anomalous-Substructure Discovery

All of the techniques that look for regions of a graph that are somehow unusual require some starting point: either a particular location in the graph from which to start, or some idea or pattern of the kind of unusual structure that might be present. There are some situations where neither of these starting points will be known, and it would still be useful to be able to find regions or substructures that are somehow unusual, and so potentially worth further analysis. To put it another way, we would like to be able to extend the idea of ranking, but so that we can rank substructures by some kind of importance or significance, rather than just ranking nodes. The ability to rank, as we have seen, is a powerful way to find interesting content in data.

Consider again the embedding of a graph into a geometric space, using a walk Laplacian matrix derived from the graph's adjacency matrix. We have already seen that the principal eigenvector of this matrix can be interpreted as a stable allocation of some distributed property to the nodes of the graph. In our example above, we thought of this property as importance. Because of the embedding, in particular the 'twist' introduced by the walk Laplacian, this eigenvector is the one associated with the $(n - 1)$-st eigenvalue and column $n - 1$ of U[35].

Another consistent and useful interpretation of the value allocated to each node in the $(n - 1)$-st column of U is that it represents the amplitude of vibration of that node in a stable standing wave on the graph. In this model, we think of the edges connecting the nodes as exerting a pull on the nodes they connect whose magnitude corresponds to their edge weights, and the graph being struck by a kind of virtual mallet that makes it vibrate. The vibration corresponding to the principal eigenvector is the vibrational mode in which large parts of the graph move small amounts; and the boundaries between different kinds of movement ('up' and 'down') represent the boundaries between clusters.

This idea of vibrational modes of the graph carries over to all of the other eigenvectors as well. The principal eigenvector is the one associated with the smallest non-zero eigenvalue of the decomposition and corresponds to large-scale, small-amplitude vibration. The eigenvector associated with the largest magnitude eigenvalue, which appears as the first column of the eigenvector matrix (U), corresponds to small-scale (typically only a single node), large-amplitude vibration. The magnitudes of the entries in this column of the eigenvector matrix reveal nodes in the graph with unusual local neighborhoods.

Recall that the rank of the embedded graph is at most $n - 1$. Each of the $n-1$ columns of the eigenvector matrix can be interpreted as describing a vibrational mode of the graph when it is struck by a virtual mallet parallel to the corresponding axis in $(n-1)$-dimensional space. Each of these vibrational modes reveals something about the structure of the graph, because how it can vibrate depends on how the nodes are connected by edges.

However, most vibrational modes are hard to interpret because they involve many nodes vibrating by varying amounts. There are three special cases, two of which we have already mentioned:

- The modes associated with the rightmost columns of the eigenvector matrix involve many nodes, but low amplitudes. They capture information about the large-scale structure of the graph.

- The modes associated with the leftmost columns of the eigenvector matrix involve few nodes, with large amplitudes. They capture information about the structures centered around particular unusual nodes.

- The modes associated with the *middle* columns of the eigenvector involve small regions of the graph, typically without obvious centers, and large amplitudes. They capture unusual structures that are unlike those corresponding to the other two modes.

Figure 6.8 is an example that is large enough to show some of these properties. In these graphs, nodes shown in black are vibrating in one direction, while nodes shown in white are vibrating in the opposite direction. Gray nodes are at rest. Differences in the magnitudes of these values are significant, but we ignore them to keep the example simple. Mode 1, corresponding to the leftmost column of U, shows clearly the unusual role of the node that joins the two chains together, acting as a kind of center from which vibrational waves go out along the arms of the graph. Mode 2 still shows that this node is a kind of center for the vibrational pattern. Mode 5 shows a typical middle-eigenvector vibrational mode, with many nodes at rest. Mode 8, corresponding to the rightmost meaningful column of U ($n-1=8$), shows the division of the graph into two clusters, using only a single cut. Mode 7 also shows a division of the graph into two "clusters", but this time requiring a more expensive cut, and with one of the "clusters" in two disconnected pieces. The other modes show other possible structures of interest in the graph. Those with high mode numbers tend to show that regions vibrating in the same direction are connected; those with low mode numbers tend to show that regions vibrating in the same direction are unconnected.

Vibrational modes that are likely to be of interest tend to be those whose overall vibrational energy is quite small. The energy of each eigenvector can be plotted, and this plot used to select eigenvectors for further attention. Figure 6.9 shows the mean absolute values of the entries in each column of the eigenvector matrix, U, showing clearly that mode 5 is a low-energy mode, and so probably interesting.

Another way to find interesting substructure in the graph is to plot the nodes of the graph using the entries of the $n-1$st eigenvector for one axis, and the entries of one of the other eigenvectors for the other axis. An example is shown in Figure 6.10 for the al Qaeda relationship data. The position of each node in the vertical direction is an indication of its importance – the most important nodes are towards the bottom of the figure. The node labelled 1 is Osama bin Laden, and the node labelled 153 is Hambali (who actually *was* more important in the graph of relationships since he linked the Middle East part of al Qaeda to the Indonesian part). The horizontal direction separates nodes based on one particular pattern of vibration, in this case associated with eigenvector 348. This eigenvector happens to separate a number of interesting subgroups: a group associated with Khalid Sheikh Mohammed and the 9/11 bombing (14, 63–66); the LAX plot (Zubaydah, 7, and Ressam, 256); the GIA (Touchent, 223); and a group of Tunisians in the top right (Dahmane, 284).

The main advantage of this kind of search for structural anomalies is that it requires no expectation of what the interesting structures will turn out

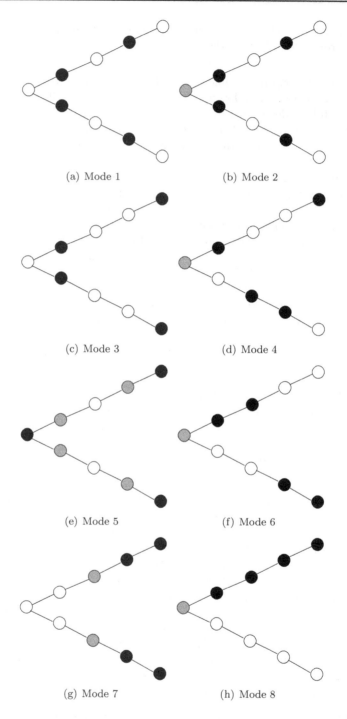

(a) Mode 1   (b) Mode 2

(c) Mode 3   (d) Mode 4

(e) Mode 5   (f) Mode 6

(g) Mode 7   (h) Mode 8

Figure 6.8. *Vibrational modes (standing waves) for a small graph with two paths. Black nodes are vibrating 'up', white nodes are vibrating 'down', and gray nodes are at rest.*

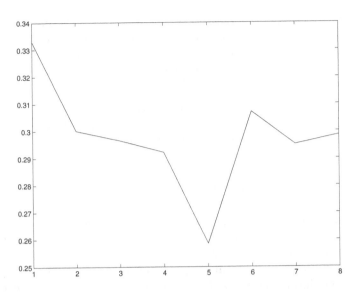

Figure 6.9. *Mean absolute energy for each eigenvector of the example graph.*

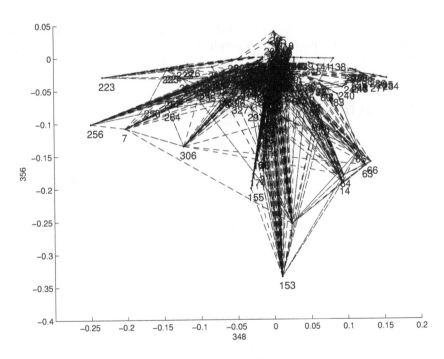

Figure 6.10. *Plot of the al Qaeda relationship graph using axes based on eigenvectors 356 and 348.*

to be. The vibrational modes depend entirely on the structure of the graph, and structures that are repeated often are likely to give rise to high-energy vibrational modes, and so can be ignored. Again, the assumption is that not everything unusual will be due to adversaries, but everything caused by adversaries should show up among the unusual.

It is hard to manipulate the data to try and avoid detection of unusual substructures because the vibrational modes that appear depend on the entire structure of the graph, and so are difficult to affect by local changes.

6.4.10   Graphs and Prediction

Prediction techniques have difficulty with data in which records have some kind of locality or spatial contiguity. For example, suppose that the data records contain some kind of geographic reference as well as the more usual attributes. It is no good training a predictor on the geographical attributes, because then the predictor is useless for similar data collected elsewhere. However, the geographic attributes are probably useful, because records from close locations are more likely to have similar or correlated attribute values, and to belong to the same class.

Very little is known about how to exploit such relational correlation among records. However, using a graph to capture this extra relational information is one way to attack the problem.

6.5   Tactics and Process

Technologies for analyzing relational or graph data are much more patchy than for prediction and clustering of attribute data, so it is not yet possible to give a full account of a robust analysis process. Table 6.1 summarizes the techniques we have discussed with respect to two dimensions: whether their main goal is the selection of interesting parts of the structure, or analysis of either a selected part or of the whole graph; and whether or not some prior information about likely regions of interest, usually nodes, is required. The boundaries between the categories are not hard; for example, social network analysis techniques could also be applied to all the nodes, with the goal of selecting those nodes that warrant further examination.

Almost by definition, the top left-hand corner of the table is empty, since the goal of selection is to provide a set of subgraphs or other structures for further analysis. Much of current relational data analysis takes place in the top right-hand corner of the table – using domain knowledge to generate a set of starting points, perhaps known persons or known configurations of nodes, and then examining all of their occurrences and neighborhoods in the graph.

	Selection	Analysis
Requires a starting place		Information retrieval; Single-node exploration
Requires no prior knowledge	Unusual region detection; Ranking; Substructure extraction; Visualization	Social Network Analysis; Clustering; Visualization

Table 6.1. *Categories of relational/graph analysis.*

While this is productive, it is also limited: because of the possibility of missed instances in the case of information retrieval, and because of the amount of analyst time consumed in the case of single-node exploration.

The bottom left-hand corner of the table is arguably the most significant as the size of relational data grows. The techniques here all try to identify parts of the graph that are somehow interesting: unusual nodes, unusual neighborhoods, or structures that are unusual just because they are rare. The goal of all of these techniques is not to explain the substructures identified, although they do sometimes have explanatory power, but to discover them in large and complex data.

The bottom right-hand corner of the table comprises those techniques that can be applied to an entire set of data, although this may often be too expensive to be practical, or to some selected substructures. As well as these techniques that are directed at explaining the graphical and relational structure, other predictive and clustering techniques can be applied to the data associated with the nodes and edges as well. Edge prediction also belongs in this corner of the table, but has rather a different flavor. It attempts to predict latent or implicit *structure* in the existing graph.

The nature of graph data has both attractive features and dangers from the point of view of analysis. Because there is really no such thing as a local property in graph data, it is extremely hard for adversaries to manipulate the data to get some particular desired effect – it is simply too hard to work out what accessible changes would create the effect. The best that they can do is to try and prevent nodes or edges corresponding to their properties or activities from being captured. On the other hand, graph data is so complex that adversary properties or activities may fail to be noticed because of the complexity of the problem. Much remains to be done in developing more-robust analysis techniques, and ways to reduce the cost of applying them, perhaps by using better selection, or by developing approximating algorithms tuned to retain unusual structure, rather than the more-conventional tendency of such algorithms to retain common structure.

Notes

[1] D.J. Watts and S.H. Strogatz, "Collective dynamics of 'small-world' networks", *Nature*, 393:440–442, 1998.

[2] S.H. Bokhari and A.D. Raza, "Reducing the diameters of computer networks", *IEEE Transactions on Computers*, 35(8):757–761, 1986.

[3] J. Travers and S. Milgram, "An experimental study of the small world problem", *Sociometry*, pp. 425–443, 1969.

[4] The problem with these experiments is that they all rely on asking some senders to try and reach a receiver, and seeing how many steps are on the successful paths. However, the lengths of the *unsuccessful* paths are not known, so the measured path lengths may be too short, that is, underestimated. Interestingly, the vast majority of the successful deliveries reach the receiver via one or two of its immediate neighbors too.

[5] D.B. Skillicorn, *Social Network Analysis via Matrix Decompositions*, in: R.L. Popp and J. Yen, (eds.), *Emergent Information Technologies and Enabling Policies for Counter-terrorism*, chapter 19, pp. 367–392. IEEE Press Series on Computational Intelligence, 2006.

[6] In fact, the additional structure that seems to disturb the overall structure of a graph least is a *path* – so the best way to add connections between adversaries is to connect them together along a chain where each knows one person on either side.

[7] A brief survey of some of the possibilities can be found in T. Coffman, S. Greenblatt and S. Marcus, "Graph-based technologies for intelligence analysis", *Communications of the ACM*, 47(3):45–47, March 2004.

[8] D. Jensen and J. Neville, "Data mining in social networks", Invited presentation to the National Academy of Sciences Workshop on Dynamic Social Network Modeling and Analysis, November 2003 and S. Donoho, *Link Analysis*, in: O. Maimon and L. Rokach, (eds.), *Data Mining and Knowledge Discovery Handbook*, chapter 19, pp. 417–432. Springer, 2005.

[9]For example, a great deal of work has been done using email, particularly since the public release of emails sent to and from employees of Enron, as part of the prosecutions of company officers. Emails reveal connections in different ways: merely by their existence since they are time-stamped arrows *from* one person to *others*; but also by their content, such as the words that are used within the email bodies. See R. McArthur and P. Bruza, *Discovery of Implicit and Explicit Connections Between People using Email Utterance*, in: *Proceedings of the Eighth European Conference of Computer-Supported Cooperative Work, Helsinki*, pp. 21–40, 2003; J. Diesner and K. Carley, *Exploration of Communication Networks from the Enron Email Corpus*, in: *Workshop on Link Analysis, Counterterrorism and Security, SIAM International Conference on Data Mining*, pp. 3–14, 2005; P.S. Keila and D.B. Skillicorn, "Structure in the Enron email dataset", *Computational and Mathematical Organization Theory*, 11(3):183–199, 2005; and J.R. Tyler, D.M. Wilkinson and B.A. Huberman, "Email as spectroscopy: Automated discovery of community structure within organizations", HP Labs, 1501 Page Mill Road, Palo Alto, CA, 94304, 2003, for some results in this area. Details about the Enron emails themselves can be found in B. Klimt and Y. Yang, *The Enron Corpus: A New Dataset for Email Classification Research*, in: *European Conference on Machine Learning*, pp. 217–226, 2004; and J. Shetty and J. Adibi, "The Enron Email Dataset Database Schema and Brief Statistical Report", Technical report, Information Sciences Institute, 2004.

[10]Human social groupings seem to show a preference for size about 150, so much useful work can be done by looking at graphs of about this size. Digital data collection, however, makes much larger graphs available. The implementations of the algorithms to compute SNA measures tend to assume that values are needed for only a few nodes. Computing many of the measures for a single node takes cubic time in the number of nodes in the graph if done poorly (quadratic number of paths ending at the node, linear average path length), so these implementations do not scale. With some cleverness, measure values for all nodes can be computed in quadratic time, which is scalable to quite large graphs, so it is important to use packages that implement the underlying algorithms well.

[11]J.J. Thomas and K.A. Cook, (eds.), *Illuminating the Path: The Research and Development Agenda for Visual Analytics*, IEEE Press, 2005.

[12]These figures are based on relationship data collected by Marc Sageman. I am grateful to him for making it available to me.

[13]A product description and some examples can be found at www.inxight.com/products/sdks/st/.

[14]For example, J. Clark, "XSL Transformation(XSLT): Version 1.0 - W3C Recommendation", November 1999, and J. Clark and S. DeRose, "XML Path Language (XPath): Version 1.0 - W3C Recommendation", November 1999.

[15]M. Harren, B. Raghavachari, O. Shmueli, M. Burke, V. Sarkar and R. Bordawekar, *XJ: Integration of XML Processing into Java*, in: *Proc. WWW2004*, New York, NY, USA, May 2004; S. Boag, D. Chamberlin, M.F. Fernandez, D. Florescu, J. Robie and J. Simeon, "XQuery 1.0: An XML Query Language - W3C Working Draft", February 2005; E. Meijer, W. Schulte and G. Bierman, *Unifying Tables, Objects and Documents*, in: *Proc. DP-COOL 2003*, Uppsala, Sweden, August 2003; and V. Benzaken, G. Castagna and A. Frisch, *Cduce: an XML-Centric General-Purpose Language*, in: *Proc. of 2003 ACM SIGPLAN Int. Conf. on Functional Programming*. ACM Press, 2003.

[16]These goals can be achieved within a single language, but only by introducing a significantly more powerful type system as described in F.Y. Huang, C.B. Jay and D.B. Skillicorn, "Programming with heterogeneous structure: Manipulating XML data using bondi", Technical Report 2005-494, Queen's University School of Computing, 2005.

[17]M. Montes y Gómez, A. López-López and A.F. Gelbukh, *Information Retrieval with Conceptual Graph Matching*, in: *Database and Expert Systems Applications*, pp. 312–321, 2000.

[18]D. Cook and L.B. Holder, "Graph-based data mining", *IEEE Intelligent Systems*, pp. 32–41, 2000.

[19]D. Jensen and J. Neville, *Data Mining in Networks*, in: *Papers of the Symposium on Dynamic Social Network Modeling and Analysis*. National Academy Press, 2002; and H. Blau, N. Immerman and D. Jensen, "A visual language for querying and updating graphs", Technical Report 2002-037, University of Massachusetts Amherst Computer Science Technical Report, 2002.

[20]R.K. Srihari, S. Lankhede, A. Bhasin and W. Dai, *Contextual Information Retrieval using Concept Chain Graphs*, in: *Proceedings of the CIR'05 Workshop on Context-Based Information Retrieval*. CEUR Volume 151, 2005.

[21]S. Muggleton, "Scientific knowledge discovery using inductive logic programming", *Communications of the ACM*, 42:245–286, 1999; and D.B. Skillicorn and Y. Wang, "Parallel and sequential algorithms for data mining using inductive logic", *Knowledge and Information Systems Special Issue on Distributed and Parallel Knowledge Discovery*, 3(4):405–421, 2001.

[22]See, for example, R.J. Mooney, P. Melville, L.R. Tang, J. Shavlik, I de Castro Dutra, D. Page and V.S. Costa, *Relational Data Mining with Inductive Logic Programming for Link Discovery*, in: *Proceedings of the National Science Foundation Workshop on Next Generation Data Mining*, November 2002.

[23]C. Cortes, D. Pregibon and C. Volinsky, *Communities of Interest*, in: *Proceedings of the 4th International Conference on Advances in Intelligent Data Analysis, Springer Lecture Notes in Computer Science 2189*, pp. 105–114, 2001.

[24] J. Galloway and S. Simoff, *Network Data Mining: Discovering Patterns of Interaction between Attributes*, in: *Advances in Knowledge Discovery and Data Mining, Springer Lecture Notes in Computer Science 3918*, pp. 410–414, 2006 and J. Galloway and S. Simoff, *Digging in the Details: A Case Study in Network Data Mining*, in: *Intelligence and Security Informatics, Springer Lecture Notes in Computer Science 3495*, pp. 14–26, 2005. Also see the company web site at `www.netmapanalytics.com.au`.

[25] Examples of the system in use can be found at `www.i2inc.com`.

[26] Home Office Large Major Enquiry System, `www.holmes2.com`.

[27] Examples of the system in use can be found at `www-306.ibm.com/software/data/ips/products/masterdata/eas/`.

[28] C. Priebe, *Scan Statistics on Enron Graphs*, in: *Workshop on Link Analysis, Counterterrorism and Security, SIAM International Conference on Data Mining*, pp. 23–32, 2005.

[29] Details can be found in K. Bryan and T. Leise, "The $ 25,000,000,000 eigenvector: The linear algebra behind Google", *SIAM Review*, 48(3):569–581, 2006, illustrating how important such algorithms can be. The number in the title refers to the expected market capitalization at Google's IPO.

[30] S. Brin, L. Page, R. Motwani and T. Winograd, "The PageRank Citation Ranking: Bringing Order to the Web", *Stanford Digital Libraries Working Paper*, 1998.

[31] These algorithms are collectively known as *spectral* graph algorithms. See, for example, D.B. Skillicorn, *Understanding Complex Datasets: Data Mining with Matrix Decompositions*, CRC Press, 2007, Chapter 4; or U. von Luxburg, "A tutorial on spectral clustering", Technical Report 149, Max Plank Institute for Biological Cybernetics, August 2006.

[32] Actually, the cosine of the angle between the vectors to each point is used. If two vectors point in roughly the same direction, then the cosine of the angle between them is close to 1; if they point at right angles to each other, the cosine of the angle between them is close to 0; and if they point in almost opposite directions, the cosine of the angle between them is close to -1.

[33] See, for example, M. Brand, *A Random Walks Perspective on Maximizing Satisfaction and Profit*, in: *SIAM International Conference on Data Mining*, pp. 12–19, 2005; and M. Brand, "Nonrigid embeddings for dimensionality reduction", Technical Report 2005-117, Mitsubishi Electric Research Laboratories, December 2005, for the use of this approach in detecting consumer preferences for films, where blockbuster movies are seen by many people because they are heavily advertised, but tend to be rated as mediocre. Their presence, however, makes it harder to see other preference relationships.

[34]D. Liben-Nowell and J. Kleinberg, *The Link Prediction Problem for Social Networks*, in: *Proceedings of the Twelfth International Conference on Information and Knowledge Management*, pp. 556–559, 2003, compares the performance of a number of algorithms, ranging from simple to quite complex, for this problem and shows that the connections discovered are often plausible.

[35]Because of the inside-out transformation of the Laplacian, it is now the smallest-magnitude eigenvalues that are most significant. The rank of the Laplacian of an n-node graph is at most $n - 1$, so the smallest eigenvalue necessarily has value zero. There may be other zero-valued eigenvalues as well, and counting them captures the number of connected components in the graph.

Chapter 7

Discovery from Public Textual Data

At first glance, it might seem odd that an adversary group would communicate in a public way. After all, public communication is always revealing, and one of the goals of such groups is concealment – of their existence, of their identity, and of their actions and intentions. Nevertheless, there are several significant reasons why public communication might happen.

The first reason is to create a desired impression of the group in some target audience. Some of the target audiences are:

- Potential members. Communication is designed for recruitment. This is common, for example, in terrorist groups.

- Sympathizers. Communication is designed to position the group in a positive way with some segment of the population. For a terrorist group this might be aimed at motivating active, or at least passive, cooperation, or to raise money. Some groups that indulge in criminal activities, for example pedophiles and drug dealers, have what amount to advocacy groups that aim to change societal opinions about particular crimes.

- Opponents. Terror can be made more effective by adding communication to actual attacks, both to increase the perception of the likelihood and severity of (further) attacks, and to increase uncertainty.

- Themselves. Self-justification is one way to deal with negative emotions that are caused by acting in ways that societies disapprove of. Terrorist groups are prone to proclamations whose purpose seems unfathomable other than as self-justification.

The second reason for public communication is because communication is somehow integral to the adversary activities. Many criminal activities require communication. For example, kidnappers must make it clear that a kidnapping has taken place, and must make some arrangements to collect the ransom. Confidence tricks depend on communication with the victim. Phishing requires communication with the intended victim. Terror attacks are usually followed by claims of responsibility and justifications.

A good example of criminal activity involving large amounts of communication is email spam. It is not difficult for anti-spam software designers to discover the latest tricks that spammers are using to try to get their spam through – this information is revealed by the very mechanism being used.

The third reason is that public communication may be the best way to implement ordinary communication among members of the group. Physically meeting creates a potentially strong signal of both the existence and membership of a group, since they are all in one place at one time. Counterintuitively, it may be cheaper and safer to communicate in a public way than to meet. This is more and more the case for groups that are loosely coupled, and that have no plausible cover reason for meeting, or those who live in societies or socioeconomic settings where personal privacy is non-existent.

Training is another activity that can be done using public communication, completely decoupling the temporal and spatial connection between the trainer, who may be well-known, and students who probably are not, and would like to stay that way.

Just because communication is public does not mean that it gives away everything that the adversaries do. Some of the reasons why public communication can remain effectively private are:

- It may be hard to find the interesting communication in the babble of constant public communication using email, instant messaging, blogs, forums, newsgroups, and web sites.

- Interesting content can be obscured either by making it seem very ordinary, or by making it very cryptic. For example, newspaper classified columns have been used for private communication via a public channel for as long as there have been newspapers.

- Authors can work hard to make sure that a communication reveals only the message that it is intended to reveal, trying to hide other factors such as the identity or character of the author.

Intelligence analysts and law-enforcement officers have many opportunities to examine communications generated by adversaries to see what can be learned from them. For example, psychological profiling is used in situations involving extortion to decide whether the threat is real or not. In this chapter, we will look at algorithmic ways to extract knowledge from communications.

7.1 Text as it Reveals Internal State

Communication can take place via a number of channels of different degrees of richness. For example, communication via high-definition video or direct observation includes not only the direct textual content of the communication, but also a large amount of side-channel information such as facial expressions and body language. Communication using speech includes not only the textual content, but also the speed, rhythm, and intonations that are used, and possibly the presence of an accent. Communication using an instant-message channel includes not only the textual content, but also the rhythm of the interactions between the two ends. Email includes only the textual content, but is usually written in a single pass, without editing. Formal writing includes only the textual content, but usually in a sanitized way, since it may have been edited carefully.

In this hierarchy of means of communication, the richest channels contain the greatest variety of signals from which useful knowledge could be extracted, while the poorest channels are limited to words used in a particular sequence. Extracting knowledge from richer channels is more difficult because of the greater volume of data, and the deeper level of analysis required. We will assume, in what follows, that we are dealing only with text, and that data gathered has been reduced to a textual form. For example, speech-to-text is now quite robust, so telephone calls and other forms of speech are included. Although we are considering text, this does not mean that we consider only text written in well-formed sentences: text from speech is filled with "um"s and other semi-linguistic features, and text from email and instant messaging is extremely informal.

Text is produced by humans in an amalgam of conscious and unconscious processes. When we speak or write, we intend to convey some specific content, and often we want to impose some tone on the way in which the content is expressed. Conscious choice is clearly relevant. However, the exact details of how a high-level idea of desired content comes out in specific sequences of words is largely a subconscious process. As a result, text reveals two aspects of the author: one related to the author's ideas about the purpose of the communication, and the other a kind of leakage of the content of the author's mind as it influences the subconscious creation process.

This hidden content is revealed in features such as:

- The sequence and order in which ideas, concepts, and words are produced;

- The actual choices of words used, especially when choices convey essentially the same meaning; and

- The way in which content usually considered as below the level of meaning, for example punctuation, is arranged.

Given an assignment to write about a particular topic, each person will write something slightly different, expressing the ideas in different ways, in a different order, and with a different emphasis. There are usually many different words that mean roughly the same thing, and each of us gets into habits of using one rather than another. Finally, we each use the machinery of a language with greater or lesser facility – for example, the choice of whether or not to put a comma at a particular place depends on an internal judgement about the flow of the sentence that is often mediated by an internal audible voice.

These differences provide information that distinguishes one person from another. Some of these markers are stable, over the medium term at least, and so provide a reliable way to indicate who generated a particular text. These markers tend also to be stable across content domains so that it becomes possible to detect that the same person wrote two different texts, even in very different contexts.

Other properties of text change depending on shorter-term variations in the internal state of the author, and so are reliable ways to understand properties such as intention, emotion, or level of arousal.

It is helpful to think of human communication as happening via two different channels. The first, which we might call the *content channel*, conveys the content of a communication via the 'big words', primarily nouns and verbs, and is the channel that we apprehend directly as readers or hearers. This channel involves the conscious minds of the author and reader, but also their subconscious minds; and its properties depend in a stable way on who the author is. The second channel, which we might call the *internal-state channel*, conveys a great deal about the internal state of the author, including both emotional state and intentions. The information in this channel is carried primarily by the 'small words', such as conjunctions, auxiliary verbs, and adverbs, which are usually viewed as less significant to the meaning of a text. Both author and reader tend to be blind to this channel, making it an extremely powerful way to extract knowledge from communication. In this chapter, and Chapter 8, we focus on the content channel. We will examine ways to extract knowledge carried by the internal-state channel in Chapter 9.

7.2 Goals

The goals of analyzing public communication mirror the dichotomy between prevention and detection that recur throughout knowledge discovery in adversarial settings. If the primary goal is prevention, then we can consider that the available data consists of large amounts of text, from which we want to extract infrequent, but important, pieces of knowledge. If the goal is detection, then we can consider that the text has been selected and collected because it is probably already relevant to the task at hand.

In the first case, the most important part of the problem is finding relevant information in what can easily be a vast sea of available text. Once found, more-sophisticated analysis can be applied to extract knowledge about content, authorship, or metainformation. In the second case, finding relevant content is less important; analysis is the central task.

A second dimension is the extent to which the analysis is hypothesis-driven or not. In some settings, it may be clear, for example, which topics are of interest; in others, this may not be known in advance. This dichotomy about whether to think about knowledge discovery as discovering the relevance of content to an existing ontology, or as discovering an emergent view of content has resulted in two, often quite distinct, streams of research.

More typical, perhaps, is an alternation between inferring plausible hypotheses, seeing to what extent the textual data supports them, and revising them, in an interactive way.

7.2.1   Finding Texts of Interest

When many documents are collected, the challenge is to find the subset that is interesting, and worth further analysis. The problem is, in many ways, similar to that of finding the most-suspicious objects in a set. Rather than trying to find exactly the subset of interesting or suspicious documents, the task is better posed as ranking documents by how interesting or suspicious they are, and then deciding, in a subsequent step, where to draw a boundary between those that will be looked at further and those that will be discarded.

The obvious first step to discovering documents of interest is to develop a list of words that are deemed interesting, and then to select messages that contain those words. For example, in 2000 the German Federal Intelligence Service[1] had a list of terms that were used to select intercepted communications for further analysis. The terms could be categorized as nuclear proliferation terms (2000), arms trade terms (1000), terrorism terms (500), and drug-related terms (400).

A simple scoring function can be applied to each communication so that those that contain an appropriate number of words from such a watch list are selected for further attention. It is probably sensible to have a threshold so that a communication that uses only one or two words is not selected; it may also be sensible to have an upper bound, since some people insert large numbers of what they believe to be suspicious terms as a form of protest against interception.

The problem with using a watch list is that it is hard to develop such a list and ensure that it contains all of the words that might be of interest. This is another version of the problem already alluded to: it is difficult to guess every possible kind of attack.

A better approach is not to rely on a watch list, but rather to rank documents by how unusual they are on the basis of their entire word usage, within some set of similar documents. This approach can be extended by using some large set of words that might conceivably make a document more interesting without having to be especially careful that this set is exactly right. Once the documents are ranked, the most unusual can be selected for further attention. As before, unusual does not necessarily mean suspicious, but common does tend to mean normal.

Adversaries will, of course, be aware of simple selection mechanisms such as a watch list. In settings where they know their audience, strategies such as replacing words that might be on a watch list by other, more innocuous words become possible. We consider this in greater detail in the next chapter. However, if the communication is intended for a wide, unpredictable audience, the content must be more or less intelligible. Various forms of locutions, such as slang, or specialized religious language, have been used historically, but these work to protect the content from the casual reader rather than from motivated opponents.

Spam provides an interesting special case. Words that are likely to trigger spam filters are often replaced by words whose appearance is similar to the original word but which, as character strings, are gibberish. For example, "Viagra" might be replaced by "V!agra", which remains intelligible to human readers but is more difficult for spam-filtering software to recognize.

7.2.2   Finding Content

The second goal of examining documents is to understand their content, broadly defined. Some of these techniques are, or may soon be, efficient enough that they could be applied to an entire set of documents before any selection of the interesting subset is made. Selection of the interesting subset could then be made on the basis of higher-level or more abstract representations of each document's content.

Although the 'content of a document' seems like a simple idea, there are actually many different kinds of knowledge that can be extracted from documents and could be called their content. We will now examine these in turn, starting with techniques that look for the plain content of documents, then techniques that look for the structure(s) that relate content within documents, and finally techniques that look at why the content is the way it is, that is, why the author chose to create the content and structure in a particular way.

- **Entities**. The entities are the important people or people-substitutes (organizations, places, objects) referred to in a document. Knowing who these 'players' are provides a quick sense of the importance of the rest of the content of the document. In English, entities are almost always signalled by the use of initial capital letters, since they are usually referred to by name. However, it is not trivial to find these named entities. For example, the same person may be mentioned near the beginning of a document as "Mr. John Smith", later as "John Smith", and then as "Smith" and it is important to realize that this is one entity, not three.

- **Concepts**. Concepts are the nouns or noun phrases that are particular to a given document. There will usually be several concepts for each document, and together they provide some indication of what the document is about.

- **Topics**. A topic is a short description of what a document is about. Unlike a concept, the words used to describe a topic may not actually have been used in the document. Such a simple description makes it possible to recognize when several texts are about the same thing, and may also be enough for rapid filtering by a human.

- **Summarization**. A summary aims to condense the content of a document into as short a form as possible, a kind of précis. This is easy to do fairly well, for example the snippets often provided by search engines with each returned URL, but much more difficult to do well.

- **Relationships**. Relationships connect some of the objects mentioned in the document together in some intelligible way. For example, a document may show that a person (named entity) has visited a place (named entity) on a particular day. Relationships indicate connections implicit or explicit in a document. Relationship information is revealed by the verbs in a document which show what the connections between the nouns are. Times are also important for showing relationships between entities. Even adverbs may be useful as they show some aspect of the quality of relationships.

- **Narrative**. At a higher level, and perhaps across documents rather than within each one, a useful goal is to understand the conversation that a set of messages represents, or the wider story that the set of documents describes. This, of course, builds on detecting the players involved and how they are connected to each other, but also looks for higher-level structures that may be of much greater interest than the individual pieces. This is a fundamental task for any analyst, but it is worthwhile seeing how much of this burden can be taken up by software. A narrative is a kind of summary of the document in a way that produces a rich awareness of the situation described by the document. The narrative

aims to strip away the extraneous and repetitive in the document, or set
of documents, but leave enough to provide a fully rounded description.

- **Intention**. Intentions are related to narratives, but focus more on the
  author than on the audience: why is the communication taking place;
  why this audience; why this language; why this content? This can help
  to understand how much of the content is believed by the author, and
  how much is being crafted to appeal to a particular audience.

- **Detecting Slant and Spin**. In a similar vein, it may also be useful
  to understand how the communication is received both by its intended
  recipients, and perhaps by others, and why it works as it does.

7.2.3   Finding Authors

The third goal of examining texts is to find out who wrote them. If nothing
is known about group membership, identifying authors at least provides information about how many people are participating. Being able to identify
authors who produce texts in different contexts is also extremely useful, since
they may not be as security-conscious in some contexts as others. For example, predators have been detected by noticing that the same individuals were
posting in teen chatrooms and predator discussion web forums.

7.2.4   Finding Author Properties

Being able to discover properties of authors other than their identities is also
useful. Because so many language properties have a subconscious component,
authors reveal their mental state and, indirectly, the mental state of other
members of their group when they write or speak. They may also reveal
something of their personal history, for example their first language, which
may aid in identifying them. Psychological profiles can be built, perhaps
revealing something about motivation and likely action.

7.2.5   Finding Metainformation

The fourth goal of examining texts is to glean extra information from the
information associated with the text, other than its content. This can include
the time and place where it was created, the place where it becomes public and,
for sets of related communications, how often they occur. These properties of
communication can provide extra insights into the structure and properties
of adversary groups.

7.3 Outline of Textual-Analysis Technology

Text comes from broadcast speech, from intercepted telephone calls, from email, from instant messaging, from web forums and blogs, from web sites, from news media, and from more-formal writing such as magazines and books. The number of emails sent per day probably exceeds 100 billion, although a huge percentage of those (perhaps more than 90%) are spam. The number of telephone calls per day is at least 20 billion. Large search engines claim to index billions of web pages, and this does not take into account the content that is created by commenting within existing web pages, nor the fact that page content can change without the page itself changing.

The different forms of texts cover a spectrum, from formal writing that follows a reasonably well-understood set of rules and so can be parsed effectively, to extremely informal texts that have little consistent syntactic structure and use vocabulary that evolves quickly. Some forms are created on the fly, which tends to make them more revealing of the subconscious thoughts of their authors; and some undergo extensive editing, allowing an opportunity for authors to try harder to remove traces of properties they would rather not reveal. (It isn't clear that such sanitizing actually helps.) So there are many different forms of text to be considered. We, as humans, can understand all of them, which can mislead us about how substantial the differences among them really are.

The available vocabulary in many languages, but especially English, is also extremely large. The working vocabulary of English has been estimated at around 100,000 words, but technical terms, acronyms, and other pseudowords probably at least double this, and perhaps even triple it. At least in informal communication, bilingual authors tend to include words and fragments from other languages when these are hard to translate, which further increases the number of words that might be present in a given text. So the number of words to be considered when analyzing text is very large.

The rules for native speakers of a language are complex and hard to encode, even for other humans. This makes it extremely difficult to distinguish normal, intelligible, but perhaps informal texts from 'word salad' that might have been deliberately generated to make the analysis task harder.

Human comprehension uses deep features of texts. It is extremely stateful, depending on extensive information about connotations of words as well as their explicit meanings, background about humans as individuals that is used routinely to disambiguate statements, and models of human culture that provide a context for interpretation. The importance of these abilities is illustrated by the difficulty those suffering from autism have in understanding ordinary communication[2].

Algorithmic 'understanding' of text, in contrast, must rely on shallower markers. Although this can, to some extent, be supplemented by powerful

	the	and	have	they	lay	vital	aids	scamp	evilly
doc1	5	4	2	1	0	0	0	0	0
doc2	4	4	0	2	0	0	0	0	0
doc3	7	0	1	0	1	0	0	0	0
doc4	3	3	1	1	0	1	0	0	0
doc5	3	1	0	0	0	0	1	0	0
doc6	6	1	1	1	1	0	0	0	0
doc7	8	2	3	0	0	0	0	1	0
doc8	5	0	1	0	0	1	0	0	1

Table 7.1. *An example of a table describing word frequencies in a set of documents.*

algorithms, the state of the art is that algorithms have difficulty extracting meaning from text. In adversarial settings, we can expect these difficulties to be increased.

However, algorithms are complementary to human understanding of texts because they can see features of texts that humans do not see. For example, as humans we are so well adapted to extracting meanings that we find it difficult to see the syntactic markers that carry those meanings. A good author can convey emotion or tone, but most readers would find it difficult to explain how it was done. In contrast, algorithms are able to 'see' such markers better than humans, even trained humans.

7.3.1 Exploring Content

The most common form in which textual data is analyzed is to extract, from the text(s), a document-word matrix. This matrix has one row for each document which might, in this context, be an entire document in the usual sense, or a meaningful piece of one, such as a paragraph or a single sentence. The matrix also has one column for each word, and its ijth entry describes the frequency of the jth word in the ith document. Each row of the matrix is a kind of profile of the corresponding textual object. Other attributes can, of course, be included. For example, the frequency of punctuation symbols might be useful as well, so extra columns can be added for punctuation symbols. An example is shown in Table 7.1. Some words, for example "the" and "and", are common; others, for example "scamp" and "evilly", are very unusual. Each column provides, in effect, a list of the documents in which its word appears, and so is a kind of index entry for the set of documents.

The entries of the matrix are usually normalized in some way to compensate for the varying lengths of different documents. This is actually quite difficult, because there are, roughly speaking, two different kinds of words. The first kind are machinery words – the longer the textual object, the more times they will tend to occur. For example, a common word like "the" occurs, on average, about every ten words. One sentence twice as long as another is likely to contain about twice the frequency of "the"s. Dividing the occurrence frequencies of such words by the length of the message provides an estimate of their relative frequency, which might be useful to measure because it varies from one author to another.

The second kind of word bears more meaning, and so the number of times it occurs in a sentence is significant in an absolute sense, regardless of how long the sentence is. If one sentence is twice as long as another, the same frequency in both sentences has the same significance. For these words, dividing by the length of the textual object obscures the importance of the frequency signal. Unfortunately, it is not easy to distinguish the two different kinds of words, so normalization often requires careful thought.

Even for a small collection of documents, such a matrix can have a very large number of columns, perhaps 100,000 as discussed above. However, most documents do not contain most words, so the matrix will be extremely sparse; that is, almost all entries will be zeroes. Both the size and the sparsity create difficulties for subsequent analysis, so it is helpful to try and reduce the matrix by eliminating less-useful words. For example, almost all documents will contain the commonest words, in English words such as "the" and "a", so the columns that correspond to them can be removed with little loss of information. Obviously, once a matrix has been created, columns that are filled entirely with zeroes, that is, those corresponding to words that did not occur in *any* document, can be eliminated. In some contexts, words whose total occurrence frequency across all documents is low can also be eliminated, although this should always be done with caution. Another approach is to compare the frequency with which each word occurs in the entire collection of textual objects with its expected frequency in the language being used, and keep only those words that occur more often than expected since they may represent the working vocabulary of the document set.

In synthetic languages, such as English, word order carries most of the meaning, so throwing it away by recording only word frequencies is a substantial loss of information. Unfortunately, preserving the word-order information is difficult. The sequence of words in a typical sentence consists of a few common words, followed by a less common word, but followed immediately by further common words, and so on[3]. Hence collecting contextual information, such as the frequencies of pairs of adjacent words, provides very little new information. If the pair contains two common words, then the pair is typically common too. If the pair contains a common word and a rare word, the frequency of the pair is close to the frequency of the rare word, and so provides little new information. And pairs of rare words almost never occur.

Looking at longer sets of contiguous words, such as adjacent triples, fails because there are too many possibilities. In one experiment[4], word triples were extracted from newly created news stories. Such triples might, intuitively, have been expected to be reasonably common – news stories are not known for their use of novel English phrases. However, when these triples were checked against existing search-engine data, almost half of them had never been recorded before. This shows that there are a very large number of word triples in common use, and existing estimates of their frequencies, even from very large sets of documents, are so poor as to be unusable.

On the other hand, word endings are not so important in languages like English, so it is common to apply *stemming*, that is treating words built from the same root word, such as *develop*, *developed*, and *developing*, as the same word. This reduces the number of columns required by a significant amount.

Analytic languages, such as Finnish, have opposite problems. Word order is not so important (or, more accurately, carries nuances of meaning rather than the primary meaning) but word endings, inflections, are critically important. Using a table of word frequencies loses less of the meaning, but separate columns may be required for all the different versions of nouns and verbs with their different endings.

A further complication is that, in most languages, words and meanings do not match in a one-to-one way. Different words can mean essentially the same thing, for example "car" and "automobile", or "doctor" and "physician", so that documents that are really about the same thing may look different because they use different words. On the other hand, the same word can have several different literal meanings, for example "bear" as in carrying and "bear" as in animal in the woods; not to mention the metaphorical meanings that many words can have. Words like this make textual objects seem similar when they are in fact quite different. When we, as humans, read documents, we rely on context to sort out these different possibilities, but even humans can find it difficult. A well-known example is the sentence "time flies like an arrow but fruit flies like a banana", which requires the reader to reinterpret the meaning of both "fruit flies" and the second occurrence of "like". Many jokes also rely on utterances with multiple meanings that have to be reinterpreted partway through.

In an adversarial setting, content can be concealed by replacing some words by others. However, this must be done in such as way as to preserve the meaning, at least for the intended audience. There is therefore a difficult and, as we shall see, intractable tension between concealment and revelation.

7.3.2 Exploring Authorship

Identifying who wrote a particular textual object can also be done from the way in which words, and other syntactic markers, are used. Because understanding the meaning of the text is not important, the problem is perhaps slightly easier. Multiple words that mean the same thing do not need to be resolved – in fact, the choice to use one rather than another may be a critical feature in determining authorship. Shallow markers such as punctuation also become more important precisely because they carry little of the meaning, and so individuals are free to use them in different ways without jeopardizing the meaning.

In a way, the *content* of a document may blur the signature of each author, since different people writing about the same topic are forced to use many of the same words. Hence the document-word matrix used for authorship may focus on many of the smaller markers in the texts.

In an adversarial setting, an author may try to conceal his or her identity or other characteristics by consciously trying to alter word-usage patterns. This is extremely difficult because so many of these patterns are subconsciously generated, and attempts to manipulate them consciously may even backfire and create unusual patterns.

7.3.3 Exploring Metainformation

The availability of metainformation depends very much on how the textual data is generated and collected. In most electronically-mediated settings, it is straightforward to get information about where and when text was created and transmitted, and sometimes by whom.

Most of the mechanisms, however, are easy to subvert. For example, cell-phone call data includes both the calling and called number, but stolen cell phones and SIM cards are readily available in most countries, and phones whose owners are not recorded can also be bought in many countries, so it is simple to conceal the originator's identity. Email addresses are also simple to conceal by using one of the web-based email services or by spoofing the sender address. Concealing IP addresses is more difficult, because communication usually requires establishing a virtual channel from one end to the other, and IP addresses can often be mapped back to locations and service providers. However, techniques for concealment are in common use. In many settings, screen names are not just common but expected, providing opportunities to conceal authors' identities.

In general, all communication comes with some form of envelope that has the potential to convey extra information. This extra information can be concealed or confused, with some awareness and care. The *existence* of the communication is harder to conceal, for the intended audience must be able to find it, so it may be more difficult to hide properties such as the total volume of communication between two people, or emanating from one person. Much of this data is naturally transformed into attributed data or relationship data and can be analyzed using the techniques of previous chapters.

7.4   Concealment Opportunities

We have already touched on many of the concealment strategies available to adversaries. They all aim to undermine the ability to find and analyze public communication to learn about those who created them. These strategies are:

- Rely on being hard to find. Because there are so many telephone calls, so many emails, so many web postings, the adversaries can hide their communications and documents in the vast noisy collection of other documents.

- Rely on making the content look as if it means something other than it does. This is the strategy to defeat all of the different forms of content extraction, but it is fundamentally difficult, since the intended meaning must be apparent to the intended readers.

  There are two diametrically opposed strategies: disguise the content so that it looks innocuous, or disguise the content so that it is so cryptic that it cannot be straightforwardly understood. Which one is better to use depends on what kind of threat the author imagines, and how robust concealment in the noise is expected to be.

  If the message can be conveyed without using any adversary language, then the communication is both likely not to be discovered, and likely to be ignored if noticed. On the other hand, if the message does not seem to make sense at all, it may be written off as the work of a crank or eccentric. This is inherently a more dangerous strategy for two reasons: the cryptic content may actually draw attention to the text; and if the text is to be intelligible to its intended audience, it is probably also intelligible (eventually) to their opponents.

  For example, one way to replace named entities is to use very general names such as "the place" and "the leader". This may be effective in propaganda where the real names that these stand for are already understood, but they are not very useful for planning an attack, since the risk of miscommunication is high. At the other end of the spectrum, the named entities could be replaced by very specific names such as "TZ" or "GL", which are unambiguous to those who know what they mean, and unintelligible to everyone else. But what channel can be used to disseminate these coded names to the readers in the first place?

Similar problems make it difficult to conceal the concepts that are discussed in a document. There are, however, some possibilities for derailing the extraction of topics and summary by including irrelevant content, as long as it is obvious to the intended audience which part of the content is irrelevant.

Relationships are harder still to conceal, partly because it seems intrinsically harder to substitute for verbs and still leave the content intelligible: verbs with similar meaning are too similar, while verbs with different-enough meanings are difficult to understand. Imagine trying to remove the relationship that a particular person was going to *visit* a particular place. Any verb with a sense of motion probably fails to conceal the relationship; but other verbs such as "decorate", "address", and so on completely obscure the intent.

Narrative extraction may well discover attempts to prevent summarization by including irrelevant content, since the extra content almost certainly disrupts the narrative. Conversely, attempts to prevent narrative extraction by, for example discursive digressions, may result in the digressions being excised by the summarization.

Concealing intention is even more difficult, as we shall see in Chapter 9, although attempts to conceal content may make it harder to discover intention.

- Rely on hiding who authored the documents or the author's properties. One way to do this is to use multiple authors, hoping to smear any signature that each author would create individually. This is slightly dangerous, since it may create a text that looks unusual precisely because of the differences in signature in different parts.

  Another approach is to use intermediaries, either human or algorithmic, as another way to smear author stylistic features. Asking someone else to write the actual text from a précis may conceal an author's habits. Using automatic translation to another language and back again may hide such features, and also features that might reveal the author's native language.

  One author using multiple identities can also make the problem harder. This strategy can be used to make a group seem larger and more powerful than it is; to make it less obvious that the espoused view is held only by a small minority; and to confuse attempts to understand the command and control structure of the group. It relies on the existence of only a single author behind the apparent multiple authors being able to remain undetectable, which is a dubious assumption.

7.5   Technologies

In this section, we examine the technologies that are being used to extract knowledge from text. Many of these technologies have existed for a long time, but what they chiefly show is how difficult it is to understand natural language, especially when it is used informally. Knowledge discovery from text in an adversarial setting has received attention only recently, except perhaps in some classified settings, so results for this special case are still limited.

7.5.1   Collecting Textual Data

At one time, collecting textual data involved reading physical newspapers and magazines, and intercepting physical mail. Now almost all text is either generated or transmitted in some electronic way, and much of it ends up stored digitally. This means that, in a broad-brush sense, collecting textual data is straightforward. The problem is really that there is so much that could be collected.

Much of the content of the web is already collected by, among others, search engines which determine the key words within each document, and build an index that is used to satisfy search queries. The technology to do the required collection relies on the fact that the protocols required by a browser or other tool to access textual content can also be executed by other software (called spiders or web crawlers) that then stores the accessed text rather than displaying it on a screen.

Some content is protected by requiring, for example, a password to access it. However, the content itself is often in a public place on the computer that holds it – all that is missing is an access path to find it. Although web crawlers associated with search engines do not do so (by agreement), there is no technical obstacle to accessing any file in a public directory. It may be possible to distinguish between an access via a browser and human, and one by a web crawler based on the timings of the requests for subpages. A web crawler can, however, be programmed to simulate human-like response times, so there is no practical way to restrict access only to browsers.

Most web servers implement password protection at the level of directories (folders), but do not check permissions recursively. If the name of a subdirectory can be guessed, which it often can by context or because of a common structure, then its contents can be discovered without a password.

Some web content is hidden by not having any links to it from other sites. Since web crawlers begin from a few 'central' sites and follow links, such sites are never discovered, and so never appear in search-engine results. The only way to find them is to know their URLs and enter them directly in a browser.

Another way to hide content from search engines is to have the content of each page generated automatically when a browser requests it. This makes it difficult for a web crawler to collect it, especially as checks can be made to see whether the request comes from a browser or some other piece of software. Other restrictions, such as insisting that the request come from a particular range of IP addresses, can also be imposed, although the use of proxies makes this potentially ineffective.

A more robust way to make content available but hide it from easy view is to use a protocol other than the web standard HTTP protocol as the access method. This requires those who want to access the content to use a different non-standard browser or other software tool to access the content. Peer-to-peer systems often use this approach to provide some level of concealment of content, but it is hard, in practice, to control who can get access to the software.

The bottom line is that there are many ways to publish content with the aim of restricting access to some people. However, these mechanisms are not robust, so content creators ought always to assume that the content is effectively public. Content that someone can get is content that anyone can get.

An exception may be concealing content inside a virtual world. Some of these virtual worlds, for example *Second Life*, are hosted by businesses that keep some track of who is using their world. However, new virtual-world systems such as the Multiverse[5] allow anyone to host a virtual world, and make it possible to teleport from one virtual world to another (or even within a single virtual world). Such systems are like the Web; they provide a network of virtual worlds through which any user can navigate using a client that plays the role of a browser.

Virtual worlds create many of the same opportunities for covert communication that the real world does, with some extra opportunities as well. The host of a virtual world can reveal hidden content to some visitors and not to others, for example by requiring the visitor to interact with an in-world avatar using a password, passphrase, or arbitrarily complex conversational template. Content may be hidden in locations in the virtual world that are hard to discover without previous knowledge.

The host of a virtual world can, of course, know everything that goes on in that world. Adversaries can set up virtual worlds for ordinary purposes that act as a cover for covert communication, and it may be hard to detect this from the outside.

A user can, in a sense, be followed from virtual world to virtual world, just as an individual can be followed in the real world. However, this virtual surveillance is much more difficult. Distance is not a necessary feature – an avatar can communicate with any other in the virtual world without being virtually close to it, so it is hard to 'see' with whom an avatar is communicating. The teleporting gateways from one virtual world to another are bottlenecks through which every individual must pass, and it is not necessarily obvious where each gateway goes. A virtual world hosted by adversaries may be crashed after an adversary has used it to teleport somewhere else, preventing anyone else from following.

The fundamental difference between a network of virtual worlds and the Web is that anyone can download a web page's source and see all of the functionality it contains – especially the other pages it links to and its content. A virtual world encapsulates its functionality in program code whose source cannot be accessed, and which cannot be forced to follow particular paths. This makes the properties and behavior of a virtual world much harder to analyze in a static way. This is new technology and requires high-end hardware and bandwidth to be usable at present. However, it seems likely that it will become more common.

A practical problem for collecting and analyzing text is the volume that could be collected. It may be difficult to store enough textual data for long enough to allow sophisticated analysis, or to allow retrospective analysis of data from the past.

7.5.2   Extracting Interesting Documents from a Large Set

Extracting simple content from texts is the core competence of search engine businesses. A typical search engine is based on:

- Crawling the web, collecting web documents in a wide variety of formats;

- Extracting every word from each document;

- Building an inverted index for each word, providing a list of all of the documents that contain it; and

- In response to each search query, selecting a list of documents that contain the specified words, and returning them in a useful order.

Search businesses are differentiated primarily by how they implement the final stage, putting the search results in a useful order, because there are typically hundreds of thousands of relevant pages for any particular query. The earlier stages use well-understood information-retrieval technology that is more or less common to all search businesses.

Search engines are the simplest way to select an interesting set of documents from a larger set, as long as the criterion for selection is the presence of a particular set of words that makes each document interesting. (Actually, each document must satisfy a boolean expression over a set of words so that it can be, for example, the presence of one word and the absence of another that makes a document interesting.)

Search engines play an important role in textual analysis because they do much of the messy work and make the results more directly available for analysis. Of course, there are reasons why, for example, intelligence analysis might duplicate some of this work. Retrieving content hidden using the mechanisms described in the previous section is one reason.

Search-engine technology is limited in two important ways. First, the standard presentation of the results is as a list, a list that has been quite carefully ordered, but still just a list. Second, although there are techniques that will help, most search engines do not do very well resolving the problems of multiple words describing the same thing, or the same word describing multiple things.

Some search engines address these issues by clustering the results based on the word-use profile of each returned document. This addresses the first problem by allowing the results to be presented in a more intelligible way, perhaps even as a visualization of the clusters. It addresses the second problem because using the entire set of words in a document to cluster it with others helps to disambiguate those particular words that are problematic, and so to diminish their confusing effect. For example, a search at Vivisimo[6] using the search term "bear" returns clusters for (among others) black bears, brown bears, teddy bears, the Chicago Bears football team, and the ex-brokerage Bear Stearns. This level of technology is easily adapted for counterterrorism and law enforcement.

A more direct way to select and analyze texts of interest is to use watch lists of words of interest, and retrieve only documents that contain (an appropriate number of) such words. This dramatically reduces the size of the problem, and may allow for deeper analysis to be applied to the selected documents simply because there are fewer of them. However, as discussed above, there are risks associated with using such a simple selection method. This, of course, is just a specialized version of using a search engine, but it is not normally implemented in the same way.

All of the preceding selection techniques work only if it is known in advance which words make a document interesting. If this is not the case, singular value decomposition can be applied to the document-word matrix to produce a representation with a point corresponding to each document. As before, distance from the origin of each document is a surrogate for how unusual the word usage of the document is. This can be used to select some documents for further analysis by, for example, selecting those whose position is greater than some given distance from the origin. Direction from the origin is also significant. This makes it possible to select interesting documents without a pre-existing model of what makes a document interesting.

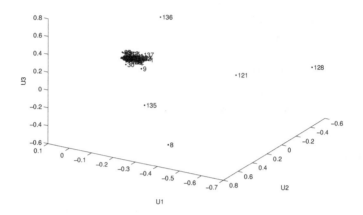

Figure 7.1. *A set of speeches in the Canadian Parliament.*

For example, the plot in Figure 7.1 shows points corresponding to a set of speeches in the Canadian Parliament, using a set of frequencies of 89 words. It is clear that the points labelled 8, 121, 128, 135, and 136 are very different from ordinary speeches in their usage of these words. Moreover, speeches 8 and 135 resemble each other; and so do speeches 121 and 128. This plot suggests that these documents are the most interesting in the set, at least based on these particular words. They do not obviously differ from the other, larger set of speeches in reading them over.

If examples of suspicious or interesting documents are already known, they can be included in the plot; and other texts that fall close to them may also be considered suspicious or interesting.

In the discussion that follows we will assume that some set of documents, possibly very large, has been extracted or retrieved. We now consider what other kinds of knowledge can be extracted from them.

7.5.3   Extracting Named Entities

Most of the time, the names mentioned in a document will be of paramount importance for intelligence analysis or law enforcement. These could include names of people; names that describe person-like entities such as organizations, businesses, or corporations; names of places, or channels between places; and names of systems or tools.

This looks like an easy problem in English, where proper names are capitalized, or sometimes acronyms, and other words are not, except for the first word in each sentence. Unfortunately, this simplicity is illusory. First, names often consist of more than one word, and it can be difficult to correctly fit the words together. Second, references to the same entity do not always look the same because of a tendency to assume that the rest of the name can be filled in from the context on the second and subsequent references – this is known as the coreference problem. Third, beginnings of sentences may be hard to find, because periods that mark the end of the preceding sentence can also appear within a sentence. For example, titles and abbreviations often use a period, so "Mr. Smith" may fail to be noticed because "Smith" looks like a capitalized word at the beginning of a sentence.

There are many commercially available named-entity recognition tools, and their accuracies can exceed 90% for relatively formal text. There are, broadly speaking, two approaches. The first is to treat the problem as a prediction problem and use any standard prediction technology with some labelled training data. The second is to exploit the sequential nature of the problem and adapt techniques such as Hidden Markov Models, using the conditional probability that the next word will be a named entity given the current left context. For example, some words such as "Mr." are strongly predictive that the next word will be a name. Approaches based more deeply on natural language are also possible. Accuracies are likely to be much lower for informal text, where less research has been done.

Many of the same ideas can be used to discover and extract entities that are not names, but rather markers for particular content. For example, in a financial domain, it may be useful to discover the type of a document, and key phrases such as "expected earnings" may make it easy to tell. If resumes are being processed automatically, finding phrases such as "employment history" may be useful. Such phrases play the role of names in a particular, specialized context.

Other entities that may sometimes be relevant but are not, strictly speaking, names are times and quantities, particularly quantities of money.

7.5.4 Extracting Concepts

In general, a concept is a phrase describing some aspect of a document's content that would not normally be considered as a proper name. Many concepts will usually be mentioned in a document.

One reasonable definition of a concept is a phrase suitable for inclusion in an ontology. Concepts tend to be treated in two quite different ways, depending on whether they are drawn from an existing ontology, or whether they are discovered, in an emergent way, from the document itself.

Particularly in specialized domains, such as medicine, large, commonly agreed ontologies already exist[7]. Finding concepts becomes the problem of finding occurrences of the already defined phrases in documents. This is not entirely straightforward, because synonyms for ontology terms can exist, but is essentially a matching problem.

If an ontology does not already exist, then the challenge is to recognize phrases that are usefully descriptive of some part of what the document is about. One helpful way to think about this is that concepts are statistically unlikely phrases. Recall that the structure of English, at least, is that rarer words hardly ever occur next to each other; they are overwhelmingly likely to be separated by much more common words. Therefore, when rare words co-occur, it is a hint that the combination is probably of interest. One way to test such combinations is to compute the likelihood ratio of any two collocated words that are each sufficiently infrequent, and so build up multiword phrases. The pointwise mutual information of the pair of words can also be used to measure their level of significance[8].

The difficulty is to decide how to compute the expected frequency of a phrase; more precisely, what the universe of comparison should be. If the universe is too large, then many phrases are unexpected because each document mentions many things that other documents do not mention – not all of these will actually be interesting. On the other hand, if the universe is small and contains mostly similar documents, only very unexpected phrases will be discovered.

This assumes that co-occurrence implies a semantic relationship between words. In languages like English, co-occurrence is a strong signal for related meaning, but this might not carry over into other languages, particularly those in which word order is less significant.

Even without an ontology, a concept-extraction system can be primed with a vocabulary of interest. This limits concepts to those containing at least one word from the vocabulary. Systems can also be primed with structural rules, perhaps described using regular expressions[9]. This is most useful in domains where there are conventions about how certain objects' properties are described. For example, species names are two-part Latin names, but the first name is often abbreviated to a single capital letter, followed by a period. A roundworm much studied by biologists is named *Caenorhabditis elegans*, but is usually referred to (for obvious reasons) as *C. elegans*. Knowing that both forms refer to the same species helps to extract concepts about it.

Another way to include semantic information without having to build a special-purpose ontology is to leverage systems such as Wordnet[10] that have already collected rules about the relationships among many words (in English in this case, but similar systems have been developed for some other languages). For example, Wordnet records hypernyms and hyponyms for each noun. Given a noun, a hypernym is a word describing a superset of similar objects. For example, the hypernym of cat is feline, a noun which also includes the big cats (lions, tigers, etc.). Similarly, the hyponym of a noun is a more specialized noun, so hypernym and hyponym are inverse relationships. Because words have several senses, most nouns have more than one hypernym and hyponym.

The GARAGE system[11] uses chains of hypernyms and hyponyms to extend the content of a document. For each noun discovered in a document, a tree is grown both up and down the hypernym-hyponym hierarchy. When another word from the document is encountered along a branch of this tree, the path is added to a graph structure and each noun on the path between them is added to the set of content words. The resulting graph of paths is then clustered and each cluster is taken to represent a concept in the document.

Concepts can play the role of automatically generated tags for a document. This can, in turn, be used to improve deeper analysis, or even search within a set of documents. However, tags such as these play a different role from that of user-defined tags, such as those defined at sites like del.icio.us, since user-defined tags often describe a document using words that come from some human-comprehensible context, and so do not actually appear within it.

7.5.5 Extracting Relationships

The next level of extracting knowledge from documents is to find relationships described or implied in the text. An entity is a single atomic object in the text; a relationship connects two or more objects and describes the nature of the connection. Many different relationships might exist in a text; not all of them are easy to discover.

One of the most obvious kinds of relationships in any document is the subject-object relationship, where the type of relationship is specified by a verb. Different families of verbs describe different classes of relationships. For example, "A hit B", "A struck B", "A attacked B" all indicate a particular kind of relation between A and B. "A told B", "A said to B", "A phoned B" indicate another kind of relation.

However, even simple relations carried by verbs can be difficult to discover in practice. First, the subject or object can be separated from the verb by other text: "A, who walked in with B and smoked a cigar, said to C" makes it difficult for software to work out who communicated to C. Second, connections across sentence boundaries often cause actors to be represented by pronouns, and working out which actors pronouns refer to is extremely difficult. Even humans have trouble on occasion and, in fact, rely heavily on contextual information about the situation being described to get this process (known technically as *anaphora resolution*) right.

Other kinds of relations may also be extracted from the text. For example, "A, and his son B, ..." tells us a family relationship between A and B. "A ordered B to ..." tells us that A has some kind of command relationship to B. Systems that are able to find instances of already-defined relations can perform fairly well on documents, but natural language contains enough variability that it is hard to perform really well.

Relations need not necessarily connect just two actors – a relation could connect three, or even more, actors. For example, from an account of a conversation, it is possible to infer a lower bound on the number of people who were present, and therefore that they have all met. From a location and a name, we can infer that a "visited" relation holds for the named person. Although it is much more difficult, it is also conceivable to infer what each person "knows" from the text of a conversation.

For relations mediated by verbs, the tense of the verb is also an important property of the relation. In preventive situations, future-tense verbs are more interesting than those in other tenses; in prosecution situations, past-tense verbs are more interesting. "A hit B" is different to "A will hit B".

7.5.6   Extracting Topics

Continuing up a hierarchy of different kinds of knowledge than can be extracted from documents, we now consider topic detection. The *topic* of a document is a high-level and simpler description of what it is *about* than either entities or concepts. In many ways, the role of a topic is to allow triage on a large collection of documents; selecting a subset of interest, discarding a subset not of interest, or clustering the set into subsets with a common focus. For example, Google news[12] produces clusters of news stories, with each cluster (more or less) about the same subject. Given the huge number of documents created each day, an analyst may wish to consider only those about a particular topic, say a particular country.

Topic detection is relatively mature, and has been exploited by many web-search businesses to improve the quality of search results, mainly by improving clustering. It can be considered as the problem of deciding what the topic of a single document is, in which case the problem is an extension of concept extraction. The topic might be the concept that is mentioned most often, perhaps. However, it is usually considered as the problem of deciding what topics a *collection* of documents is about. This works better, because the word-usage patterns across documents provide extra information about the significance of particular words.

Topic detection is clearly a biclustering problem[13]. Given a preliminary clustering of documents into topics, a clustering of the words can be performed based on how frequent they are in each of the clusters. Words that occur with about the same frequency in every cluster are unhelpful attributes and can be discarded. Words that occur primarily in one cluster are highly predictive of membership in that cluster. However, this does not make them more important attributes overall, since they provide little or no information about other clusters. Words as attributes are important when they are present, but not so important when they are absent. In other words, the clustering of the documents implies a clustering of the words.

This clustering of the words can now be used to improve the clustering of the documents, which can be used to improve the clustering of the words, and so on. It is the word clusters that are actually the interesting result of the algorithm, since these describe the topics, although it is straightforward to label each document cluster by its topic(s) as well.

There are important, and largely unresolved, issues about how to describe topics in ways that users can understand. If a topic can be described by a single term, then a description is easy. However, most topics are more complex than this. If a particular set of words describes a topic, then displaying this list is reasonable as long as it isn't too long – a list of five descriptive terms is practical, a list of two hundred descriptive terms is not.

One way to address this is to use a *tag cloud*, where words are displayed with a size that indicates their importance. This seems to make longer lists intelligible to humans. Graphical renderings are also possible, with the placement of terms indicating their importance and centrality, and the thickness of edges between them indicating the importance of their relationships. This issue has, so far, received little attention so there are surely better ways to convey useful information.

Techniques for biclustering introduced in Section 5.4.6 can be used for topic detection and document clustering by topic. However, another family of techniques has been developed, exploiting the fact that the topics in documents did not get there randomly, but were intended by authors. Furthermore, each author has distinctive word-use patterns that affect how s/he expresses content about a given topic.

These approaches all treat the topic of each document as a hidden (or missing) property that is revealed by the way in which words appear in the document. This missing information can be inferred using any one of a family of likelihood-estimation techniques. *Latent Dirichlet Allocation* (LDA)[14] is one such technique that assumes a generative model for the topics of documents. Properties such as the length of a document, and the words that appear within it are not random, nor independent, but depend on the topic(s) that the document is about. The generative model assumes that the length of the document is chosen first; then the topics are chosen; and then, for each document, one of the topics is chosen, and a word is chosen based on the topic. This is clearly not the way that documents are actually created, but it does capture the fact that words are used in documents because the words' referents are related to the topics mentioned. Some words can be used in the context of several different topics, so there is not a one-to-one relationship between topics and words.

Assuming this kind of generative model, its latent or hidden parameters can be estimated using a variety of techniques. In practice, the problem is so difficult that heuristics are needed. However, once the parameters have been estimated, the probability that each word is being used to express each topic, and the probability that each document is about each topic can be determined.

More sophisticated variations treat the identities of the authors as another set of hidden variables. The intuition is that knowing the author of a document may make it easier to predict the document's topic more robustly, because authors use words in different ways to express ideas about the same topic. This scenario can be set up as a multistage prediction problem, in which the author's identity is predicted first and this information used to predict the topic from the word usage, or the author and topic may be predicted simultaneously.

This idea can be extended further in situations, such as email or telephone calls, where the intended recipient also has an effect on the relationship between word usage and topic[15]. In other words, the same author writing about the same topic might use different words to communicate to two different readers. Again this can be set up as the prediction of author, recipient, and then topic; or all three at once.

7.5.7   Extracting Narrative and Sensemaking

At an even higher level of abstraction, we may want to extract a narrative from a document or set of documents, or perform sensemaking. These terms are intuitive, but they also have technical meanings. Extracting a narrative means finding an ordered thread through the content of related (usually temporally or causally related) events. For a single document, this is closely related to summarization, discussed below, but for a collection of documents it means pulling out one such thread in a setting where there might be many, many threads. In an intelligence or law-enforcement setting, threads that correspond to uncommon or suspicious sequences of events are most interesting.

A leading narrative-extraction system is VAST[16]. The system must be given hierarchical templates of stories that are expected in the data. For example, preparations for a terrorist attack might involve certain people crossing borders; certain kinds of communication; increases or decreases in volume of communication; increased surveillance of potential targets; and so on. A schema describing the component parts and their relationships to each other must be constructed (at present, by hand).

The fact of the occurrence of each of these events might be recorded somewhere within a large and varied set of documents. As the document set is processed, any event that matches a node of any of a set of schemas is detected and the probability associated with that node increased. Each schema node at a higher level of abstraction inherits a probability based on the current probabilities of its component pieces. Occurrences of components can be detected in the documents in any order, and the same occurrence can play a role in more than one schema.

At any stage, many different schemas can be in play, with different levels of confidence about their likelihood given the document set. When all of the documents have been processed, the most probable schemas can be assessed manually.

We have already discussed sensemaking as a way for organizations and groups of organizations to view a problem domain, and decide how to act in it. The term sensemaking is also used as a way of describing the extraction of high-level information from documents. This is similar to narrative extraction, but might focus on aspects of the content that are important for situational awareness. In a way, sensemaking or situational awareness is the union of entity, concept, and narrative extraction.

7.5.8 Summarization

Document summarization is somewhat orthogonal to sensemaking. It aims to produce a shorter version of each document that contains its essential content, but requires much less time to absorb. The goals of summarization are not as grand as those of sensemaking, and the approach is more syntactic. Looked at in another way, summarization can be seen as an extension of topic detection.

Summarization can take two forms: *extractive* summarization, where the summary is a subset of the content of the document(s); and *abstractive* summarization, where the summary may use terms that were never used in the document(s). Extractive summarization is much more common, since it can be handled as a syntactic task.

The usual approach is to treat summarization as a two-class prediction problem, where the goal is to predict whether or not to include each text fragment, typically a sentence, in the extract. Attributes used for prediction might include length of the sentence (too-short or too-long sentences are not as interesting), its position in the document (sentences at the beginning and end of paragraphs are most interesting), or the number of interesting words or concepts it contains. Support vector machines have been used for this problem.

One simple approach is to choose sentences that are highly relevant to the subject matter of the entire document. A vector describing the entire document's word usage (or better, term usage after some concept extraction, and perhaps named-entity extraction) is created. A vector is then created for each individual sentence, and the most-similar sentence is extracted for the summary[17]. This sentence has now 'covered' some of the content of the document, so the next most similar sentence is likely to be quite repetitive. To avoid such repetitiveness, the vector describing the whole document is updated by removing all of the words contained in the selected sentence; and the process is repeated, until some chosen number of sentences have been selected. This attempt to avoid repetition is obviously too draconian in many situations, since a document often introduces an idea in one sentence, and elaborates it in the following sentences. Either the introductory sentence or the elaboration are likely to be omitted from a summary built this way.

Singular value decomposition can be applied to records corresponding to the word-frequencies of each candidate sentence. This tends to cluster sentences with similar content in similar directions from the origin. A sentence from each cluster can then be selected without having to explicitly construct themes. However, for many documents, an SVD projects the sentences onto a more-or-less straight line, so a better summary can often be produced by choosing one sentence from each segment of such a line[18].

Documents are written to be read from beginning to end, so techniques that exploit this structure, especially the left context of each sentence have also been developed. One way to do this is to use a Hidden Markov Model approach[19]. Conditional random fields have also been used[20], but it is not clear whether the improvement demonstrated over Hidden Markov Models is due to the more-powerful framework or better use of available attributes.

One of the major problems in summarization is dealing with anaphora, that is, references back to someone or something using pronouns. This is very common: a person, place or thing is introduced in one sentence and mentioned in the following sentences, but not by name. This is fine, as long as only the first sentence is selected for the summary. But if one of the following sentences is selected, it will not be obvious what each pronoun is pointing to. The obvious solution is to replace each pronoun by the object it points to before beginning the summarization – but resolving what pronouns point to is so difficult that humans occasionally have difficulty, so there is little hope of good algorithmic solutions.

Resolving anaphora has been used to improve summarization but, somewhat surprisingly, does not help much in its naive form. Better results were achieved by Steinberger *et al.*[21], by treating each entity from a chain of references as an extra attribute of each sentence. Presumably, this helps to emphasize that an entity referred to in many sentences is an important entity and so the sentences in which it is mentioned are also important.

7.5.9   Extracting Intention and Slant

Another possible goal is to try and discover the role each part of a document or set of documents plays in a larger process, *from the point of view of the author*. Instead of asking questions like "what does this content mean?", questions like "why did the author choose to say this?" are more important. We will return to these issues at much greater length in Chapter 9.

7.5.10   Trends in Content

So far we have implicitly assumed that extracting knowledge from documents is a one-time act. It is also common, though, to look at the way in which content changes with time. As with other forms of temporal analysis, this could be because newer content provides new knowledge; or because the fact of the change itself is significant, regardless of how the knowledge changes.

For example, changes in entities may reflect changing personnel within a criminal group, changing targeting, or changing collaboration. Changes in concepts may reflect changing modes of attack. Changing relationships may reflect power struggles within a criminal organization, or movement to a different phase of an operation. Changes in signals of intention, such as targeting propaganda for a different audience, may reflect a changing strategy, or perhaps signal frustration with lack of progress.

Other kinds of knowledge are not as likely to change in useful ways. Although trends in topics have been well-studied, because they are important in many commercial settings, they are likely to be relevant in counterterrorism and law-enforcement settings only at large-scale and over long periods of time. A particular group involved in a particular operation is unlikely to produce much change in topic. Narratives inherently change with time, since there is no point in repeating the same story, but this does not really represent a trend.

There are a few specialized situations where detecting changes in knowledge extracted from documents is helpful:

- Detecting changing *volume* of communication. Either an increase or decrease may signal the imminence of a terrorist attack or criminal exploit; or may signal a move from one phase to another.

- Detecting the response to new methods of surveillance or counteraction. If some new technology is deployed, it is useful to detect whether what is talked about changes since this may suggest that the new surveillance modality has been detected (and so its product should not be trusted). If some action has been taken against the adversaries, changes in communication may reveal how effective it has been. Under pressure, mistakes are also more likely, so close attention at such times will be rewarding.

7.5.11 Authorship from Large Samples

Questions about the authorship have a long history, from determining the authors of biblical books, to whether or not Shakespeare's plays were written by Shakespeare. Intuition would suggest that it is the unusual words that discriminate one author's style from another, but in fact it is the way in which smaller and less noticeable words are used that makes the difference. Unusual words tend to be noticed and so can be picked up and used by other authors, either unconsciously, or as an element of parody or forgery.

Progress in determining authorship from text began when documents could be processed by computers, and properties such as the frequencies of words computed in a practical way. Some of the early success stories, in the early Sixties, were Ellegård's work[22] using frequency comparisons of 458 words to compare the style of the Letters of Junius to that of 132 contemporary authors, concluding that the attribution to Junius was in fact correct. Mosteller and Wallace used frequency comparisons of 30 words to attribute authorship of the 12 disputed Federalist Papers to Madison, and not Hamilton.

Burrows showed how to take frequency profiles of large numbers of words and use Principal Component Analysis, essentially the Singular Value Decomposition described earlier, to project this high-dimensional data into two or three dimensions, where boundaries between the documents written by different authors were detectable.

Other, more-sophisticated predictors have also been used. Matthews and Merriam trained a neural network to distinguish between the plays of Shakespeare and Marlowe, correctly with one exception, *Henry VI, Part 3*, which critics had already suggested might be a Shakespearean adaptation of an earlier Marlowe play[23].

For the Federalist Papers, Holmes and Forsyth[24] used genetic algorithms, and Fung[25] used Support Vector Machines to verify the earlier conclusion that they were written by Madison.

Rare-word frequencies *have* also been used from time to time in authorship detection, but much larger amounts of text seem to be required.

7.5.12   Authorship from Small Samples

The problem with traditional authorship detection is that, to be robust, it requires large amounts of text. In the situations we are considering, only a small amount of text by each author is typically available. Can authorship detection be extended to work effectively from small pieces of text? Recent research suggests that it can.

The first issue to consider is exactly what authorship problem we want to solve. The main possibilities are:

- Was this document (or corpus) written by *this* author or by *that* author? This is primarily the problem considered in the previous section; were the plays written by Shakespeare or the Earl of Essex?

- Was this document written by *this* author or someone else, unspecified? This is commonly the situation in forensic settings.

- Was this document written by *this* author from within a closed set of possible authors? This could be a more generalized case of the first possibility, but also comes up when a limited number of people had access to a computer or account where a document or an email was created.

- Is this given set of documents all by the same author, perhaps an author whose identity is unknown?

- How many different authors have written this set of documents?

All of these versions of the problem are of interest in adversarial situations. The problem of deciding who is the author of a document from among a smallish set of possibilities comes up whenever adversaries communicate. Is this a pronouncement from bin Laden, or has it been written by someone else and labelled as coming from him? Which member of the gang wrote the ransom note? Who is driving the recruitment effort?

Determining whether or not a particular document was written by a particular person is also common in criminal settings. Chaski gives several examples where documents were created online, and the real author claimed they had, in fact, been created by someone else with access to the computer on which they were written.

When the same individuals write in different settings, it becomes possible to connect up facts about them if it is possible to determine that the different documents were written by the same people. For example, predators may write in chatrooms where young people are present, masquerading as one of them, and also in chatrooms where predators discuss tactics. Matching the different documents to a single author helps discover the presence of the predator in the first chatroom.

It is a common tactic in chatrooms and forums for one person to masquerade as multiple people: to create more buzz, or to create better propaganda by setting up strawman arguments to demolish. Being able to decide how many authors have created a set of documents enables seeing through such facades.

The attributes that can and have been used for authorship studies can be divided into *stylistic* attributes, and *content* attributes. In general, content attributes are not as useful because the predictive models do not generalize to new content domains. Sometimes, where the content domain is expected to remain fairly constant this may not be a problem. For example, authorship prediction within jihadi web forums can reasonably rely on content since this is likely to change, if at all, fairly slowly.

Most authorship prediction relies on stylistic attributes[26]. These include:

- Lexical features, such as punctuation, capitalization, fonts, character sets, and sometimes even font color

- Syntactic features, based on the way in which sentences are structured

- Physical features, such as the way in which the text is arranged

- Frequencies of individual words or parts of speech

- The presence and frequency of different kinds of errors

- n-grams (that is, frequencies of adjacent sequences of n objects), where the objects can be characters, words, or parts of speech.

This does not completely exhaust the possibilities, and some of these attributes measure similar or overlapping characteristics of documents.

Most small documents, for example emails, telephone call transcripts, instant messaging conversations, or web forum contributions, are also informal, so we might expect that there will be much more variability than we would find in more formal writing. This probably makes the authorship problem more difficult, although a greater freedom of form might mean that authors use more characteristic idiosyncratic variations, so even this is not clear.

We are very far from understanding the problem well enough to select good attributes in advance, so most studies have begun with a very large set of attributes, typically thousands, and incorporated aggressive attribute selection into the modelling. The resulting sets of attributes associated with good prediction have not led to a deeper understanding of the problem. Each approach finds a more or less disjoint set of attributes to be useful.

Most experiments have aimed at correctly predicting authorship of a set of a few hundred documents written by a set of about ten authors[27]. Predictive accuracy in this setting tends to be somewhere between 70% and 80%. The exception is the work of Chaski[28], who achieves prediction accuracies in the 90%+ range, probably because of the use of deeper linguistic features, namely *markedness*, and punctuation boundaries.

An attempt to solve the problem of authorship when there are thousands of authors is the work of Koppel, Schler, Argamon, and Messeri[29]. They take at least a 500-word selection from the end of 18,000 blogs. Instead of building a predictive model for each author, they build three different attribute vectors, using content-word frequency, content-word presence, and stylistic-word frequency, and treat these as a simple model of each author.

A new document is classified by finding the nearest author vector using cosine similarity between its vector(s) and the collection of authors' vector(s). Of course, the prediction this produces is often wrong. The prediction accuracy varies between 20% and 40%. However, they also train a metalearner based on the pairs of (new document vector, author vector) from the training data. This metalearner is, in effect, learning when cosine similarity should be taken as reliable and when it should not.

The overall system is used as follows: given a new document, the matching author is determined from the three separate author models. These predictions are then fed to the metalearner. If the metalearner predicts a successful match for the same author from one or more models, then that author is predicted by the overall system. If not, the system returns "Don't Know". Using this approach, about 30% of documents are classified, and around 90% of these are classified correctly.

An alternative approach to modelling authors is the work of Frantzeskou et al.[30], aimed at determining the authorship of software. They collect the frequencies of character-level n-grams and, for each author, create a profile based on the most-frequent n-grams. These profiles can be compared to one another to determine the authorship of a set of programs, based on the intersection of the profiles. One of the advantages is that different profiles can be created based on the length of the most-frequent-n-gram list, and on the choice of n. For two programs, any one of these profiles should make the same prediction, so different profiles can be used as an ensemble predictor. Accuracies in the high 90% range were reported, although on quite small sets of programs.

Another attractive approach to authorship is the use of *writeprints*[31]. For each document, and a small set of related attributes, a short window slides over the document, and a record of the attribute frequencies is created from each window. Each window overlaps with the ones before and after it, so these records vary only slowly as the window slides through the document. Dimensionality-reduction techniques such as SVD are used to reduce each record to a point, and the points are plotted in two dimensions. The passage of the sliding window creates a *trajectory* through the two-dimensional space. These trajectories tend to be different for different authors because they record the way in which low-level features are used in a *local* way.

Using a different set of attributes creates a different set of records, and a different trajectory. Although authors may look similar with respect to some trajectories, it becomes increasingly unlikely that different authors will look the same for all of them. Each of the trajectories in two-dimensional space is called a *writeprint* and acts as a kind of fingerprint for authors.

Writeprints were originally conceived of as a visualization approach to authorship, but a writeprint-comparison algorithm has been developed that is able to compare a set of writeprints and determine how well they match. Accuracies in the high 90%s are reported for single messages, in a setting with a small number ($\sim$20) authors[32].

The question of whether a document has been written by a given author or by someone else unspecified, that is, when the set of possible authors is open, has been studied less. This can be thought of as a 1-class classification problem, but predictors for this problem are not very reliable, or at least cannot be demonstrated to be reliable. This makes their results difficult to use in, say, forensic settings.

One possibility is to take existing documents by a given author, and the document whose authorship we are uncertain about, and see how hard it is to tell the difference between the two, in terms of a set of attributes. If it is hard to tell the difference, or equivalently the models of each author are similar, conclude that they are written by the same person; if not, conclude that they were written by different authors.

This turns out not to work well. The model that tries to predict the difference between the two (sets of) documents will often end up using only a small number of attributes for prediction – and these attributes might be differences related more to differing purposes for the documents, than differing authorship. In other words, if an employee is sending hate email from a work account but claims someone else has used his/her computer, it may be difficult to tell. The differences between ordinary email and hate email have to do with the topic and emotional tone, which may be larger than the differences between one author and another.

Koppel, Schler, and Bonchek-Dokow[33] have developed a technique that is able to see beyond these differences and make this idea work robustly. The approach works as follows: build a predictor to learn the difference between the two (sets of) documents, including choosing attributes that are most effective discriminators. Now remove the most discriminating attribute, and rebuild the predictor. Repeat, removing another attribute each time. If the (set of) documents are by the same author, the prediction accuracy falls quickly as each new predictor is handicapped by removing attributes. If they are not by the same author, the prediction accuracy falls much more slowly. They show that, in general, six rounds are sufficient to establish clear differences.

Most work on authorship has assumed English as the target language. However, a significant amount of work has been done with Arabic[34], which presents different challenges because:

- Word length is shorter and less variable than English, making several standard measures used to differentiate text less effective.

- Most words are derived from a fairly small (perhaps 5,000) set of root words using prefixes, infixes, and suffixes. Although English has some similar mechanisms, for example adding -ly to make an adverb or -ness to make a noun of quality, this process is much less important in English. It is also different from declension and conjugation typical of Romance languages.

- Diacritical marks, roughly vowels, are not usually included in writing, their presence being inferred by the reader from the context. This is difficult to do algorithmically, making it hard to distinguish similar words.

- Elongation, the ability to insert a character that changes the intra-word spacing, can be used. This is somewhat archaic, and is often used in religious writing and poetry to create a pleasing appearance. Opinions differ about whether elongation plays a role in electronically created Arabic.

Chinese has also received some attention[35]. Because each Chinese character corresponds to a word, there are fewer lexical features available for profiling, and there is a very large vocabulary. Some work has also been done with documents in Greek and Turkish[36].

7.5.13 Detecting Author Properties

Koppel, Schler, and Zigdon[37] explored the question of whether an author's first language could be predicted from documents written in English. The intuition is that mistakes in the English text are characteristic of the properties of an author's first language. The attributes they use are:

- Frequencies of standard function words,

- Frequencies of letter 2-grams, aiming to capture spelling errors that are often characteristic of the differences in spelling between languages (for example, Spanish first-language speakers had difficulty deciding whether or not to double consonants),

- Other types of errors, and

- Rare bigrams of parts-of-speech,

for a total of 1035 attributes. 258 documents written by authors whose native languages were Russian, Czech, Bulgarian, French, and Spanish were used; the average length of each document was about 700 words. Prediction accuracies of about 80% for predicting the native language of the author of each document were achieved. As expected, the prediction model made the most errors confusing languages from similar families, for example, Russian and Bulgarian.

These results show that it is roughly correct to say that non-native speakers write, as well as speak, with an accent. There is some hope that this approach could be refined to work with even shorter documents.

Koppel, Argamon, and Shimoni[38] developed a technique to predict the gender of the author of a document with accuracies approaching 80%. They used a very large set of 1081 attributes, a mixture of function word, punctuation symbols, and n-gram frequencies, and 566 documents drawn from the BNC corpus for which the genre and author gender were known. The documents were quite long, averaging slightly more than 30,000 words, so it is not clear how well this technique would work on shorter documents. During the construction of the predictors, they were able to use attribute selection to reduce the number of attributes needed – typically sets of 64–128 attributes were sufficient. This work was extended by Koppel, Schler, Argamon, and Messeri[39] to the postings of 19,320 blog authors, with average document lengths of around 7,200 words but with high variance. Using a more-sophisticated choice of stylistic features, prediction accuracies of about 76% were achieved.

They also used the same dataset and attributes to predict the age of the authors, categorizing it into three ranges: 13–17, 23–27, and 33–47. Prediction accuracies of slightly better than 70% were achieved. As might be expected, content markers were more predictive of age than stylistic markers, since authors of different ages write about different things. These age ranges are quite wide, and well-separated, so it is not yet clear what level of accuracy could be achieved with more sophisticated algorithms. Intuitively, we might not expect writing to change in strong ways with age, so this might be a difficult problem (but see Chapter 9).

7.5.14 Extracting Metainformation

When communication is public, the records *about* the communication are unlikely to be considered sensitive, and so are likely to be public, or easily accessible, as well. There are four related categories of metainformation that are associated with entry of documents into a public space:

- The endpoint (device, account) that was used,

- The physical location from which they came,

- The time(s) at which they appeared (and the frequencies, for a set of documents), and

- The apparent identity of the authors/originators.

Most of this information is captured by logs at or close to where the document arrives in a public system. Often, some or all of the information is also captured as the document makes its way from one place to another. For example, if a user connects to the Internet via a broadband connection, goes to a web site, and posts a comment there, then a record is created when the broadband connection is made, a series of records are created as the browser communicates to and from the web site, a record is created when the user authenticates to the web site to be able to add content, and then the content itself is recorded at the web site. The low-level traffic implicit in these transactions travels over connections owned by others, and these low-level transactions can also be logged.

There are many possible ways to obscure this metainformation. Short-term email accounts are readily available, although access to broadband is associated with payment and so is harder to obscure. Similarly, access via handheld devices is associated with payments, making it harder to obscure. There are ways to access the Internet via public terminals, at Internet cafes and libraries, but the easiest way may be identity theft, or theft of an access device.

Physical location is harder to obscure because access must take place via an IP address and IP addresses can be placed at geographical locations with fair accuracy. Wireless access is even easier to localize.

Times of access can be obscured easily, because most computing systems make it possible to script the publication of the content so that it happens at some other predefined time. This decouples the moment when an author was present at an IP address from the moment when the content appears from that (or a different) IP address.

Identities are also fragile in the context of the online world. Famously, on the Internet no one call tell that you're a dog – in other words, your real identity is hidden behind the pseudo-identity implied by an online identifier.

Of course, there are technologies that make it easier to hide almost all information about who, when, and where documents are created. These are based on the use of proxies, randomized routing, and mixing traffic from different sources to make it hard to separate into its component streams. However, such systems still allow opportunities for metainformation to be gleaned. For example, requests for name service may give away where a particular user is located.

7.6   Tactics and Process

We have discussed different motives for adversaries to engage in public communication. Their desire to do so creates two kinds of opportunities for manipulation.

Public communication by adversaries cannot be effectively authenticated to the potential audience. After all, in many cases it is not clear who the audience will be. This creates the opportunity to play the role of the adversaries. In this way, the real audience can be manipulated.

Also, because the adversaries do not know exactly who their audience is, there is an opportunity to play the role of the audience. This creates the opportunity to manipulate the adversaries.

7.6.1   Playing the Adversaries

Whenever it is impossible for the potential audience to be sure who is supposed to be communicating with them, it becomes possible to play the role of the adversaries and generate communication intended for the same audience.

This creates a number of opportunities:

- **Create misleading propaganda**. Controlling content that purports to be generated by the adversaries makes it possible to alienate or mislead those who would otherwise find such content convincing. This can be done by using weak arguments, creating the impression of mental instability, justifying the unjustifiable, or reframing the issues in ridiculous ways. In short, parodying the expected real content can create an image that has the opposite effect from that the adversaries intend. Of course, this has to be done with care so that the differences between real and false channels are not easily detectable.

- **Recruit, either to neutralize or as potential double agents.** In many contexts, part of the point of public communication is to recruit. Using a false channel, some of those who might be recruited by the real adversaries may be able to be recruited by the good side instead. At worst, this neutralizes them; at best, they may be able to be used for disinformation or penetration.

- **Discover sympathizers.** Public communication in many settings tends to draw a response from members of the audience. This is useful to discover sympathizers, particularly those who might be in positions to do damage if they joined the adversaries. For example, sexual predator forums might attract 'lurkers' who deserve further attention.

- **Confuse the audience.** The ability to send content via a false channel creates many other opportunities to mislead the intended audience. Law-enforcement personnel can spread their own forms of terror, by crediting analysts with surveillance and analysis abilities far beyond what they can actually implement; by passing on rumors greatly expanded in scope or subtly altered; or by claiming that some of the real adversaries are actually law-enforcement personnel.

- **Confuse the adversaries.** The simultaneous existence of communication from the real adversaries and from a false equivalent allows many opportunities to create confusion, not only in the intended audience, but among the adversaries themselves. If the adversaries are only loosely coupled, as they will tend to be for security reasons, it may take them some time to realize that part of the communication is not coming from them – and even when they do, they may first consider that it represents some independent action by a faction.

- **Provide false training.** Training is one of the biggest motivations for creating public content. However, since there are no strong ways to validate the content of such training, there are opportunities to mistrain. This could range from simply training for incompetence, to instilling distinctive tradecraft that can then be used for detection later ("Always meet at 22 minutes after the hour"), to making training itself dangerous. For example, it has been rumored that several web sites that explain how to build improvised explosive devices contain 'mistakes' designed to make the devices explode during construction.

- **Force revealing actions.** The false content can be used to encourage actions by the audience that will either reveal who they are, or are simply pointless, defusing their resources and attention. For example, in teenager web sites, law-enforcement personnel can pretend to be vulnerable teenagers and arrange to meet predators. Target suggestions for high-profile but well-defended or apparently attractive but pointless sites can be made.

The good side can also outdo the adversaries in fervor, effectively taking over a genuine forum. If this works, the techniques described above can be implemented with better cover, since the channel was demonstrably genuine at an earlier time.

Even if the takeover does not work, enthusiasm is likely to draw attention that can be exploited in other ways. For example, recruitment of the dissembling analysts may be attempted.

7.6.2 Playing the Audience

There are also opportunities to be found in playing the desired audience. These include:

- **Finding interesting communication**. Given that, in some ways, the biggest problem is to find interesting communication, setting up an infrastructure that makes it easy for the adversaries to communicate provides an easy channel with interesting content. There is no need to search large amounts of content for something interesting; the interesting content delivers itself. There is no need to set up forums for this purpose if such forums exist already, and it is straightforward for the good side to get access to them. However, there are advantages in controlling the venue – for example, it is possible to log the actions of participants more precisely. This might make it possible to tell if the same person is using more than one screen name simultaneously. The other advantage is that it is impossible to be blocked from the site, and that anyone who arouses suspicion of being a plant can change, apparently, into someone else without needing reauthentication.

  The same process has been used successfully to identify sexual predators. In this case, there are many chatrooms and forums where teenagers spend time, so there is less need for law enforcement to set up their own.

- **Learning about the adversaries**. Acting the part of the audience encourages the adversaries to communicate further, enabling more to be learned about them. If the adversaries' motivation is propaganda, act like someone willing to be convinced; if their motivation is a confidence trick, act like a mark; if their motivation is to attract sympathizers, act sympathetic but needing to be convinced.

  For example, a site can be made to look like a jihadi forum, salted with attractive content, with some people tasked to create simulated jihadi-style conversation. If these people make sure to sound both boastful and naive, it may be hard for more hard-core jihadis to restrain themselves from correcting them.

It becomes possible to start a dialogue, either explicitly as the good side, which might sometimes be productive in a law-enforcement context, or covertly. Such a dialogue is a way to probe the thinking, planning, and mental state of the adversaries in a controlled way. With some care, it becomes possible to guide the textual data available for analysis to verify or falsify hypotheses about the situation.

For example, arguments naturally stimulate responses from the other party. Such responses may be revealing in terms of their content. But even when the content is entirely predictable, the responses also, inevitably, reveal more about their authors than they intended. We will return to this point in Chapter 9.

Questions naturally stimulate more detailed responses, making more data available, presumptively from the same author. Not many people can resist praise coupled with a desire to learn more, so the most restrained person may lose perspective and write more than caution would have suggested.

- **Learning a way in.** Playing an enthusiastic audience member may make it possible to be invited into the next level of communication. Terrorist web sites tend to be arranged in levels. Those who seem interesting in completely public forums may be told how to access a better-protected site, where less-careful conversations can take place.

7.6.3 Fusing Data from Different Contexts

We have already discussed the usefulness of biometrics as a key that allows access to other data related to a particular person. Although, as we have seen, attributing authorship is not nearly as reliable as even weak biometrics, the ability to identify an author's style can act as a biometric key. Documents created by the same person in different contexts can be associated with each other, even when some or all of them are anonymous or pseudonymous.

This ability to connect documents by the same author across contexts is very powerful, because almost everyone produces some content that is *visibly* tied to them. This makes it much harder for them ever to write anonymously again, because their anonymous writing can now be associated to them.

At present, most writing by most people no longer exists because it was done during their education, or within the context of their employment. However, increasingly, many people's writing exists in some form on the Internet and so is likely to have been archived, either via backups on server sites or as part of the Internet archive. Few college students imagine a career as a criminal or terrorist – but the presence of their early writing may eventually allow them to be identified in later life, by matching their authorship style. Little is known about how stable an authorship signature is over the course of a lifetime. However, the work on determining the authorship of documents produced by people who wrote for a living, such as Shakespeare and Marlowe, suggests that consistency over years is plausible.

Writing by the same individuals in different contexts can also be associated. When some of these contexts are public, and the person is being careful, but others are (or seem to be) more private, carelessness may reveal who the person is. This information then provides an identity for the public context.

Notes

[1] European Parliament Temporary Committee on the ECHELON Interception System, "Final report on the existence of a global system for the interception of private and commercial communications (ECHELON interception system)", 2001.

[2] Isaac Asimov wrote a series of stories whose plots hinged on the difficulty of communicating precisely enough with robots, who did not have the context that enables us to understand the meaning of what is communicated to us, even if it is not explicit. The books are *I, Robot*, Gnome Press (1950), and *The Rest of the Robots*, Doubleday (1964).

[3] R. Ferrer i Cancho and R.V. Solé, "The small world of human language", *Proceedings of the Royal Society of London Series B – Biological Sciences*, pp. 2261–2265, 2001.

[4] X. Zhu and R. Rosenfeld, *Improving Trigram Language Modeling with the World Wide Web*, in: *Proceedings of International Conference on Acoustics, Speech, and Signal Processing, 2001*, pp. 533–536, 2001.

[5] www.multiverse.net.

[6] The Vivisimo enhanced search engine, which clusters results, can be tried at www.vivisimo.com.

[7] In medicine, much of the difficulty is agreeing on basic terminology, particularly as understanding of biological processes, and forms of treatment change quickly. Some of the systems are SNOMED-CT, Systematized Nomenclature of Medicine – Clinical Terms; UMLS, Unified Medical Language System, ICD-9 and ICD-10, the International Statistical Classification of Diseases and Related Health Problems; and MedDRA, Medical Dictionary for Regulatory Activities. The LinkBase system is closer to a hierarchical ontology, and there are several other ontologies in specialized domains, for example, the GO hierarchy for genes.

[8] The pointwise mutual information measures how likely the two words are to occur together, moderated by the likelihood of the words occurring at

all. It is computed as $f(\text{word1})\, f(\text{word2})/f(\text{word1 word2})$, where f measures frequencies.

[9]X. Jiang and A.-H. Tan, *Mining Ontological Knowledge from Domain-Specific Text Documents*, in: *Proceedings of the Fifth IEEE International Conference on Data Mining (ICDM'05)*, pp. 665–668, 2005.

[10]wordnet.princeton.edu.

[11]B. Gelfand, M. Wulfekuhler and W.F. Punch III, *Automated Concept Extraction from Plain Text*, in: *AAAI-98 Workshop on Learning for Text Categorization*, 1998.

[12]news.google.com.

[13]Some examples of the application of biclustering to this problem are I.S. Dhillon and D.S. Modha, "Concept decompositions for large sparse text data using clustering", *Machine Learning*, 42(1):143–175, 2001; I.S. Dhillon, "Co-clustering documents and words using bipartite spectral graph partitioning", Technical Report 2001-05, Department of Computer Sciences, University of Texas, March 2001; F. Shahnaz, M.W. Berry, V.P. Pauca and R.J. Plemmons, "Document Clustering using Nonnegative Matrix Factorization", *Journal on Information Processing and Management*, 42(2):373–386, March 2006; and T. Kolenda, L. Hansen and J. Larsen, *Signal Detection using ICA: Application to Chat Room Topic Spotting*, in: *Proceedings of ICA'2001*, December 2001. Independent Component Analysis has also been used with some success: S. Grant, D. Skillicorn and J. Cordy, *Topic Detection Using Independent Component Analysis*, in: *Workshop on Link Analysis, Counterterrorism, and Security (LACTS2008)*, pp. 23–28, 2008.

[14]D.M. Blei, A.Y. Ng and M.I. Jordan, "Latent Dirichlet allocation", *Journal of Machine Learning Research*, 3:993–1022, 2003.

[15]A. McCallum, A. Corrada-Emmanuel and X. Wang, *Topic and Role Discovery in Social Networks*, in: *International Joint Conference on Artificial Intelligence*, pp. 786–791, 2005.

[16]S. Adams and A.K. Goel, *A STAB at Making Sense of VAST Data*, in: *AAAI-2007 Workshop on Plan, Activity, and Intent Recognition*, 2007.

[17]Y. Gong and X. Liu, *Generic Text Summarization Using Relevance Measure and Latent Semantic Analysis*, in: *Proceedings of the 24th Annual International ACM SIGIR Conference on Research and Development in Information Retrieval*, pp. 19–25, New Orleans, 2001.

[18]James Provost, personal communication, 2007.

[19]For example, Conroy and O'Leary in, J.M. Conroy and D.P. O'Leary, *Text Summarization via Hidden Markov Models*, in: *Proceedings of the 24th Annual International ACM SIGIR Conference on Research and Development*

in Information Retrieval, pp. 406–407, New Orleans, 2001; and J. Conroy and D.P. O'Leary, "Text summarization via hidden markov models and pivoted QR matrix decomposition", Technical Report CS-TR-4221, University of Maryland Computer Science Department, May 2001.

[20] D. Shen, J.-T. Sun, H. Li, Q. Yang and Z. Chen, *Document Summarization using Conditional Random Fields*, in: *Proceedings of IJCAI-07*, pp. 2862–2867, 2007.

[21] J. Steinberger, M. Poesio, M.A. Kabadjov and K. Ježek, "Two uses of anaphora resolution in summarization", *Information Processing and Management*, 43(6):1663–1680, 2007.

[22] A Statistical Method for Determining Authorship, Gothenburg Studies in English 13, 1962.

[23] An accessible discussion of these techniques and further references can be found at www.sciencenews.org/articles/20031220/bob8.asp.

[24] D.I. Holmes and R.S. Forsyth, "The *Federalist* revisited: New directions in authorship attribution", *Literary and Linguistic Computing*, 10(2):111–127, 1995.

[25] G. Fung, *The Disputed Federalist Papers: SVM and Feature Selection via Concave Minization*, in: *Proceedings of the 2003 Conference on Diversity in Computing*, pp. 42–46, Atlanta, Georgia, USA, 2003.

[26] E. Stamatatos, N. Fakotakis and G. Kokkinakis, *Text Genre Detection Using Common Word Frequencies*, in: *Proceedings of the 18th International Conference on Computational Linguistics (COLING2000)*, pp. 808–814, 2000.

[27] For example, M. Koppel and J. Schler, *Exploiting Stylistic Idiosyncrasies for Authorship Attribution*, in: *Proceedings of IJCAI'03 Workshop on Computational Approaches to Style Analysis and Synthesis, Acapulco, Mexico*, 2003, and O. de Vel, A. Anderson, M. Corney and G. Mohay, "Mining E-mail content for author identification forensics", *SIGMOD Record*, 30(4):55–64, December 2001.

[28] C.E. Chaski, "Who's at the keyboard: Authorship attribution in digital evidence investigations", *International Journal of Digital Evidence*, 4(1), 2005.

[29] M. Koppel, J. Schler, S. Argamon and E. Messeri, *Authorship Attribution with Thousands of Candidate Authors*, in: *Proceedings of the 29th Annual International ACM SIGIR Conference on Research and Development in Information Retrieval*, pp. 659–660, 2006.

[30] G. Frantzeskou, E. Stamatatos, S. Gritzalis and C.E. Chaski, "Identifying authorship by byte-level n-grams: The source code author profile (SCAP) method", *International Journal of Digital Evidence*, 6(1), 2007.

[31] J. Li, R. Zheng and H. Chen, "From fingerprint to writeprint", *Communications of the ACM*, 49(4):76–82, April 2006; and A. Abbasi and H. Chen, *Visualizing Authorship for Identification*, in: *Intelligence and Security Informatics 2006*, pp. 60–71. Springer-Verlag LNCS 3975, 2006.

[32] A. Abbasi and H. Chen, *Visualizing Authorship for Identification*, in: *Intelligence and Security Informatics 2006*, pp. 60–71. Springer-Verlag LNCS 3975, 2006.

[33] M. Koppel, J. Schler and E. Bonchek-Dokow, "Measuring differentiability: Unmasking pseudonymous authors", *Journal of Machine Learning Research*, 8:1261–1276, 2007.

[34] A. Abbasi and H. Chen, *Applying Authorship Analysis to Arabic Web Content*, in: *Intelligence and Security Informatics 2005*, pp. 183–197. Springer-Verlag LNCS 3495, 2005, and A. Abbasi and H. Chen, "Applying authorship analysis to extremist-group web forum messages", *IEEE Intelligent Systems*, pp. 67–75, September/October 2005.

[35] J. Li, R. Zheng and H. Chen, "From fingerprint to writeprint", *Communications of the ACM*, 49(4):76–82, April 2006.

[36] B. Diri and M. Fatih Amasyali, *Automatic Author Detection for Turkish Texts*, in: *ICANN/ICONIP03, 13th International Conference on Artificial Neural Network and 10th International Conference on Neural Information Processing*, 2003.

[37] M. Koppel, J. Schler and K. Zigdon, *Automatically Determining an Anonymous Author's Native Language*, in: *Intelligence and Security Informatics, IEEE International Conference on Intelligence and Security Informatics, ISI 2005, Atlanta, GA, USA, May 19-20*, pp. 209–217. Springer-Verlag Lecture Notes in Computer Science LNCS 3495, 2005.

[38] M. Koppel, S. Argamon and A.R. Shimoni, "Automatically categorizing written texts by author gender", *Literary and Linguistic Computing*, 17(4):401–412, 2002.

[39] M. Koppel, J. Schler, S. Argamon and E. Messeri, *Authorship Attribution with Thousands of Candidate Authors*, in: *Proceedings of the 29th Annual International ACM SIGIR Conference on Research and Development in Information Retrieval*, pp. 659–660, 2006.

Chapter 8

Discovery in Private Communication

In the previous chapter, we considered what could be learned from the public communications made by adversaries. In this chapter, we consider the same problem, but for communication that is intended to be, or believed to be, private.

If adversaries communicate in ways that they believe to be private, how can such communications be captured and knowledge extracted from them? There are several ways in which this can happen:

- **Naivety**. The adversaries may believe that the communication mechanism is private because they have failed to understand the underlying technology, or possible ways in which confidentiality has been compromised. For example, al Qaeda continued to use satellite phones for some time after the September 11th, 2001 attacks, failing to realize that their calls could be intercepted and their locations estimated.

- **Legal interception**. All countries have some mechanism to allow forms of communication to be intercepted by intelligence or law-enforcement organizations. In law enforcement this usually requires some judicial process based on probable cause, and is often limited in scale. In intelligence settings, much more widespread interception of non-domestic communication is common.

- **By deception**. Playing the role of an adversary or potential adversary provides a way to become an intended recipient of communications.

- **By accident**. Sometimes communications are intercepted accidentally, for example when the content of a letter drop is found.

The differences, then, between public communication, discussed in Chapter 7, and private communication are these two things: there is a different *expectation* on the part of the author about the exposure of the communication; and the *intended audience* is known to the author in a much more specific way.

Naive adversaries have the expectation that their private communications will not be intercepted and analyzed, so they have no need for concealment. This is, of course, welcome by those who would like to extract knowledge from these communications, but is also unfortunately rare.

Most adversaries are more sophisticated, and are aware of the risk and dangers of having their communications intercepted and analyzed. They know that, if a private communication happens to be intercepted, it will be analyzed by professionals, using sophisticated techniques. There is, on the other hand, no expectation that communication will be seen by ordinary people.

Knowing the intended audience brings advantages to the author of a communication. Primarily, it allows for stronger assumptions about the form that the content should take. Knowing the audience means knowing the context in which they will read the communication. For example, knowing the idioms of the readers' native language may enable subtlety of expression that is hard for non-native speakers to grasp. If the audience already knows the broad outlines of the topic of communication, references within it can be cryptic and still be intelligible to the readers. A known audience also means an audience that may have specialized knowledge without which the meaning is hidden, for example a code book. Since the invention of the telegraph, companies developed their own private codebooks to let them communicate privately over a public medium.

In this environment, two strategies are available to the adversaries. The first is to hide their communications among the torrent of other communication that takes place through the telephone system and on the Internet. In this case, they should avoid specialized modes of communication and stick to mainstream modes, pathways, and technologies. The second strategy is to somehow obfuscate the content of their communications and also, as much as possible, the metainformation associated with them. Thus if a communication is intercepted, as little as possible can be learned from it.

Both strategies can be used at once. However, there is a tension between the two strategies: obfuscation, by its nature, changes communications, and might do so in a way that makes it more likely that they will be intercepted. In fact, as we will see, this is exactly what happens.

8.1   The Impact of Obfuscation

Obfuscated communication is likely to contain markers for concealment that can be used to select obfuscated messages preferentially from the torrent of ordinary communications – they are simply more unusual as texts. This selection creates a smaller pool to be analyzed – more deeply – for knowledge discovery.

However, the extraction of knowledge from the obfuscated content will be harder since the content will be concealed somehow. Named entities might be replaced by pseudonyms, concepts concealed by replacing the nouns on which they are based and, by extension, topics obscured. Relationships might be obscured by hiding the objects involved, or by hiding the nature of the relationship completely. With much of the specific content obscured, it is not clear that even an approximation to narrative could be extracted.

With the expectation that content has been obscured, there is some hope that the adversaries might be more cavalier about metainformation such as sender and receiver identities and endpoints.

Obfuscation looks, on the face of it, to be a win for the adversaries, making it easier for them to communicate with each other privately. However, in many ways it is actually a win for the good side, since it allows them to find the adversary communications more easily than if they were not obfuscated. Having found them, it is cost-effective to subject them to extensive analysis that can perhaps discover something of what lies behind the obfuscation.

8.2   Goals

The goals of knowledge extraction in the private-communication setting are the same as in the previous chapter: extracting information from the content of communications; extracting information about the identities, and other properties, of authors; and extracting metainformation from the envelope of each communication.

8.3   Concealment Opportunities

Given that any intercepted communication will be subject to rigorous analysis, concealment opportunities for private communication need to be more robust than in the public-communication case.

The main strategy for concealment must be to hide the content-bearing words in each communication. These will typically be the proper names and the nouns; in some situations, verbs may also need to be concealed. There is one obvious difficulty – the meaning of each communication must still be intelligible to the intended receivers. This requirement imposes severe limitations on what kinds of obfuscation are possible.

A less obvious but more important difficulty is that obfuscation, by its nature, creates documents that are unusual. The unusual nature of obfuscated documents becomes a kind of signal that draws attention to the very documents that are supposed to be concealed. The way in which the obfuscation is done may also convey information about the author. To take a simple example, the level of sophistication of the obfuscation reveals something about the technical abilities of the group.

Another strategy for concealment in private communication is to create fictitious communication, intended to be intercepted. In many ways, creating this kind of disinformation is an easier problem, since the (apparently) intended recipients need to know which communications to ignore, and this requires only a single bit of information added to each communication – difficult for the interceptors to detect. The signal can even be in the metainformation – messages sent on odd dates are to be ignored.

We now look in more detail at the two main obfuscation techniques: encryption and word substitution.

8.3.1 Encryption

The best way to conceal content is to encrypt each communication. If this is done carefully, it is almost certain that the content cannot be extracted if the communication is intercepted (although there are persistent rumors of possible back-doors to common encryption schemes)[1].

However, there are also many drawbacks to the use of encryption. First, it is still the case that the vast majority of communications are not encrypted, so an encrypted message automatically draws attention to itself. Second, encryption and decryption depend on the use of keys that must be disseminated, managed with care, and occasionally revoked.

Private-key cryptosystems require a pair of keys, one for encryption and one for decryption, and both keys must be kept secure. Public-key cryptosystems allow messages to be encrypted using a public key, that is, one that can be freely known, but require a private key for decryption[2].

Public keys make it easy for an arbitrary set of people to communicate with one person. It is well structured for the situation where many members of a adversary group must report to one. The idea can be extended to allow mutual communication within the group by having each member publish a public key. The difficulty is that anyone who can get access to the public key can communicate to the central person, allowing good guys to spoof communications.

Public-key systems can also be used to create digital signatures. The sender encrypts the communication with a private key. The matching public key authenticates the message as coming from the person who owns the private key.

Neither of these situations matches what is needed by groups of adversaries: authenticated communications that cannot be decrypted if intercepted. Of course, there are ways to get both effects: sender A encrypts with his private key, and then encrypts again with B's public key. Only B can decrypt the outer structure of the message from A, and, using A's public key, B can verify that the message is in fact from A.

In private-key systems, distributing the keys causes serious logistical problems since, if they are compromised, say by interception and copying in transit, then they are valueless. Revoking keys, whether private or public, is also difficult since the revocation messages cannot be sent securely once the system has been compromised. Most public-key systems rely on distributed authentication using a public-key infrastructure of mutually trusted sites, and this is problematic for adversaries.

Man-in-the-middle attacks can be used to alter public keys as they are distributed or accessed. A sender may unwittingly use a public key forced on them by the interceptor, who now knows the matching private key that will decrypt the sender's messages.

Public keys intended for only a small group of people also create some vulnerabilities. Either the public keys must be distributed in some protected way, creating a bootstrap problem; or they are distributed publicly, say by putting them on a web site. Now watching the web site to see who downloads the public keys can be revealing.

Thus encryption provides strong protection of content, but with a significant amount of overhead. Attracting attention by encryption may also make it easier to extract metainformation such as traffic analysis or endpoints.

8.3.2 Word Substitutions

Another approach to hiding content is to replace words that would be revealing by other words, either to make it less likely that a message would be selected for attention and analysis, or to make it hard to work out what it is about if it is selected.

An obvious place to start is to replace the nouns and/or proper names with other words. There are several possible ways to do this:

- **Change the apparent story**. For a while, al Qaeda were apparently using the word "wedding" for "attack" in their communications. This is quite a good piece of social engineering, since both weddings and attacks happen at particular places and times, and require people to converge for them. For a human reader, a message planning an attack might seem like a much more innocent message planning a wedding. The adversaries' hope here is that such a message, if selected for analysis, will appear to be a false positive.

- **Replace with words from an explicit code book**. A code book allows words that might get a communication selected for analysis to be replaced by other arbitrary words that might make it seem less interesting. The existence of the book makes it possible to replace as many words, of different kinds, as required. However, disseminating the book and keeping it secure creates problems similar to those associated with encryption and decryption keys.

- **Replace with locutions, idiom, or metaphor**. Given the common knowledge of the sender and the receivers, it is possible to communicate by replacing words that might get a communication selected for analysis by some more roundabout description that makes sense for the intended audience, but does not trivially do so for anyone else, because they lack the implicit knowledge on which it is based.

  This can be effective in a limited context and a tightly knit group. However, it is difficult to convey complex or subtle content because of the inherent fuzziness of the approach. The risk of confusion increases with the length of the communication, the number of different ideas to be conveyed, and the variability in the recipients.

- **Replace with a random word**. Words that might get a communication selected for analysis can be replaced by arbitrary words, either in such a way that the recipients can work out what it intended, or using some more *ad hoc* mental codebook. This still requires some form of side-channel by which the set of substitutions is conveyed, which probably limits it to substitutions only for the most suspicion-inducing words.

- **Replace with a frequency-matched word**. Rather than replace the undesirable words with arbitrary substitutes, choose words with the same natural frequency in the language in use. This requires access to a shared frequency-ranked list of words from which to choose, but does not require more detailed prearrangement, since a rule such as "in the list, use the word five places below the word you want to replace" can be used.

These later techniques all rely on substitutions preventing communications from being selected and analyzed. If they are selected, most of these substitutions are readily detectable by humans. This does not necessarily mean that the real meaning can be inferred, but there is some risk of this.

8.4 Technologies

In this section, we discuss the technologies available for selecting interesting communications and then extracting useful knowledge from them, when some form of obfuscation by substitution has been used.

8.4.1 Selection of Interesting Communication

In this context, selection is the primary problem. The point of obfuscation is to make it as difficult as possible to see that obfuscated messages are interesting.

Watch lists as a primary detection mechanism

Selection of communications that use words from a watch list must still be done to catch communications that have not been obfuscated (those by naive authors). However, this is not simply a necessary step – the existence of such a watch list has implications for what kind of obfuscation must be done.

Adversary authors will almost inevitably be aware of the existence of a watch list. However, while they can certainly guess some words that are on the list, perhaps "bomb" and "nuclear", they can be much less sure about many other words. For example, are the words "fertilizer", "ammonium nitrate", or "Strasbourg cathedral" on the list? They plausibly could be.

This uncertainty about the length and exact content of the watch list forces avoidance behavior that is much stronger than necessary. An author *must* assume the worst and replace every word that *could* be on the watch list. This makes communication more difficult for the author, and benefits the analyst because it creates text that is further away from normal than it really needs to be.

Sentence-level measures for detecting substitution

In a communication where substitutions have been made to avoid the use of words that might be on a watch list, a human would find it easy to detect which words are substitutions. The flow of meaning in the sentence is disturbed by the replacement of one word by another.

In the examples throughout this chapter, we will use Wordcount (www.wordcount.org) as the source of frequency-ranked English words. For example, suppose that an original sentence is "The attack will be tomorrow". The next most frequent word to "attack" is "campaign", and the next most frequent word to "tomorrow" is "associated". The new, obfuscated, sentence is "The campaign will be associated", which does not make much sense. If "campaign" is considered to be too similar to "attack" then the next ranked word is "understanding", producing "The understanding will be associated". These sentences seem unusual even standing alone, but in the larger context of a document, they probably seem even more unusual.

Humans detect such anomalies in the flow of a sentence using semantic information about the words and, less obviously, mental models of the real world and the typical actions of objects in that world. The question is whether such a disturbance in the semantic flow of text can be detected using the kind of syntactic signals that algorithms are able to see. In fact, there are ways to detect these semantic bumps, but they require the use of several different measures, and access to a large text repository to estimate how common various textual constructions actually are.

The frequency distribution of words in natural language is a Zipf distribution: common words are extremely common, but word frequencies in a ranked list decrease very sharply, and rare words are extremely infrequent. One of the corollaries of this is that common words are not very useful in determining document properties, because they are present in almost all documents with consistent frequencies. Likewise, rare words are also not very useful because they occur in almost no documents. Interesting properties of documents can be found by considering words in the middle range, neither too common nor too rare. If substitutions are made, they will make a difference only if they are made for these middle-range words.

The following seven measures turn out to be useful to detect the presence of a word substitution.

Sentence Oddity (SO).   If a word 'makes sense' in the context of the sentence in which it appears, the difference between the natural frequency of the entire sentence, and the natural frequency of the sentence from which that word has been removed, should not change very much. On the other hand, if the word is a substitution and therefore out of place, the difference in the frequencies of the sentence and the sentence with that word removed should be much greater. To decide how big this difference is, an estimate of the number of documents containing the matching textual pieces can be obtained by asking a search engine.

Asking for the frequency of exact matches does not work because (a) it is extremely unlikely that a particular sentence has ever been seen before by the search engine; and (b) removing the word leaves an ungrammatical sentence anyway, so we would not expect to find an occurrence. Fortunately, treating each textual fragment as a bag of words provides usable estimates of how common, and therefore how likely, each fragment is.

Of course, asking for the number of documents that contain a particular bag of words is only a rough estimate of frequency, because it does not rely on how close together in the document the words occur, nor how many times within each document each word can be found. Nevertheless, these estimates, though rough, are good enough to be useful.

The sentence oddity of a sentence with respect to possible substitution of a particular target word is:

$$\text{SO} = \frac{f(\text{bag of words, target word removed})}{f(\text{entire bag of words})}$$

so sentence oddity should be larger for sentences containing substitutions.

We will use the following sentence as an example of the application of these measures: "The explosives will be delivered". A plausible frequency-matched substitute for 'explosives' is 'aura'. The frequency of {The explosives will be delivered} as a bag-of-words query is 1.94 million documents, and as an exact phrase is 3. With the substitution, the frequency of {The aura will be delivered} as a bag-of-words query is 1.04 million (showing some of the limitations of the bag-of-words approach, since this is an odd sentence but its words are used in many documents), and as an exact phrase is 0.

The frequency of the bag of words {The will be delivered} is 118 million, so we get:

$$\text{SO (original)} = 118/1.94 = 61$$

and

$$\text{SO (substitution)} = 118/1.04 = 113$$

Enhanced Sentence Oddity (ESO). In the definition of sentence oddity, removing the target word still matches sentences with the target word present – omitting it from the search query is not the same as excluding it. The enhanced sentence oddity explicitly excludes the target word from the search that produces the numerator value. Hence it is defined as:

$$\text{ESO} = \frac{f(\text{bag of words, target word excluded})}{f(\text{entire bag of words})}$$

Enhanced sentence oddity should also be larger for sentences containing substitutions.

The frequency of the bag of words {the will be delivered} with the word 'explosives' *excluded* is 116 million, so the enhanced sentence oddity is:

$$\text{ESO (original)} = 116/1.94 = 60$$

The frequency of the bag of words {the will be delivered} with the word 'aura' *excluded* is 115 million, so the enhanced sentence oddity is:

$$\text{ESO (substitution)} = 115/1.04 = 111$$

k-gram frequencies. We have already noted that it is hard to test the natural frequencies of exact (that is, quoted) strings using search engines because most strings of any length will never have been seen. Defining k-grams is an attempt to build patterns whose natural frequencies can be estimated in practice.

The left k-gram of a target word is the exact string from its left-hand nearest non-stopword to the word itself. The right k-gram of a target word is the exact string from the word itself to its right-hand nearest non-stopword.

The expectation is that the frequencies of both left and right k-grams will be low when the target word is a substitution. The two non-stopwords that anchor each k-gram play a similar role to the adjacent surprising words that are used in concept extraction.

The left k-gram of the original sentence is:

$$\text{left k-gram (original)} = 881,000$$

and the right k-gram is:

$$\text{right k-gram (original)} = 1,230$$

while, for the sentence with the substitution, we have:

$$\text{left k-gram (substitution)} = 1.66 \text{ million}$$

and the right k-gram is:

$$\text{right k-gram (substitution)} = 1$$

As expected, the right k-gram is much smaller for the sentence with the substitution. The left k-gram does not perform well, mostly because the left context is not actually anchored by another non-stopword.

Left and right k-grams measure different properties of sentences in English, which is not surprising given that English sentences are made to be understood based on the left context. This is very obvious for the example sentences.

Hypernym Oddity (HO). We have already discussed the concept of hypernyms and hyponyms (in Section 7.5.4), more and less general forms of nouns. Hypernyms and hyponyms define a chain above and below any word; actually a tree, because of the possibility of multiple hypernyms and hyponyms associated with different meanings. For example, one chain for "attack", from most-specific to most-general is "ground attack – attack – operation – activity – deed".

Replacing a target word with a hypernym changes the frequency of the resulting bag of words. Comparing the two frequencies provides information about whether the target word is contextually appropriate. If the replacement by the hypernym increases the frequency or leaves it unchanged, it is likely that the word is a substitution. If the replacement by the hypernym decreases the frequency, the word is probably not a substitution. This may seem counterintuitive. However, a contextually inappropriate word already tends to produce a low-frequency sentence; replacing this word by a hypernym does not change this much. On the other hand, if the word is contextually appropriate, replacing it by its hypernym tends to produce a more unusual sentence, perhaps a little more pompous, so the frequency drops.

The hypernym oddity is defined as:

$$\text{HO} = f_H - f$$

where f is the frequency of a sentence as a bag of words, and f_H is the frequency of the bag of words where the target word has been replaced by its hypernym. It is expected to be positive for an ordinary sentence, and negative for a sentence containing a substitution.

For the original sentence, the frequency of the bag of words {the explosives will be delivered} is 1.94 million, while the frequency of {the chemicals will be delivered} is 1.83 million, so

$$\text{HO (original)} = 110,000$$

The word 'aura' has several hypernyms, but the ones associated with the major meanings are 'symptom' and 'quality'. For the sentence with a substitution, the frequency for {the aura will be delivered} is 1.04 million, while the frequency for {the symptom will be delivered} is 1.9 million (and for {the quality will be delivered} is 28.2 million). So

$$\text{HO (substitution)} = -860,000$$

Each word typically has more than one hypernym, so the measure can be defined as the maximum, minimum, or average value over the possible choices of hypernym.

Hidden Markov Model. Left context is important in natural language. This measure assesses how contextually appropriate the target word is in its left context. The HMM oddity is defined to be:

$$\text{HMM} = \frac{f(\text{exact left region} + \text{target word})}{f(\text{exact left region})}$$

where each frequency estimate is for an exact string (so using a quoted string search), and is the maximum over left regions of all sizes in the sentence. In practice, frequencies for exact strings drop quickly with increasing length, so very few regions actually need to be checked.

When the target word is inappropriate in its context, and so likely to be a substitution, the HMM measure should be small.

The left context is so small in the example sentences that this measure does not tell us much. The number of documents containing 'the' is 4.6 billion.

Pointwise Mutual Information (PMI). Pointwise mutual information extends the HMM measure in two ways: considering the context on both sides of the target word, and taking into account the base frequency of the target word. It is defined to be:

$$\text{PMI} = \frac{f(\text{target word}) f(\text{exact adjacent region})}{f(\text{target word} + \text{adjacent region})}$$

where the frequencies, as before, are for exact strings, and so for quoted string searches, and + indicates concatenation in either direction. The measure is the maximum over all regions. As for HMM, all adjacent regions in the sentence are, in principle, considered, but the frequencies drop quickly to zero with increasing length.

PMI measures for words that are inappropriate in their contexts, and so likely to be substitutions, should be large.

PMI captures context in a way that is different from both k-grams, which captures only a limited context, and sentence oddity, which looks at a larger context but disregards word order.

For the example sentences, it is the frequency of the denominator that is most revealing. For the original sentence, the frequency of "explosives will" is 47,600, "explosives will be" is 22,300, and "explosives will be delivered" is 1,230. For the sentence with the substitution, the frequency of "aura will" is 58,400, of "aura will be" is 11,100, and "aura will be delivered" is 1. The denominator of the PMI measure for the sentence with the substitution gets small rapidly, making the measure large as expected.

Combining measures

Each of these measures is extremely weak at detecting substitutions at the sentence level, each individually scoring only slightly better than chance. However, each makes errors on different sentences, so using them together in an organized way makes it possible to achieve usable detection rates. An ideal boundary for each measure can be learned from labelled sets of sentences that are known to contain a substitution or not. A metalearner can then be built that uses the results of tests against these boundaries as inputs and produces an overall prediction.

In tests on several corpora, both formal and informal, prediction accuracies for substitution of about 90% were achieved[3]. However, the false-positive rate was typically about 10%. This is not usable at the sentence level, since in a set of 10,000 sentences of which 10 contained substitutions, the predictor would report 9 out of the 10 sentences that actually did contain substitutions, but almost 1000 other sentences that did not.

Extending sentence-level measures to documents

Fortunately, real documents usually contain more than one sentence and the problem of interest is to predict *documents* that contain substitutions. The rule that is used to decide when a document contains sufficient suspicious sentences to be worth further analysis can compensate for the sentence-level error rate. For example, suppose a document is considered suspicious if it contains three or more sentences flagged as containing substitutions. Messages from adversaries are likely to contain substitutions in several sentences, and so are overwhelmingly likely to match this rule and be flagged. Messages without substitutions are flagged only when there is a false positive in three or more sentences, which is much less likely. The false-negative rate at the message level increases only very slowly if we assume that almost all sentences in bad messages contain a substitution; so the false-positive rate can be made arbitrarily small. In the limit, the rule could be that *all* sentences must be flagged as containing a substitution. This would still catch almost all messages that do contain substitutions, while the false-positive rate would be $1/10^k$, where k is the number of sentences per document.

These measures require estimating the natural frequency of words, bags of words, and exact strings. Search engines approximate this because they index many documents in many different languages. The complexity and time required to access a search engine can, to some extent, be reduced by building an in-house document repository from which to make estimates. Another benefit of this is that the documents in the repository can be chosen to better represent the domain for which the 'natural' frequency is required. For example, if the pool of communications from which the messages of interest are to be selected share a property, such as being by authors for whom English is a second language, a repository that reflects this 'natural' background may be useful.

Substitution without frequency matching

So far we have assumed that the best replacement is a word with about the same frequency as the one it replaces, so that the word-frequency profile for the sentence of document remains roughly the same. What happens if the replacement is a word with a different natural frequency?

If the replacement word has much higher natural frequency, that is it is more common word than the one it replaces, then detecting the substitution becomes more difficult. This is because the phrases in which it appears have higher overall frequency, making it harder to detect the frequency changes that are the essence of the set of measures described above; and because it becomes more likely that the substitution makes sense 'by accident'. Common words tend to have multiple meanings, and so can fit into more places without creating a bump in sentence semantics.

However, the countervailing pressure is that substitution using common words also reduces the precision of the content of the communication. There are not enough common words to go around in a communication that has to mention a number of different objects.

If a replacement word has a much lower natural frequency, that is it is less common than the word it replaces, then detecting the substitution remains about the same difficulty as when the replacement is frequency matched. It may even get a little easier because the phrases in which the replacement word appears are naturally less frequent, and so several of the measures described above become more discriminating.

Detecting repeated substitutions

If several communications use the same substitutions, then the common structure this induces helps to connect these communications with one another. In other words, this could help to identify suspicious *conversations* rather than just suspicious individual messages[4].

Suppose that substitutions are frequency-matched, so that word A is replaced by word B throughout. Then the new conversation appears to be about B, when it was really about A. However, B and A have similar frequencies *because* they occur in conversations about as frequently as each other. So the new conversation will not look unusual.

However, if substitution of more than one word is made, then it may become possible to detect that the conversation is unusual. Suppose A is replaced by B, and both have natural frequency f_1; and that C is replaced by D, and both have natural frequency f_2. It does not follow that the natural co-occurrence frequency of A and C in the same document is the same as the natural co-occurrence of B and D in the same document. For example, a frequency-matched substitution for "attack" is "campaign", and for "bomb" is "contents". However, according to Google, the number of documents containing "attack" and bomb" is 12.8M, while the number containing "campaign" and "contents" is 24.4M. Of course, this example illustrates one of the difficulties: it is hard to know whether the co-occurrence frequencies will increase or decrease as a result of the substitution. For example, another pair of frequency-matched substitutions are "growing" for "attack" and "alcohol" for "bomb", but the number of documents containing the pair "growing" and "alcohol" is only 4.22M. There is a slight tendency, as the number of words involved in the substitution increases, for the co-occurrence frequencies to be lower for documents that contain substitutions.

If substitutions that replace words by much rarer words are used, then the resulting conversations rapidly become unusual enough to be detected.

Estimating natural frequencies from search-engine data finds anomalous conversations by measuring how unusual they are against a background of all (English) documents. In particular domains, this generality may make detection harder. For example, if the domain of messages being considered is email from a particular country, then there are a large number of topics that are extremely unlikely to ever be mentioned. It is conceivable to reproduce the whole machinery of a search engine restricted to each particular domain of discourse. However, it may be more effective simply to consider the set of intercepted documents as a whole. This set contains, by definition, a sample of 'ordinary' communication, possibly with a very small number of suspicious communications. Word-usage profiles can be computed for each communication in the set, and the resulting records clustered. Unusual conversations should then appear as clusters, perhaps even separated from the more ordinary topics of conversation. Substitution, especially when it is made from some global list of ranked words, is likely to insert a word that is extremely rare *in the domain of concern* and so make the document(s) containing it easy to see.

Singular value decomposition is ideal as a clustering technique in this setting because it will tend to place close to the origin documents whose content overlaps with many other documents. Documents whose content does not overlap at all with other documents will *also* tend to be placed close to the origin. This leaves documents whose word usage is correlated in a sufficiently unusual way, conversations about unusual subjects, far from the origin where they are detectable. Conversations make it easier to detect individual communications that contain substitutions.

One concern that is often raised is whether information about natural frequencies derived from search engines is sufficiently accurate to capture the usage patterns of those whose first language is not, say, English. However, search engines index so much text that they capture many examples of real usage from a wide range of users. So not only can characteristics of 'normal' usage be estimated from such repositories; so can characteristic spelling errors, English-as-a-second-language effects, and even hybrid and pidgin usage across languages.

It is clear that obfuscation is not an easy strategy for adversaries to exploit. Although it hides the content of their communications, it also creates a signal that tends to make it more likely that these communications will be selected for deeper analysis. The reason is that ordinary communication has, in some broad sense, a predictable structure of word usage. Even though there is a large vocabulary to choose from, ordinary communication has a correlational structure that can be understood by looking at large samples of text; and search engines have already collected such samples and provide a straightforward way to access the information implicit in them. Attempts to hide communication inevitably lead to variations in this implicit structure that are often detectable, and so backfire for the adversaries. Furthermore, the harder they try to conceal, the more likely it is that further artifacts are introduced, and so the more likely it is that the communications will be selected.

8.4.2   Content Extraction after Substitution

The most challenging problem in exploiting private communication is to discover the documents of interest against a background of less-interesting communication. But what can be learned from the set of documents selected, given that they have been obfuscated? We now turn to this question.

Entities

When the names of people, places, and organizations need to be concealed, new names must come from somewhere. The tendency is to do this as a two-stage process: first, choose a set from which the names can be chosen; and then choose members of this set for each entity to be replaced. For example, the sets might be other sets of names (characters from a novel[5]), colors, or days of the week. For the names of places, it may work well to choose the names of other places far away. Once the set has been chosen, then individual entities can be named by an element of the set.

We cannot use the techniques from the previous section to decide whether the collection of entity names is unusual or not because every set of names is unusual. To put it another way, global frequency information about names is not reliable because they are used in local ways associated with small collections of documents.

However, there may be something to be learned, both from the choice of the set of replacement names and the individual choices from the set. This is because these choices, made by humans, are made subconsciously, even when we think they are not. This has long been appreciated by the military, where the code names of operations are chosen in a computer-mediated way to prevent unconscious leakage of information via the choice of name. For example, the German use of *Wotan*, a one-eyed god, for the name of a radar system in World War II allowed the British to infer its single-beam properties and design a countermeasure without *any* other information about it.

Something may also be learned from the choices of particular elements of the set as replacements for particular entities. The name used for a particular person may unconsciously echo something about that person that may, with some effort, be discernible. When one set of geographical names is replaced by another, it may be convenient to use a substitution that maintains the relationships between places, such as direction or distance. Again, this may possibly be discerned.

Although entities are concealed by substitution, the unconscious aspect of language may cause some leakage from the original names to the replacements.

Concepts

Recall that concepts are short phrases, extracted from a document because their components occur adjacently with unexpectedly high frequency. We saw above that multiple substitutions are more easily detectable than a single substitution when they occur in related words because, although each individual word is frequency-matched, the combined frequencies of a set of substitutions will still almost inevitably be wrong. Concepts require multiple substitutions of *adjacent words*, which makes it even easier to detect that the combined frequency is (usually) wrong because exact string searches can be used to estimate natural frequencies.

Phrases in the same position in the document as the original concepts will be detected as concepts in the document after substitution, because the component words will co-occur with surprisingly high frequency, in fact even more surprising than in the original concept that has been obfuscated. Replacement of each word in a concept phrase by a new matched-frequency word is most likely to decrease the frequency of the new phrase. The old phrase describes an actual concept; that is why it was used. The new phrase is a more or less accidental association of two unrelated words.

For example, suppose that a concept mentioned in the original document is "explosive device". The reported frequency of this exact phrase at Google is 1.49M. A frequency-matched word for "explosive" is "adopting", and one for "device" is "minds", but the frequency of the phrase "adopting minds" is 2! Similarly, the frequency of the exact phrase "rental truck" is 450,000. A frequency-matched word for "rental" is "paving", and one for "truck" is "heels", but the frequency of the exact phrase "paving heels" is 1. These concepts will still be discovered in the altered document because the adjacent occurrence of the pairs of words "adopting" and "minds"; and "paving" and "heels" is unlikely. This suggests that concepts can be another powerful tool to detect and select documents in which substitutions have been made.

Discovering concepts in the altered document may also make it possible to guess what the original concepts were. Knowing that a particular substitution has been made using a frequency-matched word, it can still be difficult to guess what the original word was, because the precise ranking used is not usually known. A list of possible original words with similar frequency rank to the substituted word might contain several hundred entries. However, a detected concept requires two (or more) consistent substitutions, so it becomes possible to consider all pairs (or n-tuples) of possible original words against a list of known concepts. The possibilities will quickly decrease. For example, the part of the ranked list around "adopting" is: "wording, dreaming, accountancy, hm, promoter, hips, explosive, adopting, picasso, shirts, shirley, anticipation, insistence". In an adversarial situation, very few of these words look worth obfuscating. When the part of the ranked list around "minds": "turnover, observation, leisure, device, minds, economics, mortgage, ear, ok, confusion" is also considered, there are not many sensible combinations other than "explosive device", and perhaps "accountancy turnover". So using the fact that the obfuscated concept is rare, but the original concept is probably more common, combinations of terms in the same region of a ranked list whose frequency is noticeably increased are probably the original concepts.

So far we have considered only how a single concept can be used to select documents that may contain substitutions, and perhaps reverse engineer the substitutions to find the original words. Most documents contain more than one concept, so the same idea can be applied to the *set* of documents. The original document had (presumably) sensible subject matter, so the set of its concepts should occur with reasonable natural frequency. However, the apparent concepts after substitution are all expected to be quite rare individually. As a set of concepts, they should be *extremely* rare, creating an even stronger signal for the presence of substitution. In the example above, a document mentioning both "explosive device" and "rental truck" does not seem particulary unusual (although interesting from a law-enforcement point of view). In fact, Google reports 406 such documents. A document mentioning both "adopting minds" and "paving heels" is much less likely, and Google reports none at all, as expected.

This ability to use concept information as a way to select communication for further analysis makes it extremely difficult for adversaries. They have to choose between substitutions that will create plausible concepts, at the expense of poor individual word substitutions; or choose frequency-matched word substitutions that lead to outlandish concepts. For example, replacing "explosive" by "chicken" and "device" by "recipe" produces a sensible concept: "chicken recipe". However, the rank of "explosive" is 8085, while "chicken" is 4162; and the rank of "device" is 3275 while "recipe" is 6242, so the word-level substitutions become easier to detect.

Relationships

Relationships are extracted from documents using information from the properties of the verbs, and from semantic properties of some of the nouns. For example, verbs can express 1-, 2-, and 3-place relations: "I understand", "He hit her", and "He brought me the bomb". There are also some 0-place verbs in English, for example, "It is raining" where there is no actual object corresponding to "it". The number of places required for a verb is called its *valency*.

There are three possibilities for the verbs in an obfuscated communication:

- The verbs have been left unchanged.

- The verbs have been replaced by frequency-matched verbs.

- The verbs have been replaced by valency-matched verbs.

In general, it is not possible to match replacements on both frequency and valency because the frequency ranking of a verb has nothing to do with its valency, and so verbs of equal valency can be a long way apart on a frequency-ranked list.

If the verbs have been left unchanged, then the relationships are still visible in the document – but the meaning of the nodes of the relationship, carried by noun phrases, has presumably been obfuscated. The data available from the document can be thought of as a graph with edge labelling (from the verbs) but with obfuscated node labels. As we saw in Chapter 6, quite a lot can be learned from such a graph. Also, if consistent substitutions are used for the nouns, the graph from one communication can be connected to the graphs from others that use the same substitution to create a graph that captures relationships inside a conversation.

If verbs have been replaced by frequency-matched verbs, then the semantic-bump detection techniques described in Section 8.4.1 are likely to select the communication for further analysis because the substring around the verb is an inappropriate context. The measures used do not depend on the part of speech of the target word.

Parsing, and then looking up the normal valence of the new verbs is also a robust method for selecting communications, since it is unlikely that a frequency-matched verb replacement will also be valency-matched. As with nouns, detecting that there has been a substitution does not necessarily mean that the original meaning can be extracted, although similar kinds of analyses of subject-verb-object phrases might be possible.

If verbs have been replaced by valency-matched verbs, then the frequencies are likely to be very different, and local detection of semantic bumps becomes even more likely.

The properties of verbs can be divided even more finely than simply their valency. Particular verbs can take only particular kinds of subjects and objects. Only living things can eat, and what gets eaten must be some kind of food. This is called *selectional restriction*. Once again, substitutions that attempt to match only valency may violate these rules about possible subjects and objects, and so create another opportunity for selection as anomalous. On the other hand, matching subject and object type makes it harder to match frequency (although, of course, it naturally matches valency).

Selectional restriction also applies to the connections between other components of a sentence. There has been a long-running debate among linguists about whether selectional restriction is best thought of as a syntactic or semantic requirement. Access to large repositories makes this somewhat moot since, as we have seen, enough syntax approximates semantics. In fact, studies of stroke patients have shown that selectional restriction is both syntactic and semantic[6]. Other forms of selectional restriction could be used as another check on the normality of sentences.

Effective substitution requires finding a substitute that matches the original word in several different ways: natural frequency, valency, and type of subject and object. Succeeding with all three at once is almost impossible, and succeeding with one or two comes at the cost of creating a strong signal in the other(s).

If verbs have been replaced, then the graph structure of the relations can still be extracted from a document, but now neither edges nor nodes have labels. Even in this case, it may be possible to extract useful knowledge from the structure. For example, it may be possible to tell if the subject of discussion consists of tightly coupled objects, richly connected, or much more loosely coupled objects, with fewer connections – even though we cannot identify the objects or the nature of the connections. In other words, we can extract qualitative information, but cannot fill this out with details. There may also be characteristic patterns that are identifiable only from the connection structure, a possibility discussed in Chapter 6 in the context of graph information retrieval.

Substitutions of other parts of speech are limited in their ability to obfuscate relations and, like noun substitutions, tend to introduce strong signals that obfuscation has occurred, making it easier to select such communication for further analysis.

Topics

A topic is a single word or phrase that describes the content of a document. The goal of obfuscation is precisely to obscure the content of documents, so it should not be surprising that topic extraction is not going to be helpful, either in selecting documents for further analysis, or in understanding the real content of obfuscated documents.

For example, it is possible to decide that a document or group of documents are about a rare topic, rare in a particular context. But ordinary documents will also occasionally be about rare topics as well, and it seems hard to estimate, in a robust way, how rare a topic 'should' be.

It might be possible to cluster documents in some universe by topic, and look for a cluster whose topic is rare, and that seems to be too large for such a rare topic. However, it seems hard to decide, in a robust way, how large a rare topic cluster 'should' be also. One area of active investigation is to cluster a set of documents into their topics, and then see which documents do not fit into any of the clusters. The leftover documents may either be single documents about specialized content, or sets of documents about a topic which are too small or too diffuse to be detected by the clustering algorithm. In either case, they may be of interest, and should be few enough that deeper investigation is possible.

Narrative

A narrative is rather like an extended version of relationships: a collection of pieces, carried primarily by nouns and verbs, that fit together to create a coherent representation of a situation.

Although narrative, as it is ordinarily used, carries a connotation of pieces in sequence, this need not necessarily be the case. So, in the same way that it is possible to look at a graph structure, even without knowledge of the meaning of its nodes and edges, it may be possible to find narrative in (a set of) documents, even when the nouns and verbs have been replaced. Such a narrative is really a special case of a subgraph with particular structure.

Although topoi originated as specialized structures in rhetoric, they are now often considered as low-level components of a narrative. Although there are many, perhaps thousands, of such topoi, some believe that the total number is finite. In this case, extracting narrative from documents can be posed as recognizing the presence of examples of topoi. (See also the discussion of frames in Section 9.1.)

Summarization

Because most summarization techniques rely on lexical and syntactic attributes, they should produce summaries of an obfuscated document that are similar to those that would have been produced for the original document, with the corresponding substitutions, of course. These summaries are likely to seem rather odd to a human reader, but it is hard to see how this can be exploited automatically for either selection or context extraction.

Since a summary is supposed to be a short synopsis of the content of an entire document or collection of documents, it is conceivable that an entire summary could be passed, as a query, to a search engine and the resulting frequency used to make a judgement of how plausible the document or document set is.

For example, one of the snippets (the short summary that appears below the URL in a list of search results) returned by a search using the terms "explosive" and "device" is "An improvised explosive device (IED) is a euphemism for a roadside bomb. An IED is a bomb constructed and deployed in ways other than in conventional". Treating this entire snippet as a bag of words returns 10,200 pages.

Replacing "explosive" by "adopting", "device" by "minds", and "bomb" by "contents", and treating the resulting string as a bag of words produces 313 responses (showing that even highly improbable constellations of words still appear).

Of course, the number of responses has dropped sharply as the result of the substitution but, in reality, we do not have access to the original summary, and so we don't know how many responses to expect. So we don't know whether 313 is a small number of responses, or quite a large one.

This seemingly improbable response to the snippet with substitutions happens because the returned documents are all large, and contain content from a range of different topics. There is potential here to incorporate information about the size of documents as well as the number of documents into decision making, since it is inherently more likely that a given set of words will co-occur in a large document than in a small one. (Obviously, in this case treating the snippet as a quoted string returns no results.)

8.4.3 Authorship after Substitution

Authorship detection is little altered by substitution provided that it is based on lexical and syntactic attributes, rather than content. As we saw earlier, content attributes are problematic anyway, so this is the likely scenario.

Knowing an authorship signature from public communication might make it possible to select private communications that match the signature. These are likely to be little affected by obfuscation.

8.4.4 Metainformation after Substitution

Obfuscation makes no difference to metainformation since it changes only the content of communication, while metainformation is extracted from the other properties of a communication.

The improved ability to select communications of interest, however, means that better metainformation may be collected. It is also possible that senders might be slightly more careless about leaking metainformation assuming, if only subconsciously, that there is less chance of attracting attention in private communication.

8.5   Tactics and Process

The structure of the problem of selecting and analyzing communications to extract the maximal possible knowledge from them requires that the process be organized in a particular way.

As with other prediction problems, the naive assumption is that selection should be regarded as a monolithic step, distinguishing interesting from uninteresting communications. However, as before, organizing the task into a multistage pipeline provides opportunities to improve the process.

8.5.1   Using a Multifaceted Process for Selection

We now consider how to fit all of these analysis techniques together to produce an effective global process for selecting documents of interest, and extract useful knowledge from them. The techniques we have discussed are of two kinds:

- Those that are most useful for *selection*: watch-list matching, concept extraction, relationship extraction, concept co-occurrence, and topic detection.

- Those that are most useful for understanding the content of a document: narrative extraction and summarization.

Of course, some techniques are useful for both; for example, concepts and topics help with selection but are also of interest in their own right. The first set of techniques can be used as predictive models for selection. The second set of techniques are better used to support an analyst trying to understand a document.

Models that look at the simplest structures in documents, for example, looking for substitution at the level of individual words, are the weakest because they exploit the least context. Models that look for more-complex structures are more powerful because it becomes increasingly difficult to make the pieces of such structures look as if they fit together, and still conceal content. It makes sense to arrange the techniques in a pipeline, where the simple but cheaper tests are applied first, and documents that are definitely not of

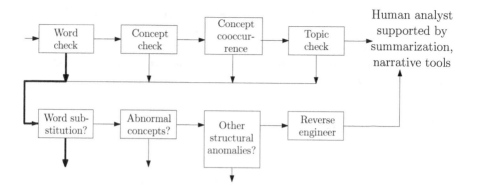

Figure 8.1. *A textual-analysis pipeline for private communication.*

possible interest are discarded. Subsequent stages of the pipeline then have to deal with smaller sets of documents, and so it matters less that they are more expensive. For any stage, it is obviously best to implement the technique as a ranking predictor, and choose boundaries so that the false-negative rate is as close to zero as possible. This avoids missing a document of interest, by applying a test too simple to notice its unusual properties or structure. The consequence of choosing such a boundary is that the false-positive rate of an individual stage will tend to be large, but this means only that the subsequent stage has to examine more documents than, in theory, it could have.

It is appropriate to build two interconnected pipelines: one to examine documents in which substitution has not been attempted, and the other in which it has. The overall process is shown in Figure 8.1.

The first pipeline relies on the existence of watch lists of properties that make a document of interest. We have already mentioned the use of watch lists of words. We suggest that this idea should be extended (if it has not already been) to watch lists for higher-level properties: watch lists of concepts, watch lists of concept co-occurrences, watch lists of relationships, and watch lists of topics. Each document flows down a pipeline that extracts, in turn, each of these structures and compares them to the relevant watch list. At each stage, a document that does not match drops out of this pipeline (and goes on to the other pipeline). A document that contains words from the word watch list is passed on to the next stage, which examines the structure of the relevant words in more detail by matching against the concept watch list. If it fails to match, the word-level match is almost certainly a false positive, and the document can be dropped out of this pipeline. For example, a document that simply contains a list of words on the word-level watch list will not produce a match with the concept-level watch list. This process continues, using analysis of more and more complex structures. Documents that are still ranked as interesting after all stages have a high probability of actually being interesting, and can be passed to a secondary phase. This secondary phase might involve a human analyst, supported by tools such as summarization and narrative extraction, as well as the results of all stages of the pipeline, that make it fast and easy to check the document's properties. Some of this functionality could probably be built into a meta-predictor eventually, but I doubt that it is well-enough understood to attempt this yet.

Documents that do not appear to contain words or higher-level structures from watch lists may still be interesting, but may have been camouflaged by substitution. The second pipeline exists to explore this possibility. Rather than relying on watch lists, the second pipeline uses *abnormality* as its measure of being interesting. As we have seen, abnormality in its ordinary sense, the unusual documents created by people with unusual style, or unusual interest reflected in content, may create signals of abnormality in some language structures, but are unlikely to do so across a set of structures at different levels. Their word and concept use may be rare, but the relationships and selectional restrictions of their documents will be perfectly normal. On the other hand, documents that have been obfuscated are likely to contain signals of abnormality at multiple levels.

The stages of the second pipeline are much the same as those of the first. Documents are first tested for the presence of word-level substitutions (that is, a test for abnormal words, rather than words from a watch list). Those documents that show no sign of such substitutions can be discarded as normal (the vast majority). This is safe to do, as long as the rule for keeping a document is sufficiently stringent – perhaps *any* sign of substitution in any sentence is enough to keep the document in the pipeline.

Documents are then tested for abnormality using a hierarchy of tests based on increasingly complex structures: concepts, co-occurrence of concepts, relationships, and selectional restriction. These tests can be arranged in a pipeline, with a low false-negative rate, or could be treated as a set of parallel tests applied to each document at once. Documents that seem normal are discarded; those that are still interesting may be analyzed with the goal of reverse engineering the substitutions they contain, and are then passed to the analysis stage: for content extraction if possible, or for other forms of analysis if not.

The heavy line in the figure shows that path that most documents will follow: most documents do not contain words on the word-level watch list, and do not show any sign of substitution at the word level. Hence, only the first stages of each pipeline need to examine all documents. The subsequent stages are all working with much smaller subsets.

Tests for abnormality require ways to access norms for many different structural properties. Many of these norms can be estimated from the data collected by large search engines, but there is obviously a role for in-house data collection to allow estimation to focus on particular language domains: particular languages, particular countries, second-language speakers, the technical language of particular domains (money laundering, drugs), and so on. It is also conceivable that some norms can be derived from a deeper understanding of how humans create language.

One of the things that this analysis makes clear is that documents consist of many interlocking pieces, fitting together at different levels of abstraction. Obfuscation is difficult, because the new document must fit together as well as the original one did, or else the obfuscation becomes obvious. To say it the other way round, ordinary documents look as if they fit together at every level of abstraction and from the point of view of every structure. It is hard to manipulate documents so as to preserve such a rich set of properties.

Notes

[1] In particular, Shamir shows that if anyone discovers or plants even a single pair of integers whose product is computed wrongly (even in a single low-order bit) by some processor, then *any* key in *any* RSA-based security program running on *any* of the computers using this processor can be broken with a single chosen message.

[2] Cryptosystems use two keys that are inverses to each other, in the sense that messages encrypted with one can be decrypted using the other. In private-key cryptosystems, both keys must be kept secret. In public-key cryptosystems, one key can be made public, since it is computationally too difficult to compute the other key from the public one. One key must still be kept secret. It can be used for decryption of messages from anyone else, or for encryption of messages that therefore must be from the person who holds the key, since nobody else could have encrypted them.

[3] SW. Fong, D.B. Skillicorn and D. Roussinov, "Detecting word substitutions in text", *IEEE Transactions on Knowledge and Data Engineering*, 20(8):1067–1076, August 2008.

[4] See, for example, D.B. Skillicorn, *Beyond Keyword Filtering for Message and Conversation Detection*, in: *IEEE International Conference on Intelligence and Security Informatics (ISI2005)*, pp. 231–243. Springer-Verlag Lecture Notes in Computer Science LNCS 3495, May 2005.

[5] For example, in Braine's novel *The Pious Agent*, the names of operatives are characters from C.S. Lewis's Narnia books.

[6] A.D. Friederici, D.Y. von Cramon and S.A. Kotz, "Language related brain potentials in patients with cortical and subcortical left hemisphere lesions", *Brain*, 122(6):1033–1047, 1999.

Chapter 9

Discovering Mental and Emotional State

In the preceding two chapters, we have looked at knowledge that can be extracted from documents, knowledge about the content, and knowledge about the identity and characteristics of authors. In this chapter, we extend this idea to look at knowledge about the *state of mind* of authors – not just who they are, but why they are writing, what they are thinking that drives their writing, and what they are feeling. The techniques discussed in this chapter are less well-developed than those in the preceding chapters, but they provide knowledge that is critically important; and the underlying technologies are developing rapidly as a result.

We will consider three broad families of techniques:

- Using *frame analysis* to learn about author intentions, how ideas and arguments are being positioned for an intended audience, and so indirectly how adversaries are thinking about their world – how they see their activities. For example, in a kidnapping it is important to know whether the victim is still alive, what the real intentions behind the kidnapping are, and whether the group that carried out the kidnapping is adhering to a plan or improvising under stress. We may want to understand whether a terrorist group sees itself as reacting to oppression, or as driving a historically ordained change, both to understand its possible targets and to understand how it might recruit.

- Using *sentiment analysis* to learn about author opinions and attitudes towards other individuals, groups, and perhaps objects and ideas. For example, we may want to know whether a crime is a hate crime or an ordinary crime using hate as a cover. We may want to know if a terrorist group directs most of its anger against a domestic government or that of some other country.

- Learning about the mental state of an author as revealed by that person's writing and conversation. For example, we may want to know if an author is depressed or elated; or if an author is being deliberatively deceptive.

These techniques all exploit the existence of an internal-state channel, by which authors reveal their mental states in ways that they are often not very aware of. Partly because this information is valuable in an adversarial setting, and partly because this channel is hard to disguise or pollute, these techniques have a great deal of potential. Although much of the technology is new, these techniques will rapidly grow in importance because they are so useful.

9.1   Frame Analysis for Intentions

Frames are a model of the way in which people understand situations, communicate about them, and in particular the way people convince, or try to convince, others. There is considerable disagreement about the exact definition of what constitutes a frame. Arguably, people use frames to project their own assumptions about how people understand their worlds and how communication works.

At their simplest, frames are explanations for how individuals structure their perceptions of the world, and therefore, in a broad social sense, what they see: how they explain to themselves the structures and motives they see in society. Frames therefore are an important part of how a group views itself, how one group convinces another, and how two groups find common purpose.

Opinions differ about whether frames should be thought of as intentional (explicit) or as tacit. If frames are intentional, then they are a bit like the metaphors that people use to represent the world to themselves. They try to convince others by arguing for a particular frame (as well as arguing within a frame). If frames are representations of tacit knowledge, we may be able to observe them, perhaps only in other people, but not much can be done with the knowledge. In this view, frames are used and assimilated more or less unconsciously.

Media studies tend to take the first position, that frames are useful tools that explain how to write effective stories. Media-studies programs often include training in how to use frames. Typical frames in the journalism setting are conflict, human interest, or economic consequences, and almost all media stories could perhaps be shoehorned into these three categories. A related position is to see frames as ways to structure arguments, similar to the topoi of rhetoric (in the sense of Aristotle). Seeing frames in this way certainly helps to explain why interest groups often talk past each other – they fail to understand that some of their differences arise from different frames, and not from the content of these frames. Their arguments to each other fail because they take place at the wrong logical level. In the 'frames are explicit' view, there are only a small number of different frames, so they can be exhaustively enumerated.

Sociologists tend to take the position that frames are tacit filters on each person's perception and understanding of the world. As such, they exist at many different levels of granularity, and there are an unlimited number of different frames of different kinds. For example, seeing a group of teenagers could trigger a frame for honor students, if they are well dressed and encountered in a high-school hallway; a frame for alienated and bored youth if encountered standing around in a mall; and a frame for a dangerous gang if encountered dressed in black on a street corner at night. Certain cues trigger these different presumptions about what the situation 'really' is, and these cues occur in sets corresponding to frames. In this view, frames are often seen as imposed (but it is not always clear how) in support of hegemony or power, although this would imply a hybrid view in which some people manipulate frames but others remain unaware of them.

9.1.1   Goals

Being able to extract and examine the frames present in a piece of writing or a conversation provides insight into how the author(s) view the world and so, indirectly at least, what their intentions are. Frame analysis can be used to:

- Understand the situational awareness of the adversaries, since it reveals what they think is important in the world from their perspective, and how they understand the meaning of events and attitudes in that world.

- Understand how they want to present themselves to sympathizers, and to the wider world, including how they approach recruitment. The kind of presentations and arguments they make not only reveal something about how they view themselves, but how they view their target audience, and to some extent their enemies.

- Discover their blind spots by exploring what their perceptual filters, as implied by their frames, miss. This can be a source of ideas for effective counteraction.

- Discover their strategic intentions (although probably not their tactical intentions) because their frames will suggest what goals they will think of as worthwhile and which they will not.

- Distinguish between people and groups who are reacting or venting in response to some perceived problem or injustice, and those who are motivated and professional enough to do something about it. For example, extremely idealistic frames may be associated with less-dangerous groups.

- Follow trends in a group's frames over time, allowing extrapolation to predict a change from, say, a reactive to a proactive mode.

9.1.2 Frame-Analysis Detection Technology

Finding and extracting frames is complicated by the fuzziness of deciding exactly what frames are. Existing work is based on the assumption that frames are primarily conscious and intentional; and most work has relied on human labelling of frames, meaning that it has been limited in scope.

Koening[1] developed a partially automated approach, assuming a fixed set of nine frames. These frames are arranged in a 3×3 grid, one of whose dimensions is based on the *form* of the frame (conflict, or human interest, or economic consequence) and the other dimension based on the *content* (ethnonationalists against one another, or liberal-individualist in contrast to a state, or harmony with nature).

He then used a four-stage process to extract the frames from a corpus. First, discourse-analysis techniques were applied to a subset of the documents, marking content such as collective-pronoun use, and national affiliations. Second, concept-extraction and mapping techniques were used to cluster the documents and so to extract markers for the frames within them. Third, these markers were used to find frames in the whole corpus; and, fourth, the corpus was clustered to validate the frames as latent factors within its documents.

Sanfilippo *et al.*[2] built a completely automatic system, using a stronger definition of frames. They define a frame to consist of four parts:

1. An intention

2. A promoter, that is an individual or group holding that intention

3. A target against which the intention is directed, and

4. An issue.

Each of these parts is selected from a possible set of options specific to each particular context. For example, intentions include criticize, request, assert, support, and judge. Issues include economy, politics, social, law, and military. Each of these parts can be described in an operational way using definitions, examples, and lexical markers. An automatic frame-extraction algorithm was built using a suite of tools for word domain recognition and named-entity extraction. This suite can find frames in documents, and fill in templates for each one with the required four parts, including probabilistic judgements for competing issues. The collection of extracted frames can then be searched using any part of the frames. The authors were able to extract trend information about the communications of a specific group that had been outlawed in its own country.

Very little work has been done on frame extraction, but there is clearly potential to learn much from documents using this idea.

9.1.3 Concealment Opportunities

Opportunities for concealment of frames depend on whether one believes that frames are generated consciously or unconsciously. If they are generated consciously, then an opportunity for concealment exists, for example using the kind of word substitutions discussed in the previous two chapters. However, the kind of content in which frames are relevant is not that of tactical messages, which is primarily what was considered in those chapters, but more strategic content, intended to persuade or align. It is not clear that obfuscation is a realistic option in these kinds of settings because part of the power of frames is the resonance they (are intended to) have with the audience, and it is not clear that this survives a deobfuscation step. In other words, if the audience has to work too hard to understand, much of the impact may be lost.

The use of word substitutions will, in the present state of the art, prevent frames from being detected, because frame-detection techniques rely on explicit verbs and other content-bearing words. For example, replacing the verbs associated with the *criticize* intention (accuse, blame for, ...) in the work of Sanfilippo *et al.* makes the corresponding frame undetectable. The difficulty is at least as great as extracting narrative from obfuscated text.

If frames are generated subconsciously, then there are no real opportunities for concealment, since authors are not aware of the frames that they use. We return to this point in Section 9.3.

9.1.4 Tactics and Process

There are two kinds of opportunities to manipulate adversaries using knowledge extracted from frame analysis. The first is extractive in nature. Discussion or argument can be used to draw out the adversaries within the particular frames in which they operate – but an awareness of these frames also makes it possible to have a discussion or argument at the higher level of the frames themselves, extracting more detailed information about these frames. This is a more sophisticated way of extracting information about an adversary using a dialogue, because knowledge of the frame enables much of the detailed content, which may not ever be made explicit, to be guessed at reliably.

The second opportunity is to use knowledge of the frames to sabotage the communication. This can be done by reframing, changing the terms of the conversation without necessarily arguing directly or changing the content. Manipulating the frame may be easier than trying to rebut arguments within the frame directly, especially if the adversaries are not fully aware of their own frames. This strategy is common in politics where political parties try to frame the ongoing dialogue in terms that make it seem most attractive to their goals. For example, reductions in government budgets can be framed as 'cutbacks' or as 'tax relief'.

Sabotage can also be implemented by forcing a *reductio ad absurdum* in the context of the frame rather than in the context of the content of the argument.

9.2   Sentiment Analysis

Sentiment analysis analyzes text to discover the attitudes, in a general sense, of the author to the content of the text, or to other objects, people, or organizations. It has its roots in advertising, where there is obvious interest in understanding the attitudes of consumers to products. Most sentiment analysis takes a simple view of attitude that is best summed up as polarity: is the attitude towards the target or object of interest positive or negative?

9.2.1   Goals

There are three primary goals for sentiment analysis, although the first has received far more attention that the others:

1. How does the author judge the target of interest, for example some object, person, or organization? This question is of interest in advertising, but also in trying to predict stock-price movements, election campaigns, popularity of films and books, and reputation of leaders or potential leaders inside organizations and in society.

2. How does the author feel about the target of interest? Judgement asks about opinions, presumptively based on some kind of rational decision making, while feelings assess the target on a less-rational basis. This is also of interest in advertising, where the appeal of certain kinds of products is not based simply on a comparison of features.

3. What feelings about the target is the author trying to create in the intended audience? This treats the content as directed towards inducing feelings that the author might not necessarily feel.

Sentiment analysis research so far has almost entirely been about determining whether an author is making a positive or a negative comment about some person or object. For example, marketers are interested in whether reviews of movies, books, CDs, or other consumer products and services are complimentary or not. Businesses want to know whether customer perceptions are positive or not. Media personalities want to measure their popularity. The huge amount of textual content created online in blogs and web forums provides a source for information about large-scale perceptions from which positive or negative opinions can be extracted.

In an adversarial setting, opinions are useful as an indirect way to gauge intent. For example, attitudes may be predictors of plausible targets either for criminals or terrorists. Attitudes towards law enforcement or government may also be useful signals of how threatened adversaries feel.

9.2.2 Sentiment-Analysis Technology

At one level, the problem is straightforward: those with opinions want to convey them to possible readers as clearly as possible, and tend to do so primarily with adjectives that have an obvious possible or negative sense. "The product is good" is easy to distinguish from "The product is bad". There are two problems that complicate this simple view.

The first is that natural language, even when used in simple declarative ways, tends to make it hard to infer whether a particular text is positive or negative about its target, at least using a bag-of-words approach. The simplest example is the use of negation: saying something is "not bad" is a weak way of saying that it is good, but a bag-of-words approach will lose the connection between "not" and "bad". There are many more complex cases. For example, "I was expecting the object to be bad, but it was good" rates the object positively, but the adjective "bad" is closest, and is in the same phrase. The danger is that over-simple analysis will make the wrong connection, and so predict the wrong polarity.

The second is the use of rhetorical devices, even in prose whose intent is declarative. For example, irony, sarcasm, and understatement may be used; different forms of nesting may dissociate the relevant adjectives from the object they refer to, and comments about features of an object may be conflated with comments about the object itself; for example, "although the special effects were poor, the movie was excellent". Extracting an author's true attitudes may require a large context: not only the full context of the text, but also a personal and societal context. For example, a faintly negative review of a product widely considered to be of high quality may be more significant than its textual content alone would suggest.

Sentiment-analysis technology has developed through a number of stages, although it is still almost entirely limited to predicting polarity. Early systems used standard prediction technology, using adjective frequencies as attributes, and developing a relevant set of adjectives either in a completely manual way, or in a semi-supervised way by choosing a small starting set of adjectives ("good", "bad") manually, and then using thesauri such as Wordnet's synonym sets to expand the set automatically. Such systems, using Support Vector Machines or Naive Bayes classifiers, have prediction accuracies in the 60–80% range when applied to documents such as movie reviews. These are easy cases in the sense that they are written explicitly to address polarity, they are fairly short, and each is written by a single author.

Another approach is to calculate the Pairwise Mutual Information (PMI) (recall from Section 8.4.1) between the object name and relevant adjectives[3]. This estimates how unusual it is for the object and adjective to be associated as they are in the text, measured against the norms of such association in large text repositories. This allows some calibration against normality, providing better estimates of polarities.

A further refinement is to try and eliminate the objective sentences from a document, expecting that such sentences may confuse the sentiment prediction. For example, movie reviews often contain a plot summary which may contain polarity adjectives, but these are not helpful in deciding the polarity of the review. A model for the difference between objective and subjective sentences is reasonably straightforward to create, at least in some domains. For example, Pang and Lee[4] use sentences from a site that collects movie reviews to provide examples of subjective sentences, and sentences from a site that provides plot summaries to provide examples of objective sentences. A model built from these sentences can be used to extract a subjective sentence summary from a movie review, and then apply polarity analysis to the extracted subjective sentences only.

More-sophisticated techniques have also been tried on a small-scale basis. For example, the polarity of adjacent sentences might be expected to be the same, and this information can be used to improve per-sentence prediction. Parsing documents[5], rather than treating sentences as bags of words, has also been used. This allows information such as subjects and objects, adverbs, and nouns to be included as attributes. Verbs can be treated as ways to transfer polarity from one object to another, for example "object A outperforms object B" or "object A runs faster than object B", and this kind of information can be captured and exploited. Finally, techniques from machine translation have been used, treating the problem as translation from natural language to "sentiment units". Kanayama et al.[6] use this approach to categorize sentence fragments as positive, negative, questions, or requests.

Sentiment analysis is used commercially. One example is the Infonic product, *Sentiment*, which targets news articles, extracting information about people, products, and companies that might affect stock prices and other tradable-commodity prices[7].

Conventional sentiment analysis can be used in adversarial settings to extract information about targeting, and opinions of one member of group about others, to the extent that these are communicated. For example, a criminal or terrorist group may discuss the merits and drawbacks of various opportunities in their communications. This information can be used for setting traps, or for target hardening. Possible points of dissension within such a group may become visible via sentiment analysis of their opinions about each other.

9.2.3 Concealment Opportunities

The objects about which sentiments are expressed can be concealed using the word-substitution techniques discussed in Chapter 8. It may be possible to detect that substitutions have occurred, and so that the opinions are really about something other than they appear to be about, but reverse engineering would be needed to work out what the actual objects were.

Obfuscation of the sentiments themselves seems much harder to do. It is, of course, possible to agree, in advance, that black is white, and everything positive should be interpreted as negative and *vice versa*. But this seems a very limited strategy. Otherwise, finding a way to replace adjectives with others in a practical and systematic way seems difficult. For example, the spectrum from positive to negative could be mapped to any other continuum, say from bright colors to dark colors. This might prevent completely automatic sentiment analysis, since the sentences might not seem to be subjective, but it is probably easy for humans to detect the underlying sentiment. Partly, we use metaphor for the positive-negative continuum already, so substitutions run the risk of accidentally using a metaphorical continuum that is already known, and so built into the analysis system.

9.3 Mental-State Extraction

People perceive themselves as largely in control of the image or persona that they present to the world. Recent psychological research is starting to show that this is not even approximately the case, and that people leak information about their mental state, broadly understood, in all of their communications[8].

This leakage of internal mental state is mediated largely by function words, such as pronouns, prepositions, articles, auxiliary verbs, and conjunctions. These words are a small set, but they are used frequently: the top ten most frequent words are function words and they account for 20% of all words used; the top 0.04% of words account for more than 50% of all words used.

Importantly, humans are not equipped to detect, except laboriously and offline, how such words are used in text and speech, in particular the norms for the frequencies of each one, and whether any given utterance deviates from these norms. This means that both author and audience are blind to any signals that are sent using this channel. Of course, counting frequencies is something that computer algorithms find easy to do, which is partly why the existence of such channels has come to light in the past few decades.

We now examine the large repertoire of aspects of internal mental state, including self-image, that can be discovered by examining the way in which words are used in texts. Not all aspects are carried by the small words, such as function words, but content-bearing words, nouns and major verbs, are usually available to conscious attention and so can be controlled more explicitly. Note the parallel with authorship determination where it is the use of smaller words that is the best discriminator among authors.

9.3.1   Goals

The goals of this kind of analysis are to discover author properties that are independent of the content of texts – the author's *style*. We have already seen one aspect of style as a signature or identifier of each author as an individual. We now turn to aspects of authors other than identity. These naturally divide into two sets of properties: personality, self-image, and emotional state; and motivation. Some of the author properties that can be extracted are:

- Age

- Personality, using several different data-driven models of personality dimension

- Gender

- In a two-person dialogue, which person has the higher status

- Aspects of health, including:

    - Health in the sense of likelihood of becoming ill
    - Personal life stress
    - Depression
    - Sense of belonging to a community

- Deceptiveness, including the range from outright lying, via spin, to negotiation.

Each of these properties is characterized by a pattern of differential word
use in text. These signatures are not yet well enough understood to form the
basis of predictive models with useful accuracy, for example, "from this text, I
predict with expected accuracy 87% that the author is a low-status male with
high blood pressure", but useful, suggestive information about authors can
be discovered, and may support knowledge discovered via other pathways.

9.3.2   Mental-State Extraction Technology

Mental-state extraction relies on counting frequencies of words, typically function words, but sometimes other words as well, and comparing them to known
models of the property of interest. Models are built empirically by taking examples of texts with known author properties, and determining, inductively,
what the differences are between the texts by authors with the property and
authors without it. Such boundaries are typically expressed in terms of the
absolute or relative frequencies of certain words or classes of words.

Many of these models have been developed by Pennebaker's group at
the University of Texas, Austin[9]. They collect large datasets, use a software
tool (LWIC) to extract frequencies of the words of interest in documents from
each class, and then use regression to find weights associated with each word
to define a boundary between documents that exhibit the property of interest
and those that do not. The deployed model then counts frequencies of words,
looking for increased frequencies for those words that are positively correlated
with the desired target class, and decreased frequencies for those words that
are negatively correlated with the class.

The weakness of this approach is that it assumes that 'increased' and
'decreased' frequencies are obvious; indeed they are defined with respect to
the pool of examples used to train the model. However, it is not always clear
that the same base frequency rates apply to texts from other domains.

Given a model that specifies that increased frequencies of some words
and decreased frequencies of others signal the desired property, a simple counting model can be extended by performing an SVD on the entire set of available
data to be classified, and then ranking the documents according to the property of interest. The benefit of using the SVD is that it takes into account
both the average for the entire set of available data in deciding what 'increase'
and 'decrease' mean, and that it takes into account correlations among different texts. Documents whose word usage is highly correlated with many
other documents in the same set, and documents whose word usage is highly
idiosyncratic are both pushed towards the middle of the ranking. Those documents that remain highly ranked not only exhibit the signature of whatever

property we are looking for, but they are also unusual among the set of documents being considered. This strategy would, of course, be disastrous if all of the documents being considered were suspicious; but if most of the documents are normal, then the effect is to make it easier to pick out the abnormal examples.

We now survey some of the properties for which results are known.

Age

As people get older, their language usage changes so that they use fewer first-person singular pronouns, more first-person plural pronouns, more exclusive words ("but", "or"), more future-tense verbs, and fewer past-tense verbs. It is clear that this is not enough to build a predictive model, but it is possible to rank a set of documents in an order suggestive of the ages of their authors. This, of course, is likely to be accurate only with large amounts of text from each author, since the context of each document necessarily restricts the possible use of these marker words to some extent.

Personality

Psychologists have developed several personality inventories that classify people into types with specific characteristics (for instance, the well-known Minnesota Multiphasic Personality Inventory (MMPI)). Adversaries are not available to answer personality-inventory questionnaires, usually based around Likert-scored questions. Hence, it is useful that personality models based entirely on word-usage patterns have been developed.

Chung and Pennebaker[10] have developed two personality models in a data-driven way, asking students to describe themselves and clustering the resulting word-usage profiles to discover latent factors that underlie them. The first model is based entirely on adjectives. From it, they extracted a seven-factor model. The dimensions are called: Sociability (words from "outgoing" to "quiet"), Evaluation (words from "beautiful" to "ugly"), Negativity ("mad"), Self-acceptance ("wonderful"), Fitting-in ("interesting"), Stability ("open"), and Maturity ("insecure" to "loving"). In each case, the word(s) in parentheses are most highly correlated with the factor. They also used a richer set of words, adding adverbs, nouns, and verbs, and built a personality model with a slightly larger set of latent factors, but several factors appeared content-filled, rather than personality-based.

The advantage of such models is that they can be applied to the documents authored by individuals to whom we have no other access. The resulting personality scoring provides some insight into characteristic modes of thought that person has. For example, Stability is an important assessment criterion for someone who may have access to weapons of mass destruction. Fitting-in may allow some insight into whether an individual feels accepted by a group, especially if this changes over time. The results of such analysis are indicative rather than determinative, at least with the present state of the art, but still potentially useful.

Gender

Recall the prediction of gender from documents discussed in Chapter 7. Surveys of gender differences in text derived empirically show consistent differences that are more extensive, but less actionable. In general, females use more pronouns, more social words (references to communication, and to other categories of humans), a wide variety of emotion- and feeling-related words, more verbs, and more negations. Males use longer words, more numbers, more articles, more prepositions, more discussion of current concerns (work, money, sports), and more swear words[11]. These results are not strong enough to predict the gender of the author of a short document, but the results of such a model may be suggestive.

Status

In a two-person interaction, the lower-status person is likely to use more first-person singular pronouns than the higher-status person. This is a useful marker, because it provides a mechanism to track command and control in adversary groups from message data[12].

Health

It is perhaps surprising that word-usage patterns reflect physical and mental health; indeed these dependencies are quite strong. Several specific cases have been investigated.

Campbell and Pennebaker[13] show that changes in the use of pronouns, and in writing style as measured using word frequencies, when writing about traumatic experience, were strongly predictive of improving physical health. It is not the use of particular pronouns, nor any particular consistent direction of change of pronoun use, but simply the flexibility to write in different ways at different times that is predictive of better health.

Consistent changes in pronoun use are also associated with stressful events, both individual and community-based. In general, successful coping with stress reveals itself by increases in third-person pronouns and movement from first-person singular to first-person plural pronouns, an other-directedness that is also related to community support. This may be used to determine whether an adversarial group, known to be under pressure, is handling it well or internalizing the stress.

Increased use of first-person singular pronouns is associated with negative emotion, especially with depression. The connection is deep – even those who have been depressed, but are not now, exhibit higher rates of first-person singular pronoun use than those who have never been depressed. This seems to be partly because use of other pronouns is a marker of affiliation with a social group; the use of first-person singular pronouns may therefore be an indirect signal of social isolation.

In an adversarial setting, we expect that members of an adversary group will feel a sense of affiliation, and so should exhibit low rates of first-person pronoun use. If this is not the case, it may suggest an opportunity for encouraging a defection from the group.

Deception

Deception in text is signalled by the following four changes[14]:

1. Decreased frequency of first-person singular pronouns, possibly to distance oneself from the deceptive content.

2. Decreased frequency of exclusive words. These words, for example "but" and "or", increase the cognitive complexity of the textual content. Those who are being deceptive face the challenge of creating a consistent story that did not actually happen, and the cognitive demands of doing so may not leave sufficient resources to make the story complex. They may also be aware, at some level, that the story will face scrutiny and they will need to recall it in order to give consistent answers if questioned.

3. Increased frequency of negative-emotion words. Such words may represent some level of discomfort at being deceptive.

4. Increased frequency of action verbs, particularly simple ones such as "go" and "going". This may be an attempt to 'keep the story moving' and so discourage deeper thought by the audience, or may be a side-effect of unusually simple structure.

This deception model was developed by Pennebaker[15], empirically, from texts in which authors were asked to write in support of positions they did and did not believe in. The complete set of words in the model is shown in Table 9.1.

The original model has been refined in a number of ways. Applying it to the Enron email dataset showed that it captured a wide range of deception, from what would be considered deceptive by everyone, through the kind of shading of the truth that is typical of politicians and advertising, to socially sanctioned deception, for example in negotiation. There is ongoing work to try and understand how the word-usage patterns change across these varying forms of deception.

The model was developed for a setting in which text was free-form. This models situations such as email, web forums, chatrooms, and even some

Categories	Keywords
First-person pronouns	I, me, my, mine, myself, I'd, I'll, I'm, I've
Exclusive words	but, except, without, although, besides, however, nor, or, rather, unless, whereas
Negative-emotion words	hate, anger, enemy, despise, dislike, abandon, afraid, agony, anguish, bastard, bitch, boring, crazy, dumb, disappointed, disappointing, f-word, suspicious, stressed, sorry, jerk, tragedy, weak, worthless, ignorant, inadequate, inferior, jerked, lie, lied, lies, lonely, loss, terrible, hated, hates, greed, fear, devil, lame, vain, wicked
Motion verbs	walk, move, go, carry, run, lead, going, taking, action, arrive, arrives, arrived, bringing, driven, carrying, fled, flew, follow, followed, look, take, moved, goes, drive

Table 9.1. *The words of the Pennebaker model of deception.*

more-formal writing. However, it does not model situations that are highly formal or structured. One particular situation of interest is court testimony and interrogation. Here, the text (usually speech) created by the putative adversary is constrained tightly by the questions that are being asked. This makes a big difference. It has long been known that non-responsiveness to questions is a sign of deception, so someone hoping to deceive cannot simply ignore the question and say something else, a favorite tactic of politicians. A response to a question cannot be free-form either; if the question is of the form "Did you ...", then the response has to be of the form "Yes, I ..." or "No, I ..." – so that high frequencies of first-person singular pronouns are expected.

Little[16] showed that a plausible variation of the basic model for deception in court testimony, derived from considering the testimony to a Canadian Royal Commission, is that deception is characterized by *increased* frequency of words in all four categories: increased first-person singular pronouns and increased exclusive words, as well as increased negative emotion words and action verbs. She showed that this model produced greater than 80% agreement with media opinions about which participants in the scandal that was the subject of the Commission might have been motivated to be deceptive in testimony. There are a number of reasons to think that increased first-person singular pronoun frequency might be associated with deception:

- Questioning of protagonists is likely to focus on *their* actions, forcing responses in the first person, while questioning of others is likely to focus on the actions of protagonists, suggesting third-person forms of response.

- Those who intend to be deceptive may rehearse their answers more extensively than other witnesses. This naturally leads to increased inner focus, and so may lead to increased first-person singular pronoun use.

- Those who are being deceptive may feel as if they are the lower-status member of the pair, of which the other member is the trial lawyer, perhaps because of guilt.

Increased exclusive words associated with deception may be due to two factors: rehearsal, and attempts to confuse the issue. With rehearsal, potential witnesses planning to be deceptive almost certainly explore multiple possible lines of questioning, and multiple possible responses to each one, naturally involving heavy mental use of exclusive words, which may spill over into actual responses. Given sufficient rehearsal, a witness may attempt to confuse the issue by refining a simple answer with multiple qualifications. There is some risk in doing this because of the need to be able to repeat a consistent story, but there is little downside to invoking hypotheticals, which do not involve this risk.

Recent work by Pennebaker[17] refines the model of deception in testimony, by looking at testimony in which the defendant was convicted, but subsequently exonerated by DNA evidence. It seems that, in emotionally charged court testimony, deception follows the conventional pattern: those being deceptive reduce their first-person singular pronoun use. However, in non-emotionally charged court testimony, Little's results suggest that those being deceptive seem to increase their first-person singular pronoun use. Ironically, juries tend to assume that high rates of first-person pronoun use are signals of guilt. This increases the likelihood of mistakes because innocent people on trial are likely to use high rates of first-person pronouns because they are more emotionally involved than a guilty defendant, and because they are not trying to be deceptive.

This has implications for detecting deception during interrogation. The implications of first-person singular pronoun frequency depend on whether the content of the questioning is judged to be emotionally charged. If it is, then decreased first-person singular pronoun use signals deception; if it is not, then increased first-person singular pronoun use signals deception. However, more work needs to be done in this area to clarify the model. It seems unlikely that exclusive-word frequencies would increase in interrogation, as they apparently do in testimony, since the need to remember and be able to repeat a consistent story is more pressing in an interrogation situation.

Work by Little[18] and Gupta[19] both suggest that Pennebaker's deception model based on 86 words can be simplified to a seven-factor model, in which the factors are: "I", the remaining first-person singular pronouns, "but", "or", the remaining exclusive words, negative-emotion words, and verbs of motion. The effect of "I" is similar to that of the remainder of the first-person pronouns, but it is a much stronger signal – perhaps because the contracted forms also contain an auxiliary verb form, and forms like "me" and "my" at least require some external focus of attention. The words "but" and "or" are used in quite different ways to each other, and to other exclusive words; it is not clear why. Verbs of motion are typically the next most important category of signal words, dominated by "go" and "going", but not nearly as much as "I" dominates the first-person singular pronouns. Finally, the negative-emotion and remaining exclusive words are very weak signals. As before, in the standard model, it is decreased frequencies of "I", first-person pronouns, "but", "or", and exclusive words, and increased frequencies of words in the other categories that signal deception.

It is interesting to consider the role of the pronoun "we" in this context. It was, at one time, believed that the use of "we" was a kind of signal of inclusiveness, and therefore tended to be associated with text written by females. It turns out that this is only partially true. Males also use "we" at high frequency, but they use it in a different way – female uses of "we" indeed tend towards inclusiveness, but male uses of "we" are a kind of royal "we", intended to soften an otherwise autocratic tone. In settings where deception is important, it might be expected that the use of "we" might be a way to diffuse responsibility away from an individual: "Did you have a gun?"; "Yes, we had a gun but I don't know who carried it". However, it turns out that the use of the pronoun "we" is not correlated with the use of any first-person singular pronouns, and does not seem to be correlated with deception either. This is consistent with other results showing that, in many settings, "we" does not behave as intuition might lead us to expect.

Although the Pennebaker model of deception is constructed by considering the factor weights of many different words with deception, once the appropriate words have been selected, the model simply counts relative frequencies of each one (in the appropriate sense). Better results can be obtained by considering the word-usage profile of each of a set of documents relative to the others in the set, especially if the majority of the set are not deceptive. This provides an empirical estimate of the norm against which 'increased' and 'decreased' frequency can be measured.

Suppose that a set of documents has been processed to extract the word frequencies for the 86 words in the deception model (or, better, for the seven classes of words in the refined deception model). The following process provides a ranking of the documents by suspected deceptiveness:

- Subtract the column mean of the non-zero entries from the non-zero entries in each column. For the 86-word model, the matrix is likely to be sparse since many of these words will not occur in any given document; but for the refined model, most entries will be non-zero.

- The entries in each column are now centered around zero, so the significance of decreased frequencies for some column values can be implemented by changing the signs of the entries in those columns, 'flipping' the data values around the origin. If this is done for the columns representing first-person singular pronouns and exclusive words, documents with large positive entries anywhere is their rows are most likely to be deceptive.

- Compute the SVD of the matrix. The early columns of the product US now contain representations for each document, from which a ranking can be extracted.

The simplest way is to truncate US at $k = 1$; in other words, project the rows onto a one-dimensional space. The ordering in this one-dimensional space corresponds to deceptiveness, but in a deeper sense than in the original Pennebaker model. First, the column normalization controls for typical word frequencies in a domain. For example, in business, rates of first-person pronoun usage may be lower across the board than in personal communication, because of different expectations, and usages such as the passive voice. Second, documents whose word-usage patterns are common tend to be pushed to the middle of the ranking, and so do documents whose word-usage patterns are eccentric. Deceptive documents are more likely to be visible at one end of the ranking, while the other end of the ranking contains documents that are decidedly nondeceptive (there tend to be few of these).

More than one dimension of the right-hand side of the SVD can be retained if it seems plausible that deceptiveness is not the only factor captured by the model, or deceptiveness is itself multifactorial. Documents can then be ranked by projecting the rows of U_k onto a line passing from the origin through the point $(s_1, s_2, \ldots, s_k)$ or, equivalently, projecting the rows of US onto a line passing from the origin through the point $(1, 1, \ldots, 1)$.

This use of correlation information can significantly enhance the model of deception. Analysis of the Enron emails using the seven-factor model produces a plot that is almost two-dimensional – the emails form a flat wedge as shown in Figure 9.1.

There is a very small set of highly deceptive emails in a small region to the left of the origin (which is marked by a circle). However, many of the emails to the right of the origin are also deceptive – the boundary between deceptive and non-deceptive emails is pulled to the right of the origin because of the large number of non-deceptive emails. The amount of deceptiveness

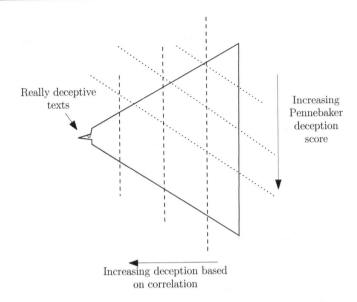

Really deceptive texts

Increasing Pennebaker deception score

Increasing deception based on correlation

Figure 9.1. *Distribution of Enron emails based on the deception model with correlation.*

decreases moving rightwards in the wedge, as suggested by the dashed lines as contours, so that the least-deceptive emails are along the right-hand edge. On the other hand, the Pennebaker model would label emails at the *top* of the wedge as least deceptive, with deceptiveness increasing moving down the wedge, as suggested by the dotted lines as contours. Emails in the bottom right-hand corner of the wedge are likely to be classified as deceptive by the Pennebaker model, but not by a model incorporating correlation.

9.3.3   Concealment Opportunities

Mental-state signals are almost entirely mediated by the subconscious. This means that authors may not realize that they are present; and even if they do, they are not able to manipulate them. Certainly it seems hard to imagine manipulating them in a consistent way; in other words, manipulation is likely to produce an eccentric word-usage pattern, rather than one that consistently signals a mental state that the author does not, in fact, hold.

There are several opportunities for manipulation that are more subtle. The first is rehearsal, something which seems to be a factor in court testimony. Rehearsal, as it usually done by actors, singers, and the like, is designed to perfect the technical aspects of a performance so as to make the creation of emotional elements easier, and more transparently visible. The goal of rehearsal in concealment is the reverse – it is designed to mute the emotional elements, while preserving the more direct purposes for communication. It is not clear that this can be done, except that, intuitively, repetition induces a certain level of boredom that might reduce emotional content across the board.

The second opportunity is for the adversaries to use their own mental-state detection system and apply it to their communications before sending them, altering them if mental-state content is detectable. The details of such models are available, so there is no difficulty in building such detection systems. There are two reasons why this strategy is not as good as it seems. The first is that, even if the model detects some undesirable mental content leakage, it is not obvious what to do about it. At some level, of course, it is: increase the frequency of certain kinds of words and decrease the frequency of others. The problem is that this must be done in such a way that the resulting document still appears normal. Because the generation of little words is so unconscious, it is quite difficult to alter a document in a desired direction without making it stilted, increasing the probability that it will attract attention as having been manipulated, and also weakening its impact on the desired audience.

The second is that an analysis technique that uses an entire set of documents to provide a baseline for frequencies, as we have suggested should always be done, means that adversaries cannot get an accurate estimate of how their documents will look because they do not have access to the context that will be used for the real analysis. They therefore never know how much alteration is enough; tempting them to overdo the manipulation and creating an anti-signature that is rare in real documents (as well as perhaps weakening the impact on the intended audience by excessive blandness).

In general, language markers that come primarily from subconscious linguistic processes are difficult to manipulate at all. We are not able to replicate, consciously, what we do easily subconsciously. Attempting to do so creates signals that strongly differentiate the resulting text from ordinary text, perhaps even more strongly than if it had been left alone.

9.4   Systemic Functional Linguistics

Almost everything in these last three chapters has been based implicitly on a model of language, as Chomsky said, as a branch of psychology. In this view of language, speech and documents are produced by following a certain set of production rules that are grammatic in character, and based, at least in part, on hardware settings in the human brain. Documents and their component sentences arise because of grammar rules which define how the pieces of each sentence can be put together, and what those pieces are: word order, declension, conjugation, mood, agreement, and so on. In particular, the view of grammar is primarily context-free, to explain why we can understand a sentence without reading the whole document it appears in, and can understand a clause without reading the whole sentence it appears in. Of course, this style of explanation is obviously not the whole story, because context, and consistency within a context, are important to understanding natural language. This approach to language has been very productive, not only leading to the kinds of analysis and results we have been discussing, but also leading to the development of computer programming languages, and to deeper understanding of how our brains work with language.

However, there is an alternative view of language, *systemic functional linguistics* (SFL)[20], which is less well-developed, but shows considerable promise as a way to understand the relationship between text and mental state that is the focus of this chapter. It takes the view that language is a branch of sociology, and so understanding how language works requires understanding how humans and human communities work as well. In particular, SFL takes the view that the string of words that appears in a text is the result of a human attempt to achieve a particular communication goal, rather than the application of a predefined set of rules.

9.4.1 Introduction to Systemic Functional Linguistics

SFL starts from the premise that the purpose of language is to make meaning. When an author sets out to do that, there are three interlocking issues that must be considered:

- Aspects of what is to be communicated that constrain what is mentioned and how different pieces of content are connected,

- Aspects of the relationship between the author and the intended audience that constrain how things are expressed, and

- Aspects of the way text binds linguistic elements together that constrain the selection and arrangement of its pieces to form a coherent whole.

In other words, when a sentence is constructed, a series of interlocking choices are made (between what would be, in some sense, equivalent ways of expressing the same meaning). These choices reflect the goal or intent of the communication, the relationships between the creator of the communication and the intended audience, and the properties of the language being used. For example, a request to pass the salt could be expressed as:

"Salt."
"Pass the salt!"
"Please pass the salt."

"Would you mind passing the salt, please?"
"I'm terribly sorry to trouble you, but could you please pass the salt?"

All of these versions convey essentially the same information, and they all have the same intent, but the forms in which they are expressed capture vivid differences in the personality of the speaker, and in the relationship between speaker and hearer. Each version also differs substantially from the others in the way in which the pieces are arranged and connected. Authors of fiction must be able to use these different forms in subtle ways to communicate the internal lives of the characters about which they write – and this is a relatively rare skill.

These examples show, in an obvious way, how context determines the form of a text, but that text also contains, embedded within it, information about a context. We are able, probably with some facility, to make deductions about the speaker from each of these short text fragments. Of course, it is this belief that text contains embedded information about author and audience that has driven the kind of analysis we have considered in this chapter.

The decisions that are made as a text is constructed can be understood as being arranged in a hierarchy. At each choice point, a decision or a set of decisions must be made; some of these decisions are exclusive (either this choice or that), but other decisions are orthogonal to each other and can be made independently. Each network of choices at a particular level of abstraction is called a *system*. Systems have been developed across many situations, and for many different languages – one of the strengths of SFL is that the same systems apply to families of languages, although the lowest-level systems are, of course, different because they rely on different detailed mechanisms.

Choices naturally form a hierarchy, because certain choices enable or disable subsequent choices from even being considered. The systems that describe these choices also naturally form a hierarchy. High-level systems distinguish between global or abstract properties of text; low-level systems distinguish between different constructions and word choices.

To analyze a text, we can parse it using systems at an appropriate level of abstraction. The result is a tree representing the choices that led to this particular document from the available systems.

However, the choices made when an author constructs a particular document are not independent choices made by an individual. Rather, some of the choices are constrained by the particular kind of communication that the document represents – *all* authors would make the same choices. For example, written letters in English typically begin "Dear X", whether or not the author feels any affection for X, and end with one of a few stylized endings ("Yours sincerely"), whether or not the author is sincere, let alone sincerely X's. Individual choices by each author are an overlay on the choices predetermined by the kind of communication, neither completely dependent nor completely independent.

These sets of predetermined choices associated with a particular purpose in a particular setting or context are called *registers*, and correspond in a rough way to the common idea of *genre*, although they are finer-grained. Registers do not represent simply particular sets of choices, but rather distributions over the possible choices at each decision point. For example, in formal scientific writing, some disciplines use a scholarly "we", but this does not preclude occasional use of the passive voice; in other disciplines, the passive voice is used exclusively. A register captures the 'normal' way in which a particular class of communications are expressed, and so are the result of a social, not an individual, process.

The choices made by an individual author are then understood as variations on those choices constrained by the particular class of communication, together with free choices whenever these are not constrained by the class of communication.

The choices that depend on the register, and those that depend on the author are not high-level choices versus low-level choices. A register may constrain the choices at a high level, but may also constrain them at a low level too. Consider the example of letters, where the constraint is on a particular individual word – the first word of the body must be "Dear". Likewise, the author choices can be made at both high and low levels.

These ideas can be used for textual and discourse analysis in the following way. Information about typical registers and the distributions of choices corresponding to each can be learned from training data, that is, from examples of text of different kinds. If registers are well-understood, it may be possible to work from examples within each, but it is probably more usual to discover previously-unnoticed registers in the course of looking at training texts. Now there are two forms of analysis. In the first, information about choice distributions can be used to predict the register(s) associated with a document, and so predict the type of text that it represents. This approach allows systemic functional linguistics to be used for intention extraction and sentiment analysis, called, in this domain, *appraisal theory*. In the second form, a document is expected to be of a particular kind, the associated register is then determined, and the expected distribution is compared with the observed distribution of choices. The difference between these two distributions is a measure of anomaly. This anomaly then reveals something about the document and its author, which could be one of a number of things: the author is inept at writing in this particular register, the author has an unusual style, or the author is trying to manipulate the audience. This second form of analysis allows some access to the mental state of the author.

One of the big advantages of this approach over the bag-of-words approach is that there is natural way to normalize the observed signals in the text to reflect the particular setting in which the analysis takes place. In the bag-of-words techniques, this is implemented by using a large text repository as an empirical oracle about norms; in the systemic functional framework, information about norms is included more explicitly, and with more control.

At present, this is actually something of a weakness, since it requires skill and time to understand and describe systems and registers; whereas text repositories are easy to query. However, the work done by systemic functional linguists is reusable (moreover often reusable across languages) so the overhead of the SFL approach will decrease with time.

9.4.2 SFL for Intention Detection

Intentions in the SFL framework refer to the intention of an author for a particular fragment of a text or document, that is, what the author is trying to achieve by making a particular set of choices. This is quite different from the kind of intentions we are interested in, things like strategies, tactics, and targets for different kinds of illegal activities.

Nevertheless, SFL provides a natural way to look for the patterns corresponding to such intentions as registers: registers corresponding to planning, targeting, selection, and so on. Such registers are potentially powerful because they can include both high-level choices and low-level choices, and expose structures that can span all scales of documents, from adjacent word choices to global structures. As far as I am aware, no work in this direction has been done, but there is an obvious opportunity.

9.4.3 SFL for Sentiment Analysis

In contrast, sentiment analysis within a systemic functional framework, where it is called *appraisal theory* is quite well-developed. The SFL system or network for appraisal is[21]:

& Attitude – relationship between subject and target object

   & Affect – emotional response to the target object

   & Judgement – evaluation of human behavior with respect to norms

   & Appreciation – evaluation of products and processes

& Engagement – positioning between subject and target audience

   ‖ Bare factual

‖ Multivoiced

  ‖ Appeal to an external voice
  ‖ Use of multiple internal perspectives

& Graduation – intensity of the appraisal

  & Force – weaker versus stronger

  & Focus – direct versus hedging

Here the use of & indicates that this is one of a set of choices at a level, all of which have to be made independently; while ‖ indicates that this is one of a set of choices at a level, only one of which must be chosen. For example, a statement of appraisal requires a choice about attitude, engagement, *and* graduation.

This system already goes well beyond the view of sentiment as simply polarity, and incorporates, in a natural and systematic way, many of the issues of rhetorical devices and the like that make conventional sentiment analysis so difficult. Each of the later choice points can themselves be further expanded, and each eventually leads to a set of words or other syntactic markers or structures that signal the set of choices that has been made to generate a particular utterance.

The resulting 'parse tree' (really a choice tree) contains information that addresses sentiment directly, or can be easily interpreted in terms of sentiment. For example, all aspects of Attitude have positive and negative markers that can be used to extract polarity, but a richer view of polarity, since it includes feelings evoked by the object, the object's usefulness, and the object's aesthetic. Issues such as bias can be extracted from the Engagement subsystem, for example, distinguishing between a consumer opinion, a magazine puff piece, and an advertisement, all of which might have the same positive things to say about the target object. Finally, the Graduation subsystem allows a different kind of judgement about the polarity, namely how strong it is and how much it is directed towards the particular target object rather than being the side effect of some wider sentiment, say about a similar class of objects. Attempts to use systemic functional approaches to sentiment analysis have begun[22].

9.4.4   SFL for Mental-State Extraction

Different kinds of mental state could be extracted from text by discovering the registers corresponding to them, and then looking for these registers. The problem is not so much to discover the registers, as to discover in which systems the registers and their differences are most obvious. It seems plausible that models for properties such as age, gender, status, and conditions such as depression might be discovered, either because the effects of these differences are pervasive across systems, or because we can make a good guess about which systems are important for each of them. For example, depression might cause changing choices in interpersonal and affect systems. Gender and age might cause different choices in a wide variety of systems.

This approach does not work so well for communication involving criminal or terrorist activity because we do usually have access to enough text of the required kind to build a robust model of the register(s) involved. For example, the pool of available ransom notes or terrorist pronouncements is small enough that the differences due to other factors almost certainly outweigh the characteristics of the typical register for that situation.

However, in situations where the characteristic of a criminal activity is a difference between their communications and normal communications of the same kind, the register idea can be used as an anomaly detector. This idea has been used to detect financial scams, in the Scamseek project[23], and in detecting the characteristics of 'Nigerian' scam emails[24]. Given a pool of registers typical of a particular domain, anomalies can be characterized as variations of these registers, or as instances of one of these registers with an unusual distribution of choices. The difference depends on whether the anomalies can be identified, that is, whether there is labelled training data for the anomaly class, and whether there are enough examples of that class to allow a robust register to be defined. The problem with single-document anomalies is making sure that they are anomalous versions of a known register (which they are trying to masquerade as) rather than some totally different kind of document.

Approaches based on systemic functional linguistics are a better fit with the kinds of problems we have been addressing in this chapter, and so we might expect that they will become important tools for extracting mental state. At present, these approaches are limited by the small number of people familiar with the methodologies, the amount of up-front work that has to be done to define systems and registers, and the difficulty of parsing. One of the biggest benefits is that, once the work is done, the effort required to reimplement in a different language is relatively small – mainly altering the low-level markers for the lower-level systems.

Notes

[1]T. Koening, "Compounding mixed-methods problems in frame analysis through comparative research", *Qualitative Research*, 6(1):61–76, 2006.

[2]A.P. Sanfilippo, A.J. Cowell, S.C. Tratz, A.M. Boek, A.K. Cowell, C. Posse and L.C. Pouchard, *Content Analysis for Proactive Intelligence: Marshalling*

Frame Evidence, in: *Proceedings of the Twenty-Second AAAI Conference on Artificial Intelligence*, pp. 919–924, 2006.

[3]T. Mullen and N. Collier, *Sentiment Analysis Using Support Vector Machines with Diverse Information Sources*, in: *Proceedings of the 42nd Meeting of the Association for Computational Linguistics (ACL 2004)*, pp. 21–26, 2004.

[4]B. Pang and L. Lee, *A Sentimental Education: Sentiment Analysis Using Subjectivity Summarization Based on Minimum Cuts*, in: *Proceedings of the 42nd Meeting of the Association for Computational Linguistics (ACL 2004)*, pp. 271–278, 2004.

[5]T. Nasukawa and J. Yi, *Sentiment Analysis: Capturing Favorability Using Natural Language Processing*, in: *Proceedings of the 2nd International Conference on Knowledge Capture*, pp. 70–77, 2003.

[6]H. Kanayama, T. Nasukawa and H. Watanabe, *Deeper Sentiment Analysis Using Machine Translation Technology*, in: *Proceedings of the 20th International Conference on Computational Linguistics*, 2004.

[7]More details of the *Sentiment* tool can be found at `www.corporasoftware.com`.

[8]And also in other modalities as well, for example, the eye-movement hypotheses of neurolinguistic programming.

[9]`homepage.psy.utexas.edu/homepage/Faculty/Pennebaker/Home2000/JWPhome.htm`

[10]C.K. Chung and J.W Pennebaker, "Revealing dimensions of thinking in open-ended self-descriptions: An automated meaning extraction method for natural language", *Journal of Research in Personality*, 42:96–132, February 2008.

[11]M.L. Newman, C.J. Groom, L.D. Handelman and J.W. Pennebaker, "Gender differences in language use: An analysis of 14,000 text samples", *Discourse Processes*, 45:211–236, 2008.

[12]Chung and Pennebaker cite this result in C.K. Chung and J.W. Pennebaker, *The Psychological Function of Function Words*, in: K. Fiedler, (ed.), *Frontiers in Social Psychology*. Psychology Press, in press, and draw attention to how well this observation is borne out in the Nixon White House where, of course, many of the interactions with senior staff were taped.

[13]R.S. Campbell and J.W. Pennebaker, "The secret life of pronouns: Flexibility in writing style and physical health", *Psychological Science*, 14(1):60–65, 2003.

[14]According to the Pennebaker model. Other relevant work on cues or markers for deception can be found in B.M. DePaulo, J.J. Lindsay, B.E. Malone,

L. Muhlenbruck, K. Charlton and H. Cooper, "Cues to deception", *Psychology Bulletin*, 9:74–118, 2003; J.R. Carlson, J.F. George, J.K. Burgoon, M. Adkins and C.H. White, "Deception in computer mediated communication", *Academy of Management Journal*, 13:5–28, 2004; and L. Zhou, D.P. Twitchell, T. Qin, J.K. Burgoon and J.F. Nunamaker Jr., *An exploratory study into deception detection in text-based computer mediated communication*, in: *Proceedings of the 36th Hawaii Intl Conference on Systems Science*, 2003.

[15]M.L. Newman, J.W. Pennebaker, D.S. Berry and J.M. Richards, "Lying words: Predicting deception from linguistic style", *Personality and Social Psychology Bulletin*, 29:665–675, 2003.

[16]A. Little, "Defining a signature for deception in court testimony", Master's Thesis, School of Computing, Queen's University, 2007.

[17]J.W. Pennebaker and D.A. Huddle, personal communication, 2007.

[18]A. Little, "Defining a signature for deception in court testimony", Master's Thesis, School of Computing, Queen's University, 2007.

[19]S. Gupta, "Modelling deception detection in text", Master's Thesis, School of Computing, Queen's University, 2007.

[20]An introduction to SFL can be found at www.isfla.org/Systemics/.

[21]www.grammatics.com/Appraisal/AppraisalOutline/Framed/Contents. htm

[22]C. Whitelaw, N. Garg and S. Argamon, *Using Appraisal Taxonomies for Sentiment Analysis*, in: *Second Midwest Computational Linguistic Colloquium (MCLC 2005)*, 2005.

[23]www.cs.usyd.edu.au/~lkmrl/ss_progress.htm and J. Patrick, *The Scamseek Project – Text Mining for Financial Scams on the Internet*, in: *Data Mining: Proceedings of the 4th Australasian Workshop on Data Mining*, Springer LNCS 3755, pp. 295–302, 2006.

[24]C. Whitelaw and S. Argamon, *Systemic Functional Features in Stylistic Text Classification*, in: *Proceedings of AAAI Fall Symposim on Style and Meaning in Language, Art, Music, and Design*, Washington, DC, October 2004.

Chapter 10

The Bottom Line

10.1 Framing the Problem

In the settings we have talked about, law enforcement and counterterrorism, the fundamental problem is to detect the traces of adversaries and their activities in data, and use them to formulate responses. These responses could range from surveillance, to prevention or interdiction, to arrest or counterattack. We have seen that there are difficult issues when the response is proactive and preventive in nature, because much of the framework of law enforcement and prosecution is fundamentally reactive – punish bad activity after it happens, rather than prevent it before it happens. Of course, there is actually a broad continuum in conventional law enforcement, but many of the most difficult social issues, including widescale data collection and analysis, arise at the more proactive end of the continuum.

The traces of adversaries and their activities have four characteristics:

1. The differences between the traces of adversaries and normal data records are unexpected, and cannot usually be determined beforehand, either from some kind of first-principles analysis, or by predicting likely behavior. This is because adversaries are constantly probing the framework of the society in which they operate for holes. Almost by definition, known holes are filled as they are discovered, so the opportunities for adversaries lie in the holes that have not yet been discovered by the wider society. This property of adversary traces makes knowledge discovery more difficult.

2. Adversaries are actively trying to manipulate the knowledge-discovery process to conceal their traces. They do this by preventing, as much as

possible, data about themselves from being collected; and by distorting the data that they cannot prevent from being collected. Doing this in a simple-minded way can backfire, creating data that looks unusual purely because of the distortions or gaps it contains. However, one of the overlooked issues in knowledge discovery is how vulnerable many of the technologies are to sophisticated manipulation of collected data. This property of adversary traces also makes knowledge discovery more difficult.

3. Adversaries are doing things that other people are not doing, and about which they may have some negative feelings, or at least trepidation because of the potential consequences. Hence data about them must differ, in some way, from data about other people. Even if they are actively trying to manipulate the data about themselves, there are some unavoidable differences because of the imperatives of their activities. This property of adversary traces makes knowledge discovery easier.

4. Adversaries must react to the presence of knowledge discovery, unless they are stupid or naive. Hence they will attempt to distort the data collected about them not only to manipulate the knowledge-discovery process, but also to try to seem as normal as possible. As we have seen, this process is far more difficult than it seems – even a knowledge of what normality looks like is difficult to reproduce for a particular data record. This property of adversary traces makes knowledge discovery easier.

These four properties of the traces of adversaries and their activities have a number of implications for the knowledge-discovery process as a whole, regardless of the particular technologies that are used. These implications are:

- Trying to build models of the *expected* differences between adversaries and ordinary people is unlikely to be effective, and runs a substantial risk of missing new adversary activities by looking for repetitions of previous adversary activities. There *is* a role for looking for repetitions of previous activity, particularly because of the well-known tendency of criminals to repeat the type and form of their crimes with amazing exactitude. However, the countervailing tendency to come up with new crimes and attacks, especially for more intelligent and motivated adversaries, needs always to be kept in mind. Pattern-based knowledge discovery can be useful, as long as it is not the only form of knowledge discovery.

- The problem of detecting the traces of adversaries in data can be reduced to two subproblems:

- **Separating the normal from the unusual.** The logic here
  is that any patterns that occur frequently in the data probably
  do not describe the traces of adversaries, because such traces will
  always be relatively rare. Hence, discovering and removing 'normal'
  records from the available data leaves a (potentially still large) pool
  within which the adversary traces remain. This first task does not
  require a model of what it means to be unusual; rather, it is based
  on a model of normality as 'frequent' or 'repeated', both of which
  are plausible surrogates.

  This phase cannot be shortcircuited; it *requires* the presence of data
  about normal activity to be able to distinguish abnormality – and,
  in a sense, the more normal data, the better. Clearly understanding, and explaining to the general public, this role for normal data
  would go a long way to relieve the minds of many – explaining that
  normal data is used as a background against which abnormality
  can be made more visible, and that such normal data is discarded
  early, as early as possible, in the analysis process.

- **Separating the bad from the eccentric.** In a sense, this stage
  does require a model for 'bad' so that it can be separated from
  the merely eccentric. However, this model does not have to be
  explicit, at least for the majority of the task. First, adversaries
  almost always act as groups, so that their traces are abnormal and
  related, whereas eccentrics tend to be eccentric alone. (A group of
  eccentrics begins to look normal as long as there are enough of them
  – another benefit of wide data collection is that almost any normal human eccentricity becomes commonplace in a large-enough
  group.) Second, adversaries react to the possibility of analysis in a
  way that eccentrics do not, creating another basis for distinguishing. Of course, this does show one of the weaknesses of knowledge
  discovery – it is not good at detecting the activity of a 'lone wolf'
  adversary.

  This second phase does create greater problems from the perspective of privacy – an eccentric is always going to be subjected to
  greater scrutiny than a more-mainstream person. (Arguably this
  is true in society already.)

  It is also plausible to try and develop a model of eccentricity, that
  is, of what it means to be unusual but innocuous. As far as I know,
  this has not yet been attempted.

- Any knowledge-discovery process needs to be built to be resistant to manipulation by those about whom the data is collected. Obviously, this
  requires an overall process that is resistant to *insider* attacks. Less obviously, it requires careful choice and design of the knowledge-discovery
  technologies so that their results cannot be altered substantially by mak-

ing changes to only a few data records. As we have seen, many technologies in use today are vulnerable in this way.

Model builders are in a cleft stick. The changing outside world requires that models should be updated regularly, to reflect changes in normality; but these updates provide the opportunity for adversaries to manipulate the outcome by forcing training data of their choosing – indirectly, to be sure, but possible by making sure that their desired records seem particularly interesting.

There is also a tension between revealing some details of how the knowledge discovery is being done, which can be used to force greater reaction from the adversaries, and revealing enough to allow the system to be manipulated explicitly. I have suggested that a certain amount of randomization is a useful way to resolve this tension and get both benefits at the same time.

- Knowledge-discovery tools should rely on attributes whose values are hard to manipulate. Such attributes are of two kinds:

  - Those attributes whose values are primarily generated *subconsciously*. Those who wish to manipulate data cannot, in general, get access to their values in a controlled way: because they are not accessible or because attempts to access them tend to create even more unusual attribute values. We have seen that many properties of communication are attributes of this kind, so analysis of text and speech can be especially revealing and hard to manipulate. However, many other attributes are also partly or largely generated subconsciously, for example habits of movement, choices of meals, physical tics, preferred times of day for certain activities; and all of these could potentially be revealing.

  - Those attributes whose values or properties emerge from the *connections* between many different records of the data. For example, the values of an attribute across many records may have a characteristic distribution in which a manipulated value seems like an outlier. The values of attributes in different records must somehow be consistent; for example, a person cannot be in two places at the same time, or taking connecting flights without the destination of one being (close to) the starting point of the other. In relational data, the affinity relationship between two records (nodes) must be consistent with the global affinity implied by all of the other connections in the data. Such attributes are extremely difficult to manipulate because the local alteration in an attribute value has to remain consistent with the values in *all* of the other records. A manipulator typically does not have access to these other records, either to see what values they contain or to alter them to match.

- Knowledge-discovery tools should *select* attributes when it can be done reliably. This is the flip-side of the previous point; some attributes are not helpful at distinguishing normal from abnormal or bad from eccentric behavior. When this can be determined, such attributes should be discarded from the data. Extra, irrelevant attributes cause two problems: they waste computational resources, and they can cause some technologies to produce substantially poorer results. The point is obvious but needs saying as a counterweight to the 'more data is better' mindset that seems superficially plausible, and tends to become entrenched.

- It is not always best to regard a dataset as a single monolithic object. There are advantages to dividing up the data in several ways: samples of the records, partitions of the records, and partitions of the attributes. This provides some computational advantages, making parallel versions of the algorithms possible, and also increasing overall performance by reducing the number of memory accesses required. However, more significantly, using ensembles provides algorithmic ways to avoid the computational analogue of group think: systems can reduce variance and bias, and are much more resistant to manipulation. Multiple models can be effective because they produce an extra piece of information: the amount of agreement among the models. Using a rule about the threshold of the number of models that must agree provides a natural way to introduce sensitivity into a knowledge-discovery system.

These implications lay out the overall structure and rules that an effective knowledge-discovery process in an adversarial setting should follow.

10.2   The Process

The first problem of adversarial knowledge discovery is to separate the normal from the unusual. We have suggested that this problem should not be treated monolithically, but rather by creating a knowledge-discovery system that uses a wide range of technological tools, each embodying different trade-offs between cost, scale, complexity, sophistication, intrusiveness, and effectiveness. Such a system, we have suggested, should be thought of as two-dimensional: in one dimension *multifaceted*, and in the other *staged*, sequenced, or pipelined.

A multifaceted knowledge-discovery system attacks the separation problem by building different models of normality, usually based on different levels of abstraction. The key insight is that normality looks normal from every direction, and at every level of abstraction. Attempts to *seem* normal can work, but only from some directions, and at some levels of abstraction. The clearest example of this is natural language, where the pieces of ordinary text must fit together as sequences of words, as verbs and their subjects and objects, as sensible content, with properly referenced antecedents for pronouns, and in an appropriate style. Getting all of these piece to look right at all of their different levels of abstraction and scales and yet carry hidden content is difficult, as we have seen.

A multifaceted knowledge-discovery system uses models based on qualitatively different attributes. A simpler version of the same idea can be built by using qualitatively different models and the same attributes, since each different kind of model implicitly looks for different kinds of structure or patterns in the data.

A staged knowledge-discovery system attacks the separation problem by winnowing the potentially unusual records from the data in stages. The early stages are based on as robust a model of normality as possible, so that records are discarded only when they are normal with high reliability (for example, exceedingly common). Later stages can apply more sophisticated models of normality. At each stage, the size of the data to be considered is reduced, making it cost-effective to apply more-expensive analysis technologies. A staged process addresses the false-positive problem since no single stage has to be right about every record. Also, a staged process provides some help with parameter setting, one of the ubiquitous chicken-and-egg problems, because information learned from early stages can be used to choose parameters for later stages.

In some problem settings, the available data is so large, and the ultimately interesting records so few, that designing the early selection stages is a substantial problem in its own right.

The second problem of adversarial knowledge discovery is to separate the bad from the eccentric, starting from the abnormal records selected by the first process. Any available knowledge of what adversary traces look like can be profitably applied to this problem; but there are also three generic properties that differentiate the two kinds of records.

The first is evidence of evasion or attempts at concealment. Ordinary people typically neither know nor care about knowledge-discovery technology that might be applied to their data in an adversarial context (except perhaps for concerns about privacy with respect to government). They therefore tend not to alter the attribute values of their records. Adversaries, however, must react to the presence of knowledge-discovery systems if only to avoid being detected by the simpler ones. This evasion, as we have seen, can often create a signature that makes them visible.

The second is evidence of manipulation. At present, knowledge-discovery tools are likely to be misled by manipulation of the data but, with awareness, this weakness can be turned into a benefit. Models can be built to be suspicious of records that are typical of manipulation, again without committing to a particular model of what manipulation should look like. For example, at present, records that lie close to some class boundary are regarded, in conventional knowledge discovery, as particularly interesting. In adversarial knowledge discovery, it might be more appropriate to regard such records as particularly (or at least somewhat) *suspicious*.

The third is to look for evidence of group structure within the abnormal records since, almost by definition, eccentrics do not form groups (if they did, they would look like all of the other groups, and so normal). Such structure may be found in *correlation* among the attribute values of different records (for example, use of the same rare words); *connections* between different records (for example, in relational data); or *emergent properties* of sets of records.

10.3   Applying the Process

For the task of prediction, we have considered three different kinds of data:

1. Attributed data, consisting of records, each with a set of values for a fixed set of attributes;

2. Relationship data, where it is the connections between records that are most significant; and each connection describes a local affinity between the two records that it joins; and

3. Textual data, consisting of descriptions of communications, text or speech.

In all of these different kinds of data, the task is similar: to predict the amount of risk or suspicion associated with each record.

For this kind of prediction, staging the task using a series of increasingly sophisticated predictors is natural. There is seldom enough knowledge of the domain and possible adversarial action to predict based on patterns. Even using the model described in the previous section of predicting normal versus abnormal, and then bad versus eccentric, there is not usually enough information to treat this as a problem of predicting a boundary. Rather, prediction is best treated as a *ranking* problem, ordering the records from most-normal to least-normal.

Given a predictor that ranks records, the decision about where to place the boundary can be made by observing the characteristics of the ranking. In particular, the ideal placement is one where there are no false negatives, that is, no adversary records are discarded as normal. Since ranking a large number of records provides a very large number of places for the boundary to go, the exact placement can be adjusted in a smooth way. For example, concerns about potentially missed false negatives can be addressed by placing the boundary 10% further down the list than its apparent best position, increasing confidence.

Placing the boundary to eliminate false negatives also tends to increase the false-positive rate. However, the implications of doing this are only on performance: more stages, and more expensive stages may be required, but consequences for non-adversaries predicted to be adversaries are not increased. Hence, although any single predictor is unlikely to have a false-positive rate below 0.01%, the entire sequence can do much better.

The use of a sequence of predictors means that early stages can use simple, cheap prediction technologies, as long as their false-negative rates are low enough. In situations where the possible datasets are extremely large, this makes a great practical difference. These predictors also tend not to have many parameters to set since they assume models that are simple, with few degrees of freedom.

The gaps between stages also provide places for useful decisions and oversight. Records considered abnormal on the basis of a basic set of attributes may have extra, more intrusive, attributes made available for subsequent stages. Procedural and judicial oversight may be exercised at these points, requiring a demonstration that the records that have not been discarded after each stage do indeed have properties of potential interest.

The use of a multifaceted process for prediction also adds more robustness to the overall system. Different pipelines of prediction can be based on different subsets, or qualitatively different sets, of attributes; or different families of predictors can be used in parallel. Each record is therefore analyzed by multiple staged pipelines.

Rules about how to regard outcomes can be created to provide fine-grained control over final decisions. We expect that a normal record should seem normal to every predictor. The question is what to make of records that are regarded as suspicious by only *some* of the prediction pipelines. In critical situations, it may be reasonable that a record regarded as suspicious by *any* pipeline should be treated as suspicious. In other situations, it may be reasonable to require that some number of pipelines should all regard a record as suspicious before acting on the suspicion.

We have also observed that the use of multiple predictors, like ensembles, creates an overall predictor that is much more resistant to manipulation than any of its component predictors. In general, the use of multiple predictors provides resistance to variance, caused by the fact that any data is *de facto* a sample from larger universe of data that could have been analyzed, and bias, caused by a mismatch between the complexity of the dataset and the power of the technology to analyze it.

For clustering, the technologies are not nearly as mature, and the goals of the process are naturally more diffuse.

Clustering attacks the problems of distinguishing normal from abnormal, and bad from eccentric in a single framework. Intuitively, we expect that normal records should form clusters filled with many records; that eccentric records should be single points far from other clusters; and that the signature of adversary traces is small clusters on the fringes of the popular clusters. We expect this signature because the activities of adversaries force attribute values that do not fit with those mainstream values that are responsible for the forming of the popular clusters; but, on the other hand, adversaries are trying to create traces as much like ordinary ones as possible.

Mainstream work on clustering for knowledge discovery has concentrated on ways to find the large clusters, and occasionally on techniques for detecting outliers. Little attention has been paid to detecting fringe records. We have also seen that clustering algorithms are very vulnerable to manipulation, often by the addition of only a few, specially constructed records. Since clustering uses all of the available data, this vulnerability is much easier for adversaries to exploit, since they have to make no special effort to get records inserted into the modelling process.

Manipulation-resistant clustering technologies are known, but they rely on using emergent, global, or correlational properties to discover the similarities and differences among records. For example, graph-based clustering is inherently more robust than attributed-data clustering because it is harder to get any desired effect by manipulating the local affinities of one, or a few, records.

A multifaceted approach to clustering is possible, and indeed helpful. The insight here is that real underlying clusters in a dataset should be visible by using *any* clustering algorithm. Of course, there will, in practice, be differences because of the differences in the underlying algorithms, but these differences should be relatively minor. Therefore records that appear in large, well-populated clusters that are much the same from clustering to clustering can be ignored as representing normality. Similarly, records that are outliers in many clusterings can be treated as global outliers. What remains are data records that are, in every sense, fringe records: different clustering algorithms vary in how they allocate them. The traces of adversaries are expected to be found among these records, a much smaller set in general.

Existing knowledge discovery in adversarial settings is typically based around one, or a handful, of analysis techniques, often based on record-by-record analysis, and sometimes requiring quite detailed expectations of what adversary traces will look like. I have argued that:

- Models cannot be based on assumptions about likely adversary behavior, but must instead be based on modelling what ordinary people do (normality and eccentricity) and then looking for adversaries in what is left.

- The extent to which individual analysis technologies are vulnerable to manipulation by insertion of crafted data records must be fully understood, and, wherever possible, more robust technologies used.

- Analysis works better when the properties of records depend mutually on the properties of other records, both because it produces better results and because it is much, much harder to manipulate.

- Individual knowledge-discovery technologies become much more powerful when they are used in systems that look in a multifaceted and staged or pipelined way for abnormality. The power of such systems is much greater than the power of the individual analysis components, but the way in which they are combined matters.

There are also many opportunities to improve the performance of individual components: resistance to manipulation has hardly been studied, strong but transparent prediction technologies are not known, clustering algorithms resistant to manipulation are scarce, and meta-technologies such as attribute selection, parameter setting, and measures for the quality of clusterings are underdeveloped.

Adversarial knowledge discovery is quite different from mainstream knowledge discovery. The basic algorithms must differ, at least in the sense of being resistant to manipulation, but often because more attention and resources need to be concentrated on regions of the data that are not considered interesting in mainstream knowledge discovery. There is thus a role for computer scientists and statisticians in designing new (versions of) algorithms. Those who use knowledge-discovery technologies need to be aware of their limitations and weaknesses, so that they do not rely on them unduly and inappropriately. Those who develop new frameworks for intelligence analysis or law enforcement need to be aware of the interplay between different knowledge-discovery technologies, and how best to combine them into systems with the greatest effectiveness. Finally, policy makers and the wider public need to understand what knowledge discovery can and cannot do, and at what cost. The discussions about privacy and intrusiveness cannot sensibly take place without some idea of the possibilities and constraints of the technology that will use the collected data.

Of course, mainstream knowledge discovery at present assumes that it is not the target of manipulation. However, as those involved become more sophisticated and aware of the benefits of knowledge-discovery systems, for example in customer relationship management, we can expect that mainstream systems will also become targets for manipulation. If a business sorts its customers into categories, some of which get better service or pricing, there will be those who want to be in those categories even though this is not in the business' interest. So adversarial knowledge discovery will increasingly become relevant to the wider knowledge-discovery community.

10.4   Open Problems

Let me end by including a personal list of some of the open problems in adversarial knowledge discovery. These will probably be of greater interest to researchers than practitioners. I have divided them into three categories: problems that relate primarily to how the knowledge-discovery process is organized; technical problems for which feasible solutions in the next few years seem possible; and technical problems that seem much more difficult.

10.4.1   Process Improvements

These are problems where the solution requires using the understanding we already have in more effective ways:

- Better overall processes for arranging knowledge-discovery algorithms. I have spent some time making the point that *defence in depth* and *defence by diversity* are important to achieving good results – there is surely more to learned by trying more algorithms and more arrangements of algorithms. Given the context of a sequence of predictors, for example, it may become obvious that some predictors are naturally most effective at particular stages of the sequence. Combining algorithms allows the weaknesses and blind spots of each to be compensated for.

- Handling multiple kinds of data simultaneously. We know hardly any algorithms for knowledge discovery using different forms of data at the same time, for example, graph algorithms that also use the values of attributes from records associated with the nodes and edges.

- Using graph-based knowledge-discovery algorithms more widely. Such algorithms are inherently more robust because they depend more directly on emergent properties. They are also more complex and expensive to execute. However, better understanding and implementation are needed to make them accessible to practical use.

- Better ways to exploit the fact that normality implies a kind of internal consistency *within* records and external consistency *among* records – consistencies that concealment and manipulation tend to break.

- Legal and social frameworks for preventive data analysis. We are having to make adjustments in many different ways to the fact that preventive data analysis is now accurate enough to be useful, but there are many impediments, some inertial and some fundamental, to using it. These need the fullest discussion with the widest possible set of stakeholders.

- Increasing the focus on emergent attributes and properties rather than directly collected attributes. Emergent attributes are powerful because they capture more-global structure, and because they are harder to manipulate.

- Finding better ways to use visualization. I have suggested that directly using visualization is ineffective because many objects are occluded by others. However, new ways to combine different forms of visualization at the same time may open up some new and powerful possibilities.

10.4.2   Straightforward Technical Problems

These problems are (or seem to be) straightforward in principle, but little or no research work has been done to address them. This is partly because many of them are not interesting for mainstream knowledge discovery. It is only in adversarial settings that their importance becomes obvious.

- Hardening standard algorithms against manipulation, both by insiders and by outsiders using data insertion. We have seen how fragile many existing algorithms are. Some can probably be adapted to be more resistant to manipulation; others may need to be discarded for adversarial settings.

- Extending predictors so that they predict "don't know" for records unlike those from which they were built. Most prediction technologies make a kind of default prediction, even for records that are completely different to those on which they were trained. Predictors need to incorporate the idea of a known region, where their predictions are at least potentially accurate; and an unknown region where any prediction they make is highly unreliable. In other words, generalization within the previously-seen region is plausible, but generalization outside it is unlikely to be appropriate.

- Better techniques for distinguishing the bad from the unusual, both to improve the knowledge-discovery process in general, and to provide a way to find lone-wolf adversaries. I have argued that it is the existence of adversary groups that solves this problem, as it creates correlation among anomalous records. However, a more direct attack on the problem of distinguishing bad from unusual could be productive as well.

- Getting graph analysis techniques to work as well as they should. Although graph algorithms have many attractive properties, they do not actually perform as well as might be expected. This is perhaps because they are sensitive to issues such as normalization that are not yet well-understood for such data.

- Strong but transparent predictors. At present, the strong predictors are opaque and the transparent predictors are weak. Confidence and explanatory power are important properties in practice, but we do not know how to get them both together.

- Clustering algorithms to find 'fringe' records. Since we expect adversary records to be found close to large, normal clusters, algorithmic techniques that search for such records directly would be useful.

- Better 1-class prediction techniques. In many adversarial settings, there are no reliable examples of adversary records, but plentiful examples of normal records. Good predictors that could be trained on the normal records, and could generalize them well, would be extremely useful.

- Algorithms to fuse records that do not share common keys but can nevertheless be associated with one another. It is clear anecdotally that records that do, in fact, belong to the same person can often be fused based on attributes that would not normally be considered identifying. The power and limits of this kind of fusion need to be understood.

- Better symbiosis between human analysis and algorithmic analysis. As we have seen, this kind of close cooperation can improve the performance of both analyst and algorithm, but very few knowledge-discovery techniques exploit this. Existing techniques either assume such large volumes of data that humans are not involved; or allow an analyst to direct data exploration ("slicing and dicing') but only for small (parts of) datasets.

- Detecting when models need to be updated because of changes in the situation that is being modelled. Almost all situations involving humans are constantly changing; this is much more obviously a problem in adversarial settings because of the adaptation of adversaries to the analysis process. Models need to be built assuming that they will be updated but, more importantly, should track themselves so that they can detect internally when they need to be updated.

- Detecting when models need to be updated because they are no longer able to represent the complexity of the situation being modelled (and perhaps never were). Models are deployed based on estimates of their performance derived from, for example, test data. In adversarial settings, newly-discovered data can not only suggest that the model itself should be modified, but that the *kind of model* should be modified. For example, it may have seemed plausible that clusters in the data were basically convex, but new data may show that they are actually quite spider-like.

10.4.3 More-Difficult Technical Advances

These problems require sustained research to tackle:

- Finding larger structures in text. We have discussed how to look for obfuscation applied at the level of individual words and within clauses. However, techniques for finding the structures in text are not able to look for more-complex structures in a robust way. Most parsing techniques assume that the structures in text are hierarchical, but this is only approximately true, and we do not have a good model for parsing long-range, non-nested structure.

- Adversarial parsing – parsing with the possibility of obfuscation wired in to the algorithms. Compilers are often able to correct small syntax errors because they 'understand' both what should be there, and what might be there as the result of common errors. There would be a great advantage in adapting this to parsing text, looking for markers of obfuscation rather than of common errors – "this otherwise nonsensical sentence makes sense on the assumption that this kind of obfuscation has been applied to it". Some work in this direction has been done for systems that teach second languages, where the characteristic mistakes of a learner are typical and so understood.

- Better authorship detection from small samples of text, and assuming large numbers of possible authors. We have seen that authorship detection can be done from small amounts of text, but not reliably enough to be able to handle large sets of possible authors. However, blogging and commenting mean that many people are now authors, and detecting who they are when the number of possibilities is large is an important problem.

- Improving unusual-region detection in graphs. In most adversarial settings, the interesting structures in graphs are at medium scale – but most of the analysis techniques are aimed either at the entire graph, or at the neighborhoods of individual nodes. We need to develop more techniques that look at the structure and properties of regions.

- Understanding and applying the systemic functional linguistic viewpoint for content and mental-state extraction from text. Almost all work with text assumes a Chomskian view of language. This has been very productive, and it is relatively straightforward to develop new applications, but the limitations of this view of language are becoming clearer. Systemic functional linguistics has some advantages in adversarial settings, but its overheads are high and there is little practical experience in its use.

Bibliography

A. Abbasi and H. Chen, *Applying Authorship Analysis to Arabic Web Content*, in: *Intelligence and Security Informatics 2005*, pp. 183–197. Springer-Verlag LNCS 3495, 2005.

A. Abbasi and H. Chen, "Applying authorship analysis to extremist-group web forum messages", *IEEE Intelligent Systems*, pp. 67–75, September/October 2005.

A. Abbasi and H. Chen, *Visualizing Authorship for Identification*, in: *Intelligence and Security Informatics 2006*, pp. 60–71. Springer-Verlag LNCS 3975, 2006.

S. Adams and A.K. Goel, *A STAB at Making Sense of VAST Data*, in: *AAAI-2007 Workshop on Plan, Activity, and Intent Recognition*, 2007.

R. Agrawal, T. Imielinski and A.N. Swami, *Mining Association Rules between Sets of Items in Large Databases*, in: P. Buneman and S. Jajodia, (eds.), *Proceedings of the 1993 ACM SIGMOD International Conference on Management of Data*, pp. 207–216, Washington, D.C., 1993.

C. Anderson, *The Long Tail: Why the Future of Business is Selling Less of More*, Hyperion, 2006.

F.R. Bach and M.I. Jordan, "Finding Clusters in Independent Component Analysis", Technical Report UCB/CSD-02-1209, Computer Science Division, University of California, Berkeley, 2002.

W.E. Baker and R.B. Faulkner, "The social organization of conspiracy: Illegal networks in the heavy electrical equipment industry", *American Sociological Review*, 58:837–860, December 1993.

C. Bellavita, "Changing homeland security: Shape patterns not programs", *Homeland Security Affairs*, II(3):1–21, 2006.

V. Benzaken, G. Castagna and A. Frisch, *Cduce: an XML-Centric General-Purpose Language*, in: *Proc. of 2003 ACM SIGPLAN Int. Conf. on Functional Programming*. ACM Press, 2003.

C. Bishop, *Neural Networks for Pattern Recognition*, Oxford University Press, 1995.

H. Blau, N. Immerman and D. Jensen, "A visual language for querying and updating graphs", Technical Report 2002-037, University of Massachusetts Amherst Computer Science Technical Report, 2002.

317

D.M. Blei, A.Y. Ng and M.I. Jordan, "Latent Dirichlet allocation", *Journal of Machine Learning Research*, 3:993–1022, 2003.

S. Boag, D. Chamberlin, M.F. Fernandez, D. Florescu, J. Robie and J. Simeon, "XQuery 1.0: An XML Query Language - W3C Working Draft", February 2005.

S.H. Bokhari and A.D. Raza, "Reducing the diameters of computer networks", *IEEE Transactions on Computers*, 35(8):757–761, 1986.

M. Brand, "Nonrigid embeddings for dimensionality reduction", Technical Report 2005-117, Mitsubishi Electric Research Laboratories, December 2005.

M. Brand, *A Random Walks Perspective on Maximizing Satisfaction and Profit*, in: *SIAM International Conference on Data Mining*, pp. 12–19, 2005.

L. Breiman, "Bagging predictors", *Machine Learning*, 24:123–140, 1996.

L. Breiman, "Arcing classifiers", *Annals of Statistics*, 26(3):801–849, 1998.

L. Breiman, "Random forests–random features", Technical Report 567, Department of Statistics, University of California, Berkeley, September 1999.

L. Breiman, J.H. Friedman, R.A. Olshen and C.J. Stone, *Classification and Regression Trees*, Chapman and Hall, New York, 1984.

S. Brin, L. Page, R. Motwani and T.Winograd, "The PageRank Citation Ranking: Bringing Order to the Web", *Stanford Digital Libraries Working Paper*, 1998.

K. Bryan and T. Leise, "The $25,000,000,000 eigenvector: The linear algebra behind Google", *SIAM Review*, 48(3):569–581, 2006.

C.J.C. Burges, "A tutorial on support vector machines for pattern recognition", *Data Mining and Knowledge Discovery*, 2:121–167, 1998.

R.S. Campbell and J.W. Pennebaker, "The secret life of pronouns: Flexibility in writing style and physical health", *Psychological Science*, 14(1):60– 65, 2003.

J.R. Carlson, J.F. George, J.K. Burgoon, M. Adkins and C.H. White, "Deception in computer mediated communication", *Academy of Management Journal*, 13:5–28, 2004.

S. Chakrabarti and A. Strauss, "Carnival booth: An algorithm for defeating the computer-assisted passenger screening system", Course Paper, MIT 6.806: Law and Ethics on the Electronic Frontier, `www.swiss.ai.mit.edu/6805/student-papers/spring02-papers/caps.htm`, 2002.

C.E. Chaski, "Who's at the keyboard: Authorship attribution in digital evidence investigations", *International Journal of Digital Evidence*, 4(1), 2005.

C.K. Chung and J.W Pennebaker, "Revealing dimensions of thinking in open-ended self-descriptions: An automated meaning extraction method for natural language", *Journal of Research in Personality*, 42:96–132, February 2008.

C.K. Chung and J.W. Pennebaker, *The Psychological Function of Function Words*, in: K. Fiedler, (ed.), *Frontiers in Social Psychology*. Psychology Press, in press.

J. Clark, "XSL Transformation(XSLT): Version 1.0 - W3C Recommendation", November 1999.

J. Clark and S. DeRose, "XML Path Language (XPath): Version 1.0 - W3C Recommendation", November 1999.

P. Clark and T. Niblett, "The CN2 induction algorithm", *Machine Learning*, 3(4):261–283, 1989.

T. Coffman, S. Greenblatt and S. Marcus, "Graph-based technologies for intelligence analysis", *Communications of the ACM*, 47(3):45–47, March 2004.

J. Conroy and D.P. O'Leary, "Text summarization via hidden markov models and pivoted QR matrix decomposition", Technical Report CS-TR-4221, University of Maryland Computer Science Department, May 2001.

J.M. Conroy and D.P. O'Leary, *Text Summarization via Hidden Markov Models*, in: *Proceedings of the 24th Annual International ACM SIGIR Conference on Research and Development in Information Retrieval*, pp. 406–407, New Orleans, 2001.

D. Cook and L.B. Holder, "Graph-based data mining", *IEEE Intelligent Systems*, pp. 32–41, 2000.

C. Cortes, D. Pregibon and C. Volinsky, *Communities of Interest*, in: *Proceedings of the 4th International Conference on Advances in Intelligent Data Analysis*, *Springer Lecture Notes in Computer Science 2189*, pp. 105–114, 2001.

N. Cristianini and J. Shawe-Taylor, *An Introduction to Support Vector Machines and Other Kernel-Based Learning Methods*, Cambridge University Press, 2000.

O. de Vel, A. Anderson, M. Corney and G. Mohay, "Mining E-mail content for author identification forensics", *SIGMOD Record*, 30(4):55–64, December 2001.

A.P. Dempster, N.M. Laird and D.B. Rubin, "Maximum likelihood from incomplete data via the EM algorithm", *Journal of the Royal Statistical Society, Series B*, 39:138, 1977.

B.M. DePaulo, J.J. Lindsay, B.E. Malone, L. Muhlenbruck, K. Charlton and H. Cooper, "Cues to deception", *Psychology Bulletin*, 9:74–118, 2003.

I.S. Dhillon, "Co-clustering documents and words using bipartite spectral graph partitioning", Technical Report 2001-05, Department of Computer Sciences, University of Texas, March 2001.

I.S. Dhillon and D.S. Modha, "Concept decompositions for large sparse text data using clustering", *Machine Learning*, 42(1):143–175, 2001.

J. Diesner and K. Carley, *Exploration of Communication Networks from the Enron Email Corpus*, in: *Workshop on Link Analysis, Counterterrorism and Security, SIAM International Conference on Data Mining*, pp. 3–14, 2005.

B. Diri and M. Fatih Amasyali, *Automatic Author Detection for Turkish Texts*, in: *ICANN/ICONIP03, 13th International Conference on Artificial Neural Network and 10th International Conference on Neural Information Processing*, 2003.

S. Donoho, *Link Analysis*, in: O. Maimon and L. Rokach, (eds.), *Data Mining and Knowledge Discovery Handbook*, chapter 19, pp. 417–432. Springer, 2005.

M. Dunham, *Data Mining Introductory and Advanced Topics*, Prentice Hall, 2003.

J. Dutrisac, "Counter-Surveillance in an Algorithmic World", Master's Thesis, School of Computing, Queen's University, 2007.

J.G. Dutrisac and D.B. Skillicorn, *Subverting Prediction in Adversarial Settings*, in: *2008 IEEE Intelligence and Security Informatics*, pp. 19–24, 2008.

M. Ester, H.-P. Kriegel, J. Sander and X. Xu, *A Density-Based Algorithm for Discovering Clusters in Large Spatial Databases with Noise*, in: *2nd International Conference on Knowledge Discovery and Data Mining (KDD'96)*, Portland, Oregon, 1996. AAAI Press.

European Parliament Temporary Committee on the ECHELON Interception System, "Final report on the existence of a global system for the interception of private and commercial communications (ECHELON interception system)", 2001.

A. Evans, J. Sikorski, P. Thomas, S-H. Cha, C. Tappert, G. Zou, A. Gattani and G. Nagy, *Computer Assisted Visual Interactive Recognition (CAVIAR) Technology*, in: *2005 IEEE International Conference on Electro-Information Technology*, Lincoln, NE, 2005.

R. Ferrer i Cancho and R.V. Solé, "The small world of human language", *Proceedings of the Royal Society of London Series B – Biological Sciences*, pp. 2261–2265, 2001.

SW. Fong, D.B. Skillicorn and D. Roussinov, "Detecting word substitutions in text", *IEEE Transactions on Knowledge and Data Engineering*, 20(8):1067–1076, August 2008.

G. Frantzeskou, E. Stamatatos, S. Gritzalis and C.E. Chaski, "Identifying authorship by byte-level n-grams: The source code author profile (SCAP) method", *International Journal of Digital Evidence*, 6(1), 2007.

S. French and C. Niculae, "Believe in the model: Mishandle the emergency", *Journal of Homeland Security and Emergency Management*, 2(1):1–16, 2005.

Y. Freund and R. Schapire, *Experiments with a New Boosting Algorithm*, in: *Proceedings of the 13th International Conference on Machine Learning*, pp. 148–156, 1996.

A.D. Friederici, D.Y. von Cramon and S.A. Kotz, "Language related brain potentials in patients with cortical and subcortical left hemisphere lesions", *Brain*, 122(6):1033–1047, 1999.

G. Fung, *The Disputed Federalist Papers: SVM and Feature Selection via Concave Minization*, in: *Proceedings of the 2003 Conference on Diversity in Computing*, pp. 42–46, Atlanta, Georgia, USA, 2003.

J. Galloway and S. Simoff, *Digging in the Details: A Case Study in Network Data Mining*, in: *Intelligence and Security Informatics, Springer Lecture Notes in Computer Science 3495*, pp. 14–26, 2005.

J. Galloway and S. Simoff, *Network Data Mining: Discovering Patterns of Interaction between Attributes*, in: *Advances in Knowledge Discovery and Data Mining, Springer Lecture Notes in Computer Science 3918*, pp. 410–414, 2006.

B. Gelfand, M. Wulfekuhler and W.F. Punch III, *Automated Concept Extraction from Plain Text*, in: *AAAI-98 Workshop on Learning for Text Categorization*, 1998.

P.B. Gibbons and Y. Matias, *New Sampling-Based Summary Statistics for Improving Approximate Query Answers*, in: *Proceedings of ACM Conference on the Management of Data*, pp. 331–342, 1998.

Y. Gong and X. Liu, *Generic Text Summarization Using Relevance Measure and Latent Semantic Analysis*, in: *Proceedings of the 24th Annual International ACM SIGIR Conference on Research and Development in Information Retrieval*, pp. 19–25, New Orleans, 2001.

S. Grant, D. Skillicorn and J. Cordy, *Topic Detection Using Independent Component Analysis*, in: *Workshop on Link Analysis, Counterterrorism, and Security (LACTS2008)*, pp. 23–28, 2008.

N. Grira, M. Crucianu and N. Boujemaa, "Unsupervised and semi-supervised clustering: A brief survey", `satoh-lab.ex.nii.ac.jp/users/grira/papers/BriefSurveyClustering.pdf`, 2005.

S. Gupta, "Modelling deception detection in text", Master's Thesis, School of Computing, Queen's University, 2007.

M. Harren, B. Raghavachari, O. Shmueli, M. Burke, V. Sarkar and R. Bordawekar, *XJ: Integration of XML Processing into Java*, in: *Proc. WWW2004*, New York, NY, USA, May 2004.

D.I. Holmes and R.S. Forsyth, "The *Federalist* revisited: New directions in authorship attribution", *Literary and Linguistic Computing*, 10(2):111–127, 1995.

F.Y. Huang, C.B. Jay and D.B. Skillicorn, "Programming with heterogeneous structure: Manipulating XML data using bondi", Technical Report 2005-494, Queen's University School of Computing, 2005.

A. Hyvärinen, "Survey on independent component analysis", *Neural Computing Surveys*, 2:94–128, 1999.

D. Jensen and J. Neville, *Data Mining in Networks*, in: *Papers of the Symposium on Dynamic Social Network Modeling and Analysis*. National Academy Press, 2002.

D. Jensen and J. Neville, "Data mining in social networks", Invited presentation to the National Academy of Sciences Workshop on Dynamic Social Network Modeling and Analysis, November 2003.

D. Jensen, M. Rattigan and H. Blau, *Information awareness: A prospective technical assessment*, in: *Proceedings of the 9th ACM SIGKDD International Conference on Knowledge Discovery and Data Mining*, 2003.

X. Jiang and A.-H. Tan, *Mining Ontological Knowledge from Domain-Specific Text Documents*, in: *Proceedings of the Fifth IEEE International Conference on Data Mining (ICDM'05)*, pp. 665–668, 2005.

S.C. Johnson, "Hierarchical clustering schemes", *Psychometrika*, 2:241–254, 1967.

J. Jonas and J. Harper, "Effective counterterrorism and the limited role of predictive data mining", *Policy Analysis*, 584:1–12, 2006.

H. Kanayama, T. Nasukawa and H. Watanabe, *Deeper Sentiment Analysis Using Machine Translation Technology*, in: *Proceedings of the 20th International Conference on Computational Linguistics*, 2004.

M. Kantardzic, *Data Mining: Concepts, Models, Methods, and Algorithms*, Wiley-IEEE Press, 2002.

P.S. Keila and D.B. Skillicorn, "Structure in the Enron email dataset", *Computational and Mathematical Organization Theory*, 11(3):183–199, 2005.

B. Klimt and Y. Yang, *The Enron Corpus: A New Dataset for Email Classification Research*, in: *European Conference on Machine Learning*, pp. 217–226, 2004.

T. Koening, "Compounding mixed-methods problems in frame analysis through comparative research", *Qualitative Research*, 6(1):61–76, 2006.

G. Kolda and D.P. O'Leary, "A semi-discrete matrix decomposition for latent semantic indexing in information retrieval", *ACM Transactions on Information Systems*, 16:322–346, 1998.

T.G. Kolda and D.P. O'Leary, "Computation and uses of the semidiscrete matrix decomposition", *ACM Transactions on Information Processing*, 1999.

T. Kolenda, L. Hansen and J. Larsen, *Signal Detection using ICA: Application to Chat Room Topic Spotting*, in: *Proceedings of ICA'2001*, December 2001.

M. Koppel, S. Argamon and A.R. Shimoni, "Automatically categorizing written texts by author gender", *Literary and Linguistic Computing*, 17(4):401–412, 2002.

M. Koppel and J. Schler, *Exploiting Stylistic Idiosyncrasies for Authorship Attribution*, in: *Proceedings of IJCAI'03 Workshop on Computational Approaches to Style Analysis and Synthesis, Acapulco, Mexico*, 2003.

M. Koppel, J. Schler, S. Argamon and E. Messeri, *Authorship Attribution with Thousands of Candidate Authors*, in: *Proceedings of the 29th Annual International ACM SIGIR Conference on Research and Development in Information Retrieval*, pp. 659–660, 2006.

M. Koppel, J. Schler and E. Bonchek-Dokow, "Measuring differentiability: Unmasking pseudonymous authors", *Journal of Machine Learning Research*, 8:1261–1276, 2007.

M. Koppel, J. Schler and K. Zigdon, *Automatically Determining an Anonymous Author's Native Language*, in: *Intelligence and Security Informatics, IEEE International Conference on Intelligence and Security Informatics, ISI 2005, Atlanta, GA, USA, May 19-20*, pp. 209–217. Springer-Verlag Lecture Notes in Computer Science LNCS 3495, 2005.

C.F. Kurtz and D.J. Snowden, "The new dynamics of strategy: Sense-making in a complex and complicated world", *IBM Systems Journal*, 42(3):462–483, 2003.

A. Lazarevic and Z. Obradovic, *The Distributed Boosting Algorithm*, in: *KDD2001*, pp. 311–316, August 2001.

A. Lazarevic and Z. Obradovic, "Boosting algorithms for parallel and distributed learning", *Distributed and Parallel Databases, Special Issue on Parallel and Distributed Data Mining*, 11(2):203–229, 2002.

M. Lazaroff and D. Snowden, *Anticipatory Models for Counter-terrorism*, in: R.L. Popp and J. Yen, (eds.), *Emergent Information Technologies and Enabling Policies for Counter-terrorism*, chapter 3, pp. 51–73. IEEE Press Series on Computational Intelligence, 2006.

J. Li, R. Zheng and H. Chen, "From fingerprint to writeprint", *Communications of the ACM*, 49(4):76–82, April 2006.

D. Liben-Nowell and J. Kleinberg, *The Link Prediction Problem for Social Networks*, in: *Proceedings of the Twelfth International Conference on Information and Knowledge Management*, pp. 556–559, 2003.

A. Little, "Defining a signature for deception in court testimony", Master's Thesis, School of Computing, Queen's University, 2007.

J.-F. Lyotard, *The Post-Modern Condition: A Report on Knowledge*, volume 10 by *Theory and History of Literature*, University of Minnesota Press, 1984.

J.B. MacQueen, *Some Methods for Classification and Analysis of Multivariate Observations*, in: *Proceedings of 5th Berkeley Symposium on Mathematical Statistics and Probability*, volume 1, pp. 281–297. University of California Press, 1967.

R. McArthur and P. Bruza, *Discovery of Implicit and Explicit Connections Between People using Email Utterance*, in: *Proceedings of the Eighth European Conference of Computer-Supported Cooperative Work, Helsinki*, pp. 21–40, 2003.

A. McCallum, A. Corrada-Emmanuel and X. Wang, *Topic and Role Discovery in Social Networks*, in: *International Joint Conference on Artificial Intelligence*, pp. 786–791, 2005.

S. McConnell and D.B. Skillicorn, *SemiDiscrete Decomposition: A Bump Hunting Technique*, in: *Australasian Data Mining Workshop*, pp. 75–82, December 2002.

E. Meijer, W. Schulte and G. Bierman, *Unifying Tables, Objects and Documents*, in: *Proc. DP-COOL 2003*, Uppsala, Sweden, August 2003.

B. Mezrich, *Bringing Down the House: How Six Students Took Vegas for Millions*, Arrow Books, 2002.

M. Montes y Gómez, A. López-López and A.F. Gelbukh, *Information Retrieval with Conceptual Graph Matching*, in: *Database and Expert Systems Applications*, pp. 312–321, 2000.

R.J. Mooney, P. Melville, L.R. Tang, J. Shavlik, I de Castro Dutra, D. Page and V.S. Costa, *Relational Data Mining with Inductive Logic Programming for Link Discovery*, in: *Proceedings of the National Science Foundation Workshop on Next Generation Data Mining*, November 2002.

S. Muggleton, "Scientific knowledge discovery using inductive logic programming", *Communications of the ACM*, 42:245–286, 1999.

T. Mullen and N. Collier, *Sentiment Analysis Using Support Vector Machines with Diverse Information Sources*, in: *Proceedings of the 42nd Meeting of the Association for Computational Linguistics (ACL 2004)*, pp. 21–26, 2004.

T. Nasukawa and J. Yi, *Sentiment Analysis: Capturing Favorability Using Natural Language Processing*, in: *Proceedings of the 2nd International Conference on Knowledge Capture*, pp. 70–77, 2003.

M.L. Newman, C.J. Groom, L.D. Handelman and J.W. Pennebaker, "Gender differences in language use: An analysis of 14,000 text samples", *Discourse Processes*, 45:211–236, 2008.

M.L. Newman, J.W. Pennebaker, D.S. Berry and J.M. Richards, "Lying words: Predicting deception from linguistic style", *Personality and Social Psychology Bulletin*, 29:665–675, 2003.

D.P. O'Leary and S. Peleg, "Digital image compression by outer product expansion", *IEEE Transactions on Communications*, 31:441–444, 1983.

B. Pang and L. Lee, *A Sentimental Education: Sentiment Analysis Using Subjectivity Summarization Based on Minimum Cuts*, in: *Proceedings of the 42nd Meeting of the Association for Computational Linguistics (ACL 2004)*, pp. 271–278, 2004.

J. Patrick, *The Scamseek Project – Text Mining for Financial Scams on the Internet*, in: *Data Mining: Proceedings of the 4th Australasian Workshop on Data Mining*, Springer LNCS 3755, pp. 295–302, 2006.

L. Pietronero, E. Tosattib, V. Tosattib and A. Vespignani, "Explaining the uneven distribution of numbers in nature: the laws of Benford and Zipf", *Physica A: Statistical Mechanics and its Applications*, 1–2:297–304, 2001.

C. Priebe, *Scan Statistics on Enron Graphs*, in: *Workshop on Link Analysis, Counterterrorism and Security, SIAM International Conference on Data Mining*, pp. 23–32, 2005.

J.R. Quinlan, *C4.5: Programs for Machine Learning*, Morgan-Kaufmann, 1993.

A.P. Sanfilippo, A.J. Cowell, S.C. Tratz, A.M. Boek, A.K. Cowell, C. Posse and L.C. Pouchard, *Content Analysis for Proactive Intelligence: Marshalling Frame Evidence*, in: *Proceedings of the Twenty-Second AAAI Conference on Artificial Intelligence*, pp. 919–924, 2006.

B. Schneier, *Why Data Mining Won't Stop Terror*, in: *Wired*, 2006.

T.E. Senator, *Multi-Stage Classification*, in: *Proceedings of the Fifth IEEE International Conference on Data Mining*, pp. 386–393, 2005.

F. Shahnaz, M.W. Berry, V.P. Pauca and R.J. Plemmons, "Document Clustering using Nonnegative Matrix Factorization", *Journal on Information Processing and Management*, 42(2):373–386, March 2006.

D. Shen, J.-T. Sun, H. Li, Q. Yang and Z. Chen, *Document Summarization using Conditional Random Fields*, in: *Proceedings of IJCAI-07*, pp. 2862–2867, 2007.

J. Shetty and J. Adibi, "The Enron Email Dataset Database Schema and Brief Statistical Report", Technical report, Information Sciences Institute, 2004.

D.B. Skillicorn, *Beyond Keyword Filtering for Message and Conversation Detection*, in: *IEEE International Conference on Intelligence and Security Informatics (ISI2005)*, pp. 231–243. Springer-Verlag Lecture Notes in Computer Science LNCS 3495, May 2005.

D.B. Skillicorn, *Social Network Analysis via Matrix Decompositions*, in: R.L. Popp and J. Yen, (eds.), *Emergent Information Technologies and Enabling Policies for*

Counter-terrorism, chapter 19, pp. 367–392. IEEE Press Series on Computational Intelligence, 2006.

D.B. Skillicorn, *Understanding Complex Datasets: Data Mining with Matrix Decompositions*, CRC Press, 2007.

D.B. Skillicorn and Y. Wang, "Parallel and sequential algorithms for data mining using inductive logic", *Knowledge and Information Systems Special Issue on Distributed and Parallel Knowledge Discovery*, 3(4):405–421, 2001.

R.K. Srihari, S. Lankhede, A. Bhasin and W. Dai, *Contextual Information Retrieval using Concept Chain Graphs*, in: *Proceedings of the CIR'05 Workshop on Context-Based Information Retrieval*. CEUR Volume 151, 2005.

E. Stamatatos, N. Fakotakis and G. Kokkinakis, *Text Genre Detection Using Common Word Frequencies*, in: *Proceedings of the 18th International Conference on Computational Linguistics (COLING2000)*, pp. 808–814, 2000.

J. Steinberger, M. Poesio, M.A. Kabadjov and K. Ježek, "Two uses of anaphora resolution in summarization", *Information Processing and Management*, 43(6):1663–1680, 2007.

P.-N. Tan, M. Steinbach and V. Kumar, *Introduction to Data Mining*, Addison-Wesley, 2006.

D.M.J. Tax, *One Class Classification*, PhD Thesis, Technical University Delft, 2000.

J.J. Thomas and K.A. Cook, (eds.), *Illuminating the Path: The Research and Development Agenda for Visual Analytics*, IEEE Press, 2005.

J. Travers and S. Milgram, "An experimental study of the small world problem", *Sociometry*, pp. 425–443, 1969.

J.R. Tyler, D.M. Wilkinson and B.A. Huberman, "Email as spectroscopy: Automated discovery of community structure within organizations", HP Labs, 1501 Page Mill Road, Palo Alto, CA, 94304, 2003.

L.G. Valiant, "A theory of the learnable", *Communications of the ACM*, 27(11):1134–1142, November 1984.

U. von Luxburg, "A tutorial on spectral clustering", Technical Report 149, Max Plank Institute for Biological Cybernetics, August 2006.

D.J. Watts and S.H. Strogatz, "Collective dynamics of 'small-world' networks", *Nature*, 393:440–442, 1998.

C. Whitelaw and S. Argamon, *Systemic Functional Features in Stylistic Text Classification*, in: *Proceedings of AAAI Fall Symposim on Style and Meaning in Language, Art, Music, and Design*, Washington, DC, October 2004.

C. Whitelaw, N. Garg and S. Argamon, *Using Appraisal Taxonomies for Sentiment Analysis*, in: *Second Midwest Computational Linguistic Colloquium (MCLC 2005)*, 2005.

C. Yu and D.B. Skillicorn, "Parallelizing boosting and bagging", Technical Report 2001–442, Queen's University Department of Computing and Information Science Technical Report, February 2001.

L. Zhou, D.P. Twitchell, T. Qin, J.K. Burgoon and J.F. Nunamaker Jr., *An exploratory study into deception detection in text-based computer mediated communication*, in: *Proceedings of the 36th Hawaii Intl Conference on Systems Science*, 2003.

X. Zhu and R. Rosenfeld, *Improving Trigram Language Modeling with the World Wide Web*, in: *Proceedings of International Conference on Acoustics, Speech, and Signal Processing, 2001*, pp. 533–536, 2001.

Index